Natural
Prophets

Natural Prophets

From Health Foods to Whole Foods— How the Pioneers of the Industry Changed the Way We Eat and Reshaped American Business

JOE DOBROW

RODALE.

Rodale books may be purchased for business or promotional use or for special sales. For information, please write to:

Special Markets Department, Rodale, Inc., 733 Third Avenue, New York, NY 10017

Printed in the United States of America

Rodale Inc. makes every effort to use acid-free ∞, recycled paper ♻.

Book design by Amy C. King

Library of Congress Cataloging-in-Publication Data is on file with the publisher

ISBN-13: 978-1-62336-179-2

Distributed to the trade by Macmillan
2   4   6   8   10   9   7   5   3   1   hardcover

We inspire and enable people to improve their lives and the world around them.
rodalebooks.com

Contents

PROLOGUE
THE TIPPING POINT

Whenever you played the late doubleheader at Broome Park, you always had to be worried about the lights.

For one thing, they were terribly inadequate. A few lonely stanchions were presumably all that Montgomery County, Maryland, had deemed affordable, or politically feasible, when they had converted this former middle school into a two-field softball complex, tucked into the tidy Twinbrook neighborhood of neo-colonials, Cape Cods, and ranch houses about 15 miles northwest of Washington, DC. The result was typical rec league low wattage— no problem for the teams playing the early games, but a real challenge for those whose first contest began at 8:30 p.m.

And then there were the timers. In a deal undoubtedly negotiated with the Twinbrook neighbors at the time Broome was converted in the mid-1980s, all lights were put on timers that would snap off at precisely 10.45 p.m , with all the subtlety and forgiveness of motel bathroom heat lamps—leaving the field in primal blackness no matter the status of the games.

That was a concern for the players of the Fresh Fields Naturals as they arrived at the field on Tuesday, June 11, 1996, and began stretching and playing catch in preparation for their games. But the talk was of something else.

"Did you guys hear the news? Company's being sold to Whole Foods," said Tom Kovack, the team's pitcher, as he warmed up his arm behind the first base dugout. Kovack worked at the Fresh Fields warehouse, managing teams of workers who, in a masterful ballet of logistics and sweat, received tons of organic produce and natural foods from incoming 18-wheelers throughout each day, moved the products around the warehouse on pallet jacks, and then shipped them off to the company's 22 stores the next morning. "They asked us to run another shift tomorrow to clean up the warehouse so it'll be ready for *visitors*," he said, his voice tinged with—what? resentment? resignation?—as he fired a warm-up toss a little bit harder.

"It's true," added shortstop/grocery manager Brian Bishop with the confident tone of someone who has been on the receiving end of a shocking rumor and now wants to be among the first to pass it along as fact. "I heard Ordan was down in Texas last Friday signing the papers."

And so, as game time neared, some murky shadows began shifting fitfully across the field, and across the future of the company.

To most of the Fresh Fields players—marketing managers, information technology specialists, and others from the corporate office—this was a baseless rumor, just a bunch of foam and froth. How could it possibly be true? Fresh Fields was thriving! Founded only 5 years earlier by Harvard Business School graduates Mark and Kathy Sklar Ordan, legendary grocer Leo Kahn, and Kahn's longtime operations mastermind Jack Murphy, Fresh Fields had already grown faster than anything the natural foods industry had ever seen: It was now pushing $250 million in sales, second only to Whole Foods Market's $496 million from that company's 47 mostly-west-of-the-Mississippi stores, and gaining fast. Stores in Bethesda, Maryland, and Tysons Corner, Virginia, were racking up among the nation's highest supermarket sales per square foot. Fresh Fields had been praised lavishly in the press, earning *Money* magazine's Store of the Year honor in 1993 and considerable attention from the *New York Times*' Marian Burros ("These gleaming new supermarkets . . . bear about as much resemblance to the to the grungy, 1960's fern-bedecked natural-foods co-op . . . as McDonald's does to Lutece.").[1] The company also had a powerhouse board of directors that included Howard Schultz, CEO of Starbucks; Dave Fuente, CEO of Office Depot; and leaders from not one but *three* top financial companies: The Carlyle Group, Tiger Management, and Goldman Sachs. And so, not surprisingly, covert discussions had begun about an initial public offering (IPO). True, Fresh Fields had not yet turned a profit. But others had filed for an IPO while they were still in the red, including Boston Chicken, which had gone public in 1993 and seen its stock jump an amazing 143 percent on the very first day. Most observers thought Fresh Fields had that kind of potential (and if the rumors were to be believed, Whole Foods thought so, too). Somehow, Fresh Fields just had to keep the investors happy and the competitors at bay.

But now came this scuttlebutt, this hardball rumor on the softball field, apparently backed up by incontrovertible details—and instantly, all thoughts turned from day to night, from IPO to sale, from glory to obsolescence, from immense pride to prospective unemployment.

Indeed, much hung in the balance on that June night in 1996 as the Fresh Fields Naturals took the field at Broome Park, and as Fresh Fields the company fought for its life. The question was, would the lights go out before the game was over?

The fact that such machinations were even being contemplated was in many ways astonishing.

Just 2 decades earlier, the natural foods industry was still in its infancy, a hippie sideshow to the serious business of food production and retailing that, in the years since World War II, had fueled America's growth and transformed us from a nation of bread lines into the breadbasket of the world. Through the 1960s and 1970s, there had been little more than a sprinkling of dreary health foods stores across the country, offering a laughably small selection of wheat germ, tofu, brown rice, and other products that were decidedly lacking in mainstream tastes, and for that matter lacking in taste altogether.

But then something happened, something dramatic and completely unexpected: Spurred by the unrelenting idealism of a few visionaries and by a series of food scares that laid bare the presence of dangerous chemicals in everyday foods like apples and diet soda, society began to rediscover the world of natural and organic foods, the very same world in which it had unwittingly operated for centuries before science and agribusiness reinvented our diets with synthetic additives, preservatives, pesticides, and herbicides and allowed chemicals to infiltrate every last link of the food chain. Natural foods became more abundant, more accessible, more sophisticated, more palatable, more desirable . . . and soon became a bellwether of the late-20th-century shift toward more enlightened business attitudes, as well as a badge of merit for aspirational consumers.

In the vanguard of that movement were pioneers like Mo Siegel of Celestial Seasonings, John Mackey of Whole Foods Market, Steve Demos of WhiteWave, and Gene Kahn of Cascadian Farm, who combined a passion for changing the world with the practical vision and business acumen to actually do so. Through their efforts to educate customers about the risks of chemical additives and the benefits of healthy eating, and through their innovative developments in merchandising, packaging, and product quality, natural foods began to reclaim at least a foothold in our pantries, in our menus, in our diets, and more importantly in our consciousness.

It was never easy. These Natural Prophets faced most of the obstacles trailblazing entrepreneurs usually encounter—no access to capital other than friends and family, no road map, no established market for their products. They also met with the staunch opposition of Big Food and chemical companies; the limitations created by government programs like the Farm Bill that reinforced the status quo; plus the biases of a nation that, through the efforts of Madison Avenue, had come to favor catchy advertising jingles over ingredient lists, and that still seemed to believe the Woodstock generation mostly just needed a safety razor and a can of Ultra Ban 5000 deodorant.

More fundamentally, the reflexive idealism of the industry's early pioneers had begun to run headlong into the gathering forces of opportunism. Second-generation entrepreneurs who, at first, cared less about food purity than about pure profits saw huge potential in the industry; in the late 1980s and early 1990s, hundreds of new products were launched, and big retail chains like Wild Oats and Fresh Fields were born. Then, once natural foods showed real signs of promise, money began pouring in. The newfound government surpluses and prosperity of the Clinton era created optimism among investors and an eagerness to find places to use their ample cash reserves. (The Dow Jones average was about to enter the steepest growth period in its 18-year bull-market run, and while technology companies like Microsoft, AOL, and Apple were enticing, the "dot-com boom" was still a couple of years away.) Hedge funds, private equity firms, venture capitalists, and the investment wings of pension funds jumped in. "Green" and "socially responsible" funds were being created by mutual fund companies like the Calvert Group and investment banks like Adams, Harkness & Hill. The natural foods industry, once derided by the head of biochemistry at the Vanderbilt School of Medicine as consisting of "the organic gardeners, the anti-fluoride leaguers, the worshippers of 'natural foods,' those who cling to the philosophy of a vital principle, and other pseudo-scientists and faddists,"[2] was suddenly an attractive investment option.

Now it was 1996, and the natural foods industry was simply *exploding*, as millions of consumers seemed to have awakened suddenly to the benefits of healthier eating. There were more than 6,600 natural/health foods stores in the country, many of them fancy "yupscale" supermarket-sized palaces like Fresh Fields, tallying $9.17 billion in sales. Although this was just a tiny fraction of the overall retail food business in the United States (Kroger alone had 1,356 stores doing $25.2 billion in sales),[3] natural foods had grown at an amazing compound annual rate of approximately 17 percent over the previous 5 years, roughly four or five times the rate of the conventional side of the business.[4] Moreover, some of the leading natural foods brands—like Earthbound Farm salads, Stonyfield Farm yogurt, Celestial Seasonings tea, and Frookies fruit-juice-sweetened cookies—had all crossed over to become mainstays in conventional supermarkets, as well.

The year 1996 had already seen several momentous leaps forward.

There had been the announcement that Mountain People's Warehouse, the largest natural foods distributor in the West, and Cornucopia, the largest one in the East, had joined forces to create a new company called United Natural Foods, Inc., or UNFI. The creation of UNFI portended a new day in natural foods, not far off in the future, when efficient logistics would at last come to this traditionally fragmented, unreliable, ragtag industry. Costs would come down, in turn lowering retail prices, and thus perhaps attracting a much larger group of consumers.

In March, there had also come word of the purchase of the organic baby food company Earth's Best by the H.J. Heinz Company for $30 million. While this was certainly not the first time that a Big Food company had invested in a natural foods company—that honor probably went to Kraft and Smucker's, which purchased Celestial Seasonings and the R.W. Knudsen juice company, respectively, in the appropriately Orwellian year of 1984—it was nevertheless a milestone moment that, as it turned out, would usher in a furious period of investment in natural foods companies by Big Food: Before the end of the 20th century, less than 4 years away, Mars, General Mills, Kellogg, and Dean Foods, among others, would all buy their way in.

But the biggest news of the year so far was that the Boulder-based retailers Alfalfa's and Wild Oats had announced their intention to merge and then go public. Alfalfa's, founded in 1979, had earned a stellar reputation for its store operations, food quality (especially in natural meat), and convivial social environment; it had grown slowly and steadily, and by 1996 had 11 stores spread out in Colorado, Santa Fe, Seattle, and Vancouver doing a combined $120 million

annually. Wild Oats had been founded in 1987 by Mike Gilliland, an enterprising but somewhat aimless entrepreneur who had lately been running some convenience stores with his wife, Elizabeth "Libby" Cook. But this was the right
time, and Boulder was the right place. Between 1989 and 1993, the company
grew 544 percent. It made the *Inc.* magazine list of the 500 fastest growing
small companies in 1994, and by 1996 had more than two dozen stores throughout the West and was generating about $150 million in sales.[5] Thus, the merger
of Alfalfa's and Wild Oats would create a combined company (operating as
Wild Oats) with 39 stores and $270 million in sales, leapfrogging past Fresh
Fields into second place and challenging Whole Foods' healthy hegemony
from the West.

And now—well, now these rumors about a Fresh Fields IPO being replaced
by rumors about Fresh Fields selling out to Whole Foods? Even those who were
caught up in the day-to-day fight recognized that a seminal moment had
arrived in the natural foods revolution. For the question of who would emerge
triumphant in the retail battle had ramifications beyond just that of a land grab
or a play for market share: The companies also represented radically different
philosophies. Whole Foods was a product of the old guard, a recognizable evolutionary varietal descended from the health foods movement, nurtured lov-
ingly by natural foods zealots; Fresh Fields was a meticulously engineered
corporation, built with MBA genius and Wall Street money; Wild Oats was an
opportunistic response, a business version of throwing spaghetti on the wall to
see if it sticks. Whole Foods was consensus-driven and decentralized, while
Fresh Fields was closely controlled and tightly structured; Wild Oats, expedient
and protean, fell somewhere between the two. It was mission against money,
idealism against opportunism, the school of bootstrap entrepreneurship against
Harvard Business School, with a Wild card thrown in for good measure.

So it was that the humble little natural foods industry—product of the
counterculture movement, viewed for so long by so many as just a fringe group
of tofu-wiggling, wheat-germ-crunching food faddists—had come of age. A tipping point was clearly at hand, as the Era of High-Minded Idealists had begun
to yield to the Age of Opportunists, and a movement gave way to a legitimate
industry. New products and big brands were emerging and crossing over into
the mainstream. Giddy investors were lining up. Consolidation was the order
of the day. And on the retail side, a three-way struggle for supremacy was shaping up, with IPOs and mergers threatening to shift the balance of power wildly

one way or the other. The very direction of the natural foods industry, perhaps even its soul, was at stake.

———•——

We have come a long way since that pivotal moment. Whole Foods Market is now an enormously influential Fortune 500 company. Fresh Fields lives on only as a Facebook "fans and alumni" page. Wild Oats is gone, though a new ownership group has bought the name and may be planning to bring it back. Yet today, if you shop for groceries, or dine at a restaurant, or prepare meals for a child, or just stop off for a beverage at a gas station convenience store, then natural foods are probably a part of your life. Whether you shop at Whole Foods or Walmart, whether you go out to eat at Chipotle or McDonald's, you will find natural and organic foods options everywhere.

Having lived through that food revolution, and having fought on its front lines as the top marketing executive for several of the combatants at one time or another, it began to dawn on me that there is far more depth to this tale than just an arcane history, far more significance than just a struggle among competitive brands. It is actually a big, sprawling story of popular movements and unpopular products, of entrepreneurs and industries, of idealists and opportunists, and of how their efforts to build companies worked, and didn't. It is a story that begins to explain the competitive/cooperative contradictions of modern business, one that in some ways neatly pegs the changes in consumer priorities that have come to define us in today's world. It is a story from which much can be learned—about entrepreneurship, about how missions drive business, and about the American character itself. And it is a story that most people have never heard.

The fact is that from its early roots as a reaction against the postwar proliferation of chemicals, to its philosophical but impractical development by idealistic children of the sixties, to its conversion in the eighties and nineties into a modern business by a group of ambitious opportunists, to its current state as bubbling crucible of mission-driven entrepreneurial activity, the natural foods industry has proven to be both fascinating and unduly influential. It has sparked a revolution in food production, marketing, and consumption. It has focused our attention on health, and on ways to remedy our personal and collective failures to look after ourselves and our planet. And somewhere along the way, without our really noticing that it was happening, the natural foods industry has helped to change the way a lot of 21st-century business is conducted, and the manner in which many companies now organize themselves around principles instead of products.

It can be argued, and I do in this book, that some of the natural foods pioneers—people like John Mackey of Whole Foods, Gary Hirshberg of Stonyfield Farm, and Drew and Myra Goodman of Earthbound Farm—have made a larger contribution to the health and sustainability of this planet and the human beings who ride on it than just about anyone else in the modern era, including the usual targets of our hero worship in that apotheosis of entrepreneurship, Silicon Valley. (The natural foods pioneers' stories are also *vastly* more entertaining.)

Just as importantly, the business legacies of the many influential companies in this industry run deep. If indeed we are now living in a changed world—one in which mission-driven values, corporate social responsibility, transparency, and authenticity have gone from being marketing gimmicks to requirements—then in my view, we have natural foods companies like Whole Foods, Stonyfield Farm, Organic Valley, Earthbound Farm, and Honest Tea to thank.

Of course, a topic as expansive as the birth and growth of an entire industry does not easily lend itself to a single book. For although the natural foods industry developed in a rather concentrated period of time, there were still a great many people involved, a great many brands born, a great many events unfolding more or less concurrently in different parts of the country and the world. Hence, more so than with most histories, one's narrative depends on one's perspective—on the point of entry into the tale and on which story lines are chased down and which ignored.

For example, in looking at the "natural products industry"—a catchall term encompassing natural and organic foods, body-care products, vitamins and supplements, and housewares such as cleaning supplies—I chose to focus mainly on natural foods, because it is the largest and best-known sector. Organics, by this definition, are a subset of natural foods. Natural body-care products make a cameo in this book, but only a cameo, since the fact remains that many core natural foods customers view the mouth as the Maginot Line of their greater health awakening, and continue to freely use topical products that contain all sorts of artificial ingredients. Similarly, I chose not to spend time focusing on the vitamin and supplement industry, for although it was an important precursor to the natural foods industry, it was largely subsumed into it.

Also worth noting is that given the modern economics of book publishing, no one could include information about all of the important food companies in a single volume; the industry is simply too vast. Some of the founders were impossible to reach or declined to participate; other stories seemed to add little value to the narrative. Hence, some well-known companies are not prominently featured in this book, despite their undeniable appeal and success.

What I have written falls somewhere between scholarly history, popular history, biographical memoir, and corporate profile. Because of my own background in the industry, I was able to tap into some unusual archival material and perhaps provide some insights into various characters' personalities and motivations. But because I was trained by great historians such as Howard R. Lamar of Yale University and the late John L. Thomas of Brown University, I approached the topic dispassionately and always attempted to consider the people and events in the context of their place and time through the use of more than 300 outside sources as well as the recollections—gathered during interviews—of nearly 100 industry pioneers. I have made an effort to verify, validate, and corroborate the material gleaned from these interviews, though it has not always been possible, because some of the events discussed happened decades ago and even a natural foods diet heavy in ginseng and ginkgo biloba cannot stave off the effects of Father Time.

Still, whatever the perspective and methodology, this book tells an entertaining story, and a meaningful one. It provides insights into the food industry, the world of retailing, the entrepreneurial mind, the management tool kit, and the kitchen pantry—as well as a rollicking ride in the Wayback Machine through some of the more memorable developments in American business and society of the past 50 years. And, just maybe, by looking back it offers a road map forward into a more natural future. For as the early 19th-century German writer and philosopher Friedrich von Schlegel said, "The historian is a prophet in reverse."

Joe Dobrow
July 2013

CHAPTER 1

THE MILKMAN
OR THE COW

T his morning, hundreds of thousands of people sat down to a bowl of Post Honey Bunches of Oats cereal. Maybe even you. It is, after all, one of the most popular breakfast cereals in America, second in sales only to Honey Nut Cheerios. Perhaps you chose the Tropical Blend Mango Coconut flavor in the orange-and-turquoise box with the palm trees on it. Or the one that reassuringly includes "real strawberries."

The Post brand dates back to the late 19th century, and is legendary in the cereal business. A farm-implement-manufacturer-turned-real-estate-developer named Charles William (C.W.) Post founded the company after a stay at the Battle Creek Sanitarium run by John Harvey Kellogg, in an attempt to get his nervous and digestive issues under control. Post was impressed by the dietary products he sampled at Battle Creek, and in 1895 launched a product of his own, a "cereal beverage" called Postum. It was pitched to consumers as a caffeine-free alternative to coffee. A 1903 advertisement made the straightforward case: "Coffee causes Heart-Failure, Dyspepsia, Brain-Fag and Nervous-Prostration. These will leave you when you use Postum Food Coffee."[1]

In 1897 Post came out with a new cereal product called Grape Nuts, and in 1904 with a corn flake cereal originally called Elijah's Manna, prudently renamed in 1908 as Post Toasties. In later years, as the company evolved and became known as General Foods, there would be many more storied cereal products: 40% Bran Flakes, Raisin Bran, Alpha-Bits, Spoon-Sized Shredded Wheat, Honeycomb, and in 1971 the immortal Fruity Pebbles.

In fact, one could look at the Post portfolio of cereal products and brands and trace nearly the entire history of the modern American health foods industry through their advertising—from brain-fag to Euell Gibbons to Fred Flintstone. And back: Starting in 2004, Post reduced the amount of sugar in some of their popular cereals, and in 2011 their new packaging boldly trumpeted the gluten-free version of Fruity Pebbles. Yabba dabba don't.

Honey Bunches of Oats was launched in 1989–1990, around the same time that General Foods was being married to Kraft by parent company Philip Morris, creating a $30 billion, 55,000-employee colossus that C.W. Post could never have imagined. The cereal's current ingredient list reflects some of the tempering effects that the healthy foods revolution has had on the cereal industry, but also the extent to which a multitude of inputs (in this case, at least 30) still define our highly processed world: corn, whole grain wheat, sugar, whole grain rolled oats, brown sugar, rice, high oleic vegetable oil (canola or sunflower oil), wheat flour, malted barley flour, salt, corn syrup, whey (from milk), honey, malted corn and barley syrup, caramel color, natural and artificial flavor, annatto extract (color), and BHT [butylated hydroxytoluene] added to the packaging. There are also added vitamins and minerals, including reduced iron, niacinamide, vitamin B_6, vitamin A palmitate, riboflavin (vitamin B_2), thiamin mononitrate (vitamin B_1), zinc oxide, folic acid, vitamin B_{12}, and vitamin D.

The Post Toasties your grandparents may have eaten—admittedly before labeling laws had been enacted to require full disclosure, but also before modern-day innovations like code dates, fortification, and Recommended Daily Allowances brought a flurry of new ingredients to each box—bore this simple statement on the front of the package: "Made from corn grits, sugar and salt."

And what about the milk with your Honey Bunches of Oats? You might have added some 2 percent milk from your local dairy (which is probably a few hundred miles distant). Or perhaps some raw milk, or Silk soy milk, or calcium-enriched whole milk Lactaid, or maybe even Organic Valley fat-free organic milk fortified with omega-3 fatty acids sustainably sourced from wild ocean fish. Your grandparents' milk? It likely came from the milkman—probably with cream on top—or from the cow.

In just one or two short generations, food production and procurement have been completely transformed in nearly every corner of the world. Natural and organic foods, once the norm, have given way to synthetic and chemical foods so thoroughly, so absolutely, that we have all but forgotten how things used to be. Only through the heroic efforts of a small group of entrepreneurs in recent years have we begun to turn back the tide of artificiality and to rediscover the foods, processes, and principles that our forebears would have recognized.

The fact is that from the time *Homo sapiens* first appeared on the planet at least 200,000 years ago up until nearly the present day, *all* of the food we ate was "organic," which is to say: as it was found in nature, with the only modifications coming from preparation (separating, cutting) or from the alchemy of ingredients and creative genius we think of as "cooking." But the raw elements? They were pure and natural for roughly the first 199,900 of those years. Whether it was big game meat scavenged by the Neanderthals, shoots and grains carefully cultivated by our Mesolithic forebears, a béchamel sauce prepared in the court of the Sun King during the late 17th century, or the box of Post Toasties in your grandmother's pantry, all food was taken as a gift more or less straight from nature. Chemicals never factored into the equation. There was no equation at all.

Since about the time of World War II, however, *Homo sapiens* has become incredibly . . . sapient. And we have shifted almost in toto to a diet of chemically treated crops and animal proteins, and highly processed foods with lengthy polysyllabic ingredients lists. Some 80,000 new chemical compounds have been introduced in the United States in that time,[2] many of which are used in the production, packaging, and storage of food. In particular, chemicals are used as pesticides, herbicides, fungicides, and fertilizers on 930 million acres in the United States, or roughly 96 percent of the farmland, and on 3.8 billion acres globally.[3]

Among the class of pesticides alone, US farmers use an estimated 5.6 billion pounds per year, a tenfold increase since World War II, in part because evolutionary forces keep fighting back: There are now hundreds of pesticide-resistant insects, whose biology has proven to be more potent than the chemical cocktails we feed them. A 2004 study also showed the existence of 286 herbicide-resistant weeds. Despite the epic battle fought with these tens of thousands of chemicals, crop losses due to pest and weed damage have nearly doubled since World War II, and now amount to about 37 percent of the total grown.[4]

The ingenious laboratory work of companies like Dow Chemical, DuPont, Monsanto, and American Cyanamid has brought enormous benefits to farms, economies, and, arguably, the human race. Farm productivity has increased beyond all mathematical reason. Farmers are able to plant more densely, extend the growing season, yield more food per acre, and reduce their labor costs. Chemicals have also helped agronomy advance in the developing world to the point at which some soil-poor nations are now better able to feed their starving masses.

But there has also been an almost unfathomable cost. For after the lid of Pandora's pesticide box was flipped open, some residue remained inside. Because some of these chemicals are fat-soluble, they can penetrate the cells of the plants on which they are applied, and can "bio-accumulate" into each successive member of the food chain that consumes the plants. Many other chemicals enter our bodies through the environment, such as the common herbicide Atrazine—also known as 2-chloro-4-(ethylamino)-6-(isopropylamino)-s-triazine—which, according to the *New York Times,* "has become among the most common contaminants in American reservoirs and other sources of drinking water."[5] Thus, almost every single person in the country now has traces of pesticides in the blood; most newborns have at least 232 chemicals in their bodies.[6] Indeed, it is estimated that the average American now consumes about 9 pounds of chemical additives each year.[7] Many of these compounds have been linked to brain and lung damage, cancer, developmental disabilities, and a host of other diseases, conditions, and afflictions.[8]

But that is the only the start of our chemical dependency. Here in the 21st century, nearly 70 years after the synthetic revolution began, the transformations in our food are not just molecular, but genetic and societal, too.

First, consider the genetic level. With Daedalian ingenuity, and what critics would say is hubristic indifference, scientists in the postwar period discovered that DNA could be transferred between two different organisms, thus opening up the possibility that the genetic makeup of foodstuffs could be engineered to breed for desirable characteristics. There were some experiments with antibiotic-resistant tobacco plants in the 1980s. Then scientists at a company called Calgene developed a tomato whose ripening process was slowed down by adding a gene from the *E. coli* bacterium that interfered with the normal production of an enzyme responsible for breaking down pectin in the cell walls. The effect would be to make a tomato that was resistant to rotting, and which could theoretically be allowed to remain on the vine longer than most tomatoes (which are typically picked when under-ripe and then allowed to ripen in transit or with the addition of ethylene gas). This test-tube tomato was called CGN-89564-2, but was better known as the Flavr Savr—the first commercially produced "genetically modified organism," or GMO. With the approval of the Food and Drug Administration (FDA), it was born on May 18, 1994.

It turned out that vowels were not the only thing missing from the Flavr Savr. The fruits were smaller than most other tomatoes, the yield per acre was terrible, and the product ultimately had to be cross-bred to achieve a better flavor. Calgene was eventually sold to Monsanto.

But CGN-89564-2 unleashed a torrent of additional interest, research, and development in genetic food engineering that would remake the food landscape forever. Crops could now be engineered that were drought resistant, or that had greater rigidity to enable denser planting, or that could minimize the need for excessive application of pesticides and herbicides. Soon, genes from the flounder were being bred into certain tomato crops to make them more resistant to frost; the company Ventria Bioscience even used genes found in human saliva and breast milk to engineer a type of rice they said could be useful in treating children with diarrhea.

Today, a mere 20 years later, an estimated 91 percent of all soybeans, 85 percent of all corn, and 88 percent of all cotton grown in the United States comes from genetically modified seeds. Monsanto alone controls 90 percent of US soybean production and 60 percent of US corn through patented seeds that, because they must be repurchased every year instead of being allowed to regenerate, have in turn remade the whole economics of the agricultural system.

Second, there is the societal level—for the gains made in productivity on the farm in the chemical era set off a chain reaction that ultimately toppled some unintended dominos.

As Michael Pollan illustrated so dramatically in *The Omnivore's Dilemma*, chemical innovations led to greater productivity from cornfields. More corn produced meant more need to find uses for corn. One such use was as livestock feed. Only about 10 percent of the world's grain in 1900 went to feed livestock, but that number doubled by 1950, doubled again by the late 1990s, and has now surpassed 60 percent in the United States. Cattle came off the range and into dense feedlots, concentrated animal feeding operations, or "CAFOs" in industry parlance, that produced a surge in the supply of beef, which in turn generated a change in the American diet—from per capita consumption of about 112 pounds in 1909 to about 271 pounds by the mid-2000s, when it peaked.[9] Additionally, fewer cattle on the range meant fewer small family farms (down by more than 300,000 since 1979), and the absence of cattle on mixed-use farms meant less manure, which meant more need for synthetic fertilizers.[10] Single-use "monoculture" farms became the rule, and biodiversity suffered.

Another use for the corn surplus was as a sweetener: high-fructose corn syrup (HFCS), introduced in 1980. Cheap to produce (one bushel of corn yields 33 pounds of HFCS), and just as sweet as sugar, HFCS quickly became a staple of the American diet. By 1984 it had replaced cane sugar in the sacrosanct recipes of both Coke and Pepsi. By 2012, the average person was consuming almost 55 pounds a year of HFCS without any corresponding decrease in sugar consumption, in turn contributing significantly to a surge in adult type-2 diabetes and the current epidemic of obesity.[11]

Hence, because of a dotted line extending straight back to the emergence of chemical agriculture, our diets today bear little resemblance to those of earlier generations. Early humans got 65 percent of their calories through fruits and vegetables; modern Man derives only 7 percent of calories from the combination of fruits, vegetables, legumes, whole grains, nuts, and seeds. Instead, 51 percent of our food energy comes through processed foods.

So in the span of one or two human lifetimes—a mere heartbeat, evolutionarily speaking—we have gone from a world of authentic to synthetic, from connate to construct, from pure to processed. Post Toasties are gone; postmodern—as surely evidenced by Fruity Pebbles made from red 40, yellow 6, yellow 5, blue 1, blue 2, artificial flavors, genetically modified soy lecithin, and high-fructose corn syrup—is at hand.

Skull-and-crossbones-laden chemical concoctions used to stimulate agricultural abundance . . . unpronounceable ingredients in our food . . . food products that are neither local nor possibly even terrestrial . . . Faustian trade-offs made to get it all. . . . None of this would have been at all comprehensible to our grandparents or great-grandparents. Yet, the water slowly heating to a boil around us, we seem not to have noticed the change.

How in the world did we get here?

In the United States and most of the developed world, natural food was the norm even well into our accessible history. In the early 20th century, America was still a predominantly rural country where most of the food was grown on small farms that operated in much the same way they had since agriculture was invented 12,000 years earlier. Fertilizer, for example, came mostly from the manure of livestock, guano, crop residues, and the application of natural elements such as potash, phosphorus, and nitrates.[12] Livestock were still being raised on untreated feed and pastureland; the regular use of antibiotics and growth hormones as feed supplements was still years away. Weeds were controlled primarily through mechanical methods (hoeing, tilling, flooding, burning, etc.), or through "cropping" or biological means, such as the introduction of parasites;[13] salt, ashes, and a few compounds like sodium nitrate or calcium cyanamide were being used selectively, but chemical weed control was still in its infancy.[14]

There were some chemical pesticides in use, notably the arsenic-based paint pigment Paris Green, which had first been used against the Colorado potato beetle in 1867. In fact, lead, mercury, arsenic, and cyanide were all hailed as beneficial insecticides for many decades. To a modern reader, the insouciant use of such poisons might seem startling. But as Will Allen demonstrated in his fascinating 2008 book *The War on Bugs,* the editors of magazines such as *American Farmer* and *The Cultivator* and rural journals like *California Farmer* actively and reassuringly promoted the use of chemical pesticides. By the 1920s, Standard Oil even hired the cartoonist Theodore Geisel— aka Dr. Seuss—to help popularize its home pesticide, Flit, and the cartoon campaign increased household pesticide use tenfold.[15] Nevertheless, the use of such new-fangled insecticides by farmers was by no means routine. Farm manuals of the day were just as likely to recommend pyrethrum powder (made from ground chrysanthemums), or natural methods, such as cutting the first crop of alfalfa when it buds in order to kill the weevil larvae by starvation or exposure to heat.

Away from the farm, there were a few large food processing companies such as General Mills, Kraft, Heinz, and Del Monte, as well as many smaller regional ones, producing some canned goods and packaged items. Some of the common packaged foods were Pillsbury's Best flour, Eagle Brand condensed milk, Uneeda biscuits, Heinz tomato soup, and Hershey's chocolate bars. Most of these were pure and simple products that had not yet been reformulated in the laboratories for enhanced color and flavor or extended shelf life. Food in the early 1900s, and right up through our grandparents' generation, was still recognizably food, the unsullied bounty of Mother Nature.

However, "progress" was certainly coming to both farm and factory—and in the land of Manifest Destiny, where faith in technology was an inherent trait, it would be almost universally welcomed.

Airplanes were first used to dust crops with pesticides in 1921. Chemists developed ever more effective pesticide compounds; by 1929, 29 million pounds each of lead arsenate and calcium arsenate were helping to control insects each year.[16] Synthetic nitrogen, which accounted for less than 5 percent of the nitrogen used for fertilizers at the turn of the century, began to grow in popularity after World War I.[17] Urea was synthesized in the lab in the 1930s and was soon put to use in stimulating growth of livestock. Such advances were generally regarded as positive developments, just a few more points on an upward continuum that had already recorded the invention of the cotton gin, the railroad, the telephone, and the gas-powered tractor, and would soon include extension of the electrical grid into rural areas through the Tennessee Valley Authority.

Similarly, though processed food had not yet become an essential part of everyday life for our grandparents' generation, a number of developments were beginning to pave the way for its infiltration into the American food pantry by the mid-1940s.

First, food manufacturing processes were advancing rapidly.

Steam-powered steel rolling mills had replaced the ancient stone grain mills, and as early as 1884 Pillsbury was capable of producing as much as 5,000 barrels of flour a day, or about 980,000 pounds. Manufacturing companies like Hobart invented labor-saving machines that made large-scale industrial food preparation much cheaper, such as the electric mixer, food cutter, and potato peeler. Great advances were made in the pasteurization of milk, the hydrogenation of oils, and the extraction of juices.

Second, there was a revolution in food preservation.

Although people had been curing, drying, and salting foods for thousands of years, canning had become the preservation method of choice in modern times. The canning process was first developed by French chef Nicholas Appert, using glass jars to preserve products like soup, vegetables, and dairy goods for the French military during the Napoleonic Wars. The science of canning advanced in the latter half of the 19th century, in part through the efforts of companies like Nestlé and Heinz. The first fruits and meats in tin cans began appearing on US store shelves around 1880.

In the early 20th century, both food preservation and processing were significantly aided by the development of refrigerators and what were commonly called "deep freezers" or "deep-freeze units." Companies like Kelvinator and Electrolux—still around today, though radiating little more than the quaint glow of long-forgotten brands from a simpler time—were the early leaders in refrigeration, along with General Electric, which introduced the first mass market model, the Monitor-Top, in 1927. Some of these models contained usage meters, and advertised payments as low as 15 cents per day. Around the same time, a former taxidermist named Clarence Birdseye invented a process for flash-freezing foods in waxed cardboard boxes, and sold the patents and trademarks to—who else?—the Postum Cereal Company, along with what was then known as the Goldman-Sachs Trading Company, for $22 million.[18]

Eventually, as the scientific community turned its attention to the processing and preservation challenge, there would be a fundamental shift away from the simplicity of mere canning and freezing, and into technologies of altering the food itself to meet the demand of the emerging convenience- and consumption-driven society for more volume, more variety, and more shelf life.

Third, there was the development of the mass marketplace, through the combination of retailers, advertising media, and Americans' increased mobility.

In the towns and urban centers, far away from the farms, a patchwork of dry goods stores, green grocers, butcher shops, poultry marts, and bakeries had long dominated the retail food industry. But with more Americans moving to the cities, there was a greater need to supply food for the teeming masses. Chains of small groceries exploded in popularity: By 1929 there were 15,709 A&P stores alone.[19] The first of the "combination stores" or "supermarkets," King Kullen, opened in Jamaica, New York, in 1930. Founder Michael S. Cullen wrote of his plan to build "monstrous stores . . . away from the high-rent districts" that would employ aggressive price-cutting tactics.[20] Other chains like Safeway, Kroger, Ralph's, and Publix soon followed suit.

These stores mostly sold fresh, local fare—because, after all, there was no interstate highway system to facilitate delivery of meat or dairy or out-of-season goods, and no regular commercial trans-American air service to fly in mangos and coconuts. This was, in some respects, still the era of Elijah's Manna. Honey Bunches of Oats Tropical Blend would have to wait for another day.

Newspaper grocery ads reflected the mix of local goods and branded packaged foods. For example, on June 1, 1935, Cobb Markets in Phoenix featured a selection of mostly local perishable items such as jumbo local strawberries, Arizona seedless grapefruit, eggs ("strictly fresh, all white"), broilers ("dressed and drawn"), as well as a few symbols of the dawning age of consumerism, such as packaged products from Del Monte (asparagus, jams, pears, even salmon), Libby's potted meats, Philadelphia cream cheese, and Kraft Velveeta. Their competitor, Safeway Pay'n Takit stores, advertised local strawberries, grapefruits, carrots, and blackberries. Another merchant, A.J. Bayless, included items like Arizona Star flour, Maricopa butter, Morning Bracer coffee ("we grind it to suit your individual requirements"), and of course Post Toasties—two packages for 15 cents.

Soon there would be many more packaged products, as new technologies helped stimulate the demand and create the means to connect it to the supply. Radio consoles from the likes of Philco, Zenith, Westinghouse, and Crosley dropped in price to an affordable average of $47 in 1933, and soon extended into nearly 60 percent of all households, creating an opportunity for advertisers to reach millions of homes.[21] Widespread use of color printing also made this a golden age for magazines and for those who would advertise in them. And, despite a manufacturing slowdown during the Depression years, about one in every five Americans owned a car in the 1930s—creating a degree of mobility that helped to get laborers to farms and food and consumers to stores. The first "farm-to-market" road, christened in Texas in 1937, presaged the development of the transportation network to come.

By 1940, products such as Borden's homogenized milk, B&M brick-oven baked beans, Peter Pan peanut butter, Maxwell House coffee, Hotel Bar butter, Sunsweet prune juice, Campbell's cream of mushroom soup, Pepperidge Farm cookies, Arnold bread, Spam, and hundreds of others would become household names. Most, of course, were still made without any artificial additives.

—·—

Although agricultural products in the prewar era may have been predominantly fresh and natural, they were teased from the earth at great expense and with excruciating labor and unpredictable results. Farming was no Elysian existence; those who live by the plow have always led hardscrabble lives, and this was never truer than in the years of the Dust Bowl and the Great Depression when drought, soil erosion, and bad husbandry and agronomic practices all contributed to crippling drops in productivity on many of the nation's 7 million farms. Even without these additional encumbrances, the age-old farming methods—plowing and harrowing by mule, weeding by hand, spreading manure as fertilizer, and utilizing some combination of crop rotation, trapping, praying, and scarecrows to ward off pests—were backbreaking and inefficient. If the rains didn't come, or if the corn borers and thrips did, an entire season's crop could be lost. So by the end of the 1930s, American agriculture was primed and ready for improvements of any sort. And the industrial chemistry labs had just the answer.

The theory of using chemicals on the farm dated back at least a century. Justus von Liebig was a German chemist and teacher who had studied in Paris with one of the pioneers of modern chemistry, Joseph Louis Gay-Lussac. Liebig focused his work on soil fertility, and in particular the importance of nitrogen, phosphorus, potassium, and a few other minerals. A depletion of these nutrients below a certain minimum, argued Liebig, adversely affected crop yields. Through enthusiastic promotion of his sometimes rather narrow and specious theories (which ignored factors such as microorganisms, pH levels, and crop rotation), he became what author Will Allen called "the first great propagandist for chemistry and for chemical-industrial agriculture."[22] Liebig's 1840 book, *Organic Chemistry in its Applications to Agriculture and Physiology,* was the essential text on the subject. For a time, Liebig exerted considerable influence, especially at the scientific schools at Harvard and Yale. The work of one of his disciples, August Wilhelm von Hoffman, also led to breakthroughs in the development of chemical pesticides and fertilizers by the German companies Bayer, BASF, and Hoescht. Nevertheless, as Allen showed, the pointy-headed academics aside, those who actually tilled the soil in the United States were resistant to "book farming," and Liebig's theories fell out of favor.[23]

But everything changed in 1939, when a Swiss entomologist named Paul Müller discovered that a chemical compound called dichlorodiphenyltrichloroethane—DDT—was perhaps the most potent broad-based insecticide ever seen, effective even on pests that had developed a resistance to the old standby, arsenic. This was a breakthrough discovery that would ultimately lead us on a path from the blissful ignorance of our agricultural idyll, to "better living through chemistry," to a book that awakened a generation, to the natural foods revolution it all spawned.

DDT had first been synthesized in 1873, but no real use had been found for it until Müller's discovery. During World War II, the US military and the War Production Board used DDT to control the spread of "louse-borne typhus" in Europe and malaria in the Pacific, to great effect. It was then released from military control for farm and household use right after the war, and quickly became the standard for insecticides.

"Painted or sprayed on the walls of a cow barn, it will kill every fly that lights there for the next 30 to 60 days," read one giddy editorial.[24] "DDT is good for me-e-e!" sang a group of cartoon animals, vegetables, and people in an ad run in *Time* magazine in 1947. "The great expectations held for DDT have been realized," the ad continued. "During 1946, exhaustive scientific tests have shown that, when properly used, DDT kills a host of destructive insect pests, and is a benefactor of all humanity."[25] The 1949 book *Principles of Field Crop Production* contained 15 separate mentions of DDT and recommended it for use in controlling such pests as the Australian wheat weevil, saw-toothed grain beetle, Indian meal moth, European corn borer, Great Basin wireworm, potato leafhopper, and velvetbean caterpillar—albeit with some cautions, such as avoiding feeding DDT-treated hay to dairy cows "because the DDT consumed by cows is secreted in the milk."[26] In 1948, Müller was awarded a Nobel Prize for his work on DDT. By the mid-1950s, DDT became the most widely used pesticide in the country, replacing arsenic.[27]

DDT was not the only by-product of the war machine that would rapidly transform the food supply:

- British scientists at the Rothamsted Experimental Station, working to improve crop yields to help feed a hungry nation at war, developed an herbicide called 2,4-dicholorophenoxyacetic acid, also known as 2,4-D or Tributon, which would have revolutionary effects on weed control after it was released in 1946.

- Pharmaceutical companies that commercialized penicillin to treat war wounds would parlay that work into the development of antibiotics for livestock.

- Chemical companies that produced weapons like napalm bombs for the Air Corps turned their attention to agricultural uses after the war, and would churn out all kinds of new potent broad-spectrum pesticides.

- As the tide of fighting turned in Europe, more and more chemical secrets and processes from the highly regarded German industrial sector fell into Allied hands. Research done for the production of nerve agents—much of it by the members of the German chemical conglomerate I.G. Farben—led to the development of a whole new class of organophosphate agricultural chemicals (including the soil fumigant DD and the insecticides parathion and malathion), as well as to carbamates, among the deadliest substances ever produced.

Throughout 1944 and 1945, government committees were working on plans to transfer the remarkable military production capacity—which by war's end would produce more than 41 billion rounds of small arms ammunition and 5.8 million tons of aircraft bombs—away from materiel and over to peacetime production. Agriculture was the primary beneficiary. For example, the huge munitions plant in Muscle Shoals, Alabama, which was left with a surplus of ammonium nitrate from the production of explosives, was converted in 1947 to a factory for the production of fertilizer.

It was, as a DuPont Farm Chemicals brochure of the 1950s boasted, "Man against the soil . . . [a] rise from savagery to civilization."[28]

Most of these new agricultural chemicals were known to be highly toxic, although the specific risks—such as bio-accumulation in humans, development of birth defects, creation of algal blooms in the oceans, and destruction of the stratospheric ozone layer—would not be discovered for many years. As a result, a culture of acquiescence and blind faith in science permeated much of society. The Depression and Dust Bowl were distant memories, the horrors of war were over, televisions were everywhere, and Uncle Miltie was there to make us laugh. This optimism and toe-the-line Levittown loyalty were part of a postwar consensus that, according to author Mark Hamilton Lytle, "encouraged social and political conformity, respect for governmental and community authority, uncritical patriotism, religious faith, and a commitment to a vague notion of an American way of life defined by prosperity, material comfort, and a secure home."[29] Thus, weren't the chemicals that were starting to generate miraculous gains in productivity on the farms just part of the inevitable American march of progress?

The gains really did *seem* miraculous. Herbicides greatly reduced the need for farm labor, and from 1920 to 1955, farm output per labor hour jumped by 146 percent.[30] From 1935 to 1955, corn yields per acre increased 58 percent, milk per cow, 21 percent, and eggs per hen, 42 percent. By adding antibiotics to livestock feed, and administering female sex hormones to bulls, calves could be brought up to "slaughter weight" in as little as one quarter of the time it used to take.[31] By fumigating the soil with methyl bromide and chloropicrin, strawberries could be planted in the same fields every single year instead of every 10.[32]

Farm productivity took off exponentially, creating a surplus of some $6.6 billion in food at a time when, according to a *Life* magazine article, "most of the semistarved half of the world is still using Biblical methods of agriculture."[33]

There was also an explosion of processed foods, many now improved and enhanced with chemical discoveries by the growing class of food technologists. Using the latest scientific and synthetic advancements, orange juice could now be concentrated and frozen, and whipped cream could be made Reddi in an aerosol can. Cheese was an especially vulnerable category. By 1930, 40 percent of all cheese in the United States was processed in some way. In the 1950s, spray drying of milk (atomizing it to convert it into a powder, then drying it with a hot gas) became a widespread practice, leading to the development of imitation cheese slices made mostly from vegetable oil and water; by the late 1960s, the addition of sorbic acid also gave these slices antimicrobial properties. Kraft introduced Cheez Whiz in 1953, thanks to the help of some non-cheese additives like stabilizing agents, emulsifiers, citric acid, and flavoring compounds.[34]

Frozen foods also developed into a huge category, as 6.5 million Americans owned "deep freezers" by the mid-1950s.[35] The technologists found that with the right blend of emulsifiers (calcium carbonate), stabilizers (carrageenan), preservatives (sodium benzoate), neutralizing agents (lactic acid), and flavor enhancers (monosodium glutamate), just about anything could be frozen and made palatable. C.S. Swanson & Sons proved this, with the introduction in 1954 of an entire turkey dinner that could be frozen and packaged for consumption in front of the TV, for the very reasonable price of 98 cents.[36] Within a year, they had added three more entrées and were selling 25 million TV dinners annually.[37]

A particularly fascinating example of the popularity of frozen foods was Seabrook Farms, a vegetable growing and freezing operation on 50,000 acres in southern New Jersey at the head of the Delaware Bay.

The farm had been founded in 1893 when Arthur Seabrook, a sharecropper who had been selling vegetables door to door, purchased 57 acres. Arthur's son, C.F. Seabrook, built up the operation by contracting with other local farmers, adding 35 miles of roads, two railroads, and a power plant. Although he ran out of money and lost the business in 1924, he bought it back by 1930 and began freezing vegetables as a contractor for the Postum Cereal Company, which had just been rechristened as General Foods and which had purchased Birdseye's flash-freezing patents.

C.F. Seabrook's primary need had always been labor, because his idea was to apply modern factory methods to farming—a concept that earned him the nickname "the Henry Ford of agriculture." In the 1920s, he ran an ad looking for "people who are mad enough to desire a quiet, comfortable home with modern conveniences, in the country, and a chance to save money, rather than high wages with dirt, noise and uncertain employment. The place has nothing to recommend it except good treatment, healthful living, steady position, and an opportunity for everybody to work their way up in a new and growing business. No sulkers or people with touchy feelings need apply."[38]

During the war, with manpower scarce, C.F. cleverly recruited people of Japanese ancestry who had been in internment camps; more than 2,500 ended up moving there to work on his operations, and in a single year they helped provide 60 million pounds of frozen vegetables to the US military.

By the mid-1950s, the combination of advances in chemical farming, mechanization, and the burgeoning market for frozen produce had built Seabrook Farms into a $25 million operation producing 100 million pounds a year. *Life* dubbed it the "biggest vegetable factory on Earth" in its issue of January 3, 1955—ironically, just 80 days after Hurricane Hazel had blown through, destroyed the entire spinach crop, and set in motion a series of financial pressures and family squabbles that would ultimately lead to the sale and dissolution of the business. (Today there is virtually no trace of Seabrook Farms. There is just the unincorporated community of Seabrook, which C.F.'s grandson John described as having "the forlorn look of a company town without the company"; some spinach fields; and a population of 1,484—many of Japanese ancestry.)[39]

In this same time period there was also extraordinary growth in infrastructure and technology, which further facilitated the development of the new food industry. Vacuum techniques repurposed from the war effort were used to pack and ship fresh produce on railcars with less spoilage; by 1950 iceberg lettuce from California was available from coast to coast and became the most consumed vegetable in the country.[40] Other dividends of the war were showing up in America's kitchens, including Corningware, Pyrex, Tupperware, and other plastics. Gas stoves became popular. Soon there were also mechanically cooled refrigerated trucks to help move perishable items over greater distances. In 1956 the Federal-Aid Highway Act provided $26 billion for the construction of 41,000 new miles of high-speed roads. All of this brought more products to more stores more quickly: Whereas the average supermarket in the United States stocked 3,000 items in 1946, by 1957 the number was up to 5,144.[41]

By the end of the 1950s, the chemical revolution and the march of progress had almost completely transformed the way food was grown, prepared, shipped, and sold. American agricultural industry and ingenuity had become the envy of the world, as evidenced by the behavior of none other than Soviet premier Nikita Khrushchev. During a visit by Vice President Richard Nixon to an exhibition of American consumer goods in Moscow's Sokolniki Park in July 1959, the two leaders openly debated the wisdom of America's headlong rush toward synthesized and mechanized abundance. Khrushchev mockingly asked, "Don't you have a machine that puts food into the mouth and pushes it down?" But by the end of the visit, he was posing with a bottle of Pepsi.[42] Two months later Khrushchev visited the United States, and was photographed looking inquisitively at a cellophane-wrapped bag of apples during an impromptu visit to a San Francisco supermarket. The memorable Associated Press lead that accompanied the photograph described the scene, including the crush of curious customers and reporters, as "like the happy hour in a manic depressive ward, like the year of the locusts, like the bull in a china shop, like the night the dam burst, like crazy, man."[43]

But as Henry Drummond, the fictitious version of Clarence Darrow in Jerome Lawrence and Robert E. Lee's 1955 play *Inherit the Wind,* said, "[P]rogress has never been a bargain. You've got to pay for it."[44]

And so it was with food. For all of these breakthroughs and gains came at a price, a price that was only starting to register among the select few whose voices had been drowned out by the fulminating sounds of President Dwight Eisenhower's military-industrial complex.

One of those voices belonged to Jerome Irving "J.I." Rodale, who had been born Yakov Cohen in 1898 in the back of his father's 10 by 40-foot grocery store on the Lower East Side of New York. Rodale always had a fascination with the natural world, even in the tenements and concrete canyons of New York, where he grew flowers on the fire escape and thought about growing mushrooms underneath his bed. A peripatetic entrepreneur even from an early age, he worked as a runner on Wall Street, sang in choirs, collected installments for Singer Sewing Machines, sold colored Christmas tree bulbs, traded stocks while still in high school, worked as a tax auditor for the Internal Revenue Service, and started a successful electrical manufacturing business with his brother, Joe. During the Depression he moved to eastern Pennsylvania, where he took up manufacturing, farming (he bought a rundown 63-acre site in the town of Emmaus called Reinhart Farm for $7,000 in 1940), and, later, publishing.

Always an iconoclast, Rodale rejected the modern improvements to agriculture, choosing to focus instead on "organic farming," a term coined in 1940 by Lord Northbourne and used to describe the natural, regenerative methodologies long practiced and lately detailed in the books *An Agricultural Testament* by Sir Albert Howard and *Bio-Dynamic Farming and Gardening* by Dr. Ehrenfried Pfeiffer. In 1942 Rodale launched *Organic Farming and Gardening* magazine (shortened to *Organic Gardening* after five issues), explaining in his very first article that "organic methods of farming . . . increase the fertility of the soil, produce much better tasting crops, crops that are healthier for man and beast, reduce weeds, [and] do away with the necessity of using poisonous sprays. . . . " He railed against "the liberal use of chemical fertilizers," tied agricultural chemicals to health risks, linked the deterioration of the soil on American farms to the decline of Rome, and presciently looked ahead to a day when "the public is going to wake up and will pay for eggs, meats, vegetables, etc., according to how they were produced."[45]

The magazine was not an instant hit. Rodale printed 14,000 copies and sent them to farmers in the hopes of attracting subscribers; only 12 responded. Thus began J.I. Rodale's frustrated cries in the wilderness—a pursuit of "legitimacy" and a receptive audience for his unconventional ideas that would last for the rest of his life, and well into the lives of his descendants. But through *Organic Gardening*, he did slowly begin to find his voice. The question was: Had the world already moved too far along to be able to hear him? Thus, in a *New York Times* book review of his 1945 work *Pay Dirt,* in which Rodale collected some of his *Organic Gardening* arguments and warned about the dangers of DDT, Russell Lord, editor of *Land* magazine, wrote: "Much of the stuff he cites seems to me the outcome of a flaming will-to-believe, and a bit 'screwy'; but most of it makes sense, plainly."[46]

Despite the carping, *Pay Dirt* was a breakthrough of sorts, and sold more than 50,000 copies. "It more or less made me 'Mr. Organic,'" Rodale later wrote. "I was considered the leader of the movement. I was called on to speak all over the country. . . ."[47]

That "will-to-believe" never flickered in Rodale. He experimented with organic methodologies on his farm, persisted with *Organic Gardening,* launched the organic-based Rodale Diet in 1947, wrote more books, and in 1950 created a health-related magazine called *Prevention,* which attracted 50,000 subscribers from the very start and went on to become the first big commercial success for Rodale.

Throughout that decade, with his son, Bob, at his side, Rodale grew more convinced about the evils of chemical farming, and more evangelical about the benefits of organic. *Organic Gardening,* which had 60,000 subscribers in 1951, grew to a circulation of 135,000 by 1957. In the 15th-anniversary edition, in June 1957, J.I. noted that although "our voices have sometimes been blotted out," and despite the fact that the USDA "and pretty nearly every part of the widely-spread agricultural activity of our country" have "regarded us with a cold skepticism" and "looked upon us as invading carpet-baggers who have come to intrude upon . . . the monopoly of opinion," nevertheless, tremendous strides had been made. "The fact of the matter is that the organic method is [now] known in every nook and corner of our land, from the halls of congress down to the smallest country town P.T.A."[48]

As his granddaughter, Maria, would later write in her book *Organic Manifesto,* he "was ahead of his times in many ways, but he was also a part of his time. His magazine served as a voice for a growing chorus of concern, and back then, if you wanted to eat food without chemicals, there was only one way to do it: Grow your own."[49]

As an appropriate coda to the decade, in 1959 Rodale published an article by Ruth Adams that blasted Tang, the new General Foods orange juice–flavored powdered drink that actually contained no juice at all. "The best thing that you can say about this product is that if you drink it with enough water, it won't kill you," she wrote. When, shortly thereafter, Rodale's ad sales chief went to the General Foods' agency, Young & Rubicam, to inquire about placing ads for Postum in *Prevention,* the Tang tirade not surprisingly got in the way.[50]

One hundred thirty miles to the west of Emmaus, in the town of Penns Creek, Pennsylvania, the voice of another Natural Prophet was also starting to be heard.

Paul Keene was a Yale graduate who began his career teaching math at Drew University in New Jersey. During a 2-year leave to teach in the missions in India starting in 1938, he met Mahatma Gandhi, who was then working at a rural school, and accompanied him on his morning walks. Keene was deeply impressed by Gandhi's philosophy of simple living, village enterprises, and desire to seek out a larger framework for life. Keene was also influenced by the organic farming theories of Sir Albert Howard, who was at the time also in India.

When Keene and his wife, Betty, returned to the United States, the former teacher found that "mathematics was rapidly losing ground to thoughts of fields and streams, of proper foods and rural living." They spent 2 years studying organic farming at the School of Living in Suffern, New York, where they learned "a kind of decentralized, self-sufficient, back-to-the-soil, do-it-yourself home-steading," and then an additional year near Philadelphia at Kimberton Farms, a small organic farm school—the only such facility in the country—which was run by Dr. Ehrenfried Pfeiffer, one of the other fathers of organics. While at Kimberton Farms, they met J.I. Rodale, who attended a short lecture course and spoke about starting *Organic Gardening*. Keene was a marvelous writer, and Rodale asked him if he wanted to become the assistant editor for the magazine, but Paul declined; he had his heart set on farming.

In 1946, Paul and Betty borrowed $5,000 to buy a dilapidated 100-acre former pig farm in Penns Creek called Walnut Acres. There was no furnace or even plumbing, the tin roof was rusted through, the house and barn hadn't been painted in 20 years . . . but to the idealistic and lyrical Keene, it was utopia. "Never was a new-born babe more beautiful to a relieved mother than was Walnut Acres to us as we rattled proudly up the winding lane on that bright March moving day," he would later write. "Oh, the wonder of it all. We had a house and barn and outbuildings and a hundred acres. Did you hear? One hundred acres!"[51]

Their goal was not just to farm the land organically, but to produce and package organic goods that could be sold by mail order—a remarkably innovative business model that had the Sears Roebuck catalog in its roots and the seeds of Webvan and Fresh Direct hiding deep in its DNA. "Had we known beforehand what lay ahead we would have been scared to death," he wrote of the experience. "But nature kindly keeps our destinies from us. One grows but gradually into one's future."[52]

The first Walnut Acres product they created was an apple butter cooked in an iron kettle over an open fire, which they called Apple Essence. The year's output: 100 quarts, which they sold for $1 each. Clementine Paddleford, the influential food editor of the *New York Herald-Tribune*, found out about Apple Essence and wrote about it, attracting scores of letters and considerable interest in Walnut Acres. Later, they started selling potatoes, carrots, beets, chickens, and eggs. The eggs were shipped in metal containers specially made for parcel-post handling, which would be returned by the customers when they were done. Each egg was cushioned in its metal shell with crumpled pieces of paper. "If fate decreed a rare unhappy journey, we gave credit for each broken egg," wrote Keene.[53]

The business grew slowly but steadily. The draft horses were replaced by an old Ford 9N tractor. They purchased their first stone mill in 1949 to make fresh whole flours and cereals. The old barn was eventually converted to a grinding mill and store. The farm expanded and would reach 500 acres in size, then 660.

As products became available, Paul would type up "price lists" and send out mimeographed copies to interested customers.[54] There would be spaghetti, granola, pasta sauces, soups, peanut butter, and other products made from ingredients grown organically on Walnut Acres and on other farms.

Throughout the 1940s and 1950s, as the Big Food producers were churning out one synthetic product after another, Paul began speaking throughout the Northeast. In turn, many organic acolytes made the trek to Penns Creek. "People everywhere seem to be relearning that which should have never been forgotten," wrote Keene.[55]

In each edition of the Walnut Acres mail order catalog—successor to the price lists—which reached 100,000 customers and had a total annual distribution of 2 million,[56] he wrote eloquently and insistently about his farm, family, and philosophy.

In July 1958, for example, he lamented after paying a visit to a modern chicken farmer about the "full cages of up-and-coming, lay-or-bust, now-or-never, do-or-die chickens" and was aghast at the list of ingredients on their feed, which included chlortetracycline hydrochloride, nicarbizin, arsanilic acid, and the preservative butylated hydroxytoluene. "Heaven only knows what it does to the persons who eat these capons. All I can say is: Not at our place. NEVER at our place."[57] In October 1959, he wrote: "The wheat ground is worked. Very soon the new turn of the wheel will begin. Again the seed will be planted. Take a handful of that soil, or stretch out flat with your face over it, and draw in life's odors. Can you explain what the smell of living earth does to you? Will the agriculturists give us a formula for it? Ah, the completeness, the synthesis, the balance of it all. These will, thank God, forever and ever defy analysis and elude description."[58] And in January 1966, he let loose with another poetic polemic: "Oh polluting factories, combustion engines, tightly packed chimneys—spewers forth of lung-searing, earth-befouling byproducts of humanity's search for wealth and comfort—stay your unrelenting push into our paradise. Let purity, simplicity, and freshness abound, until the sun rises on the day of humanity's awakening and humbling."[59]

Still, chemical-based farming and the processed productions of Big Food owned the day. It was, as the DuPont Corporation promised, "Better Things for Better Living . . . Through Chemistry." In the span of just 2 decades, the chemical companies had revolutionized the American food business, producing better yields, greater abundance, and a bounty of new, longer-lasting products—and 130,000 *Organic Gardening* readers and 100,000 Walnut Acres catalog customers did not a protest movement make. They were just a bunch of Luddites and back-to-nature buffs who were not about to motivate many people in Mainstream America to question the safety (or sagacity) of all those chemical additives. Not against a backdrop of suddenly plentiful iceberg lettuce, Seabrook Farms, happy housewives, Tupperware parties, and millions of people tuning in to watch *Kraft Television Theater*, *The Adventures of Rin Tin Tin* (sponsored by Nabisco), *Space Patrol* (sponsored by General Mills), *The George Burns and Gracie Allen Show* (sponsored by Carnation), or, not to be outdone, *The DuPont Show with June Allyson*.

Fear, as it turns out, would be a much stronger motivator.

In 1956 the government initiated a spraying campaign in Michigan, New York, New Jersey, and Pennsylvania to try to eradicate the gypsy moth, an annoying pest that had been imported into the country years earlier in an ill-conceived scheme to bolster the domestic silk industry, but which had escaped the lab and begun defoliating the suburban canopy of trees. A mixture of DDT in fuel oil was sprayed by air somewhat indiscriminately, covering crop lands, dairy farms, marsh ponds, suburban homes, commuters at railway stations, and millions of acres. This proved deadly to birds and bee colonies, and led to numerous tests of milk and crops in which DDT was showing up at the rate of at least 14 parts per million, more than twice the legal limit. This resulted in a protracted lawsuit by a group of prominent and vocal Long Islanders, which drew a great deal of publicity.[60] According to J.I. Rodale, this was the first time "the highly populated northeastern areas of the United States had dramatized to its populace the extent to which the chemical industry is today influencing our environment."[61]

The following year, the USDA began a campaign to eradicate fire ants in the South, using two relatively new pesticides called dieldrin and heptachlor, which were many times more toxic than DDT, but about which little was known. Poultry and pets died. Cows perished, and so did some of their calves who had been fed only milk since birth. On one tract of land in Alabama, half of the birds were killed. In Hardin County, Texas, the populations of raccoons, opossums, and armadillos were annihilated.[62]

Then, just before Thanksgiving in 1959, residues of the widely used herbicide aminotriazole were found in Oregon cranberries. Aminotriazole was known to have caused thyroid cancer in laboratory animals, and although medical experts disputed the threat to humans, the US Food and Drug Administration (FDA) issued a ban on these cranberries. The Department of Health, Education and Welfare later issued a ban on all aminotriazole-treated cranberries from 1957 to 1959. The thought of a toxic Thanksgiving dinner *2 years in the past* must have been a bit unsettling to those who learned about it on *Douglas Edwards with the News*—prior to the regularly scheduled CBS broadcast of *The DuPont Show with June Allyson*.

All of these events, and many more, were chronicled in Rachel Carson's book *Silent Spring*, which began appearing in serialized form in the *New Yorker* in the spring of 1962. Carson, a marine biologist, was an insightful naturalist and gifted writer whose 1950 book, *The Sea Around Us*, a lyrical description of the marine world from the point of view of those who live in it, stayed on the *New York Times* best-seller list for 86 weeks, 39 of them in first place. In *Silent*

Spring, however, Carson moved away from the mellifluous marine language of her earlier works, and turned visceral, urgent, and not so vaguely threatening. Her description of 11 orange pickers in Riverside, California, poisoned by parathion—reduced to "retching, half-blind, semi-conscious misery"—conjured the writing of Ambrose Bierce or Stephen Crane. She told of puppies and little boys dying due to pesticide exposure, "the appalling destruction of wildlife," and asked us to imagine a sterile future world in which "no witch-craft, no enemy action had silenced the rebirth. . . . The people had done it themselves."[63]

Carson turned social critic as well, methodically building the case for the dangers of DDT and chemical agriculture, castigating the chemical industry for spreading flawed information, and lambasting the government for its close ties to the industry and lack of perspicacious oversight. As Mark Hamilton Lytle wrote in his biography of Carson, *The Gentle Subversive,* her work "call[ed] into question the paradigm of scientific progress that defined postwar American culture. She faulted the legion of scientists and corporate interests who, through arrogance or carelessness or willful ignorance, employed chemicals, a weapon 'as crude as a cave man's club . . . against the fabric of life.'"[64]

It also provided encouragement to the small cadre of people who were starting to advocate for a return to organic farming and natural foods. *Silent Spring,* Paul Keene wrote, "began to suggest a growing awareness, a built-in rectifying spirit of common sense that seems to be ever a part of life."[65] Many of those who would go on to join Keene in the production of natural foods would cite Rachel Carson as one of their primary inspirations.

Silent Spring was a selection of the prestigious Book of the Month Club, received wide coverage and critical acclaim, and was on the *New York Times* best-seller list for 31 weeks.

The work also drew raging criticism. While *Silent Spring* was still in the stage of *New Yorker* serialization, the Velsicol Chemical Company, sole manufacturer of heptachlor and chlordane (pesticides that were attacked by Carson), threatened to sue if the magazine moved forward with another installment, though nothing ever came of it. The Velsicol general counsel argued that chemicals were essential "if we are to continue to enjoy the most abundant and purest foods ever enjoyed by any country of this world."[66] William Darby, head of biochemistry at Vanderbilt School of Medicine, argued that Carson's call for restraint on pesticides would bring about "the end of all human progress, reversion to a passive social state devoid of technology, scientific medicine, agriculture, sanitation."[67]

To the generation of Americans that had been born into the optimism of the postwar years and had been raised in an era of paternalistic government, but who were now coming of age and beginning to openly question the tenets of society, *Silent Spring* was like a bolt from the blue. And the criticism the book received from the entrenched captains of capitalism and crew-cut members of the Establishment—all of which reeked of ulterior motives—only served to deepen their skepticism. Before long, *Silent Spring* would prove to be the most influential book of its generation, a sort of countercultural codex that served as the touchstone for the young high-minded idealists in the tumultuous decade ahead. For them, *Silent Spring* passed directly into the Summer of Love, and ultimately to the fall from grace of conventional foods.

CHAPTER 2

A FEW GNARLY
PIECES OF FRUIT

D efiantly un-springlike, the sixties came in like Lamb Chop and went
out like Elsa the Lioness.

With the clamor and discord of an especially noisy era, the
homespun early sixties wholesomeness embodied by Shari Lewis's sock puppet
gradually turned cloying and quaint, while the ecological protest symbolized
by Joy Adamson's leonine *Born Free* heroine eventually found its voice. In
between came roiling years of change that took us from black-and-white TV to
Day-Glo tie-dye, from space shots to acid trips, civil rights to civil unrest, love
to Haight, Jack Paar to Laugh-In, JFK-and-Jackie to Sonny-and-Cher, and from
the two-finger peace sign to the one-finger salute. "By the end of the decade,"
wrote cultural anthropologists Jane and Michael Stern, "it seemed that everybody was furious with everybody else."[1]

Entertainment, fashion, sex, religion, government, education, music—
every aspect of society got caught up in the social revolution, as generations
new and old forced each other into a fundamental reevaluation of what they
thought they knew and held sacred. America quickly mutated from a society
in which the amiable family physician made house calls with a few palliatives
in his black bag, to one in which the CIA began covertly experimenting with
LSD in search of a truth serum—and soon many others joined in. Joan Baez
appeared on the cover of *Time* magazine, as did Julie Andrews and Jackie

Gleason and a bikini-clad epoxy resin sculpture of Raquel Welch; but so did the question "Is God Dead?" and the Vietnam War—35 times.

Thus, a decade that began with the joyful and somewhat innocent exercise of a new set of cultural values rapidly descended into protest, provocation, violence, and a profound national identity crisis. And it was at precisely this time that the generation of people who would become the pioneering Natural Prophets of the latter 20th century was coming of age.

———•———

Among the things called into question as the decade transitioned from open expression to open revolt was the very ground on which people were standing, and farming.

The agricultural industry was of course already in the throes of its own dramatic chemical metamorphosis. *Silent Spring* did have a major impact in beginning to curb DDT use, but the pesticide's usefulness had diminished over time anyway. Many insects, it turns out, produce three or four generations in a single year, and can quickly build up a resistance to chemicals. So those "cow barn" flies that were initially being killed by 60-day-old applications of DDT quickly underwent a Darwinian miracle: As early as 1949, just 4 years after the pesticide's release into general use, 87 percent of all flies in the United States were resistant to it.[2]

Thanks in large part to the stern defense of chemical agriculture mounted by the scientific community and other vested interests, there was always another pesticide formulation hitting the market. As Rachel Carson had noted, the production of synthetic pesticides in the United States quintupled from 1947 to 1960, to a total of almost 638 million pounds, and it continued to grow after that; today the total exceeds 5.6 billion pounds a year.[3] Throughout the sixties the agrichemical companies began building all kinds of better mousetraps, including Alar and Atrazine and Dursban and Kelthane and Furadan—each of which received millions of applications, and each of which would eventually be banned or severely restricted.

Meanwhile, hormones were added to the farmer's toolkit when it was discovered that the synthetic estrogen diethylstilbestrol, or DES, which had been prescribed to women for 30 years to help prevent miscarriages, had the curious effect of causing cattle to gain weight quickly when pellets of DES were implanted behind their ears.[4] Thus began the routine use of hormones and antibiotics in livestock for purposes much different from those for which they had been developed.

And in the laboratories, all kinds of new food additives were being developed to help food look prettier, taste better, and last longer. One that became extremely popular was cyclamate, an artificial sweetener dozens of times sweeter than sugar that had been discovered in 1937 when a University of Illinois graduate student working in a lab rested his cigarette on a bench and noticed a sweet taste as he put it back in his mouth. It was commercially introduced in the 1950s and was put into wide use in the 1960s—until 1969, when it was proven to cause cancer in lab animals, and thus became the first food additive banned by the FDA.

All of this chemical euphoria was good news for Big Food companies. General Foods, under the leadership of Chairman Chauncey William "C.W." Cook—a post–C.W. Post "C.W."!—invested heavily in the development of processed foods with a full complement of the latest artificial additives. General Foods soon began spending millions advertising products like Shake 'n Bake, Cool Whip, freeze-dried Sanka, and, for good measure, D-Zerta, a low-calorie artificially sweetened version of Jell-O, which itself was sort of an artificially flavored version of gelatin or pudding.

Indeed, despite the vivid footage from Vietnam and the menacing news of riots delivered each night by the stern visage of Walter Cronkite, this was a time of cheery consumerism throughout the food business. The suburban diaspora had begun, creating larger homes with larger pantries and the need for wood-paneled station wagons to ferry home more and more goods from the store. About one out of every eight grocery stores in 1963 was now large enough to be called a supermarket, and they accounted for 69 percent of all grocery sales. New supermarkets opened that year averaged 19,900 square feet, twice the size of prewar stores, and they were filled with aisle upon aisle of the newest packaged goods.[5] And new they were: 50 percent of the items available in those aisles in the early sixties did not exist 10 years earlier.[6] Where once there had been wonder expressed at each new food creation (instant coffee! pre-baked beans!), now the industry had matured to an inevitable new phase in which competitive knockoffs were everywhere (Folgers, Maxwell House, Nescafé). So the battle for profits in those supermarket aisles would be fought not by what was *in* the can, but by what was *on* it and what could be projected onto it: the brand.

Soon, two-thirds of newspaper revenue and half of TV revenue would be coming from food advertising.[7] Millions of dollars were funneled to Madison Avenue to create snappy jingles that could get lodged in the minds of those who sat captive in front of the television. A 1965 study found that the typical consumer had an astonishingly high 34 percent recall of TV ads.[8] With some 541 commercial TV stations (nearly all carrying the programming of CBS, NBC, and ABC) beaming to the rabbit ears of 90 percent of the homes in America, it was the very definition of a mass market. This was perfectly suited to the Big Food companies, which were built to create huge volumes of undifferentiated products; the more people they could reach with a single message, the higher their sales would go. Thus, if you were one of the 12 million people watching an episode of *Gunsmoke* or *The Beverly Hillbillies,* before very long there was simply no way to avoid knowing that Almond Joy has nuts (Mounds don't), or that things go better with Coke.

Those who were unpersuaded by Madison Avenue's catchy tunes and wanted to seek out foods with better ingredients had their work cut out for them. Without any requirements for ingredients to be listed on labels, there was often no way to tell what additives had been included. In passing a 1958 amendment to the Food, Drug, and Cosmetic Act called the Delaney Clause, which required the FDA to ban any food additives shown to cause cancer in laboratory animals, Congress had grandfathered in nearly 1,000 chemicals "generally regarded as safe (GRAS)," which comprised just about every additive then known.[9] None of these had to be singled out on a package, and in most cases would hardly have made sense anyway: Wonder Bread, the popular product that kids liked to ball up and bounce, had some very un-breadlike ingredients, now identified as the bleaching agent azodicarbonamide and the dough emulsifier know by the acronym DATEM. (The Fair Packaging and Labeling Act of 1967 introduced some labeling requirements, but as late as 1980 only about 10 percent of supermarket products had full ingredient labels.)[10] As long as the additives were on the GRAS list, they could be concisely summarized by innocuous-sounding phrases like "artificial flavorings."

Moreover, very little attention was being paid to the natural foods category. The food marketplace was beginning to cleave into segments, none of which were terribly worried about purity. On one end, Julia Child went on the air in 1962 as *The French Chef,* promoting French cooking techniques and sparking an interest in the continental menu and gourmet food; she was much more concerned with taste than with nutrition. On the other end, urbane young women (a group Jane and Michael Stern characterized as "perky girls," symbolized by Marlo Thomas in *That Girl* and Sally Field in *Gidget*) were no longer majoring in home ec. They had careers to pursue and parties to plan, and were more likely to buy convenience foods and throw together pauper's pizzas and other dishes that, the Sterns noted, "required little culinary skill but were as amusing as driving an orange motor scooter to work."[11] Shake 'n Bake and Cool Whip were just the ticket. In between those poles lay the reliably bland meat-and-potatoes Middle America, phlegmatically loading up on homogenized groceries at the Big Bear or Piggly Wiggly three times a week.

Beyond a few progressive outposts, mostly on the coasts and the outskirts of college towns, there simply weren't many people clamoring for natural or organic foods. The "compost and ladybug" routine advocated by the Rodales was not for everyone. Nor were the parcel-post eggs of Walnut Acres. Furthermore, the news media and other standard-bearers of established society, reflecting prevailing Cold War sentiments, made it clear that "progress" in agriculture and food production was a good thing, not to be questioned. "The US farmer now approaches a mastery over nature," *Life* magazine proclaimed in 1962. "[He] alters nature almost at will, breeding his animals and plants to consumer preference, growing gardens where climate and soil had all but outlawed life, changing the very chemistry of the earth to feed the ravenous roots of his bumper crops."[12]

The real showcase of progress, the 1964 World's Fair at Flushing Meadows Park, New York, featured many examples of that "mastery over nature." There was Chunky Square, where candy bars were made on site; agricultural pavilions that featured the latest farming innovations; the Better Living Center, with exhibits that included Sunshine biscuits and Hershey's chocolate (and, curiously, one called Natural Foods, Inc.); and, of course, an enormous presence by the postmodern Postum Cereal Company, General Foods. For sheer blithesome radiance, however, nothing at the '64 Fair could top the "Wonderful World of Chemistry" pavilion from DuPont, which included a live performance by a group of clean-cut, Pepsodent-perfect young dancers doing the Watusi and singing lyrics like, "You know we all have a smile on/That started with Nylon."[13]

But underneath the surface society, the magma of a disenfranchised generation was simmering. The polite strumming protests of Peter, Paul and Mary gave way to the dissonant overdrive of Jimi Hendrix, the riots in Watts, and the cultural chaos of Haight-Ashbury. In October 1967, the 82nd Airborne was called out in full riot gear during the huge antiwar march on the Pentagon. There were protests on hundreds of college campuses, some of which turned violent. With the development of a throbbing counterculture, it was unsurprising to also find the appearance of what social historian Warren J. Belasco called a "countercuisine." Characterized by whole grains, organic agriculture, a sprinkling or two of philosophy, and a lot of brown foods (brown rice, whole wheat bread, soy, turbinado sugar) suitable for a culture that was no longer so Orval Faubus white, the countercuisine gradually came to form "a coherent set of dietary beliefs and practices"[14] that stood in stark contrast to the synthetic chemicals that were overtaking the farms and the additive-laden convenience products that the Big Food companies had begun creating en masse.

By 1965 there were about 500 health foods stores, food co-ops, and workers' collectives that had popped up around the country (compared to 30,000 or more supermarkets).[15] Most of them were small groceries, no more than about 1,000 to 2,000 square feet. They were frequently located in building spaces that were ill-suited for retail use or which had failed in any number of other incarnations. They were usually no-frills affairs, with wood slat floors, low ceilings, bad lighting, and wooden barrels filled with serve-your-own brown rice or honey or peanut butter. Many even lacked refrigeration.

Some of the health foods stores were run by straight-laced dowagers with an old-world commitment to pure foods. There was New Age Foods in Boulder, Colorado, started in 1957 by the 44-year-old Hanna Kroeger, featuring natural products as well as herbal healing classes. In Los Angeles, there was Lindberg Nutrition, founded in 1949 by Gladys Lindberg and her husband, Walter, out of concern that modern children were malnourished and not as robust as prior generations. Lindberg's 11 stores featured jewelry-type display cases and pecan wall paneling, juice bars and nutritional counseling areas; the employees all wore pink and the store used the tagline, "Keep in the pink."

But by the mid-sixties, when peyote and peacock-colored paisley were in the ascendancy, the health foods stores and co-ops were more likely to be run by hippies who were dropping out and dripping with the idealism of the age. They had all of the earnestness of Kroeger and Lindberg, but often no particular business goals other than to feed themselves and to do things in precisely the manner in which the typical businesses would not. This could take the form of collective buying efforts, co-ops in which traditional roles of management were thrown out, and even quasi-nonprofit structures where the proceeds of the business were considered to be an unfortunate by-product and were given away to charity. Some had tinges of religion or mysticism. Most had counter-cultural elements, and many even bore the idealistic (and one might speculate pharmaceutically inspired) names of the age: Back to Eden, Earth Stone, People's Grainery, Co-Opportunity, Mother Truckers, Joyous Revival, the Sun and Earth Shop, Food Conspiracy, Nature's Children, Wholly Foods, Yellow Sun Natural Foods, and Beautiful Day Trading Company.

To a post–Bay of Pigs America, this sort of collectivism may have smacked of communism. But inside the four badly spackled walls of the health foods stores, a participatory process seemed as natural as the foods they were selling, even when it turned dysfunctional. There were, for example, many debates about just what foods to sell under the health foods store rubric (all organic, or just preservative-free? all good-for-you, or were natural snacks loaded with calories okay?)—fundamental issues that would hound the natural foods industry for decades, the resolution of which would ultimately come to define a new era in the industry in the 21st century. Warren Belasco noted that "differences were often discussed to the point of exhaustion and schism. With everything connected—food, health, politics—it was hard to establish priorities. The chief problem lay in balancing economic and idealistic goals, price and ideology, pure shopping and pure revolution."[16] This, too, would be a legacy carried forward in the natural foods industry.

The staples of the health foods store were items like cranberry beans, fava beans, azuki beans, sunflower seeds, wheat germ, bulgur, sprouted mung beans, carrot juice, yogurt, comfrey tea, granola, and earthy loaves of bread sprinkled with poppy or sesame seeds. Asian-inspired soy products such as tofu and tempeh were also common. And almost all of the health foods stores had a field bin or two with a few gnarly pieces of organic fruit, which, because the art and science of organic farming had not yet been rediscovered, lacked the robustness, uniformity, and overall visual appeal of nearly everything farmed conventionally. If there were still some dirt clinging to the fruit, or some bugs on it, all the better. Additionally, some health foods stores sold vitamins and supplements like garlic oil perles, but most were limited to food and left those items to the "pill shops," of which there were quite a few.

There were also a few branded items in the health foods stores. One line was called Carque's, developed by a German immigrant named Otto Carque, who began selling dried fruits out of his "health wagon" in 1912. They offered the Carque's California Fruit Bar, as well creamed papaya, apricot mango juice, nut butters, and more. Carque was one of the first people to promote natural foods and to speak out against pesticides. He opened three natural foods stores in California by 1926, and published a book called *Natural Foods: The Safe Way to Health*—a full 53 years before John Mackey would also riff on the name of one of the country's largest grocers with the opening of Safer Way Foods.[17]

Customers at a health foods store might also find products by Hain. Harold Hain founded Hain Pure Foods in 1926 in Stockton, California, marketing carrot and celery juice. He sold the company in 1953 for $100,000 to an entrepreneurial pharmacist named George Jacobs, who expanded the product line to include safflower oil, pure nut butters, fruit juices, and more. There was exactly zero indication at the time that this would go on to become the biggest name in the natural foods manufacturing business.

Other early health foods brands included Lundberg Rice, which had been around since 1937, and Alta Dena—a line of dairy products produced by the Stueve family utilizing "natural" standards, starting in 1945. But there were no Bac-Os, no Awake synthetic orange juice, no Moo imitation milk, no Carnation Instant Breakfasts, as there were in all of the conventional supermarkets of the 1960s. Not even any Post Toasties, which may have had a few ingredients added over the years but which were ostensibly still a "clean" product. In the health foods stores, the ingredients mattered less than what the brand represented, which meant that virtually everything produced by Big Food was out.

Of course, this meant that most of America was out, too. To the Establishment, the health foods stores were dens of iniquity, the "health nuts" were well left of normal, and the health claims of those who promoted natural and organic foods sounded like flummery spewed by hucksters who were directly descended from the snake-oil salesmen of a few decades earlier.

Certainly there had been good reason in the past to question or at least temper the enthusiasm of the sunflower seed set, which had produced its share of charlatans and Chicken Littles. The story of Sylvester Graham—a

19th-century Presbyterian minister who preached that vegetarianism and a high fiber diet could help cure alcoholism and prevent masturbation—was still well known, and recounted in the media as his namesake graham crackers grew in popularity. In the 1920s there had been a small chorus of health foods advocates who had spoken out against iodized salt. Two decades later, there were others who offered specious claims that lecithin could lower cholesterol, and they were roundly attacked by the medical community. More recently, health foods of one sort or another had been enthusiastically offered up as cures to arthritis, cancer, impotence, old age, and just about every other malady known to humankind.

This sort of boosterism—reminiscent of the heavy-handedness of the early railroad men and Western promoters, who urged settlers to go farm in the arid country because "rain follows the plow"—did not sit well with the Establishment. Health foods promoters were called "faddists" and "nuts" and "worshippers." The phrase *natural foods* was often set off in quotation marks, as if it were some whimsical concept invented by Lewis Carroll—though in truth there was no strict definition for it, or even for organic foods: The rules that began to develop in each state were all different. In Emmaus, Pennsylvania, the Rodales sensed this threat, and sought to layer some legitimacy onto the organic movement with a Rodale Seal of Approval for any farm whose soil humus content proved to be 3 percent or greater when tested by an independent lab.

Some of the boosters argued that organic and synthetic fertilizers were indistinguishable, and even that pesticides shouldn't be a threat to humans because, as the food author and encyclopedist James Trager wrote in *Vogue* magazine in 1971, they "can and should be biodegradable, not persistent."[18] No one knew for sure, any more than they knew whether smoking truly caused lung cancer. As late as 1972, the major magazines were running articles with titles such as "The $2 Billion Health Food . . . Fraud?" and "What's So Great about Health Foods?" *Life* magazine noted that "[h]ealth food stores come in all shades of scrupulousness."[19] *Harper's Bazaar* called health foods "one of the costlier rip-offs of these times" and quoted Dr. Frederick J. Stare, chairman of Harvard's Department of Nutrition since its founding in 1942, as saying that nothing at all could be gained from a diet of organic foods. "*All* foods are composed of chemicals," Stare said. "You and I are composed of chemicals. And strictly speaking, *all* foods are organic."[20]

Yet no part of the health foods world was castigated more frequently in the sixties and seventies than the macrobiotic diet, popularized in the United States by a unique Japanese immigrant named Michio Kushi and the company he and his wife, Aveline, launched in 1966 called Erewhon.

The roots of macrobiotics date back to ancient Greece, where Hippocrates used the term in his essay "Airs, Waters and Places." Herodotus and Aristotle also wrote about it. It was revived in Germany in the late 18th century, and then in Japan in the 19th century. The basic concept is that one can live a long and vigorous life by moderating and balancing the approach to diet, spiritual, and social matters, each of which has countervailing "yin" and "yang" elements. The macrobiotic philosophy that Michio and Aveline had learned from modern macrobiotics master George Ohsawa, and began teaching in the United States in 1955, saw the changes in food quality as "the basic cause of the breakdown of modern civilization."[21] The diet itself emphasized traditional foods such as whole grains, beans, locally grown vegetables, soy foods, some white meat fish and shellfish, sea salt instead of refined salt, and natural grain sweeteners such as rice syrup and barley malt instead of refined white sugar. The macrobiotic diet excluded red meat, alcohol, and dairy products. On its own, that dietary regimen—there were 10 different macrobiotic levels—was not far off from what many people in the counterculture were eating, especially the growing number of vegetarians.

Some doctors and nutritionists issued warnings about the macrobiotic diet, pointing out that strict adherents to macrobiotics were at risk because of inadequate amounts of liquids and vitamin B_{12}, and should not rely on brown rice as the "perfect food." Macrobiotic children, they noted, tended to be in only the 10th to 30th percentiles for height and weight. Furthermore, public concerns were raised by the news in 1965 that a 24-year-old New Jersey woman named Beth Ann Simon, who had been following the cereal-heavy macrobiotic diet 7, had withered to 70 pounds and starved to death.[22] Soon thereafter, the FDA shut down the New York branch of the Ohsawa Foundation, which at the time was the leading center for macrobiotics in the country.

This was a setback to the macrobiotic community, which, like the larger natural foods community to which it was related, was craving legitimacy. Some quietly mumbled that Beth Ann Simon had been using heroin, and that the government crackdowns in the wake of her death were merely further evidence that there was some sort of conspiracy among Western medicine, Big Food, the FDA, and the agrichemical industry. But the setback was only temporary. Fueled by 1960s juju, the macrobiotic movement gained strength in places like San Francisco; Los Angeles; Ann Arbor, Michigan; Seattle; and especially in Boston, where the community that the Kushis had built around Erewhon and their *East West Journal* was strong, and where by 1972 nearly 20 percent of the estimated 10,000 macrobiotic followers in the United States lived.[23] The diet became known in many parts as "Zen macrobiotics," and was often practiced in "macrobiotic study houses" and other communal living situations. A cookbook published that year listed 368 different macrobiotic stores and restaurants.[24]

Where macrobiotics became a bit more threatening to a Western audience was in its behavioral, philosophical, and cosmological elements. "Macrobiotics," Kushi wrote, "embraces behavior, thought, breathing, exercise, relationships, customers, cultures, ideas, and consciousness, as well as individual and collective lifestyles found throughout the world."[25] Kushi urged adherents to chew their food well ("at least fifty times or more per mouthful"); when eating, to "sit with a good posture and take a moment, inwardly or outwardly, to express gratitude for your food"; and whenever possible, to walk barefoot on the beach or grass, "as this stimulates energy flow in the body."[26]

Wally Gorell, who went to work for the Kushis, expressed the macrobiotic philosophy this way: "We were intent on changing the world, nothing less, so we saw *everything* we did—eating, tripping, dancing, loving—as vitally important. Reading Timothy Leary, Jethro Kloss, Alan Watts, George Ohsawa and others, we learned that we had to change ourselves before we could change anyone else. So we determined to change ourselves, to *embody* change."[27]

Macrobiotic thinking occasionally veered out of standard earth orbit altogether. Kushi was intent on "recognizing universal laws and principles—the infinite order of the universe—as the foundation of all existing world philosophies, religions, cultures, economic and political systems, and arts and sciences." He created pages upon pages of dreary documentation of the biological and social decline of modern society, citing statistics on headaches, psychiatric disorders, birth defects, and amputations.[28] By the 1990s, Kushi's writings about macrobiotics even had a Steven Spielberg vibe to them. If things continued on their present path, he wrote in *Macrobiotic Diet* (1993), "humankind will inevitably face total collapse within the next fifty years," and he could also foresee that "as human abilities are replaced by artificial ones, fierce competition may arise between robots and humans and between the semi-humans or semi-robots that could arise from their union as the result of advances in recombinant DNA and other biogenetic techniques."[29]

But in its early days, most of the focus of macrobiotics was on food. And so in 1966, with DDT and cyclamate still very much on the mind, macrobiotics' emphasis on "clean" foods provided a boost to the natural foods movement. Michio and Aveline opened a macrobiotics store on Boston's Newbury Street in April of that year, in a tiny 200-square-foot space below street level. They named it Erewhon (pronounced AIR-wahn), an anagram of the word *nowhere* that had been invented by Samuel Butler in his 1872 novel *Erewhon: or, Over the Range*. They sold obscure macrobiotic products like the sea vegetables agar-agar and kombu, and stone-ground sweet brown rice flour. There were miso and tamari, most of which had just been sent in tins as gifts by the Kushis' friends in Japan, and didn't go through customs. Evan Root, the first store manager, recalled that "the store defied all business reason as so few people came through the doors to shop. It was principally a place where people came to talk and wonder about our place in the universe, and how macrobiotic practice could align us with that order." The store brought in less than $100 a day for the first year.[30]

But Erewhon was not like all of the mom-and-pop health foods stores around the country, because retail was only a small part of its business model.

One difference was the educational mission. Erewhon was founded "not on the profit motive but out of a desire to serve the public," recalled onetime store worker and *East West Journal* writer Ronald Kotzsch. "From the outset it had two primary aims: to make available the highest quality natural whole foods, and to educate the public in the importance and proper use of these foods. The store was a natural and necessary extension of the educational activities of the Kushis. . . . "[31]

Another key difference, of course, was that there was a business model at all. Unlike so many of the progenitors of co-ops and patchouli parlors, the Kushis and the people they hired were strategic thinkers who wrote books, founded institutes, published journals, and more—in today's parlance, "parallel entrepreneurs." What they realized was that the staples of the macrobiotic diet—whole grains, brown rice, sea vegetables, Asian soy products—were very hard to get in the United States. With their ties to food producers and (legitimate) exporters in Japan, and with some scrambling to establish relationships with US growers, Erewhon sought to become a true vertically integrated company that could manufacture, sell, and distribute products to the emerging network of natural and/or macrobiotic stores and restaurants. And if that worked, it could then expand horizontally to open other retail stores, as well. The anagram for nowhere was getting somewhere.

Distribution was the key. At the time there were only a handful of natural foods distributors, such as Kahan and Lessin in Los Angeles, Landstrom in San Francisco, Balanced Foods and Sherman Foods in New York, and Health Foods, Inc., in Illinois. None of them had any vertical business operations. By packaging some products in bulk (50- or 100-pound bags of brown rice), developing their own "private label" for other products, printing up a price list or catalog (a la Walnut Acres), and acquiring a few trucks, Erewhon would be able to create some economies of scale and provide a valuable service to others.

The links to macrobiotics were always there, as in the leaflet Erewhon offered that started out with the psychedelic-sounding principle that "everything is the differentiated manifestation of one infinity."[32] But to a certain extent, Erewhon became part of the larger natural foods industry. Thus, the label on its organic brown rice bulk bag contained a mix of Zen and organic messages:

> We at Erewhon are happy to offer these whole natural foods to you. Since food is basic to good health, and since good health is the foundation of a happy and creative society, we treat our food with the greatest respect and care. Since the effects on man of many of the chemicals which are presently being used on farms may not be known for many years hence, and since their effect on the delicate ecological balance of man and his environment is not beneficial, we are following that path which will take us towards a renewal and regeneration of our land and natural resources.[33]

In 1968 Erewhon began formally importing products from Japan and moved into a much larger (2,000 square feet!) retail store farther down Newbury Street. Soon it was carrying more exotic items like lotus root tea, charred eggplant, sesame shampoo, and barley-soy paste. By March of 1970, there were 96 items in the order catalog. Erewhon added a 40,000-square-foot warehouse and processing facility in South Boston. Sales grew to about $8,700 per week, enough to warrant expansion.

Aveline Kushi soon moved to Los Angeles and established Erewhon-West as a retail/distribution company. It still mostly offered products in bulk, such as the 100-pound sacks of brown rice that sold for $16.50 each. The Los Angeles outfit sold about 1,200 of these per month, with 90 percent of them going to retail stores and universities.[34] Aveline also began to attract a bizarre mix of health-minded Hollywood celebrities to her home, including Cicely Tyson, Frank Zappa, Lenny Capizzi (cocreator with Bobby Pickett of "The Monster Mash"), and silent film star Gloria Swanson—who, more than 20 years earlier, had been photographed in a stylish black dress and heels, visiting none other than J.I. Rodale on his farm.[35]

Erewhon's overall sales totaled just under $500,000 in 1970, $1.9 million in 1971, and an estimated $3.2 million in 1972.[36] As demand soared, Erewhon scrambled to keep up with the supply. It took over the rice contract that the California macrobiotic company Chico-San had set up with Lundberg Rice, after Chico-San's facilities were lost in a fire; by 1973 Erewhon had contracted with 57 farms in 35 different states to provide a wide variety of organic products.[37] To meet the needs of the many natural foods stores it served, Erewhon also began to carry some natural foods that were *not* macrobiotic, such as yogurt, frozen meat, and vitamins. Sales reached $6.8 million in 1976, and topped $10 million for the first time in 1978—but, because the company now had the carrying costs of more than 4,000 items in inventory, and the additional expense of a union contract that was authorized in 1979, it started losing money. Erewhon, in the view of Ronald Kotzsch, had succumbed to "the intoxicant of growth."[38] Like so many of the entrepreneurial natural foods companies that would follow in its wake, Erewhon ran out ahead of its infrastructure and ran short of cash.

What made Erewhon finally unravel were the internecine rivalries within the industry. Around 1975 Erewhon began to distribute to co-ops. Some of the retail stores complained that this was undercutting them, because it was tantamount to "selling directly to customers at wholesale prices." Several stores began to boycott Erewhon in 1976, and in turn Erewhon sued. Erewhon won the case, but racked up a quarter-million dollars in legal bills, debt from which it was never able to recover.[39] Owing creditors $4.3 million, the company filed for Chapter 11 bankruptcy protection on November 9, 1981.

In the end, as onetime shop manager Jimmy Silver wrote in the preface to the *History of Erewhon,* "As a business entity, Erewhon failed. As a business idea, it was wildly successful." [40]

Certainly Erewhon's influence on the natural products industry was substantial.

First, its focus on the primacy of distribution (often, but not always, as part of a vertically integrated company) became a model for the industry. Erewhon influenced many others to follow the same path, including Eden Organic Foods in Ann Arbor, Michigan; Essene in Philadelphia; Food For Life in Chicago; Janus in Seattle; Laurelbrook in Forest Hill, Maryland; The Well in San Jose, California; and Westbrae Natural Foods in Berkeley, California. The distributors paved the way for steady growth on the retail side: The total number of health foods stores, which in 1965 had been just 500, reached 2,000 to 3,000 by 1972.[41] No less a tool of the Establishment than the *Wall Street Journal* predicted that natural foods would be one of the 10 highest growth industries for the decade of the 1970s. Even Sears Roebuck got into the act, with a separate catalog for "health and organic foods."[42]

Second, many people who worked at Erewhon in its early days would become influential in the new progressive world. Among them were Paul Hawken (called by *Fortune* magazine "the original hippie entrepreneur," he would go on to found the garden supply chain Smith & Hawken, sell millions of copies of his books about environmentalism, and win many awards and honorary doctorates);[43] A.C. Gallo (who would go on to work at Bread & Circus and become the co-president of Whole Foods Market); Doug Rauch (who became a top executive at Trader Joe's); and Eric Utne (who left Erewhon to create a restaurant at the University of Minnesota called Whole Foods—years before the creation of either Whole Foods Company in New Orleans or Whole Foods Market in Austin, Texas—and later founded *The Utne Reader*).

Third, Erewhon established New England, and Boston in particular, as one of the centers of the natural foods movement. This would provide some of the intellectual capital and the market for the many natural products manufacturers that would pop up there in years to come, including Stonyfield Farm, Tom's of Maine, Lightlife, and Seventh Generation. Even more importantly, Erewhon became a major supplier to, and influencer of, the Irish immigrant Anthony Harnett and the chain of New England natural foods supermarkets he developed called Bread & Circus.

Finally, to this day the Erewhon name lives on as a brand, producing well regarded if somewhat obscure organic cereals and graham crackers. The brand merged with U.S. Mills in 1986, was acquired by Attune Foods in 2009, and then sold once again in January 2013. The new owner? A little company that in 2007 had been spun off from Kraft (General Foods), called Post Cereals.

—•—

Throughout these years, the Rodale family continued their quiet, persistent campaign for organic agriculture and natural foods. On the farm near Allentown, Pennsylvania, they experimented with composting and organic techniques, and welcomed visitors who wanted to learn more. They published more books and magazines, and even a weekly newsletter called *Health Bulletin*. They began talking about "the organic way of life," an extension of the farming philosophy into health and fitness and even occupation. This was sort of an eastern Pennsylvania version of the Buddhist concept of "right livelihood" that was starting to gain currency in certain circles. Bob Rodale captured it well in 1962, noting that some people "are not satisfied with the way they are spending their lives and would rather do something that would give them the feeling that their daily plan of life is in keeping with nature and not in conflict with it."[44]

The *Organic Gardening* subscriber base grew to about 300,000 by 1962—an encouraging development for J.I. and Bob, who knew there were still many critics out there who deemed them "some kind of rabid religionists."[45] To go organic, Bob wrote, "you must align yourself with the minority. You must reject the opinions of the experts and the professors and stand up to occasional charges that you are a crackpot or faddist."[46]

But the criticism kept coming. In 1964, the Federal Trade Commission took Rodale Press to court for false and deceptive advertising related to its book, *The Health Finder* (an ad for which had said that the information in the book "could add years to your life"). This was the start of a trend, continuing to this day, in which the government seemed more concerned about the claims related to health foods than about the safety of chemicals and additives actually *in* food—most of which were, after all, "generally regarded as safe."

At nearby Walnut Acres, Paul and Betty Keene were encountering similar resistance. FDA standards for peanut butter permitted the use of 10 to 15 percent non-peanut products, such as sugar, salt, and hydrogenated fats, but also stipulated that the peanuts had to be blanched. Walnut Acres had begun manufacturing peanut butter using nothing but whole, *unblanched* peanuts (including the nutritious peanut skin and germ), and no non-peanut products. The FDA objected, and told them they would have to label their product as "imitation peanut butter." The Keenes thought this was the height of absurdity, and encouraged their customers to write to Washington; they eventually got the FDA to change its standards for peanut butter, but similar battles would be fought over Walnut Acres whole grain spaghetti, and over numerous other pieces of legislation that seemed to be anti-organic. According to Paul Keene, "Walnut Acres seems to have borne the brunt of the battle over food labeling for small producers in general. Every few years proposals would come up in the Senate that, if adopted, would have put us out of business. Proposed bills would have required us to analyze every batch of every product we made in order to determine the percentages of major nutrients therein. Doing so would have cost us about a half million additional dollars at a time when our annual profit was just a few thousand dollars."[47]

The Rodales fought the deceptive advertising charge, mostly on principle since only about 240 copies of the 1957 book remained in print, and eventually prevailed on a technicality—but not before they had racked up $200,000 in legal bills and Bob had spent the better part of a year working on it.

By this time, J.I. had turned most of the day-to-day business over to Bob so that he could pursue other experiments and interests. J.I. fought against a plan to fluoridate the water in Allentown, and won. He wrote plays that had some transparently activist characters in them (in *The Hairy Falsetto,* a riff on Little Red Riding Hood, the wolf character testifies: "Your honor, I will prove to the satisfaction of this court that whenever Little Red brought groceries to her grandmother, they were the kind of packaged goods heavily loaded with chemical additives, homogenized with insecticides, and fungicides, alkaloids, propiolates, polyoxyethylene monostearates, prokylene oxides, methyl bromides and assorted diacetate compounds, benzoate of soda and 2, 4-D.").[48] And, as noted in a lengthy profile of him in the *New York Times* on June 6, 1971, the 72-year-old took 70 supplements a day, stopped work every hour for deep knee bends, and for 10 to 20 minutes each day sat in a contraption that emitted shortwave radio waves that he believed would boost his body's supply of electricity, which he theorized had been depleted because of society's steel girders overhead and insulation underfoot. His eccentricities and larger-than-life legacy thus immortalized for all time by the paper of record, J.I. Rodale went on *The Dick Cavett Show* 2 days later, declared during the taping "I never felt better in my life" and "I've decided to live to be a hundred," and died of a heart attack on the set. The show never aired.

———

The incipient natural foods movement of the sixties and early seventies was also bolstered by a somewhat more unexpected voice, whose earlier protestations could now at last be heard.

Adelle Davis was no organic farmer, but neither was she a long-haired Timothy Leary groupie in a fringed vest. Davis was a well-educated 50-something nutritionist and mother who, by 1960, had already published six books on health-related topics, including *Let's Cook It Right* (1947) and *Let's Eat Right to Keep Fit* (1954). She had earned a degree in household studies from UC Berkeley in 1927 and a master's in biochemistry from USC in 1943. "You are what you eat," she had often said, and she did not eat enriched white bread, packaged mixes, refined sugar, or soft drinks. Davis was an especially staunch supporter of whole wheat bread, noting at one point that the 40 nutrients humans need daily can all be found in wheat, but that the modern milling process removes most of them. "The reason weevils can't live in [white] flour is the same reason humans can't live on it," she told the *New York Times*.[49] She grew her own fruits and vegetables, and advocated for the use of supplementary vitamins, earning the nickname "Vitamin Davis" during 2 years at Purdue University. She reportedly took dozens of vitamins (as well as brewer's yeast) daily at a time when, J.I. Rodale aside, that was still an unusual practice.

Davis had worked as a consultant and personal nutritionist for many years. Yet despite her experience and her books, her views about the linkage between diet and health sometimes went unheeded by the food and medical community and the public at large.

Some of her ideas *were* a bit radical. She insisted, for example, that even mental and social ills (including alcoholism, crime, and divorce) could be tied to poor nutrition. She had also suggested that France fell to Germany at the start of World War II because the black bread and beer of the Germans were nutritionally superior to the white bread and wine of the French.[50] (Later, she would note that the Manson Family had subsisted mainly on

candy bars.) She also was somewhat sloppy with her research, and sometimes drew conclusions based on anecdotal evidence.[51]

In the post–*Silent Spring* era, however, with *Organic Gardening* reaching
700,000 subscribers by 1971, America was waking up to the new realities of its
changed diet and agricultural system. Adelle Davis found a new audience and
became a much more active crusader. Lecturing on college campuses at first,
and in the early seventies during a string of appearances on *The Tonight Show
Starring Johnny Carson, The Dick Cavett Show,* and *The Mike Douglas Show,*
Davis came across as a wizened matriarch with glowing skin, a bun of gray hair
pinned up on her head, and a slightly kooky zeal for healthy eating. Her message began to catch on, and she ended up selling more than 10 million copies of
her books. (Like J.I. Rodale she would be cruelly betrayed by her own body—
succumbing to bone marrow cancer in 1974. When she was first diagnosed, she
reacted with "shock and disbelief," according to the *New York Times.* "I thought
this [disease] was for people who drink soft drinks, who eat white bread, who
eat refined sugar and so on."[52])

The words of Rachel Carson, J.I. Rodale, and Adelle Davis had provided the
intellectual underpinnings for the fight against agribusiness and Big Food. Erewhon had created some commercial momentum through its business model
and rapid growth. And soon enough, the flower children of the sixties—who
had been born into postwar conformity and affluence, but who had come of age
viewing the world through the dark lens of Vietnam and civil rights struggles
and the kaleidoscope of pharmacological freedom—would mature into a generation of idealistic entrepreneurs. But for these disparate skirmishes to
coalesce into a battle, and for the battle to intensify into a revolution, it would
still take one more factor: the development of a mass market.

It materialized seemingly out of nowhere.

First, there was a series of gatherings, concerts, and protests that attracted
hundreds of thousands of people, and a great deal of publicity, too.

On January 14, 1967, a date one astrologer projected would be when the
world's population would exactly equal the number of dead people in human history, between 20,000 and 30,000 people showed up at San Francisco's Golden Gate
Park for an event called the "Human Be-In." Among them were counterculture

icons like Timothy Leary, Gary Snyder, Jerry Rubin, and Allen Ginsberg. Five months later, the Monterey Pop Festival was even more of a mainstream hit, with performances by Jimi Hendrix, The Mamas and the Papas, Janis Joplin, The Who, Jefferson Airplane, and Simon & Garfunkel; a documentary of the concert was released the next year. In October more than 100,000 people converged in Washington for the march on the Pentagon.

Then, throughout 1968, the protests spread to college campuses. Many of these were organized by the dozens of chapters of Students for a Democratic Society, which mounted a one-day strike on April 26 in which more than 1 million of the nation's 7 million college students took part.

Martin Luther King, Jr., was assassinated in April of that year, Robert Kennedy in June. Things had heated to a rolling boil by August, when the Democratic convention was held in Chicago. The Youth International Party, or Yippies, a radical protest group, threatened to pollute the city water system with LSD and did manage to spread feces on the rugs of the Hilton Hotel, raise the North Vietnamese flag in Grant Park, and elicit a muscular response from Mayor Richard Daley and the Chicago police that included tear gas and clubbings—images of which were beamed "via satellite" into the living rooms of a horrified Middle America, chowing down on their Swanson TV dinners. Fifty weeks later, 400,000 people showed up on Max Yasgur's farm in Bethel, New York, for the Woodstock Music and Art Fair.

Next, fear reared its head once again. In January 1969, a major leak from Union Oil's well A-21 sent oil and natural gas spewing over 800 miles of pristine California coastline, from Santa Barbara to San Diego. In June Cleveland's Cuyahoga River caught fire—not the first time this had happened, but set against the TV news pictures of napalm and Agent Orange lighting the jungles of Southeast Asia aflame, as well as the first color photo of the lonely blue planet earth drifting in space, taken in December 1967, it was a potent symbol. Some people began to worry about a pending "ecotastrophe."[53] Suddenly there was more scrutiny of the issues of pesticides, synthetic additives, and "plastic" food.

In response, 20 million Americans participated in the "teach-in" event called Earth Day on April 22, 1970.[54] Later that year, President Nixon announced the establishment of the Environmental Protection Agency (EPA). And one of the first major actions the EPA took was to ban DDT, on June 14, 1972.

The motivations of the millions of people who participated in concerts and protests—and the many millions more who were there only in spirit and failed memory—differed wildly. But taken together, these events led to the fairly rapid evolution of a group consciousness, born from the counterculture movement, that had the potential to develop into a commercial market. It would take time and money and infrastructure and a few visionary people, but the components were in place to establish one of the great ironic twists in modern history: The generation of freaks, hippies, protestors, and idealists would produce some of the most successful capitalists of our time and the most consumptive society the world had ever seen.

CHAPTER 3

THE RISE OF THE
HIGH-MINDED IDEALISTS

A s the cartoon editor of the *New Yorker* since 1997, Robert Mankoff has provided his readers with many wry and whimsical social commentaries about the incongruities of modern life, but none better than a cartoon he himself drew in 1979. It depicts a large gathering of clean-cut, middle-aged people standing around in a field, wearing suits and ties and prim skirts, sipping beverages, chatting amiably . . . and it was captioned "10th Anniversary Woodstock Reunion." So goeth the revolution.

Woodstock happened in the last half of the last year of the 1960s, just 3 weeks after JFK's destiny had been fulfilled by landing a man on the moon and returning him safely to the earth. What a stark contrast! Three men crammed into a capsule in the loneliest, quietest corner of the known universe, and 400,000 people noisily spilling over the back roads and porta-potties of Bethel, New York; Neil Armstrong's all-American Navy haircut and gleaming white space suit, and a whole county's worth of hip-length hippie-dos, mutton-chop beards, and mud-splattered tie-dye. Woodstock may not have been the finish line of the long and winding road through the sixties counterculture, but it was one small step.

Those born in the first wave of what would later be called the Baby Boom generation, from 1945 through about 1954, grew up in a convulsing society, with conformity in the rearview mirror of their Edsels and individualism out on the road ahead of their VW Microbuses. Many, of course, went off to war; some 50,000 of them came back in body bags. Some of those with more favorable draft numbers (or connections, or deferments) stayed the course and slotted themselves into the prescribed positions of society and career, the arc of which was still rooted in the fifties and which they therefore thought they understood.

But there were others still, those who may have been raised in a paternalistic cocoon of comfort and affluence, yet for whom *Silent Spring* and Adelle Davis and LSD and the Warren Commission and the My Lai massacre and the 1968 Democratic convention were all turning points. Those events and many others combined to cast profound doubts in the minds of this smart, disaffected group of young people, doubts about just whose interests government and industry were truly serving. The world was failing them, and the more its stodgy scions tried to defend the status quo, the further away the kids of the sixties turned. For them, it was less a matter of personal expression than moral compunction that drove them to reject materialism, vilify the notion of capitalist competition, and look for more idealistic alternatives. Thus, as they reached adulthood and started their careers in the late sixties and early seventies, their goal was singular and humble: Save the world.

———•———

To those who know him, it comes as little surprise that Mo Siegel ultimately scaled such great heights.

He was born in 1950 in the town of Salida, Colorado, 9,000 feet up in the Monarch Pass of the Rocky Mountains—a spot where his parents had stopped en route from Chicago to Albuquerque and decided to buy a dairy ranch. The Siegels later moved to the town of Eagle Lake, north of Colorado Springs, a 7,200-foot-high "snow belt" in a region that always knew a lot of snow, at least until chlorofluorocarbons started punching a hole in the ozone layer and warming things up a bit. "Lots of people say, 'I had to walk a mile and a half through the snow to get to school every day,'" said Mo. "But no, *I had to walk a mile and a half through the snow to get to school every day.*" His eyes sparkle gently in telling the story, but his feet shift around a bit; they remember.

Siegel's mother died when he was 2 years old, at which point his 9-year-old sister, Sherry, took responsibility for raising him. His father eventually remarried and was a very busy man, so the Siegel kids were often on their own. Mo spent a lot of time outdoors, hiking the mountains and studying the natural world around him with more than just a child's wonderment: Starting at age 7 or 8, he began picking wild berries in the mountains and selling them to some of the local ladies, who would make jam out of them.

Born Jewish, he nevertheless attended The Abbey, a monastery and preparatory school in Cañon City, Colorado. There, searching for some sort of stable ground amid the rumblings of society, he became interested in a different kind of spirituality through *The Urantia Book,* a 1955 work that presented an integrated view of science, philosophy, and religion based upon the teachings of Jesus. Siegel went on, briefly, to Western State College in Gunnison, Colorado, but, profoundly distressed by the world he saw unraveling around him, he dropped out in 1969 and moved to Aspen. He had no particular plan. He lived on the cheap, hiked Red Mountain or Buttermilk whenever he could, got high, learned all about health foods, followed the course of world events through the newspaper and just shook his head. In order to earn a little cash, he sold posters (Jefferson Airplane, Peter Max, Alice's Restaurant, Marc Chagall, peace signs, etc.) out of a small storefront.

Soon these interests began to converge. Siegel moved his poster business into a tiny health foods shop called Mother's Natural Food Store, and began working there for the founder, a fellow named Roy Rickus. Mother's offered standard-fare health foods for the times—brown rice, whole grains, dried fruits—but also brewed an herbal beverage that Rickus called Moo Tea, which was offered free to all of the shoppers. Siegel was intrigued. He knew that herbal tea was popular in Germany and elsewhere in Europe, but it was virtually unknown in the United States, where traditional black teas like Lipton had defined the category for decades. Moreover, wild herbs, as he well knew, grew abundantly in the nearby mountains; whereas the traditional black tea plant, *Camellia sinensis,* was almost nonexistent in the United States, outside of a few plantations in South Carolina.

He began reading books about plants, and trekking into the mountains with botanists in search of herbs. Siegel learned how to identify edible herbs like chamomile, wild peony root, devil's club, and osha, and how to avoid some of the poisonous ones like lupine, larkspur, and black nightshade. But mostly what he developed was a nose for herbs that could make money, as he found that some of the tea blends he created proved to be very popular back in town. "Wow, you really ought to sell that tea," people would tell him. "That stuff is really great!"

But there was no particular reason to think that a real business was rustling around in the weeds. America was a coffee-drinking nation—per-capita consumption was still high, between 2 and 3 cups per day, and new freeze-dried instant brands like Maxim and Taster's Choice were being marketed with $10 million each in annual advertising.[1] Meanwhile, Lipton dominated what tea market there was with its traditional black tea products. But to a young idealist and self-described "tree-hugger" and "health fanatic" like Mo Siegel, the dream was not so much about making money, not yet; the little boy who had once picked and sold wild berries had a bigger mission. "I was convinced that part of the social trend that needed to happen in America was for people to eat healthy food and that the junk food bandwagon was just a horrible thing," said Siegel. Tea brewed from freshly picked wild mountain herbs, free of caffeine and additives, could almost be a subversive beverage—an alternative to lab-created coffees, sugar-laden sodas, and chemically enhanced juices. A few months later, he left his posters and everything else he owned behind at Mother's and hitched a ride with friends 200 miles east to Boulder, where, between Hanna Kroeger's New Age Foods and the Green Mountain Grainery, there was a bit more of a health foods scene.

Still in need of money, Siegel sold carrot juicers door to door. But he continued to hike into the mountains, often with his girlfriend (soon to be his wife), Peggy, friend Wyck Hay, and Wyck's girlfriend, Lucinda. Siegel sold Hay on the merits of herbal tea, and they decided to create a company, which they named Celestial Seasonings. Working out of a tiny A-frame and a country barn given to him by a friend, Siegel would go off and pick wild herbs with Hay, and then dump them onto screen doors to filter them and let them dry. Then they made blends such as "Mo's 36" with just herbs and natural ingredients; no artificial flavors, colors, or preservatives. They packed the tea into muslin bags, sewed them by hand, and tied them with elastic they had salvaged from scrap telephone wire. In their first year of business, they sold 10,000 tea bags to Green Mountain Grainery—a surprising success, though one that Siegel knew was not scalable. They would need some money to change that.

Of course, in any industry, respect is hard to come by for newcomers. The existing players use every tool at their disposal to erect costly barriers to entry and keep new competitors at bay. Access to capital is limited. And if your product is founded upon anything other than pure, bare-knuckled capitalism, you are at a further disadvantage; idealism has no place.

These were some hard lessons for Celestial Seasonings in its early years.

Celestial needed more space, and approached a company called Early Bird Cereal—the only other natural foods company in Boulder—for help. The landlord of Early Bird's building refused to rent space directly to Mo Siegel's little tea company, fearing it wouldn't be around for long, but he did agree to rent new space to Early Bird and let them sublease to Celestial. Early Bird subsequently went bankrupt.

Seeking capital, Siegel teamed up with Wyck Hay's brother, John. "He came in with all the big money," said Siegel. "He sold his car and the equity left was $500." Mo and John decided to apply for a loan, and set up an appointment to meet with the manager of the local bank. They walked into his office—which had solid glass walls that allowed him to look out into the lobby of the bank—wearing jeans, smelling of herbs, and armed with Tupperware containers of Mo's 36 and Sleepytime blends. They had a business plan that envisioned a $100 million company, and a request for $25,000 to get it all going. Mo thought the pitch went well, especially when, toward the end of the meeting, the manager said, "I need to bring the other executives in to hear the story. Would that be okay? Would you mind repeating your story?" The executives came in, listened patiently to the story of Mo and the wild herbs and the screen doors and the "natural foods industry," and then the meeting ended. They shook hands and left. And as Mo and John were walking through the lobby toward the exit, they looked back at the glass office and saw all of the executives laughing hysterically. Apparently, they had been asked to repeat the dog-and-peony show for sheer entertainment purposes.

The bank ended up giving Celestial Seasonings a $5,000 loan. They made John's mother co-sign for it.

Another humbling moment came on the road trip Mo Siegel took around 1971, from Colorado to New York. He stopped in Chicago, and wound up at a dinner party being thrown by Bob Bauman, a family friend of Mo's wife, Peggy. At the party was none other than C.W. Cook—the post–C.W. Post "C.W.," chief executive officer of General Foods, the erstwhile Postum Cereal Company. Mo was introduced to C.W., and the conversation began pleasantly enough. *Young Mr. Siegel had driven in from Colorado? He was in the tea business? Wasn't that interesting?* General Foods had many successful beverages, noted C.W., including

Tang, the artificially colored and flavored powdered drink mix that had been going into space since John Glenn's mission in 1962. "One of these days," Siegel remembers C.W. saying optimistically, "*all* of our food is going to be made in the labs out of chemicals." There would be no need to eat apples off trees. Vitamins would be regulated and problems like salmonella poisoning would be eliminated.

This was, of course, nothing more than the Voice of Progress itself, sounding faint echoes of Justus von Liebig, DDT cow barn fly ads, "better living through chemistry," and "We've all got a smile on/That started with Nylon." But to a high-minded idealist like Mo Siegel, it struck just the wrong note. Headstrong, full of the ideas of his generation, emboldened by the modest successes Celestial Seasonings had racked up, Siegel launched a rhetorical counteroffensive—arguing that chemicals and food additives were endangering our health, and that the companies producing them should be held accountable for those costs to society. C.W. laughed derisively, stunned by the naïveté and insolence. "Why don't you give up your goofy little tea company and get a *real* job and come work for me at General Foods?" Siegel shot back: "You keep up that attitude and the natural foods industry is going to explode!"

One can only imagine the horror that must have been felt by the hosts, Peggy's family friends the Baumans, as they watched the seasoned CEO and the upstart herbalist locking philosophical horns. "I probably ruined their dinner party," laughed Siegel in remembrance, "because at the end of that hour we were deep into it." But it proved to be a seminal moment in Mo Siegel's life, and by transference in the history of Celestial Seasonings and the entire natural foods industry: The Enemy had been identified, a critical requirement for any mission-driven company. In the months and years to come, when Celestial struggled to make payroll and didn't know whether the company would still be there in the morning, Mo would think back to that confrontation with C.W. Cook. "He turned out to be one of the inspirations of my life. I'd think of his words . . . and it just invigorated me to get up the next morning and solve whatever problem was in our way."

————

While Mo Siegel was in the midst of his odyssey from Eagle Lake to Aspen to Boulder, Gene Kahn was on an idealism-to-capitalism journey of his own.

It had begun on the South Side of Chicago, where Kahn was raised. His father, a trained pianist, had given up his creative aspirations in order to support his growing family and become a grocer. Gene attended Roosevelt University in Chicago, a 20-year-old college that had a curriculum steeped in social justice, a history of radicalism, and a faculty that included Charles V. Hamilton, the distinguished civil rights political scientist who had just coauthored the book *Black Power* with Stokely Carmichael. Kahn studied literature and poetry, simply because he had an interest in those topics. But there was an edge to Gene Kahn, a curious amalgam of intellect, South Side pugnacity, the spurned follow-your-heart ambitions of his father, and a deep disenchantment with the way the world was unfolding before him. "I actually thought society was completely crumbling, and I had an extremely alarmist perspective on the world."

During the summer of 1968, when the Democratic convention was held in Chicago and quickly degenerated into chaos, Kahn was right there in Grant Park, where the Yippies raised the North Vietnamese flag in protest and were confronted by the Chicago police. "That was a key turning point where I lost all hope and faith that society as we knew it was going to have a good outcome. Things were unraveling. And it was hopeless to participate in the affairs of that society. One had to go out and start something new."

Despite his BA and vague plan to pursue a graduate degree in English literature, Kahn drifted a bit, unsure of whether the world he had been training to enter was really worth the effort. In April 1969 he headed out to Berkeley, where several hundred people had taken over an empty city park owned by the University of California, planted seeds, passed the hash pipe, and erected a sign that read: "People's Park: Power to the People." Governor Ronald Reagan soon called out the National Guard, and a standoff ensued for 2 weeks.[2] Kahn said that he was simply drawn there. "I suppose in retrospect I had intent. It was just: That's where one needed to be."

He did enroll in the English lit grad program at the University of Washington, but never saw it through. Instead, he became intrigued by the work of the Cooperating Community, a sort of loose collectivist network of businesses that aimed to be self-supportive and in so doing rewrite the traditional capitalist/profit-centric business structure. There was a need for farms to provide produce and grains to the community, so Gene Kahn decided to go back to the land to help—though his only previous experience on a farm had been occasional stints in his grandfather's fruit orchards in South Haven, Michigan, where he mostly just liked to sit on the tractor. But he had read *Silent Spring,* read Frances Moore Lappé's *Diet for a Small Planet,* subscribed to Rodale's *Organic Gardening.* Their combined influence led him to believe that to save the world, you had to start by changing the way food was grown and how the food system was structured.

"I had a strong anti-business bias," he said in reflecting on his move, "and felt that I was going to be part of a new reconstruction, or a new construction of society. . . . We would bring to urban America this notion of collective farming." If you weren't going to be a pianist, or a grocer, or an English professor, or a businessman—and the headstrong Gene Kahn was most certainly not—then a career in organic farming made a lot of sense.

In 1972 he leased 51 acres in the Skagit Valley, along the North Cascade Mountains 80 miles north of Seattle, and, as it turned out, one of the more difficult places on earth to farm organically—because the temperate rain forest and moist conditions nurtured weeds and promoted agricultural diseases. He called it the New Cascadian Survival and Reclamation Project, Cascadian Farm for short. It was a bit of an in-joke, since virtually every business in the surrounding towns of Rockport, Marblemount, and Concrete was named Cascadian-something. That fed Gene Kahn's increasingly subversive sense of humor.

Kahn was not thinking big; he had a hard enough time just figuring out how to farm organically, and there were several early crop failures. Distribution, for example, was not a huge problem for him, the way it was for Celestial Seasonings, because his goal was simply to support the Cooperating Community, and perhaps some additional communities in Washington and Oregon. Retailers, as part of the profit-centric business model, were also not part of his calculus. The Seattle-based Puget Consumer's Cooperative (PCC), which had started as a food buying club in 1953 and evolved into a co-op with 1,887 members in 1973,[3] was an important partner. But in general, retailers were an afterthought. "They were sort of a necessity for dealing with my goals. I mean, retailing was like, 'Oh God, I have to go see these guys? These are the last people I want to go talk to.' You know? I was focused on changing agriculture."

Since synthetic pesticides, herbicides, and fertilizers had completely revolutionized American farming, there weren't many remaining models for learning how to do things organically—much as there weren't many resources for learning how to manufacture buggies and horse-drawn wagons, had someone still wished to do that.

Bob Rodale was offering small-scale tips through *Organic Gardening* and his Rodale Seal of Approval program ("We don't want this important industry ruined by a few charlatans," he said).[4] Cascadian Farm was one of the first farms to earn the Seal, and they placed it prominently on the company's very first invoice, #101, for $89 to PCC.

But a more useful model for Gene Kahn was Walnut Acres, which by 1972 had expanded to 360 acres and was operating as a true vertically integrated company: farming its own crops organically, contracting with outside farms to bring in other products, manufacturing processed goods, and marketing them. Kahn, the erstwhile student of poetry and English literature, was charmed by the musings and insights of Paul Keene in the Walnut Acres catalogs, and went to visit him. "What was so exciting about him was his understanding of the relationship between organic farming and husbandry or care for the earth, and his constant, very poignant associations between the art of farming and what we'll call 'earth caretaking.'"

Once the agricultural theory of Cascadian Farm began to succeed—organic farming really did work—the business soon followed. Cascadian began processing its own foods—for example, freezing some of the vegetables it grew, turning berries into jam, and pickling some of the cucumbers. Little by little, the business began to take off, spilling over the collectivist walls of the Cooperating Community and the farm stands and farmers' markets of Skagit County, and becoming a household brand in the seventies and eighties. Before long, Kahn began to expand the "home farm" onto 250 acres of adjacent land. Thus, the South Side poet, son of a grocer, reluctant visitor to his grandfather's farm, and disaffected child of the sixties began to find his calling as a leader of the nascent organic foods movement, nestled uncomfortably between the worlds of idealism and capitalism.

—◆—

Some of the organic bounty of the New Cascadian Survival and Reclamation Project ended up in a little health foods store in Portland, Oregon, called Nature's Food and Tool. It had been started by two friends who had gone surfing in California, discovered the natural foods scene there, and decided to bring it back to Portland. They opened it in a converted one-car garage in the Lair Hill Park section of town, fountainhead of Portland's hippie movement; the adjoining one-car garage housed the city's first head shop, the Psychedelic Supermarket.

When a fire destroyed the building, Michael and Kay Greer bought the business and relocated it to a relatively large 5,000-square-foot space on SW Corbett Street, next to the Willamette River. The building had weaving wood floors that kept an underground stream at bay, most of the time. Michael and Kay moved into the apartment above the store, drilled a hole in their floor, and ran a string to the store below with a bell attached to it. If a customer came into the store and no one was around to help them, a pull of the string would summon the owners.

The store, which came to be known around town as Nature's, was divided into three sections. The center, which took up about half the total space, was the retail bay, where the food and gardening tools were shelved. There was also an herb room, with a shag carpet and dark lighting, and then some "warehouse" space to house the back stock. (Eventually, they got rid of the tools, opened the whole store up as a retail sales floor, and renamed it Nature's Fresh Northwest.) In co-op like fashion, people could work at the store and earn purchase credits. Susie Walton, wife of Portland Trailblazers' red-headed star Bill Walton—a counterculture figure in his own right, who went to so many Grateful Dead concerts that he became known among "Deadheads" as "Grateful Red"—was an employee. In 1975, the year in which Stan Amy started working there, Nature's racked up $300,000 in sales, an impressive figure for a small store.

Like Mo Siegel in Colorado and Gene Kahn in Chicago, Amy had been born right after the war (1947) and had come of age in the sixties questioning everything as his family bounced from California to Vancouver to Houston and then to Portland. His father, an *Encyclopedia Britannica* salesman who had been wounded during the war in the Aleutians, divorced from his mother when Stan was 12. It was, said Stan, a very left-wing family: His uncles helped found the longshoreman's union in Vancouver, and his mother left her job at the Fred Meyer supermarket company to take a job at the VA hospital, where the very real effects of the war in Vietnam could be felt. Though he was, in his words, somewhat "socially ill-adept," Stan became active in the antiwar movement, especially after he enrolled at Portland State.

There, however, life took another unpredictable turn. The college was expanding rapidly through the urban renewal programs of the Department of Housing and Urban Development, and this resulted in Stan being evicted three or four times in his first 2 years there. In response, he initiated a student-run class, which produced a paper on the impacts that students had on the low-income housing market and argued for the creation of a nonprofit company to help them. At the age of 19, he became the first president of Portland Student Services, which provided housing for 3,000 students and ended up building a 16-story high-rise. He never finished school; his newfound mission—to promote the radical concept of aggregating the purchasing power of a disenfranchised group (students) to build a community—was far more interesting.

During this time, he had begun living with friends in a macrobiotic communal house just outside of town. Michael and Kay Greer were there as well. Intensely analytical and very much a product of his times, it didn't take him long to graft his entrepreneurial experience onto the fledgling business with which Michael and Kay were involved. Natural foods producers, retailers, and customers had no power in the world of agribusiness and Big Food, which by 1969 had become the country's largest industry, with $350 billion in assets, 23 million workers, and 3 million farms, selling $100 billion worth of food to 200 million consumers.[5] But if you could somehow aggregate the purchasing power of people who had concerns about pesticides and food additives and consolidate it, then maybe, just maybe, you could begin to influence what actually got produced in the first place—and how.

Stan left Portland Student Services, and before long went to work for Nature's.

Although he grew up in a typical middle-class household in Sacramento, Michael Funk came armed with a spirit—and a name—that were made for cultural rebellion. These were the incense-burning, kaleidoscope-turning, karma-learning, convention-spurning 1960s. "What made it all so charismatic," noted the cultural anthropologists Jane and Michael Stern, "was the newborn hippies' sense of mission, their conviction that the flashing light shows, happy hallucinations, and far-fetched philosophizing were keys to something really big."[6]

With a name like Funk, he had no chance at a straight-laced career as, say, an accountant, especially not after the revelation he had as a young boy, sitting out in his front yard and watching the garbage man come by. "Here comes this long-haired, bearded guy who must have been one of the earliest hippie-dazed people. He was slapping cans in the back of that truck and I thought, 'Well isn't that cool? A guy can look any way he wants and do that job.'"

Beginning in his senior year in high school, Michael grew his hair long—in preparation?—and, sure enough, became "an employee of the county" after graduating, right alongside the can-slapping anti-material materialization of his youth.

He hauled garbage for a couple of years, attended anti-nuclear rallies, and became "a big herb fan." In 1973, when a downtown buying club came together and formed the Sacramento Natural Foods Cooperative, with a store at 16th and P streets, Michael Funk became a regular. The people who were running these kinds of co-ops—another one had opened in nearby Davis, California, and was known initially as the People's Food Conspiracy—had no retail expertise, and had never even contemplated the idea of "merchandising." Mostly, they had volunteers who drove to places like Tony's in West Sacramento (for cheese) and the Abdallah Produce Company, picking up goods, bringing them back to the store, and setting them out as-is.

Funk remembers the fruit well. "There were people running around looking for abandoned orchards, figuring they had never been sprayed. But it meant that the fruit was, you know, beat up. In many cases over-ripe. And it was bug-infested. Let's just say fruit flies buzzing, that was a badge of honor." In fact, he said, "it was amazing that people came back to those stores with such poor selection and such poor quality. No wonder the industry grew so slowly during those years."

Then in 1974 he moved to Belize, where he bought 10 acres for $50 an acre and decided to homestead. "I wanted to live a back-to-the-land sustainable lifestyle," he recalled. "I was looking for a different way of life, and it was the only place I could afford." It also happened to be a place where the land was still largely untainted by chemical farming. For 18 months or so, he grew his own foods and foraged in the jungle. But he missed the California culture, and moved back. Needing a job, he went to the local agricultural office, where they gave him the once-over and said, "Yeah, you want to work? Go pick apricots."

For someone who had actually aspired to be a garbage man, the thought of a little manual labor posed no problem at all. But, based on everything he had read and what he had experienced in the co-ops and in Belize, he was intimidated by the thought of all the pesticides and herbicides on the fruit he would be picking. So before he headed out to the Valley and into the apricot orchards, Michael Funk did what he considered to be the only sensible thing: He put on gloves. That slightly haughty act—the white glove treatment for the dirty chemical industry!—proved to be one of his last moves of forethought before he found himself bopping through a carpe diem existence, into an unplanned career, in an undefined industry, that would ultimately land him at the top of the heap of the most important distributor in the natural foods industry, United Natural Foods, Inc. (UNFI).

———

While some aspects of the sixties counterculture were walled off into self-contained gardens—communes, for example, or San Francisco's Haight-Ashbury neighborhood, aka Hashbury, which attracted Grey Line bus tours in 1967 billed as "the only foreign tour within the continental limits of the United States"[7]—others found their way into the mainstream.

In education, for example, there was a movement toward more freedom and less rigidity of structure. Some elementary schools began experimenting with "open classrooms," which utilized a free-flowing curriculum and team-teaching, and invested the students with the power to choose and guide their own studies. There were also inter-age classrooms, combining multiple grades. San Francisco State College and others pioneered new ideas about teaching students how to think instead of just memorizing facts, and interdisciplinary programs like Brown University's 1969 "New Curriculum" began ushering out older and more traditional approaches.

So it was with Hampshire College, a small liberal arts school—*very* liberal—located on 800 acres in Amherst, Massachusetts. Established in 1965, it began accepting students in 1970 using an unusual system. Students would design their own curriculum, and progress through their college years by doing a series of projects in which they would contract to do a course of study. A committee of professors would either agree that they had fulfilled that contract, or push the students for more. No majors. No grades. No requirements. No credits. It was all very entrepreneurial, and that's what made it the perfect place for Gary Hirshberg.

Born in Manchester, New Hampshire, in 1954, the eldest of five children, he was a high-energy kid from the start—building tree houses, falling out of those trees, ski racing, playing tennis and soccer, always getting into some kind of mischief that drove his mother crazy. In thinking about her kids, she always said that it was "Gary and the other four." His parents divorced when he was 14, and "I sort of became the CEO of the house even though neither my mother nor my siblings wanted that."

Beneath his thick hair, blue-gray eyes, and aquiline nose, he developed a facile mind and a rhetorical style that left people feeling at once endeared to him and outwitted. Mostly, he just saw the world for the way it was—flawed—and, ignited by both stubbornness and idealism, pledged that he would put his considerable energies to work to try to fix it.

As an experimental college, Hampshire was a crucible of far-flung intellectual theories that attracted some of the most creative people in the country, including quite a few Hollywood progenies, budding film producers, and actors. Among Hirshberg's classmates in Hampshire's third-ever class were Ken Burns, who would achieve fame as a documentarian, and Jon Krakauer, who would become an outdoor adventurer and writer. Yet while many of his classmates felt the push-and-pull of the "movements"—antiwar, civil rights, feminism, drugs, rebellion against authority, back-to-the-land—it was environmentalism more than anything else that sang to Gary Hirshberg's soul. He wrote his thesis about the expansion of alpine tree lines, which was being caused by what we now refer to as climate change. He was moving in the direction of advanced climatologic research and a PhD. But then he had a revelation: "I realized I didn't want to further advance my knowledge of the problem; what I really wanted to do was work on the *solution*."

After graduating, he went off to the New Alchemy Institute, which had been started in 1969 on the site of a former dairy farm on Cape Cod. The goal of the Institute was to create a model for small-scale food production using renewable energy (solar heating and wind power), aquaculture, and organic farming techniques such as integrated pest management and solar-aided composting. Since Hatchville, Massachusetts—close to Cape Cod's "heel," near Falmouth—is not exactly a temperate zone, New Alchemy constructed greenhouse-type structures dubbed "bioshelters" so it could conduct year-round experiments in food production and pest control, monitoring energy flows, water, and nutrients every step of the way. Much as the Rodale family was doing on its farm near Allentown, Pennsylvania, and as Paul and Betty Keene were doing at Walnut Acres, New Alchemy began to prove anew what the world had once taken for granted: that you could produce good agricultural yields with very low inputs and no toxins. And people started to come see it for themselves: The New Alchemy Institute attracted 25,000 visitors a year.

Hirshberg arrived in 1977 as an intern, promising to barter his writing and editing skills in exchange for the experience. He started writing grant proposals, and helped bring in some money; he also developed an expertise in building windmills, and eventually wrote a book about that. By 1979, at the age of 25, he became the executive director, after the founding director decided to leave and pursue his own independent research.

Replacing a founder—as Hirshberg would soon learn, and would rediscover many times later in his career at Stonyfield Farm—is one of the more challenging entrepreneurial moves one can make. "It was a very sixties kind of consensus place where hierarchy was [frowned upon]," recalled Hirshberg. "They needed and wanted an executive director, but they didn't really. It was a place that sort of ate and chewed up leaders."

In 1980 Ronald Reagan swept into the White House, and one of his first acts was to slash the Community Services Administration, which was the principle source of funding for the New Alchemy Institute. Along with other cuts in programs like organic research at the USDA and renewable energy research at the Department of Energy, this created a domino effect of pressure on private support—and that combination spelled trouble for Gary Hirshberg and New Alchemy. "That led me to really question not only whether that's what I wanted to keep doing, fighting with the system, but it also got me realizing that unless I was involved in creating enterprise, business, that could take these ideas to the marketplace, I would be forever dependent on philanthropy. Which was not a very exciting prospect."

Hirshberg was mulling this over in 1982 when he took a trip to Florida to visit his mother, who by then had become a senior buyer at Disney's Epcot Center. Together they toured an exhibit called the Land Pavilion, sponsored by Kraft. (Kraft was still 6 years away from joining the bloodlines of Postum Cereal through the merger with General Foods, but as the manufacturer of artificial food products like processed American cheese slices, Cheez Whiz, Parkay margarine, and Miracle Whip, it was already a kissing cousin.) Gary saw what he described as a "cartoon scene of chemistry gone mad," including "rivers of chemical fertilizers, herbicides, and pesticides swooshing around the naked roots of anemic-looking plants grown hydroponically in plastic tubes." There was also a scene eerily reminiscent of the DuPont's Wonderful World of Chemistry exhibit at the 1964 World's Fair, a musical number called "Kitchen Kabaret" featuring, among other things, an animatronic robot named Miss Yogurt.[8] He was aghast.

Fortunately for Hirshberg, there was another prospect waiting in the wings, for he was serving on the board of an organic farming institute in his native New Hampshire. The school's founder, Samuel Kaymen, was a brilliant and inventive man who had been a "clean room" engineer, designing dust-free, bacteria-free rooms. But he also had an enduring interest in food and sustainable farming. He had worked on developing pickles, beer, and wine, and for nearly a decade had been toying with a recipe for yogurt that he had learned from some of the old Hasidic Jews back in Brooklyn. At the board meetings for the school, he would often serve the yogurt. Then one day he or Hirshberg—they have never been able to agree on who took the fateful first step—decided that maybe they should start selling the yogurt as a way to raise funds for the farming school. Indeed, they could probably be more effective educators by selling a high-quality organic product line than by pro-ducing all of their workshops and publications. It was, in Hirshberg's ironic words, a case of "the tail wagging the cow."

Thus, Stonyfield Farm Yogurt was born, in April 1983, even though they didn't really know what they were doing or getting themselves into. Kaymen secured $35,000 in loans from some Catholic nuns and burned right through the cash. On August 1, Hirshberg told Kaymen that he would partner with him, but only after he returned from a consulting trip to China. Over the next 6 weeks, when checks came in, Kaymen cashed them to buy more feed or fruit or yogurt cups; when bills came in, he put them in a pile for Hirshberg to deal with upon his return. So in September 1983, Gary left New Alchemy to explore the newer alchemy of his partnership with Samuel Kaymen, and arrived on his first day to find a pile of unpaid bills. "I discovered by the time noontime came and we had opened all the mail that we were $75,000 in the hole. We were basically bankrupt, and I hadn't even had lunch yet." Thus, the product of one of the world's most entrepreneurial educations now began his real education in entrepreneurship.

———

Throughout the country, on farms and in university towns, in urban centers and in progressive enclaves, this is how the natural foods industry inched for-ward: one entrepreneur at a time. It was like an intricate symphony, played out on a national scale, with people in disparate cities contributing their own musi-cal signature in a gradually swelling crescendo toward a harmonic convergence.

Only, most of them were at best vaguely aware of the presence of a score: Everything felt like a solo.

Back in Colorado, good things started to happen for Mo Siegel and Celestial Seasonings.

For one, the distribution network began to grow. At first this was just through the natural foods channel, as Erewhon discovered Celestial Seasonings tea and decided to start selling it in their stores and offering it to other retailers through their catalog.

"When we got the stamp of approval from Erewhon, a bunch of other small little distributors, such as Laurelbrook Foods in Maryland and Stow Mills in New Hampshire, fell in line, and it sure made our lives a whole lot easier," recalled Siegel. "Erewhon was kind of the spark plug for all of that natural foods distribution."

The conventional supermarkets were not far behind. Unlike most natural foods products of the era, tea was familiar to the mass audience, so there were few barriers to acceptance. More importantly, Celestial Seasonings' distinctive packaging made it look legitimate. Having abandoned the unmanageable muslin bags with the phone wire, Siegel had created boxes with unique, vibrant artwork and inspirational "words of wisdom" from the likes of Goethe, Thoreau, and Sanskrit proverbs. There was nothing like it in the marketplace. Siegel said that the idea for this type of packaging "came right out of my being," and it created a popular framework that helped the products to cross over easily into mainstream supermarkets. "I had the full intention to trick people into good health. [I wanted] the packaging to be so adorable that they were going to like it and then wake up and go, 'Oh, by the way, that's really healthy.'" Celestial Seasonings thus became the first company in the natural foods industry to develop a multichannel strategy, targeting natural and conventional retailers simultaneously.

The impact of the packaging was even more profound in the natural channel. The few small companies that were making packaged goods in this industry (such as Arrowhead Mills or Hain Pure Foods) had struggled mightily just to get into production; package design was viewed at best as an afterthought, and more likely as a prohibitively expensive burden.

Moreover, the stores themselves were drab, with brown foods and wood fixtures and poor lighting. Effectively, the health foods business—despite being aligned with the kaleidoscopic visions of *Yellow Submarine* and the psychedelic sixties—was a black-and-white affair, especially when compared to the super-markets filled with cleverly packaged products like Hamburger Helper, whose ads were now being brought to you in living color on NBC. When the adorable teddy bear made its debut on the side of the lavishly illustrated Celestial Season-ings Sleepytime Tea package on the wooden shelves of stores like Green Moun-tain Grainery, it was as if the natural foods industry had just landed in Oz.

And there was one other decidedly bold departure from the norm made by Mo Siegel and Celestial Seasonings: to focus obsessively on flavor. Since taste is the most important characteristic of food, it might seem obvious that all new product development would focus on the flavor. But this was not true of the countercuisine. Many early health foods products seemed to have been devel-oped for a consumer base with malfunctioning taste buds: The very fact that products like wheat germ and tofu were relatively flavorless seemed to infuse them with nobility among the health foods crowd. In turn, this led to endless parodies among the media and mainstream population about the "sticks and twigs," "cardboard," and "acorns" that were sold in health foods stores. The very mention of yogurt, dandelion soup, desiccated beef liver, and even organic produce was enough to draw the outlines of the caricature and elicit some chuckles from mixed company.

Even when the mainstream food world tried to tap into the health foods ethic, it sometimes resulted in unwitting parody. And here, once again, it was General Foods in the center ring, with its ad campaigns for Grape-Nuts, the healthful cereal invented by C.W. Post himself that actually contained neither grapes nor nuts. Way back in 1910, an ad had suggested that Grape-Nuts con-tained "phosphate of potash" that would help build brain and nerves; later ads stated that Grape-Nuts prevented diseases such as malaria and appendicitis. All of these claims were baseless, but the product continued to wear a healthy halo.[9]

It was the Grape-Nuts TV ads in the early 1970s featuring outdoorsman Euell Gibbons that created the biggest comic backlash. Gibbons had written popular books like *Stalking the Wild Asparagus* and *Stalking the Good Life* that promoted the "new" idea of foraging for foods in the wild. But it wasn't until General Foods put the 60-year-old Gibbons on TV—trekking through the snow in a sheepskin jacket in search of some "high bush cranberries" to add to his bowl of Grape-Nuts, "my back-to-nature cereal," with a flavor that "reminds me of wild hickory nuts"—that he rose to fame, part of the new class of second-tier health celebrities like J.I. Rodale and Adelle Davis who made the circuit of the

TV talk shows. The earnestness and passion of these "health nuts" proved to be an effective comic foil, as Dick Cavett and Johnny Carson would cock their heads and stare dumbfoundedly at some of the things being said. Carson joked about sending a "lumber-gram" to Gibbons, and Sonny and Cher awarded him with an edible plaque, which he promptly took a bite of.[10] Thus, although Grape-Nuts was an old brand and was the seventh best-selling cold cereal in the country, through the Euell Gibbons ads it came to be conflated with the taste-less new-age health foods, and this started its decline into near obscurity.[11]

As an avid health foods consumer, Siegel knew that the reason the health foods parodies were so funny was because they hit very close to home. "People were so gung-ho about health," remembered Siegel. "[But with most natural food] you might as well have been grazing on your lawn, the way it tasted."

He chose to steer his fledgling company in another direction. "At the end of the day," he said, "people are going to buy what tastes good. They are going to want to buy what's healthy. But you marry those two and you have a winner." So as the company grew, expanding beyond the limitations imposed by foraging among Rocky Mountain flora, Celestial started to source natural ingredients from around the world, which opened up all sorts of new flavor possibilities. And the company quickly found that with some effort, it was possible to be both natural *and* great-tasting. In 1972 Celestial introduced Red Zinger Tea, with ingredients like hibiscus, peppermint, West Indian lemongrass, lemon verbena, and cherry bark. It was an instant hit, and remains one of the company's most popular products more than 40 years later.

With its attractive packaging and inventive herbal flavor blends, Celestial really stood out from the humdrum old reliable teas on the grocery shelves, like Lipton, Tetley, and Bigelow. Sales reached a few hundred thousand dollars in 1972 and 1973. But then a fortuitous event really blew the lid off the tea kettle.

One day in 1973, Siegel received a letter from Susan Saint James, co-star (with Rock Hudson) of the popular TV show *McMillan & Wife*. She loved Celestial Seasonings products, and also loved to ski in Colorado; could she come by to visit on her next trip? The meeting was arranged, and Saint James showed up with her manager and an offer to invest some money in the company in exchange for stock. Siegel didn't think it was an especially favorable deal, but he needed cash. Saint James told him: "Don't worry, I will pay you back. You wait and see. I will take care of this deal."

A few months later, Siegel received a call from Saint James: "Watch Johnny Carson on Monday."

As it turned out, Carson was not hosting *The Tonight Show* on Monday, February 25, 1974, but someone better was behind the desk: John Denver, the singer-songwriter who loved Colorado so much he had changed his name to reflect it. Denver was a friend of Siegel, and a health foods nut as well. As Siegel recalled it, when Denver introduced Susan Saint James on *The Tonight Show*, she came through the multicolored curtains carrying a tray.

"What do you have there, Susan?" asked Denver.

"Red Zinger Tea!" she said excitedly.

"Red Zinger Tea? Far out! Far out!"

It was exactly the push that the company needed. The next day, supermarkets that had been ignoring the sales calls from Celestial Seasonings began ringing up the office. Before long, Saint James also provided entrée for Siegel to other TV shows, and he started making the rounds himself. Sales would surpass $1 million in 1974 for the very first time, and Celestial Seasonings— mission-driven creation of a mountain-climbing child of the sixties, just a few short years removed from the days of hand-sewn muslin bags in the A-frame— was on its way to becoming the first truly successful "big" company in the natural foods industry. Suddenly that $100 million goal that had been such a knee-slapper to all those bank executives in the glass office . . . it wasn't so funny anymore. Mo Siegel's vision of truth (the quotes on the packaging), beauty (the artwork on the packaging), and goodness (healthful and pure herbal tea) was becoming a winning business proposition.

At its core, the company remained quirky and rebellious, the classic idealistic anti-business born whole from the sixties like Athena from the head of Zeus. Mo Siegel rode to work each day on a bicycle. Some employees walked around in bare feet. Barney Feinblum, a production manager who later became Celestial's CFO, arrived at work one day to find that there had been no production by the night shift, only to learn that they had taken a "moon break" because of the full moon. Still, the product was good and the demand was growing. The company hit $3 million in revenue in 1976 and couldn't make enough tea to keep up with demand; most stores ordered on allocation. Feinblum kept seeing large orders come in from Mountain People's Warehouse and wondered, "Who is this company that keeps growing and keeps buying more of our tea?"

By 1983, with significant distribution through conventional channels, sales had jumped to $27 million; this was no longer Mo's goofy little tea company. Feinblum encouraged Siegel to bring the company to Wall Street through an initial public offering (IPO)—an unheard-of concept in the natural foods industry.

Through a friend, Feinblum brought in Goldman Sachs, one of the gilded leaders of the investment banking world, to underwrite the IPO. But while the deal was in registration, disaster struck: A woman in Mississippi who had broken her hip tried to take a large dose of Celestial Seasonings Comfrey Leaf tea to help her bones knit, and she fell ill. She claimed that the tea contained belladonna, a naturally toxic substance.[12] Goldman felt its reputation was at stake, and withdrew the offering shortly after it had started trading.

To Wall Street and all the pillars of the Establishment, this was just another retelling of The Little Engine That Couldn't. They should have known better: The natural foods industry was flaky. Ephemeral. A fad. The people behind it were crackpots and charlatans. The health nuts, like J.I. Rodale and Adelle Davis, had died from disease just like everyone else. Over the long haul, the Establishment doubters knew, American consumers were not going to reject "progress," and they were not going to willfully overpay for foods. "That," remembers Feinblum dolefully, "restricted capital flow to our industry for almost a decade."

But it did not stop Celestial Seasonings. The very next year, 1984, the company was sold to Kraft for $40 million, or roughly $39,999,990 more than Mo Siegel had gotten for the berries he had sold to the local ladies back in Eagle Lake.

Gene Kahn's idealistic goal of changing American farming remained intact, but he began to see that the way to do that was going to be from the inside; in effect, you couldn't really influence the Democratic convention from way out in Grant Park. Cascadian Farm would have to grow and prove the worthiness of its model through the one thing that the Otto Carques and Erewhons of the earlier natural foods movements had never achieved: commercial success.

By the 1980s, Cascadian started to use outside packers, which changed the scale of the enterprise entirely. With high-speed equipment and production lines, the challenge became how to get enough raw ingredients. Kahn began to set up a network of other farms, in more appropriate microclimates, to grow a larger volume and greater diversity of organic foods. The problem was, there was still very little organic farmland and even less organic knowledge. So he created a team of extension specialists, which in later years he would name the "Organic Mujahadeen"—a weed scientist, a plant pathologist, an agronomist, and an entomologist. "We would go to the 'evil' large conventional growers, bring them contracts, and convert them."

Additionally, Kahn created a highly unusual business model in which Cascadian would provide guaranteed payments to these contract farmers, effectively taking on all the production risks himself. If there were too much rain, or an untimely freeze, or if the cutworms and loopers had an especially destructive season, the strawberry crop might be lost; but the farmers would still get paid. This enabled him to attract some of the most talented farmers anywhere into the Cascadian "custom farming" system. It was, he began to see, all about leverage. More than 97 percent of all the farmland was being managed conventionally, that is, in the post–World War II style. If he could bring business to these so-called despoilers of the land, these conventional farmers who were so hard-working and committed but had come to rely on chemicals as a labor-saving economic lifeline, then he could persuade them to "go organic." Only then would there start to be some kind of real commercial chance for organic farming and organic foods.

Then, as it had so often before in the food business, fate intervened.

Apple farmers had been using chemicals like arsenic, DDT, and fluorine for decades to try to regulate crop growth. Many of these substances had generated great controversy, as for example when the Boston Health Department had insisted on destroying arsenic-contaminated apples for 3 years in a row from 1919 to 1921.[13] But apples are big business, and are hard to grow well, so the chemicals kept coming. In 1963 the Uniroyal Chemical Company introduced daminozide, a new growth regulator that could be sprayed on apples (and cherries, peaches, peanut vines, and more) to improve their chances of success. Sold under the brand name Alar, this chemical could increase the size of the fruit, produce more pronounced tips, and keep it on the tree longer so it could ripen. By the mid-eighties, more than a million pounds of Alar were being used each year, part of the total of 1.1 billion pounds of chemical pesticides being applied across the country.[14] The EPA raised questions about the safety of Alar because of gaps in the toxicological and environmental tests, but in 1986, under pressure from the growers, declined to restrict its use (some states, such as New York, Massachusetts, and California, passed their own restrictions). The testing went on, however, and the Natural Resources Defense Council issued a report in 1989 that highlighted government studies showing that Alar caused tumors in lab mice and posed an "intolerable risk" to children, who consumed large volumes of apple products. Six thousand preschoolers might eventually get cancer from Alar and other chemical pesticide residues, they suggested. The real hullaballoo erupted on February 26, 1989, when CBS ran a segment on *60 Minutes,* calling Alar "the most potent cancer-causing agent in the food supply today."[15]

The reaction was swift. Parents started dumping applesauce. Schools in New York and Los Angeles canceled their orders for apple juice. Supermarkets pulled apples off the shelves. As a result, apple prices fell to their lowest level in years, $7 for a 42-pound box, well below the break-even point. Soon the EPA decided to initiate its long-discussed ban on Alar.

But the impact went way beyond apples. Within weeks, red grapes from Chile were found to be laced with cyanide. Reports came out questioning the food safety of broccoli, beef, chicken, pork, milk, fish, eggs . . . even popcorn. Conventional supermarkets like D'Agostino's in New York began offering organic produce for the first time. Senator Patrick Leahy and his working groups picked up the pace on their legislation that would create national organic standards to replace the hodgepodge of state laws that were gradually coming on line. And *Newsweek* ran a special report on March 27, 1989, entitled "Warning! Your food, nutritious and delicious, may be hazardous to your health," which included a sidebar story about the "desperate" rush by consumers to find pesticide-free foods: "Suddenly, It's a Panic for Organic" read the headline.[16] The sleeping giant of the mass market had been rudely prodded from its slumber.

Gene Kahn welcomed this turn of events; he went out and bought 20 copies of *Newsweek.* Cascadian Farm was running a bit low on cash, and this news would surely help. In fact, he viewed it as a time to double-down. If the public at large had finally come around to the need for organics, which in turn would trigger the conversion of more acres of farmland over to organic methods, his little operation would need to expand. He began selling container-loads of organic apples to conventional supermarkets throughout the country, and even to Japan. He quickly began borrowing money to fund the expansion—and then, almost as soon as he did, the "panic for organic" ran its course, the hysteria subsided, and people largely returned to their usual ingredient-blind shopping patterns. It was a new lesson in leverage for Kahn, this time about debt; soon he needed to sell his company for the sake of the larger mission.

In 1990 the Welch's National Grape Cooperative came along to bail him out. They had seen the impact that Alar had on other juice companies, especially Treetop, the largest apple processor, and thought that an organic food producer like Cascadian Farm could be a sort of insurance policy against other as-yet unknown but potentially damaging news. Kahn was thrilled. "I couldn't have had a better partner than a farmer-owned cooperative," he said. Over the next few years—a time period Kahn referred to as "my business school"—he learned from Welch's about formal business planning, branding, marketing, retailing, manufacturing . . . all the disciplines that had never been part of the curriculum for an English lit major and bootstrap farmer/entrepreneur.

News of the modest success of Celestial Seasonings and Cascadian Farm reached Stan Amy just as he began his new life as a retailer at Nature's (after shoring up the floorboards to keep the water out). And so the man who had so carefully analyzed and dissected the student housing system in Portland realized that, similarly, all of the elements were in place for an explosion of the natural foods business, except perhaps for that one final spark.

"We were responding to a movement," he said, "and it was a movement grounded in community. The community consisted of food activists, thought opinion leaders, fans of Rachel Carson, and a broad base of consumers who were concerned about things having to do with their food that was not currently being recognized in the food production system or being labeled on food," he said. By creating a place, a venue for that spark to ignite, he sensed that a revolution could be started. "You could *feel* that there was power there to tap," he recalled. "You didn't have to go see that business model."

Nature's grew from about $300,000 in 1975 to more than $800,000 in 1978. Amy could clearly see that there was an opportunity to open multiple units, and he bought out Michael Greer's share of the company. But what convinced him of its potential was the fact that the conventional supermarkets that were his chief competitors were such . . . conventional thinkers. "They were unresponsive to consumer demands, and actually structurally hampered in trying to be responsive," he said. Traditional supermarkets competed with each other by selling commodity products based on promotional pricing—advertising wars, coupons, S&H Green Stamps, and things like that—so their profit margins were slim. "Their organizations all got built around materials handling and efficiency," noted Amy; "cost-control was their driver, and that's not how you add attributes to products."

This was driven home rather dramatically by a chance encounter. They had no photocopier at the Nature's store on SW Corbett Street, so every couple of weeks Amy would walk five blocks to an office complex, where he would pay an architect on the second floor 5 cents each to make copies. And each time he made that walk, he passed by an anonymous door on a building, with nothing more than lettering that read SAFEWAY EGG BUYER. This struck him as odd, and finally he had to investigate. Inside was a plain office occupied by one man and a secretary. Amy told them that he ran a weird little store down the street, and learned that in this office they were brokering egg purchases for Safeway all up and down the West Coast.

"Would you ever consider buying brown eggs?" Amy asked.

"No way," said the man. "How would I work them into the system? They would sell in some stores, and they wouldn't sell in other stores. There isn't enough supply for me to do it uniformly across the system."

They chatted some more, and then Stan Amy walked out and allowed a broad smile to engulf his face. The conventional supermarkets had an impossibly inflexible system geared toward uniformity and efficiency, and that was great news for the natural foods retailers. "That is when I began believing that a key competitive advantage for us was building systems that had a tolerance for complexity," he said. "That was very different than what they were doing, and so there was the opportunity."

Soon Stan Amy the urban planner and community builder set to work on growing the natural foods business. But creating that "tolerance for complexity" was difficult.

He joined Gene Kahn on the board of the Food Alliance, a group that sought to increase production by, in part, establishing a "sustainable" classification for certain agricultural products that would be just below "organic"; it was a battle royale, since many of those in the organic movement felt that it would devalue their efforts.

Then, on a whole series of occasions, the anti-establishment focus that had brought employees into Nature's in the first place turned into navel-gazing or acrimony. For example, when Amy redesigned the Corbett store to eliminate the "warehouse" bay and put all of the product out on the sales floor, some employees resisted the change. Similarly, in 1983 Nature's surveyed its customers to see how they would feel about adding certain products that were taboo among the natural foods purists: coffee, beer, wine, fresh fish, and some baked goods with refined sugar. About 3 percent of the respondents vowed that they would never shop in the store again. In another instance, when he introduced vitamins into the store, some of the employees demurred, saying it was just a health foods rip-off. "Look," he told the dissenters, "we all have screwed-up ways of thinking about money. From my perspective, money is a tool. It's like a hammer. You can use it to build a house, or you can use it to break somebody's head. And if those of us who have values don't learn how to use hammers to build houses, they will all be in the hands of people who want to break heads." Finally, to those who adopted the communal war cry of "food for people, not for profit," Amy came back with wink-and-a-nod T-shirts that said "food for people *and* for profit" and "no margin, no mission."

In 1980, when Nature's opened a second location, a 7,000-square-foot store on NE Fremont Street, it fell into the common expansion trap: All of the energy shifted to the new store, and the old one began to falter. It was now a real business, and would have to be managed differently. Amy went back into the Corbett store himself to help save it. He reflected: "The entrepreneurial style is really appropriate for a very creative phase in the business, at the beginning. But once a business gets past that point, once you've got multiples, care and feeding becomes the bigger issue. The need for administration rises, and the likelihood that an entrepreneur's style is going to work and lead an organization diminishes."

Thus, two steps forward, one step back, Stan Amy and his team grew the Nature's business. They opened five more stores, including some larger-format ones (20,000 square feet), and several of them were generating $200,000 or more a week—roughly two-thirds of the *annual* output of the Corbett store when Stan Amy had first joined the company in 1975. And by the time GNC came knocking in the mid-nineties, looking for a strategic investment to complement its vitamin store business, Nature's Fresh Northwest was a valuable commodity; the sale occurred, as did so many others, in 1996 . . . for $17.5 million.

When Michael Funk returned from the apricot orchards, he would turn right around and sell the fruit on the side of the road, or sometimes to retail stores. The tool of his trade was a red VW Microbus that he had bought for $400 on a trip to North Dakota. ("It was good on gas and could hold 50 boxes of fruit or something, but it couldn't take a lot of weight.") For the time being, that was as far as his logistical planning—and ambition—went.

"Back then we were living with a kind of week-to-week type mentality. You know, there was some fruit to pick, there was some fruit to sell, there were some other nuts to buy. When we finally opened a business checking account and bought a truck, you know, those were all conscious decisions that we were in business. But 'business' was a bad word. I didn't want to be called a 'business-man.' And I wasn't sure that this was going to be my work."

What he had discovered, though, was a gaping hole in the natural foods commerce cycle. There was certainly a surge in consumer interest. There were lots of little companies starting to produce natural foods, like Cascadian Farm and Westbrae and Barbara's Bakery. There were plenty of retail-type outlets to sell the food, including co-ops, country communes (whose ranks had multiplied fivefold since 1965), and a whole new crop of small natural foods stores, slightly larger than the health foods stores of yesteryear, and distinctly different from the pill shops that sold bottles of vitamins; by 1972 there were more than 3,000 such stores, up from just 500 in 1965.[17] What was missing, however, was a large and reliable distribution system to get the foods from the manufacturer to the retailer. Because, after all, small farms and food producers didn't have the wherewithal to be able to deliver directly to multiple locations across the region or the country; the retail buyers didn't have the time or scope to be able to source so many new products coming from so many places; and without some volume, the costs of the inefficient system would keep the retail prices far above the plastic pabulum being sold in the conventional supermarkets.

The existing distribution system had evolved out of necessity, not planning, and was therefore regionalized and highly fragmented. At first there were small companies like Harvest Provisions in Boston, Earthly Organics in Philadelphia, NutraSource in Seattle, Kahan and Lessin in Southern California, and Rock Island in the Bay Area. They were classic wholesale middlemen, buying goods from the manufacturers and selling them to the retailers. But since the supply and demand were still so small, many of them carried only a few hundred products, often within a single category like frozen foods or vitamins or produce—meaning, a fleet of small trucks would show up at the natural foods stores, often at unpredictable times. There was no scale to the business at all. Inventory out-of-stocks were a weekly occurrence.

Then there was Sunburst, a spiritual community near Santa Barbara, California, that had been founded by Norman Paulsen, disciple of Parahansam Yogananda, author of *Autobiography of a Yogi*—a book that over the years has influenced everybody from George Harrison to Steve Jobs to Dr. Andrew Weil.[18] Sunburst operated a 150-acre organic farm it called Lemuria, as well as a variety of farms, retail stores, restaurants, and other businesses. In its prime, Sunburst was also a major organic produce distributor, and although it was already in decline by the time Funk got going with his business, he nevertheless looked to it as a model. "It was impressive," he remembered. "But it wasn't around long enough for any of us to say 'That's where we want to go.'" Mostly, it made him realize one of the great lessons of the entire natural products industry: "You've really got to get some scale to make this thing work."

Funk and a couple of partners decided to create a distribution business of their own, with a name straight out of the mid-seventies collectivist Yellow Pages: Sacramento People's Produce. It was based out of a small building near the freeway in downtown Sacramento, and, using a single 18-foot bobtail truck cab, Funk began making delivery runs up into the little towns of the Sierra Nevadas: Grass Valley, Nevada City, North San Juan. It was real back-to-the-land heaven, with stores like Mother Truckers, Nature's Way, Earth Stone, and the Briarpatch Co-op, as well as plenty of buying clubs. Sometimes Funk would show up at a truck stop or church parking lot, and families would meet him there and buy their groceries directly from him. But at the end of a truck run, he would have to drive back into Sacramento, and the smog and congestion drove him crazy. Before long, he and his partner decided to split the business into city and mountains. Funk, of course, took to the hills, and renamed his business Mountain People's Warehouse.

Very slowly, he added some real trucks and built the business to scale. His fleet would pick up produce and bulk goods (and eventually packaged goods, too) at the source, warehouse some of it, and slot deliveries to natural foods stores throughout the West—much as other regional companies were doing elsewhere, like Stow Mills and Cornucopia in New England, and Tree of Life in

Florida. He knew that he had to stop thinking small. "Well before 'local' was a buzzword, there were still romantic tendencies about having the local distributor that handled the product. But distribution is about scale. Everybody needs to have the lowest cost possible, the widest selection possible, the most efficient deliveries possible. All those things are more possible the larger you are. It's just the way it works."

In time, these distributors also played other roles besides wholesaling. One was a sort of "data warehouse" function for the retailers. The retailers often had ancient cash register systems, many of which did not even scan barcodes (which began to come into usage in June 1974, and were omnipresent by the eighties); consequently, they had no idea how much they had sold of each item. But Michael Funk knew, because he had reasonably good records of what got loaded onto each truck. So Mountain People's was eventually able to help the retailers by supplying reports of "warehouse pulls."

Another role played by the distributors was that of credit banker. Although the industry was growing fast, there was very little available cash. A lot of the retailers were able to survive simply by floating credit through the distributors: taking in cash from customers, but delaying by 30 or 60 days before paying the distributor for the next round of purchases. The distributors, somewhat reluctantly, accepted this role.

It was not until 1984, 8 years in, that Mountain People's Warehouse finally turned a profit. But that didn't matter to Michael Funk. He knew he was providing a vital service that was helping to promote natural and organic products, by bolstering both the growers and the retailers. He wasn't interested in being an entrepreneur who starts one business after another. "It takes so much energy to bring these things to life and nurse them," he said. "It's like bringing a child into the world. I wanted to start one business and stick with it; that was enough for me."

He was helping to change the world. And he was able to do it all without a haircut or a shave.

Gary Hirshberg had spent his entire life to that point pursuing knowledge, resolute in his belief that concepts like studying alpine tree lines, removing toxins from farming, and building windmills could somehow heal the planet.

But nothing prepared him for the harsh realities of becoming an entrepreneur, building a business from scratch, and trying to make a profit from little cups of yogurt. "Having an organic yogurt business in 1983 was great," said Hirshberg in a joke told so often he has developed the perfect syncopation for it. "There was just no supply and no demand."

After returning from China in mid-September 1983, he paid off the $75,000 debt that Stonyfield had run up in his absence by raising some money from his former funders at New Alchemy, and by borrowing money from his mother. "I was in the spider's web at that point; I slowly but steadily descended into this trap."

Once they got into the flow of things, Hirshberg and Kaymen would be milking cows in the morning, and producing and delivering yogurt in the afternoon, a couple of cases here and a couple there. They went around town in a little van with an insulated box to hold the yogurt. "We just drove fast. Who could afford refrigeration?" At night they would hand out free samples in the five Stop & Shop stores that a buyer had reluctantly allowed them to test. They came to find that these "demos" were vital, part of the "indispensable hand-shake with the customer" that elevates one product over another because it creates some kind of emotional connection.

The key to their success was not just that the yogurt tasted great, but that the mission behind the products was simple and powerful: As Hirshberg told one trade magazine, "Food ought to be good for people, not just okay for peo-ple."[19] No artificial ingredients, of course. None of the added sugars of, say, Columbo or Dannon, two of the leading yogurt brands. A gradual shift from natural ingredients to organic ones, with a commitment to pay local organic farmers a 10 percent "quality premium." And an overall commitment to social responsibility by supporting charities, employee education, and recycling efforts. "We were leading with our mission, leading with our values, but abso-lutely leading with our chins," Hirshberg said.

The main problem for Stonyfield, as with nearly every other natural foods company of the era—and indeed, of startups in any new industry—was that there were no models. No road maps, no manuals. Imagine being plopped down in some foreign country, tasked with some difficult project, handed the keys to a vehicle you don't know how to drive, and given no navigational aids. That was what starting Stonyfield Farm felt like to Gary Hirshberg and Samuel Kaymen. Because there really was no precedent for establishing an all-natural or organic branded perishable product for sale in a network of natural foods stores. No articles in some obscure publication in the reading room at the Londonderry Public Library that would tell them how to produce the yogurt. No guidelines for setting up a distribution network, or reaching out to supermarkets. Nothing. And if the folks at Columbo knew anything that could prove helpful, they certainly weren't going to share it. "We had no idea what we were doing," conceded Hirshberg, a lament heard from so many natural foods entrepreneurs. "If I had known what was going to be happening over the next few years, the pain that we went through and the difficulty that we put our family and friends through, I would have run in the other direction. . . . I got swallowed in the vortex of the business."

Prospective funders would tell him that he needed to write a business plan. He had never done that before, but pegged away at it, eventually coming up with some 30 different variations. "I would produce one and get it done and hand it to them, and I could tell it would just be wrong. Capital W Wrong." What he came to learn was that "the product wasn't the point of the business plan. It was the process, the process of trying to think through and understand break-even points, key targets, and gross margins. Things we didn't understand that were absolutely critical benchmarks for success. And we just kept missing those benchmarks."

Hirshberg's charm and passion opened many doors, so Stonyfield went through the typical progression of "friends and family" money to "angel investor" money to equity partnerships. "I was neither patient nor virtuous in this period," recalled Hirshberg. "I was under severe duress. I was running on adrenaline and fear. I was damned if I was going to lose my mother-in-law's money."

In 1987 a deal to expand production to a western Massachusetts dairy owned by friends turned into a "near-death experience" when the dairy went bankrupt 3 months into the arrangement. Hirshberg and Kaymen hadn't looked into the dairy's finances closely enough and had to pull production back to their original farm, and then start building a new factory from scratch; they lost $3.5 million in the process. Hirshberg noted, "The common thread across this entire era was hopeless infinite naïveté about cash flow," for Stonyfield and for nearly every other natural foods company. "Because you can go a long time without profits, but you can't go any time without cash."

Once the hard work began to pay off, with a contract to sell to all 230 of the Stop & Shop stores and accounts at hundreds of small health foods stores throughout the Northeast, Stonyfield Farm finally began to shed its entrepreneurial skin and operate like a real company. A carpenter friend of Hirshberg put it succinctly: "You can't bullshit a nail." You can only invent new solutions for so long before you come back around to the obvious and logical conclusion that you can't "entrepreneur" your way out anymore. You need to hire experts in sales and logistics and quality control and marketing, people who aren't always "inventing on the job." Hirshberg said that it was only when he and Kaymen began to hire people who knew more than they did that Stonyfield finally started to become a company. "The art," he said, "was in finding not just the right skill set but the right person." There were, for example, some very talented people who came on board who looked at Hirshberg and Kaymen and thought they could take advantage of them. "I tended to assume the best in people. But that's part of the [entrepreneurial] learning curve. You learn that's not the best approach. You have to let people prove themselves before you hand over the keys."

Stonyfield had terrible shortages of cash, and of labor, and of experience. In all these regards, it was the prototypical entrepreneurial company. But Hirshberg had absolutely no shortages of wacky promotional ideas.

One of the earliest promotions was an "adopt-a-cow" program: Customers who mailed in five yogurt lids would be sent a certificate naming them as the co-owners of a cow. The cow would send a photograph and a couple of letters over the course of the year. It was pure country kitsch, but it worked: The *Boston Globe* ran a big article about it, Joan Rivers adopted a cow live on national television, and Stonyfield was able to build its brand awareness without having to resort to expensive advertising campaigns.

On one occasion, Hirshberg's 30th birthday in 1984, he held a party with his Hampshire College ultimate Frisbee team. He blew out the candles on his cake, and said, "It's great that you guys have come, but if you want to give me a really great gift, go down to Bread & Circus and ask for our yogurt. They're not carrying it yet." That was on a Sunday. On Wednesday, Mary Carol Skinner, the buyer at Bread & Circus, called and said, "Gary, I don't know what is going on but demand has gone through the roof suddenly! Get it in here right away." On another occasion, when a talk radio DJ bashed Stonyfield on the air, saying he would rather eat camel manure than yogurt, Hirshberg went to Benson's

Animal Park in New Hampshire, filled a yogurt container with camel manure, and delivered it to the radio station. These were not the sorts of things that Columbo would ever stoop to do.

By 1989 sales reached $3.4 million. They nearly doubled the next year, and then topped $10 million in 1991. Still, there was the constant struggle for respect, epitomized by the raft of articles that misspelled the name of Stonyfield's New Hampshire hometown as "Londonberry." Then the Fresh Fields stores came on the scene and opened up a huge new outlet for Stonyfield. "It looked like heaven on earth," said Hirshberg. "It looked like we had finally arrived."

In 1992, 9 years into the venture, Stonyfield Farm turned its first profit.

———

There were many Mo Siegels and Michael Funks in the natural foods revolution—unapologetic hippies who found a higher calling, because commerce-with-a-purpose was mightier than the protest. There were also plenty of Gene Kahns, Stan Amys, and Gary Hirshbergs—intellectual rebels who simply came to believe that food and health were linked, and were sacrosanct, and thus found their purpose in purity.

There was, however, only one John Mackey. While the other high-minded idealists raged against the machine, hacking their way through the business wilderness illuminated by little more than their brightly burning mission and occasionally stumbling into success, Mackey used his vision and capitalistic ambition to blaze new trails.

Shaggy-haired and decidedly counterculture, he appeared to have come right from central casting in the Age of Aquarius. He had dropped out of both the University of Texas and Trinity University multiple times and had gone to live in a vegetarian co-op called Prana House. Then, along with girlfriend Renee Lawson Hardy in 1978, the 25-year-old Mackey had opened a small health foods store-cum-restaurant with the stick-it-to-The-Man name of Safer Way Foods (Safeway was the nation's largest supermarket at the time), in a three-story Victorian house in Austin, Texas. The store was on the first floor, the restaurant on the second, and they lived in a showerless apartment on the third, forcing them to bathe in the nearby Barton Springs Pool.

But this was a reconstructed idealist, an entrepreneur of a different stripe, more empire-builder than castle-builder. He may have been a bit of a drifter, but he was also ambitious, curious, well-read, whip-smart, and highly savvy about the ways of business (his father, Bill Mackey, was CEO of a hospital management company that he would sell in 1984 for nearly a billion dollars). Having seen the potential in supermarket-sized natural foods stores during a 1979 scouting trip that included upstarts like Mrs. Gooch's in Los Angeles and Bread & Circus in Boston, Mackey approached Craig Weller and Mark Skiles—the partners of another Austin health foods store called Clarksville Natural Grocery, with whom he had sometimes teamed up on ordering—with an offer so logical that they couldn't imagine a reason to say no. Mackey had found a new location for Safer Way, at 10th and Lamar, a former nightclub and Big Bear supermarket that had burned down and been rebuilt. It was close to Clarksville, and would be four times its size.

"If you don't come in with me, I may put you out of business because I can sell cheaper than you can," Mackey reportedly told Skiles.[20] It wasn't a threat, just a statement of inevitable fact in the World According to Mackey: part Don Corleone, part irrefutable logic. Since Weller had long thought that the site would be a great place for a natural foods store, a partnership was soon formed. The store, renamed Whole Foods Market, opened in September 1980.

Whole Foods thrived at the new address, tallying $200,000 a week in sales after just a few months in business, making it the highest grossing natural foods store in the country.[21] A Memorial Day flood in 1981 that destroyed the store and most of its inventory proved to be little more than the legendary fodder for future storytelling: Friends and customers pitched in to clean it up, and the store was able to reopen a month later. By year's end it had 100 employees, and the partners were already beginning to think about ways to replicate their success elsewhere. Mackey, Weller, and Skiles expanded to a second location in North Austin a year later, and soon to Houston and Dallas.

By 1992 there were 12 Whole Foods Market stores doing $92 million in sales, and in January of that year the company went public—a seminal event that brought an infusion of $23 million in capital, money that would put some carrot-and-stick behind Mackey's entreaties to competitors and bankroll the company's buying spree over the next few years. Under the leadership of its complex, hypercompetitive CEO and cofounder, Whole Foods would come to display a voracious appetite for growth, especially the kind that came through the vanquishing of a competitor.

Whole Foods Market was still a tiny company in a fringe sector of the food business, but it was starting to make some noise. Clearly, a new day was about to dawn in the natural foods industry, one in which a sudden transformation in the shape and scope of retailing would point the way toward viability for an industry that had always been long on ideas but short on profits.

CHAPTER 4

THE BOULDER MAFIA

L ike Colorado itself, US Route 36 starts in the plains and ends in the Rockies.

The road originates in Ohio, but when you pick it up at the Kansas–Colorado line, it runs 206 desolate miles while some anonymous-sounding roadside encampments sail by: Joes, Cope, Last Chance. It joins up with the interstate, runs through Denver, then Boulder, ascends into the Front Range, and then beyond Estes Park undergoes another engine-churning climb into Rocky Mountain National Park. It ultimately disappears into Route 34 at Deer Ridge Junction, surrounded by geologic features whose names are as stalwart as the plains towns were meek: Tombstone Ridge, Bighorn Mountain, Sundance Mountain, Spectacle Lakes.

The 25-mile stretch from Denver to Boulder opened up in 1952 as a turnpike, with a 25-cent toll. Today it is a heavily traveled corridor that runs past Denver's sports palaces, skirting its gritty warehouses and refineries, and continues on past the pleasant Anywhere, USA, retail centers of Broomfield, revealing vast open spaces rimmed by dense subdivisions.[1] But as you crest the ridge near Louisville, at mile marker 42.2, the dull yellow hayfields with their prairie-dog villages yield to a spectacular sight: the sandstone Flatirons formation a few miles ahead, with the pine-covered foothills of the Front Range beyond and the Boulder Valley splayed out below.

From this vantage point you can see the massive brick red University of Colorado dormitory towers at Williams Village, 15 stories and 164 feet high, dwarfed like Lilliputian Legos by the mountains of the Front Range—which in

turn appear meager against the snow-capped peaks of the *real* Rockies of the
Continental Divide. The scale is simply hard for the parietal cortex to process.
It is a sight at once inspiring and intimidating, the fusion of plains and moun-
tains, settlement and wilderness, all evident in one sweeping glance.

Beyond the ridge, as you descend into Boulder, the perspective is different.
Very different. For Boulder is a town that is so progressive, so hip, so weird, so
politically charged, it has often been called "twenty-five square miles surrounded by reality," or the "Gore-Tex Vortex," or the "People's Republic of
Boulder." And while it has sometimes been grouped with Denver in the same
metropolitan statistical area (a demographic measurement tool), it is in many
ways an entirely different universe.

Boulder's quirky cultural vibrancy stands in stark contrast to the geologic
grandeur around it. In town are the University of Colorado, Naropa University
(founded by Tibetan Buddhists), a lively music scene, schools of Rolfing and mas-
sage therapy, several federal government offices, the Chautauqua lecture series,
even a Shakespeare Festival. Democrats outnumber Republicans two-to-one—
and seemingly in every other driveway, leftist bumper stickers hold together
rusted old Subarus. Boulder was an early leader in "progressive" social policies,
including gay rights, same-sex marriage, and anti-smoking legislation. *New
York Times* writer Florence Williams referred to the town's "unshaven roots"
and "veneer of adrenaline-jacked grooviness," and noted that columnist David
Brooks had unleashed a savage parody of Boulder "as a latté town of bourgeois
bohemians with their in-your-jowls liberalism and an uncanny ability to accrue
wealth while pretending to care only about following their creative visions."[2]
And while that recalcitrant population has grown by 150 percent since 1960, to
about 100,000, the town itself has not, courtesy of a series of ordinances that
have restricted building. In fact, in 1967 Boulder became the first city in the
United States to tax itself in order to preserve open space.[3]

All of Boulder's eccentricities are on display on the Pearl Street Mall, an
open-air pedestrian walkway lined by gentrified old buildings that is the spiritual heart of the city. There are independent restaurants and bookshops, stores
that sell wind-up toys and others that offer somewhat more adult toys ("Boudha's
Goudhas" calls itself "an enlightened smoke shop"). There are buskers playing
didgeridoos, happy dogs with bandanas, guitar-strumming guys in wool hats,
and young people with matted hair just sitting around and talking. Underem-
ployment, it would seem, runs rampant.

This curious mélange has attracted considerable media attention. In recent years, national magazines and Web sites have ranked Boulder as America's #1 "town to live well" (*Forbes* magazine), the #1 "city to raise an outdoor kid" (*Backpacker* magazine), the #1 "brainiest city" (Portfolio.com), the #1 "happiest city" (CBS *Moneywatch*), the #6 "healthiest city to live and retire" (*AARP* magazine), the #1 "foodiest town" (*Bon Appetit* magazine) . . . and the one of which Boulderites are perhaps most proud, the #40 "worst-dressed city" (*GQ* magazine).[4]

There is *something* about the people, and it seems to be tied up in the majesty of the place.

Boulderites embrace their beautiful surroundings and have an outlook as big as all outdoors. Many of the rusted Subarus have ski racks on their roofs. North Face jackets and Lululemon yoga pants are de rigueur. There are 43,000 acres of protected open space surrounding the city. Boulder Creek Path runs right through the center of town, bringing glacial melt water tumbling out of the mountains and bisecting a park that is alive with bicyclists and runners and Tai Chi classes.

There is a humility that comes with living in such a place. Surrounded by such resplendence, implied though it is—from within the city's midst, Boulderites can see only some of the mountains—they cannot help but understand Man's relative insignificance in the scheme of things. Appreciation for the natural order is all but a residency requirement.

And so, not surprisingly, that passion for the natural world also extends to food. Boulder has what is certainly the highest concentration of per capita natural foods stores in the country, including one building at the corner of Broadway and Arapahoe that over the past 30 years has gone from Alfalfa's to Wild Oats to Whole Foods to a new iteration of Alfalfa's; only the presence of tofu on the shelves has remained constant. Today the ALFALFA's sign wraps around the corner of that building, so that Broadway is illuminated at night by the letters ALFA, an appropriate if unintentional label for the store that started it all in the town that started it all.

It was not always this way. Like so much of the West, the region was originally viewed as a resource to be plundered. One of the earliest settlers, Captain

Thomas Aikins, remarked in 1858 that "the mountains looked right for gold and the valleys looked rich for grazing."[5] The South Arapaho chief, Niwot, told Aikins: "Go away; you come to kill our game, to burn our wood and to destroy our grass." This came to be known as "Niwot's Curse," a notion that the valley was so beautiful that people who saw it would want to stay, and would then be its undoing. (Today the "Curse" has been co-opted as a sort of Chamber of Commerce tagline to mean that those who visit Boulder will never be happy anywhere else.)

Boulder offered most of the trappings of frontier life that attracted fortune-seekers and bred stout souls. There was the battle between the white men and the Indians, with predictable results: Niwot and many of his tribesmen were killed in the Sand Creek Massacre of 1864. There was a brief gold rush, followed by a longer history of silver and tungsten mining once the narrow-gauge railway arrived in 1879. Boulder had its saloons and its red-light district. It also had frontier lawlessness, remedied by the mining district's "club rules," which doled out punishment to transgressors by shaving one side of a man's beard and the other side of his hair, and then kicking him out of town.[6]

But starting in 1877 it also had the university, an active Women's Club (Colorado women were granted the vote early, in 1893), and a forward-looking vision that included a remarkable degree of city planning and parks creation. Boulder even went "dry" in 1907, 13 years before Prohibition, and remained so until 1967. The unusual combination of frontier independence and civic progressivism, along with the ever-present sense of solidarity with nature, would attract many dynamic people to the Boulder area, and set the stage for its starring role in the natural foods revolution.

One of the first to arrive was one of the least likely. Prem Pal Singh Rawat was born in India in 1958, son of a revered spiritual leader. When his father died in 1966, the young boy immediately assumed the title of Satguru, The True Revealer of Light and Spiritual Master of the Divine Light Mission, and became known as the Guru Maharaj Ji. He told the mourners, "Dear children of God, why are you weeping? The Perfect Master is among you. Recognize him. Obey him and adore him."[7]

Following his father's teachings, he encouraged people to renounce their worldly possessions and receive "the Knowledge," which was described as "a direct and concrete experience of inner peace and joy" that "eradicates hatred, greed, and fear" and "contains a solution to every problem at present facing humanity."[8] The Satsang meditation involved four techniques, which one was supposed to practice for 2 hours each day: the Light (pressing your thumb and forefinger against closed eyes); the Music (putting thumbs in your ears, closing your eyes with your pinkies, and concentrating on inner sounds); the Nectar (rolling your tongue back in your mouth as far as possible); and the Word (deep, even breathing while concentrating on the sound of the unspeakable name of God).[9] He soon articulated a rather simplistic vision of world peace and love that resonated with many. On November 8, 1970, at the age of 12, Guru Maharaj Ji addressed a crowd of more than 1 million followers at Delhi's India Gate and said, "I declare I will establish peace in this world." Before long, he claimed 6 million followers worldwide, including 40,000 in America who organized themselves in 54 ashrams, or communities, throughout the country. He established the US headquarters of the Divine Light Mission just down US Route 36 from Boulder, in a seven-story office building in Denver.

Certainly he was not the first guru to find a receptive audience among westerners, whose search for meaning through a belligerent and provocative era had often turned eastward for answers. The Hare Krishna movement began in New York in 1965. *Life* magazine had even declared 1967 "the year of the guru" after Maharishi Mahesh Yogi came to the United Kingdom and led a weekend of "spiritual regeneration" centered on Transcendental Meditation for a group that included the Beatles and Mick Jagger.[10] In 1968 the Maharishi added Donovan, Mia Farrow, and Mike Love to his impressive roster of followers.

But the Guru Maharaj Ji exerted an influence that was even more extraordinary, given that he was just a pudgy teenager. One middle-aged woman reflected the spirit in an interview captured in the 1974 documentary *Lord of the Universe*.

"I was very happy. Had a family. Beautiful children, grandchildren, 14 grandchildren, very, very happy. Beautiful husband, beautiful friends. I didn't realize I was searching, really. But I am through searching. I have found that thing that we are all searching for."

An old woman next to her asked, "I'd like to know, how did he get so many people to follow him?"

The first woman giddily answered: "Because he gives that true experience of God. He gives a true experience of God. You see light, you hear music, you taste nectar, and you feel the word. . . . This is the day we have been waiting for. He's here! He's here!"[11]

Today, hearing the accounts of the "Premies"—those who pledged themselves to Guru Maharaj Ji—conjures up frightening associations with the People's Temple in Jonestown, Guyana; the Branch Davidians in Waco, Texas; or
another cult that was making news from 1969 to 1970, the Manson Family.
Such was the starry-eyed nature of their devotion. And certainly there were
those who viewed the young guru as a fraud, someone who quickly accumulated an incredible amount of wealth when applicants signed over their insurance policies, mortgages, inheritances, and trust funds to the DLM. Before
long, Guru Maharaj Ji had Rolls-Royces and Jaguars in London, a chauffeured
Mercedes limousine in Denver, and mansions in Long Island; Denver; and
Malibu, California. He also had an insatiable thirst for Western culture (Hawaiian Punch, Baskin-Robbins ice cream, Batman comics, a digital watch, squirt
guns, and a motor bike that he liked to drive into his mother's hotel room).[12]

But the Premies' love and devotion was generally sincere, attracting not
just lost souls but smart young seekers with college degrees. And the DLM was
serious business. It included 10 retail thrift stores, a restaurant in New York, a
movie production company, a monthly magazine, three airplanes, WATS and
Telex lines to connect its 154 branch offices, an IBM computer system to keep
track of every Premie's skills and background, the Cleanliness Is Next to God-
liness janitorial service, and, in order to feed all those people in the ashrams, a
network of sophisticated natural foods co-ops called Rainbow Grocery.[13]

———

Mark Retzloff was one of those college graduates who moved to Colorado to see
what the DLM was all about. Born in Indiana in 1948 and raised in Michigan,
he could have been the poster boy for the Wonder Bread—and carefully bred—
Midwestern middle class: the responsible eldest of four children, the bright kid
who couldn't stay in his seat, the son of an automotive engineer who grew up in
the suburbs of Detroit where everyone worked for Ford, GM, or Chrysler and
looked forward to their pension.

Retzloff was and is a serious person, a deep thinker who sees the systems
in life, not just the surface. It is hard to coax a smile from him. Thoughts flow
from his mind smoothly, emerging as fully formed paragraphs.

As a teenager in the sixties, he put those cognitive skills to work trying to
analyze how he could make a difference in a world that he viewed to be in

peril. He read *Silent Spring*. He was granted conscientious objector status, and became active in the antiwar movement.[14] He pursued a degree in conservation and resource planning at the University of Michigan. He carefully followed the protests at the 1968 Democratic convention while driving back from a summer of work in California. Back in Ann Arbor, Michigan—where the student protests of 1968 and 1969 were getting heated, fueled by the increasingly violent activities of Bill Ayers's and Tom Hayden's Weathermen, a splinter group of Students for a Democratic Society (SDS)—he got arrested, along with 240 others, at a sit-in at the county courthouse on behalf of Aid to Dependent Children.

In the spring of 1969, he married a woman he had met at the sit-in, and along with three others they moved into a house in Saline, about 10 miles south of Ann Arbor, and began pursuing a macrobiotic lifestyle. Through his environmental studies, Retzloff was already deeply concerned about human impact on the world, and macrobiotics gave him a strong foundation in how food fit into that equation. At first it was hard to find macrobiotic foods. They had to drive 100 miles round-trip to Detroit. But then they discovered that they could purchase foods through Erewhon, and before long they simply decided to go into business for themselves. Later that year, they teamed up with two others who were starting a co-op in Ann Arbor and opened a small store over a bike shop at the intersection of Williams and State Streets, right next to the campus. They called it Eden Foods.

"My role at Eden was to go out and talk to the farmers and convince them to grow organically," said Retzloff. "We didn't really know what organic was, but we knew it was without pesticides and chemicals. And at that time there were still lots of farmers who had taken over from their father or their grandfather . . . and they weren't so sure about what the seed salesman and the fertilizer salesman were telling them."

The goal wasn't to make money; Retzloff and his partners viewed this as a sensible lifestyle, something that fit in with their set of values. "It was really what we truly believed. We were doing it in all parts of our lives, whatever clothing we were wearing, where we were living, how we were living, all those types of things were part of it. So it got infused deeply into who we were as individuals."

Retzloff graduated in December 1970 and poured his energy into Eden Foods for a year. Then he moved to Seattle, where he ran an Erewhon grocery store, started a spring water business, and drove a truck once a week making deliveries in Washington and Oregon for the natural foods company Chico-San. "I was seeing these stores and meeting these people," he recalled, "and had these little businesses that I was working on. So I was gaining the experience and the confidence that if I set myself in the right direction, I could be successful."

Not long after that, however, he found out about the Divine Light Mission, and was attracted to its sense of orderliness, community, pursuit of peace, and ties to the natural foods business. "People were searching for meaning and what was making sense out there. And the young, you have a lot of aspirations of what should be going on and happening in the world. So it made sense that there was something over here that said, 'Well, you know, here is the meaning of life.'" Retzloff gave up his worldly possessions, including his ownership stake in Eden Foods, and moved into the ashram in downtown Denver.

———

Retzloff's talents did not go unnoticed by the very practical leadership of the DLM. He was smart, organized, entrepreneurial, and had solid experience working in food procurement and retailing. He was put in charge of all work involving filming, publications and recordings, and food operations. At the time, the DLM was like every other small community of people searching in frustration for supplies of natural and organic foods. They bought brown rice, bulk beans, and flour from the Seventh Day Adventists, a denomination founded in Battle Creek, Michigan (with strong ties to the sanitarium where C.W. Post first got his breakfast cereal ideas from Kellogg), that stored and sold food. They bought barrels of honey from a farmer in New Mexico. They negotiated for a few organically grown apples from some hippie farmers on the Western Slope. But it was piecemeal procurement, and as the ashram grew to about 350 or 400 people, that was not going to work.

Yet that was small change compared to what was to come. In 1973 the DLM decided to stage a massive event at the one place in America that was big enough and important enough to accommodate it: the Houston Astrodome. Millennium '73 would be a 3-day gathering of Premies and supplicants, "the most holy and significant event in human history," featuring Guru Maharaj Ji's proclamation of 1,000 years of peace. The guru would "present to the world a plan for putting peace into effect," read their press release. "He will announce the founding of an international agency to feed and shelter the world's hungry. He will initiate the building of a Divine City that shall demonstrate to the world a way for people of all sorts to live together in harmony."[15] With massive crowds expected to fill the 50,000-seat stadium, the DLM needed people who had experience with food—so they sent several of their best coordinators, including Mark Retzloff, as well as a slender 24-year-old of Pakistani-British heritage named Shahid "Hass" Hassan, who had been working at a DLM ashram in Boston. The two men recognized their intellectual common ground and complementary skill sets, and quickly became friends.

Millennium '73 was a lavishly prepared and highly anticipated event. It was over-the-top and under-the-dome. The lead-up was accompanied by the "Soul Rush" publicity campaign that implied that something unprecedented would happen in Houston—perhaps even the appearance of aliens. Thirty-three jets were chartered to bring in faithful followers from around the world. A band called Blue Aquarius, led by Guru Maharaj Ji's 20-year-old brother, Bhole Ji, performed "Satisfaction" by the Rolling Stones, wearing powder-blue leisure suits. Guru Maharaj Ji himself sat on a throne in white robes or a Nehru jacket, with ornate headwear, and when he wasn't engaged in Darshan—a practice where supplicants kissed his feet—he was giving news conferences and bantering with the press in perfect idiomatic American English ("What's up? What do you want?" . . . "You just don't like guys fooling around"). Rennie Davis, a prominent 32-year-old activist who had been one of the "Chicago Seven" prosecuted for their roles in disrupting the 1968 Democratic convention, opened the event by declaring, "It is not possible to understand the Middle East, or Watergate, or UFOs, or the super comet in the sky, unless you understand the central event on this planet around which all other events now spin." He also said that the political and cultural revolution of the sixties, for which he had fought so hard, "was really all a warm-up . . . for the greatest transformation in the history of human civilization."[16] An op-ed in the *San Francisco Sunday Examiner* wondered whether Davis had been lobotomized, and suggested that if not, he might consider it.[17]

In the end, though, Millennium '73 was a total bust. Only about 20,000 people attended; 7 weeks earlier, the hokey "Battle of the Sexes" tennis exhibition between Billie Jean King and Bobby Riggs had drawn 30,472 people to the Astrodome. The press coverage of Millennium '73 and the Guru Maharaj Ji was devastating. *Rolling Stone* magazine ran a story entitled, "When the Lord of All the Universe Played Houston, Many are Called but Few Show Up."[18] Worse, the DLM was left with a debt in excess of a half-million dollars. It had to cut staff and tighten up its operations, including the way it procured food.

The DLM needed the buying power of a mass market—and that was where the concept for Rainbow Grocery came in. Over the next couple of years, Mark Retzloff helped the DLM to open seven or eight Rainbow Grocery operations around the country, serving the ashrams and the local communities as for-profit operations. He called his friend Hass, whom he had met in Houston, and invited him to come out to Denver to manage the co-op there. Then Retzloff hit the road. Meeting with farmers and food producers, retailers and distributors, he began to piece together a more sensible system for procurement. Along the way, he began to see that although the natural foods world was still small and fragmented, it held the promise of community. "It helped me to understand that I didn't have to do it myself. There were a lot of other people who felt the same way, who were on a similar path. And therefore, we had that common interest. Getting together with them, we could do more."

Hassan, meanwhile, found a better way to organize the retail side of things. In the past, the ashram had always taken food orders from individual house-holds and aggregated them to figure out what would be needed for the week; then they would go out and buy the food and divide it into household orders. It was classic co-op. When he first arrived, Hassan and one other person would perform these functions, splitting up the food purchases in an old garage and delivering them to the ashram families on Capitol Hill in an old VW Microbus. But the operation was shut down by the Health Department, and it was at that point he realized an entirely different model might work. "We decided that the organization we had was incapable. It was [two of us] doing a food co-op thing for all these people. 'You know, this is silly, there has got to be a better model. Oh yeah, retail stores!' You put the food in one place, and people come to you. And you don't have to do the ordering and the delivering."

Once Rainbow Grocery was housed in a retail store, Hassan also found that it began to serve another purpose, as a meeting place for like-minded people. "The idea was: Let's do a retail store where we create this sense of community, where we are answering a need in people's lives and where people feel like, 'Oh, that is my community place where I see my neighbors and I see my friends. And the people that work there are not this foreign race of people that I don't relate to. These are people with whom I share values and am friends.'"

The concept was a success. By 1977, however, changes in the tax code forced the DLM to divest itself of the profit-making Rainbow Groceries. Retzloff borrowed some money from his parents, and he and Hassan bought the store at the corner of York and Colfax in Denver. They operated it for about a year, and then realized that a much more fertile market for natural foods awaited them 25 miles up US Route 36, where Hanna Kroeger and Green Mountain Grainery had been operating small health foods stores for years, and where a company named Celestial Seasonings had grown into a $5 million business, a kingmaker in the natural foods industry.

Hassan had been painting houses in Boulder and, given his background, appreciated the town's entrepreneurial spirit. "I had come from England in the seventies, which was in the worst of times, in a lot of ways. Hung over from the sixties, depressed, terrible weather, the economy was really bad, Margaret Thatcher was battling the unions. It was like there was a hangover from the end of the empire and the class system. And I came to Boulder and I was like, 'Wow! If you have an idea, and you want to do something, people do it. There aren't the levels of societal constraints. . . . ' In the West there was this attitude that I loved, which Boulder exemplified, a sort of freedom and creativity and new ideas and people actually taking those ideas and doing something with them."

So Retzloff and Hassan moved to Boulder, and in 1979, after pooling together $300,000 from their own savings and a small group of investors, opened a 5,900-square-foot store at 1825 Pearl Street that they called Pearl Street Market.

Retzloff and Hassan had learned a tremendous amount about growing, buying, and merchandising food. They had an instinctive feel for what would resonate with the changing consumer attitudes. And they were becoming aware of what was happening elsewhere with stores like Nature's Fresh Northwest in Portland, Oregon; Mrs. Gooch's in Los Angeles; Bread & Circus in Boston; and Whole Foods Market in Texas. So with Pearl Street Market, they created a true natural foods supermarket, featuring a wide variety of healthy foods in a shiny store with straight aisles wide enough for two shopping carts to pass, bright lighting, and electronic cash registers—all of which would appeal to conventional shoppers. They bought turkeys from local farmers, arranged with independent truckers to bring in produce from California, and flew in specialty cheeses from New York. They sold natural foods, but were not as strict as Mrs. Gooch's or Bread & Circus. "We try to stay away from preservatives, chemicals, and added sugars," Hassan told one interviewer.[19] Pearl Street Market grossed more than \$1 million in its first year, and took off from there. By year three, they knew they needed more space, and in 1983 moved into a 12,000-square-foot site at the corner of Broadway and Arapahoe, which they named Alfalfa's. For almost a year, they tried to run the two stores in tandem, but when it became obvious that everyone was shopping at the new location, they sold Pearl Street Market and set off on careers that would eventually cycle through many similar and successful turns—the merry-go-round ride of a lifetime.

Meanwhile, the forces that had brought them to Boulder slowly dissipated. Eden Foods followed in the footsteps of Erewhon, becoming a distributor and eventually a brand manufacturer. Rainbow Grocery would stay in business for a few more years, before being purchased by the major East Coast distributor Cornucopia, which shortly thereafter became part of United Natural Foods, Inc. And the Guru Maharaj Ji? In 1983 he renamed the Divine Light Mission "Elan Vital" and closed the ashrams. But he continued to spread his message of peace through speeches, broadcasts, and events—piloting himself around the world on a *leased* private jet—and does to this day.

By the time Pearl Street Market opened, Barney Feinblum had already moved to Boulder, ditched his Samsonites, and talked his way into a job at Celestial Seasonings.

Born in Brooklyn in 1947, Feinblum had grown up in Levittown, the cookie-cutter community on Long Island that was the ultimate tribute to post-war Establishment planning. Barney was a good Jewish boy with an upbringing that was kosher in every respect. He studied. He was good with numbers. He played hockey. He went to Cornell. Ithaca, New York, however, was another hotbed of protests in the late sixties, and in his junior and senior years normalcy was disrupted and the university cancelled final exams. Barney had a deep desire for social justice, but was conscientious about the way he expressed it. "I was part of the SDS establishment that was trying to maintain order and keep things from escalating. I remember telling my mom I had to get off the phone because I had to go take over Barton Hall. She told me to make sure I dressed warm." When the National Guard shooting at Kent State happened in May 1970, Feinblum expressed his outrage by writing a letter to the *Cornell*

Daily Sun explaining why this sort of activity was worthy of protest (subsequently, he found out that one of those killed was his high school hockey buddy, Jeffrey Miller). Then he went out and joined the National Guard himself, in order to avoid the Vietnam War.

After college, the boy from Levittown worked for three different companies in the modular housing industry, each of which went broke. The last of them was in Denver, where he had been lured by a college friend named Joe Parent who was working on his PhD and had become interested in Boulder's Buddhist community. Feinblum himself had always been drawn to Eastern religions, perhaps because the yin-and-yang in his own life (red-headed Jew, individualist who grew up in the most generic town in America, athlete who played a violent sport but attended peace rallies) was so obvious. At one point, while they were still in New York, Joe had even taken Barney to practice meditation in the Bronx. "We tried to do that while the subways were rumbling by," remembered Feinblum. "It was not exactly ideal."

Feinblum fell in love with Boulder, and earned an MBA at the University of Colorado. He then landed a job as a night-shift foreman at the Samsonite factory in Denver, where suitcases would come off the production line with a tag that said "BUILT UNDER THE SUPERVISION OF BARNEY FEINBLUM." But at the same time, he was being coaxed into the natural foods world by his wife, Julie— so when she found an ad for a job at Celestial Seasonings in 1976, he put on a suit and tie and went for an interview. The secretary who greeted him there was barefoot, and told him that she lived in a tepee in the mountains. She took him to meet the personnel director, who was wearing shorts and a T-shirt. Mo Siegel, the mountain-climbing, bicycle-commuting CEO, told him that the salary for the new position would be two-thirds of what he was making at Samsonite. Feinblum sucked in some air through his teeth, loosened his tie, and settled in for what would become a wild ride. Another member of the Boulder Mafia was about to be initiated.

———•———

Steve Demos was 28 when he moved to Boulder in the summer of 1977, seeking to learn more about Tai Chi Chu'an, the Indian-Chinese blend of meditation and yoga.

Demos had always been a "seeker." As a boy, he used to ride the SEPTA trains into Philadelphia to visit the Penn Museum and see the displays of the Egyptian mummies and Buddhist and Chinese cultures. He became fascinated with cooking and by the age of 10 was tackling pie baking on his own. He attended Bowling Green State University, in Ohio, right in the midst of all the campus turmoil of the late sixties and early seventies, and his inquisitiveness began to turn to querulousness. He reacted sharply to the events happening about him, especially when it came to food and the rapid growth of additives, junk foods, and petrochemicals in agriculture. "There was more than an *awareness*," he recalled, still bristling at the affront of the Big Food companies. "It was a revolt. This wasn't a trusted evolution. We had been organic until 1940-something. Why in the world did we have to become experimental guinea pigs during our lifetimes?"

Demos went to India, and spent 4 years hitchhiking around with Pat Calhoun, whom he would later marry, and divorce, and partner with in business. ("I was once offered two pounds of opium and a camel for Pat, and I have reminded her many times in this life that she was two goats away [from being traded].") Demos studied Buddhism, became a vegetarian, and internalized the concept of "right livelihood"—the notion that one could live a productive and fulfilling life without harming others, and that even businesses should have to follow the Golden Rule: "Good for me, good for you, good for everyone who touches it." He returned to the United States and started a natural foods co-op in Lahaska, Pennsylvania, a few hundred square feet that were jammed with vegetarian products, bulk herbs and grains, teas, and a couple of glass refrigerators of dairy products. Demos bought some of his goods from Erewhon, some from a place in Philadelphia called Walt's Beautiful Foods, and once or twice a week he would get up early to make some purchases at the produce market in Philadelphia.

But the seeking continued. He sold the co-op for the value of its inventory, returned to India, moved to New York, and then spent a couple of years living in the Sant Bani ashram in Sanbornton, New Hampshire, before heading out to Boulder.

The town promised to be a comfortable place for Demos, perhaps somewhere he might actually stay for a while. There was the Buddhist community and its Tai Chi disciples, and plenty of likeminded spirits. "The incredible beauty and remoteness . . . lures that adventure spirit. I think everybody who moved here in the late seventies [came] for the exact same reason, and that was: This is the new frontier. Boulder had some magnetic draw to it."

It had also begun to develop a reputation for alternative diets. Celestial Seasonings was a legitimate company. Green Mountain Herb was big. And there were a few small retailers, including Green Mountain Grainery, Down to Earth Produce, New Age Foods, plus the Carnival Café. "I figured this was going to be the mecca of natural food," said Demos. "The attitude that people came in with was an expectation that living here was about quality of life. And high on that quality of life was what you ingest."

He borrowed $500 from a neighbor and began making tofu in his apartment, with an eye toward selling it on Pearl Street, and in the rest of the known universe, for that matter. He and Calhoun called their company WhiteWave Foods. The goal was pure high-minded idealism, with a slight Eastern twist: Change the world by proving that a right-livelihood-based business could compete with the traditional capitalist model, which, in his view, had "desecrated" the food business.

Though it had already emerged as the consummate symbol of mockery with which the mainstream critics lampooned the natural foods industry, tofu had become fairly well established in America. Large Asian companies, like Hinode out of Los Angeles and Azumaya out of San Francisco, were distributing products into ethnic stores and some supermarkets. According to Demos, some 270 other small companies began making tofu around the same time as WhiteWave. "I always believed it was going to be a big deal. Right from day one I was convinced that everybody was going to love tofu. That's how deluded I was."

And so, filled with entrepreneurial energy, but lacking a business plan and a real market for a product he believed would sell, Demos flailed about for some winning formula—because in the end, right livelihood is no livelihood if it can't be sustained. He made bricks of soft and firm tofu. He flavored and baked them. He made miso and tempeh and seitan. He experimented with frozen products, like Polar Bean soy ice cream, Polar Pals soy ice cream sandwiches, and ToFruzen; nothing caught on. Like all of the pioneers in the natural foods industry, he had no one to turn to for help. "No metrics. No mentors. We didn't have anybody that we could talk to. It was a joke. You just invented everything."

Rail-thin, slight of stature, sporting a classic seventies bushy mustache, flowing brown-blond curls, and an intense gaze reminiscent of what the author Wallace Stegner once called "eyes that bore into the camera like . . . zealot grandfathers in old tintypes,"[20] Demos became known all over town. He started the GoodBelly Deli, and a nut butter company called Naturally Nuts. He opened a small shop on Pearl Street, right across from the Pearl Street Market, called The Cow of China, where he made artisanal tofu in the back and sold sea vegetables, almond milk, and other items out front. And after Retzloff and Hassan moved their store, Demos shared a delivery truck with them—the WhiteWave logo on one side, the Alfalfa's logo on the other, and a curtain that could be moved to cover up the Alfalfa's logo should Demos need to make a delivery to Safeway. It was classic bootstrap, do-whatever-it-takes entrepreneurship, and it wasn't easy. "They forgot to tell us that 'small is beautiful' but highly unprofitable," Demos said in his slightly raspy, declarative voice. And then he laughed in the self-effacing way that only someone who has wallowed in obscurity truly can.

"You know, as the idealistic hippie out to change the world, there were a few dents and bruises along the way," he remembered. WhiteWave almost went bankrupt, and had to call every vendor to work out a payment plan. The company borrowed money from Demos's father and mother-in-law. WhiteWave also incurred the wrath of town leaders when it was discovered that their effluents were hitting the county's waste treatment plant, "like flushing one giant toilet every day." Demos struggled on, putting his house up as collateral, and earning just $35,000 a year in salary year after year.

Adding to the complexity was that Demos's partner was his ex-wife. Of course, entrepreneurs frequently turn to their spouses and family as a source of readily available skill and cheap labor, before the companies grow more professional and realize that these relationships usually sour a business. Divorced partners upped the ante. However, it worked. "There was an absolute trust already established," said Demos. "She did all the bookkeeping and the finance, and I did everything else. She fired me 10 times but I fired her 15. You know, shut the door and have a screaming, hollering match. No problems!"

The company grew, slowly, reaching about $6 million in sales by 1996. "Eighteen years of hell," Demos called it. Mostly he was trying to come to grips with the message the world was sending him: that maybe his idealism was too big for his business. "After a while I adjusted to the idea that it was okay to grow a business that became respectable and sizeable and produced the things that it was supposed to produce, and that was livelihoods for people, enough to pay mortgages and to raise families. And that became the mantra for a number of years, and the goal. Because I was committed to getting people to live lower on the food chain; this was my mission in life. If I wasn't going to change the planet today, then I was sure my efforts were going to have some impact way down the road when this stuff became popular."

It would be many years before that day would come, and the "stuff" that became popular was not what he had imagined it would be. But when it did, it was not only a game-changer; it was an industry-changer.

The concept was not squirmy, formless, bland bean curd, but something infinitely more familiar to Americans: a smooth, creamy white beverage, packaged in gable-top containers so that it could be poured over breakfast cereal. But it didn't come from a cow; it came from a soybean. He called it Silk, an onomatopoetic contraction of soy and milk. It would go on to become one of the most recognizable brand names of the era and, along with Earthbound Farm and Horizon Organic, one of the top three best-selling organic brands in the history of the natural foods industry.

Soy milk was not a new product. Vitasoy, Edensoy, and Westbrae, among others, had been selling it in boxy cartons for years. But by ingeniously packaging it in milk containers, designed to live right next to the cow's milk in the dairy section of the grocery store, WhiteWave instantly paved the way for the product's rapid expansion in merchandising sets, and for its repositioning in the minds of consumers as a viable and perhaps healthier alternative to milk.

"When I launched Silk, I knew that I had strapped myself to a rocket ship and that all those fantasy visions of being very large were actually going to come true." He was so sure of the prospects of his new product that he didn't even conduct any market research, doing all the taste-testing himself. He took in millions of dollars of investments from Dean Foods. He built nine independent operating systems in six factories, and in a stroke of genius, located his extraction operations next to milk processing plants, running a pipe through the wall, so that they could produce their soy milk during the night on the same equipment that the dairies would use for their cow's milk during the day, after it had been sanitized. This drove costs out of the system, and allowed White-Wave to produce Silk very cheaply. "For $9 million," said Demos proudly, "we got to use somebody's $250 million asset."

The production system was revolutionary. The packaging and store placement were inspired. The name was brilliant. After a little bit of experimentation, the flavor and consistency were perfected so that the product became a crossover hit with everyday consumers in conventional food stores, too. Even the timing was good, as numerous reports were hitting the press about the health benefits of soy. By 1999, when the Food and Drug Administration released a landmark report linking consumption of soy products to heart health, WhiteWave's sales had more than doubled to $14.2 million. They would more than double again in 2000. And in 2001. And in 2002.[21]

Demos noted that the town played a big part in his success. "I don't know if I would have made it in a whole lot of towns other than Boulder," he told a reporter in 2005. "Because who was buying tofu in 1977?"[22] There was also a supportive group of people who, like him, had survived their days of protesting and drug-taking and seeking, and paved the road from idealism to capitalism. And, perhaps most importantly, there was Celestial Seasonings. "When I started out that was the golden castle on the hill," said Demos. What they were achieving was "astronomically grand. They definitely changed the world of consumer packaged marketing by [using] wit, humor, and art. So they instilled in me, by observation, sort of an axiom: Get them to buy the package without any product inside and you have made great strides in brand loyalty." That was precisely the bit of innovation that would be needed to make Silk such a stunning commercial success.

———•+•———

Over the years, the intersecting careers of Mark Retzloff, Hass Hassan, Barney Feinblum, and Steve Demos would take more twists and turns than Boulder Creek as it comes cascading out of the Rockies.

When Retzloff and Hassan needed money for their move over to Broadway and Arapahoe in 1983, they initially sold shares to local investors in $5,000 units, but burned through that quickly and then turned to Celestial Seasonings—which made a $250,000 investment, and installed Barney Feinblum on Alfalfa's board to protect it. Feinblum would also join Demos on the board of WhiteWave. After Retzloff left Alfalfa's in 1990 to start Horizon Organic Dairy, Feinblum went to Horizon and became CEO. Years later, Feinblum would became a founding partner of Hassan's British-based natural foods retail company, Fresh & Wild; Retzloff, Hassan, and Feinblum would join together in the creation of Greenmont Capital Partners, a natural products investment fund; and in 2011, with undiminished idealism, Retzloff and Feinblum would team up to open a new version of Alfalfa's, in the old space at Broadway and Arapahoe. (Indeed, there were many companies "built under the supervision of Barney Feinblum.")

"You had this whole thing happening," remembered Retzloff about the magnetism of Boulder. "It was a small town. We all knew each other, we started talking to one another, we were using each other's services." According to Feinblum, their common goals encouraged them to set aside any competitive jealousies in support of a larger cause. "We would kind of meet socially, we shared values, and we tried to help each other out. You know, the retailers would give manufacturers ideas on products that they thought consumers wanted. The whole industry started to try to help each other compete against this conventional monolith that seemed almost insurmountable."

This same sort of symbiosis among like-minded entrepreneurs developed in a few other outposts of the natural foods movement, albeit on a smaller scale.

New England, for one, had a long history in health foods, starting with Sylvester Graham, the 19th-century minister in western Massachusetts who had believed that vegetarianism could help prevent masturbation, and whose "Graham bread"—free of chemical additives such as alum and chlorine—was the forerunner of graham crackers.

Of course, from its earliest settlement by Europeans, New England had been built upon reformist principles. And while the separatist tradition of the Pilgrims of Plymouth Colony was distinct from the righteousness of the Puritans who followed, and different still from the religious tolerance preached by Roger Williams when he broke to form the Rhode Island Colony, the character of the people was shaped by tendencies toward rebellion and self-sufficiency that suffused the settlements and transcended the generations. The heroic New England archetype was the yeoman farmer—independent, resolute, silent except when compelled to protest, hand-plowing his rock-stubble fields, fighting the elements, taking up the musket if need be, working so that his sons would be able to attend the Boston Latin School and Harvard College.

Strains of many of those elements were passed down to each successive generation with only slight evolutionary modifications. The New England character of the latter 20th century was thus recognizably Puritan in its industriousness, pragmatism, stubborn sense of fatalism and parochialism, though the slight non-conformism and belief in the primacy of education steered it in decidedly liberal intellectual directions. The modern New England was the

Yale graduate Paul Keene and his literary appreciation of the world about him, later reflected at Walnut Acres. It was Helen and Scott Nearing, whose life of homesteading in a hand-built stone house in Vermont led to their book *Living the Good Life* and inspired many who were interested in the back-to-nature movement. It was Michio and Aveline Kushi, settling in a place that was ready to hear their macrobiotic philosophy and that had the educated populace to make Erewhon a success. It was the maverick founders of Hampshire College and its no grades/no majors curriculum, which attracted the likes of not just Gary Hirshberg, but also Jeffrey Hollender, who would found an innovative Vermont-based company called Seventh Generation that produced natural cleaning products. It was the New Alchemy Institute on Cape Cod and its research in alternative energy and food production. It was the Boston branch of the Guru Maharaj Ji's Rainbow Grocery, lately attended to by Hass Hassan. And it was Anthony Harnett, whose open-minded yet cheeseparing Irish ways fit in well in Boston and made Bread & Circus an early titan in the natural foods business.

New England had all the necessary commercial starter dough: a tradition of polemics, a dense population of well-educated people, and an entrepreneurial legacy. The mass market understood the value of natural foods and was willing to pay a bit more for them. This stimulated enough demand to warrant the creation of several retail outlets, whose presence and marketing efforts generated further awareness and demand. With a conduit to the market, numerous leaders emerged on the product side, including Stonyfield Farm, Ben & Jerry's, Lightlife, Smartfood, Annie's Homegrown, Tomsun Foods, Nasoya, Putney Pasta, Lake Champlain Chocolate, After the Fall, Burt's Bees, Seventh Generation, and Tom's of Maine. As homegrown players in a region that drips parochial pride, their standing in the business community was elevated beyond what their sales might have warranted. And then, to connect manufacturer to retailer, a relatively strong network of distributors developed, including Stow Mills in New Hampshire and Cornucopia in Rhode Island. Massachusetts even became home to the Organic Trade Association. Absent any one key element, nothing as significant would have arisen. But with all of these factors in place, New England became a vital center for the natural foods industry, second only to Boulder, whose aura, timing, talent, and Rocky Mountain holy water had made it the industry's true cradle of development.

———•———

The Pacific Northwest was another nexus of natural living—and here, too, the character of the land was infused into the people and ultimately into their corporate creations.

There has long been a trailblazing spirit among people in the Northwest, with a dotted line all the way back to Lewis and Clark. The area's massive scale, mighty rivers, towering old-growth forests, volcanic peaks, active wildlife, and Pacific flank always rendered it intimidating and indomitable; human beings have had to learn to live with nature in the Pacific Northwest, not master it. Yet that very beauty and insuperability also attracted many settlers, and by and large those who were drawn to the area were hearty souls, capable of handling a crosscut saw or reloading a Winchester '73. The endless dreary weather has also engendered in its people a spirit of patience and understanding of the cycles of nature. Under such conditions, the East Coast notion of self-reliance gave way to a Northwestern acknowledgement of interdependence, which in the earliest days of settlement was manifest in the active fur trade and the Hudson's Bay Company, and in more modern times as the unusual easy-going pleasantness of its people, characterized by *Pacific Northwest* magazine as "the comic after-you-no-please-after-you traffic merge."[23] In today's Northwest, the politics are progressive, the attitudes tolerant, the cities dangerously hip, and the symbiosis of humankind and nature so ingrained that it is said that when strangers meet at a party, instead of asking "Where did you go to school," as they might in Boston, they ask, "What do you do for recreation?"

By the second half of the 20th century, these characteristics created just the right conditions for a natural foods revolution. There were the first-generation pathfinding retailers, Puget Community Cooperative and Nature's Fresh Northwest, as well as a good crop of small health foods stores that included New Day Natural Foods in Oregon (co-managed by Terry Dalton before he moved to Florida to start natural foods restaurants and eventually Unicorn Village), and the Erewhon store in Seattle that Mark Retzloff briefly managed. There were iconoclastic back-to-the-landers like Gene Kahn, whose New Cascadian Survival and Reclamation Project ended up "reclaiming" not just thousands of acres in Washington and Oregon for the organic movement, but also plenty of space in the supermarket freezer case that had been overtaken by artificially flavored and colored products like Eggos and Kool Pops.

There were also pioneers like Arran Stephens in British Columbia and Chuck Eggert in Oregon. Stephens's father, Rupert, had literally done ground-breaking work in organic soil development on their family farm on Vancouver Island. Arran opened the first natural foods supermarket in Canada, Lifestream, in 1971, and 14 years later founded Nature's Path, one of the most successful organic cereal companies the industry has ever known. Eggert started Pacific Natural Foods in 1987 as a co-packer of soy milk and built it into the top soup company in the natural channel. When he saw an opportunity for vertical inte-gration—supplying vegetables, milk, and meat to Pacific—Eggert turned into a latter-day Cincinnatus, returning from the commerce wars to the farms (he now owns several), where this unusual CEO/CPA/MBA/farmer is raising 1,200 dairy cows, 150,000 chickens, and 12,000 American Bronze Heirloom turkeys using organic methods that are both ancient and state-of-the-art. His turkeys, for example, are free to roam, and have cleared 35 acres of hillside covered in black-berries; and all of his cows wear wireless transmitters so that their every step through the organic pastures is measured. "We think organic will eventually be more profitable than conventional," he said.

Then there was the California transplant Bob Moore, who had discovered the charming artistry of stone grinding grains back in Redding at what he called Moore's Flour Mill. Moore blazed an Oregon Trail of his own, moving to Portland to attend a seminary—only to stumble upon a dilapidated old mill by the railroad tracks in Milwaukie, Oregon, which he bought, painted red, and called Bob's Red Mill. That building burned to the ground in an arson in 1988, but the 59-year-old Moore had a spirit as big as the redwoods. He started over, and then remarkably grew Bob's Red Mill into a $120 million business selling a wide variety of wholesome stone-ground grains, flours, and cereals.

Popular natural products also came from the Springfield Creamery in Eugene, Oregon (makers of Nancy's Yogurt, starting in 1970), Kettle Brand Potato Chips (1982) out of Salem, Oregon, and Washington's Stretch Island Fruit Company (1976).

—◦—

There were other smaller pockets of entrepreneurial natural foods activity as well.

In Ann Arbor and Austin, the presence of an important company (Eden Foods, Whole Foods Market) and a major university helped stimulate the market.

In Northern California, many of the key elements were in place for an explosion in natural foods, including proximity to the farms, a key distributor (Mountain People's Warehouse), several natural foods manufacturers (Lundberg, Westbrae, Barbara's Bakery, Traditional Medicinals, Santa Cruz Naturals, Imagine Foods/Rice Dream, R.W. Knudsen, Fantastic Foods, Hain Pure Foods), and the influential presence of Alice Waters and her restaurant, Chez Panisse; but it ended up being a slower build. This was largely because the retail side of the equation was lagging. Safeway, headquartered near Oakland, owned a dominant share of the market. Raley's, one of the conventional competitors, was among the first mainstream chains to bring in some natural foods. But none of the smaller health foods stores that had been born in the wake of the counterculture movement grew into anything big. New Age Foods, first opened in Haight-Ashbury by a former chemical salesman named Fred Rohe, expanded to three other locations. New Age's neighbor in the Haight, Far-Fetched Foods, achieved some notoriety but no commercial success. Another Bay Area retailer, Living Foods, had three stores, one of which was run by a tall, handsome, cerebral Stanford grad named Walter Robb who later went on to greatness at Whole Foods; but it didn't have the wherewithal to get too far.

In Southern California—haven for fortune-seekers, immigrants, Okies and other Dust Bowl refugees, and ultimate destination for those in search of the sun-dappled, sea-breeze-cooled, palm-tree-lined "Good Life"—health had nearly always been an industry. As early as the 1870s, California was "prescribed" as a part of the solution for those suffering from tuberculosis, and a network of sanitariums popped up to meet their needs.[24] Otto Carque had been among the first to commercialize the health food trend, with his 1912 "health wagon" and three retail stores, but there was fairly widespread interest in the industry. When Carque died in 1935, a memorial photo was published that contained the names of 77 companies and individuals involved in the health foods business who paid tribute to him.[25] Wisconsin-born Mildred Lager opened a store called The House of Better Living in downtown Los Angeles in 1933, and a newsletter and catalog to help market it ("Have you tried Olson's 100% whole wheat raisin bran bread?" read the issue of September 11, 1935, in part. "We also have all the Soy Bean products, soy cookies, crackers, and Bill Baker's soy and lima bean bread.").[26] The *Los Angeles Times* was filled with many columns and correspondents' articles about healthy eating, and there was even the industry's first true magazine, *California Health News*, published by

Irwin Clarke in the 1930s. Vitamin and supplement companies abounded. Thanks in large part to the huge number of farms in Southern California and the adjacent San Joaquin Valley, the region would become a major center for organic produce and for other natural foods companies (Bragg, Health Valley, Albert's Organics, Cedarlane Foods, Kashi, and many more).

But the Southern California marketplace was vast and eclectic, and until Mrs. Gooch's came around in 1977, no natural foods retailer was able to gain much traction. Lacking the capital to create scale, stores like Lindberg's Nutrition, Frazier Farms, and Sunburst never attracted more than a localized following. The Irvine Ranch Farmers Market, founded as a roadside stand in Orange County by Jon Hubbard in 1968, was more of a gourmet store than a natural foods operation. It grew to 11 locations at its peak, but of these, only the one at the upscale Beverly Center in Los Angeles made any money. With some bad leases and overly aggressive expansion, the company racked up $17.5 million in debt, and filed for bankruptcy protection in July 1988.[27]

One other Southern California retail chain that started to shift into natural foods at this time was a curious hybrid that had been built by a former Rexall Drug manager named Joe Coulombe. In 1958 Rexall had appointed the 26-year-old Coulombe to run a convenience store chain called Pronto Markets. It did well, but by 1966, facing competitive pressure from 7-Eleven, Rexall opted to exit the convenience store business. Coulombe purchased the stores, and in 1967 began converting them to South Seas–themed groceries selling affordable but upscale goods, something he called Trader Joe's. The idea, he later told *Forbes* magazine, was "to appeal to the well-educated and people who were traveling more."[28]

According to Bob Johnson, who worked with Coulombe as a store manager and buyer for 20 years, "He didn't want to sell things for which he just turned the machine on and never turned it off. There was no excitement in that for him." So as early as 1971, with the introduction of a few types of organic granola under the Trader Joe's private label, Joe Coulombe began to shift into natural foods. True to their convenience store roots, Trader Joe's stores continued to sell mass market items like Coca-Cola and Budweiser, and plenty of standard fare from the wholesaler Certified Grocers; however, by 1977 the competition had grown so intense that one grocer or another was always selling six-packs of Coca-Cola for 99 cents on the weekend, and Trader Joe's could not keep up. Johnson remembered that when they got rid of Frito-Lay products, the

Frito-Lay truck driver told him, "You can drop me but I guarantee you I'll be back here within three months and we'll be filling the shelves again."

It never did happen. Trader Joe's kept adding more natural and organic items, mostly under its private label, as the company grew to more than 20 neighborhood-based specialty stores. In 1979 Coulombe sold Trader Joe's to the German billionaires Karl and Theo Albrecht, and with the infusion of their capital the enigmatic and hard-to-define company began to expand beyond California, on its way to becoming the largest specialty food chain in the country, and an important player in the natural foods industry.

Back in Boulder, there were other influential people in town, consiglieri among the Boulder Mafia. Mo Siegel, of course, was in many ways the godfather of the natural foods industry in town, although with five kids and the largest business in the industry, he didn't have much time for socializing. Then there was John Elstrott, a founder of Green Mountain Herbs, who also served as the CFO at Celestial before Feinblum. Even though he left Boulder to teach at Tulane, he never left the industry, and in fact remained so influential that he would become the chairman of the board at Whole Foods. Another influential pioneer was Sheldon Romer, who founded a company in Boulder in 1976 that he named after Swami Rudrananda, leader of an Eastern ashram: Rudi's Organic Bakery. Several years later, in 1984, an enterprising 26-year-old one-time Air Force cadet named Mike Gilliland came to town, opened three convenience stores, and then in 1987 jumped into the natural foods business by purchasing a store called Crystal Market—the successor to Pearl Street Market, at 1825 Pearl—and later changing its name to Wild Oats. Other Wild Oats stores followed in Boulder, and so did more than 100 others elsewhere in the country.

But of all the tributaries that fed Boulder Creek, none added quite as much volume and froth as a media company that in 1988 relocated to an office on Pearl Street from a little town in Pennsylvania, not far from the Rodales' farm, called New Hope.

New Hope was the brainchild of Doug Greene, a visionary trade media specialist from Arkansas whose southern gentility was balanced by a peripatetic mind. Greene had grown up in Little Rock, competed in track and field, drove a Wonder Bread truck for a while, and earned a degree in advertising. He was from the sixties, but not of the sixties, for while his intellectual fidgetiness played like fingers on guitar frets, he didn't so much question authority as question how things worked—and how they could work better. He had a unique ability to connect the dots of the business world and project their forward arc, in order to be there out ahead of everyone else once the times caught up with him. His mind was always in overdrive, thoughts forming well ahead of his sentences, words firing off like a Gatling gun.

Greene worked in New York for a while, and in Malibu, selling ads for sporting goods and other retail trade publications and attending industry trade shows. His passion wasn't for the content of those publications, but for the systems behind the industries. What worked? Why did Herman's World of Sporting Goods succeed in building a chain of 250 stores while so many others stayed independent? Could market forces lure Herman's west of the Mississippi and Oshman's east of it? And what were the implications if a non-sporting goods store like Kmart started selling fishing rods? Doug Greene wanted to know.

He was turned on to natural foods by two friends who were holistic doctors, one of whom he met on a chance encounter at a restaurant in Mexico in 1974. He immersed himself in the topic, and soon swore off coffee and white sugar and meat. And what he began to realize was that while there were plenty of companies starting to produce natural and organic foods, and more retailers starting to carry them every week, there really was no natural foods *industry*. In order to take off and truly challenge the entrenched interests of Big Food, the natural foods companies needed a framework for sharing information and learning about how real businesses were run. They needed communications vehicles. They needed heroes and role models. They needed a trade magazine. And they needed a trade show of their own, separate from the tiny little shows then in existence (such as the National Natural Foods Association Show in Las Vegas), which were still dominated by the vitamin industry.

Having seen the way such elements could form the connective tissue in other industries, Greene knew he was onto something. So, his feet planted firmly on the ground and his gaze far off into the future, Doug Greene launched *Natural Foods Merchandiser* magazine in 1978, and the first Natural Products Expo in 1981.

Greene was way ahead of his time. Peter Roy, who was running a small store in New Orleans called Whole Food Company and would later become president of the much larger Whole Foods Market, remembers the first issue of *Natural Foods Merchandiser* just showing up in his mail. "What the heck is *this?*" he thought. But he read the cover story, about Sandy Gooch of Mrs. Gooch's Natural Foods Market in Los Angeles, and said, "I *have to* go see this store." As soon as he could find the time, he flew to San Francisco to visit friends, and then decided to splurge and have his wife, Gillian, and 12-week-old daughter, Emma, join him, so they could drive down Highway 1 to Mrs. Gooch's in LA. They rented a Pinto, and along the way decided to stop off at the headquarters of *Natural Foods Merchandiser* to learn more about this exciting enterprise and meet the publisher. He followed the directions, exited off the Ventura Freeway toward the town of Agoura Hills, and realized he must be in the wrong place as he pulled up to a residential home. But there was Doug Greene: He was running "NFM" out of his garage. Thus began a lifelong friendship between the two.

Roy visited Mrs. Gooch's the next day and found it eye-popping. "It was the first natural foods store that I had ever been in that was selling protein. They had their big fresh meat department. A seafood department. And that was just revolutionary. I had never seen anybody merchandising produce in the way they were merchandising produce, really stacking it high. It was electric. I just was transformed." He didn't get to meet Sandy Gooch on that trip, but on the recommendation of Greene, he did visit Sunburst, and met with Bill Frazier of Frazier Farms in San Diego, too. Doug Greene was connecting the dots.

"I used to envision myself as having a stepladder," recalled Greene, his still-youthful eyes darting about the room in a never-ending search for more data points. "And I went and found the most interesting things happening in the country. I got on the ladder and held up a mirror and I shined it down on what they were doing, so everybody could look in that mirror once a month and say, 'Wow! Look what *they* are doing! That's really cool.'"

The Natural Products Expo became wildly successful, even more so than *Natural Foods Merchandiser* and the other publications Greene started cranking out. Greene's company—by now relocated close to his Pennsylvania in-laws and named for its town, New Hope—put on a polished and professional show at the Anaheim Convention Center, and expanded to do a second annual show in Washington, DC (later, Baltimore), in 1985. Hundreds of natural foods companies bought booths to show off their latest products and packaging, hoping to expand their business from local to regional or even national, and from the slow build of case-by-case sales to the triumph of selling pallets or truck-loads. This, in turn, would attract thousands of retailers, and in an era before discount airlines and e-mail and Web sites, the Expos quickly became the primary means for meeting other people in the business and learning about best practices.

By 1986 the business had outgrown New Hope, Pennsylvania, and Doug Greene spent the next 18 months looking for a more suitable home. He considered St. Augustine, Florida, where the growing distributor Tree of Life was based. "We knew that being close to them would mean we would have a lot of good people coming to our office." He looked at Austin, Texas; Ann Arbor, Michigan; Santa Barbara, California; and Sebastopol, California. He fell in love with Bellevue, Washington, for a while. But there was really only one place for a company like New Hope Communications: the land of Subarus and gurus, ancestral home of Chief Niwot of the South Arapaho tribe, current home of Celestial Seasonings and Alfalfa's and WhiteWave, that place where US Route 36 descends from reality—Boulder, Colorado, USA.

CHAPTER 5

SPONTANEOUS COMBUSTION

Although soil fertility was his favorite topic, and his 1840 *Organic Chemistry in its Applications to Agriculture and Physiology* became the leading text on the subject, the German chemist Justus von Liebig had other fascinations.

One was the rather macabre phenomenon wherein an otherwise seemingly healthy human being reportedly bursts into flames—"spontaneous combustion." Even by the mid-19th century, there had been numerous sensational accounts of this occurrence, such as that of the Italian countess Cornelia Bandi, who in 1745 went to bed after dinner, saying she felt "dull and heavy." The next morning, her maid found nothing but the countess's legs protruding from a smoldering pile of ash. In 1853 the Victorian magazine *Notes and Queries* included a summary of 19 reported cases of spontaneous combustion, mostly linked to high alcohol consumption; and in his novel of that same year, *Bleak House,* Charles Dickens used spontaneous combustion to kill off Mr. Krook.[1]

Von Liebig was not convinced. He studied more than 40 cases, tried unsuccessfully to burn anatomical specimens that had been stored in alcohol, and wrote articles in the *Times* and the *London Medical Gazette.* "The opinion that a man can burn of himself is not founded on a knowledge of the circumstances of the death, but on the reverse of knowledge—on complete ignorance of all the causes or conditions which preceded the accident and caused it."[2] In order to understand the effect, he was saying, one must study all the antecedent factors.

It was a curious conclusion to be drawn by a man who a few years earlier had deduced that poor crop yields could be traced to a single antecedent: an imbalance of nitrogen, phosphorus, and potassium in the soil. But while reports of spontaneous combustion in humans have never been explained, in this respect, at least, von Liebig was right: For something to catch fire, the conditions have to be right.

———•———

Certainly the conditions were right for a figurative spontaneous combustion in the natural foods industry in the 1970s and 1980s.

There was great passion for the mission of returning American farms and food to a purer state. There were philosophical inspirations from *Organic Gardening* and Walnut Acres and Erewhon. There was the legacy of the counterculture, which had eroded trust in the Establishment, created an environmental consciousness, and spawned a boom in health foods stores and co-ops. There was a growing marketplace of activist consumers. There were entrepreneurial role models like Mo Siegel and Gary Kahn and Gary Hirshberg, who were beginning to prove that practicing good values did not preclude creating value. There was the framework of industry connectivity beginning to take shape under the guiding hand of Doug Greene, *Natural Foods Merchandiser,* and the Natural Product Expos.

And, of course, there was also a common enemy in Big Food. Synthetic pesticides and herbicides were now being deployed on a massive scale: 50,000 different pesticides alone had been approved for use by 1972. By 1986 it was estimated that farmers were using more than 1 billion pounds of pesticides annually, an increase of 500 percent since the 1950s. And as *Newsweek* magazine frighteningly pointed out, "[L]ess than 1 percent of the poisons reach their target pest; the rest wind up as contaminants in water, residues on produce and poisonous fallout on farm workers."[3] The most celebrated of these, DDT, was finally banned in 1972, although exceptions were made for some crops like sweet potatoes (furthermore, DDT remained a problem because it lingered in the soil, and continued to be used in many other countries around the world, some of whom exported produce to the United States); but there were plenty of new concoctions to take its place. To those in the natural foods movement, Monsanto—the Missouri company that in one way or another had already been responsible for popularization of the artificial sweeteners saccharin and aspartame, the Flavr Savr tomato, the herbicide-defoliant Agent Orange, many pesticides including DDT, and would later bring the world the synthetic bovine growth hormone Posilac as well as the brave new world of genetically modified seeds[4]—became "Mon-satan."

Additionally, antibiotics and hormones were now regularly being administered to livestock, creating a quiet swell of protest in America and a larger one around the world: In 1979 Europe banned imports of antibiotic- and hormone-treated meat from the United States.

Meanwhile, "plastic" food was everywhere, as processed goods now dominated supermarket shelves. Most of the products contained some combination of artificial colors, flavors, sweeteners, preservatives, sequestrants, surfactants, thickeners, stabilizers, bleaching agents, and buffers whose safety was regularly being questioned. In 1969 the *Whole Earth Catalog* sounded a sardonic but by then familiar note when it said that "BHT is a legal, inexpensive, non-addictive, non-psychoactive, non-nutritious, anti-oxidant chemical that may make you live twice as long as the other mice."[5] By 1972 there were 1,800 additives in use, with annual per capita consumption amounting to 5 pounds; the normally staid *Fortune* magazine ran a huge article entitled "The Hysteria about Food Additives" that chronicled concerns over possible links between additives and cancer or genetic mutations.[6]

Ironically, those very synthetic elements were also beginning to create the economic conditions necessary for more expensive natural foods to gain acceptance. The wholesale use of pesticides and herbicides had obviated the need for some farm labor, reducing production costs; and cheap chemical additives like saccharin had replaced more expensive raw ingredients like sugar cane. As a result, food costs declined sharply, and the amount of disposable personal income Americans spent on food dropped from more than 23.5 percent in 1947 to 13.4 percent in 1977 to 11.5 percent in 1987.[7] This opened the door for more expenditures on "luxury" items, which before long would include natural and organic foods.

In response to all this, more and more entrepreneurs started to create natural foods companies, modeled after the increasingly successful and visible efforts of Celestial Seasonings, Cascadian Farm, Stonyfield Farm, and other early pioneers. For example:

- In 1970 a former benefits counselor at Aetna Insurance named Tom Chappell, who had relocated to Kennebunk, Maine, from Philadelphia in an effort to simplify life for his family and find unprocessed foods and unadulterated products, launched a company called Tom's of Maine using a $5,000 loan from a friend. The first product was a phosphate-free laundry detergent called Clearlake, with a label drawn by his wife, Kate. Soon Tom's added vegetable glycerin soaps, shampoo, toothpaste, and deodorant, with sales approaching $2 million by 1983.

- At the age of 17, Barbara Jaffe tapped into her college fund to open up Barbara's Bakery in a storefront in Palo Alto, California; it went from a small retail bakery to a larger wholesale one within a year, eventually becoming a major natural foods brand of cookies and cereals.

- Coming off the modest success of his retail store, Morning Dew Organic Food Market in St. Louis, Robert Nissenbaum created a rice-based beverage and frozen dessert he called Rice Dream. Developed in relative obscurity in the Missouri countryside in 1982, Rice Dream might not have gone much further, but he took it to the Natural Products Expo in Anaheim, California, and it became a smash.

During this same time period, the tiny organic agriculture movement began to mobilize. *Life* magazine reported in 1970 that there were perhaps 5,000 farmers who were growing crops commercially "without modern aids."[8] And although Rodale's 1972 effort at measuring organic farms' humus content and rewarding them with a Seal of Approval resulted in only 56 certifications, more initiatives would follow, reflecting the growing interest in organics and the increase in conversion of conventional acreage. California Certified Organic Farmers (CCOF) came into existence in 1973 and certified 635 organic farms that year. Oregon Tilth arrived on the scene as another major certification organization in 1974. An alphabet soup of others followed, including OGBA (Organic Growers and Buyers Association) in 1977, FVO (Farm Verified Organic) in 1979, OCIA (Organic Crop Improvement Association) in 1984, and QAI (Quality Assurance International) in 1989.[9] By 1992 there were more than 3,500 certified organic operations spanning nearly 1 million acres, and the *real* growth was only just beginning: Over the next 5 years organic acreage would increase by 45 percent, and over the next 15 years by 359 percent.[10]

The problem was that there was still no consistent legal definition for what "organic" meant. Through the seventies and eighties, the states had been left to define it for themselves—deciding, for example, the precise amount of time needed between cessation of chemical use and organic certification. California's Organic Law, passed in 1989, was often thought of as the gold standard, but with each state defining things somewhat differently, and a passel of certification organizations weighing in, there was an understandable amount of confusion and cynicism among consumers. If something were labeled organic, what did that mean? What was the difference between California organic and Pennsylvania organic? Since there was no national standard, and no one to police it, might it just be a marketing ploy by growers and food producers wishing to capitalize on the higher retail prices that organic could command?

Urged on by trade groups,[11] and with their considerable help, Congress passed the Organic Foods Production Act of 1990, directing the US Department of Agriculture to develop a set of national standards. In turn the USDA set up a group called the National Organic Standards Board (NOSB) to work on this task. It took years.[12] Still, throughout the process there was a sense of inevitability and growing confidence in the organic industry that set the stage for a boom in supply. And the irony of the entire episode was not lost on many: Natural foods, whose growth had long been stymied by government policies that had always favored Big Food and agribusiness, had now become perhaps the only industry in history that actively sought out greater regulation from the federal government.

———•———

One major issue for the natural foods manufacturers was the fragmented nature of the retailers, estimated to number about 3,000 in the early seventies. If you were, say, Barbara Jaffe, creating baked goods out of a storefront in Palo Alto, California, you might reasonably be able to drive some products around to health foods stores in San Francisco and the East Bay. As you generated some cash to expand production, you might be able to supply local restaurants and food service operations as well, and perhaps reach stores in Sacramento or Fresno. But if your goal was to become a larger regional company, or a national one, how were you supposed to tell all those independent stores about your products . . . and how could you deliver?

Gary Hirshberg had this problem in the early days of Stonyfield Farm. "We used to go to the natural foods show, and [meet] these tiny, tiny stores all over the place without the volume. We couldn't make money shipping to all of these places. We started working with [all] these distributors, what eventually became UNFI, but it was tough slogging."

Things were very different in the conventional foods industry. General Mills, for example, was producing many items that were nominally in the same categories as Barbara's, such as Lucky Charms cereal and Bugles corn snacks. Because the company had teams of salespeople to call on the major supermarket chains like Kroger and Supervalu and could just ship directly from its manufacturing plant to the retailers' big warehouses, it was easy to achieve rapid growth for these products. Bugles, which were introduced in 1964, reached national distribution by 1967, and sales topped 2.4 million pounds per year by 1975.[13] But Barbara's had no big manufacturing plant, no team of salespeople to call on the health foods stores, and had to rely on the patchwork quilt of brokers and distributors to get both the word and the product out. Even in the early 1990s, when chefs Dana Sinkler and Alex Dzieduszycki launched Terra Chips, they had to deal with a hornet's nest of distribution issues. "We must have had a network of 110 distributors and 40 brokers," Sinkler recalled. "You can imagine what I did all day long. It was get on the phone and get bitched out about 'Why is this guy selling at this price?'"

Certainly there was some potential to sell those natural products through conventional supermarkets. The awareness and appeal of natural foods had grown steadily since World War II, to the point at which a 1980 Federal Trade Commission report noted that 63 percent of people polled agreed with the statement that "natural foods are more nutritious than other foods," and 39 percent said they regularly buy food because it is "natural."[14] The awareness had come not just through the ominous words of *Silent Spring* and the periodic crises (aminotriazole-laced cranberries, cyclamate in soda), but through the burgeoning self-help movement that played well in Middle America. The success of Rodale's *Prevention* magazine was strong evidence of this, but Adelle Davis and a cadre of other self-help pseudo-celebrities used the national media stage to reach the masses. Dr. Carlton Fredericks, a nutrition advocate, broadcast his *Design for Living* radio program 6 days a week on WOR in New York (and syndicated elsewhere) beginning in 1957 and continuing to 1987. Gaylord Hauser—a German-born doctor who had provided nutrition advice to Gloria Swanson even before Rodale and Aveline Kushi did so, and who had written the popular book *Look Younger; Live Longer*—created a popular column for the Hearst newspaper chain.[15]

But the movement began to grow populist roots. By 1970 *Life* magazine was reporting about "The Move to Eat Natural," noting that "new converts to organic food are sprouting up all over" as "the movement sheds the fanatic fad image that health foods used to have." (However, the article's author, Elizabeth Lansing, cautioned, "On a mass scale, organic foods and a supermarket economy are incompatible."[16]) At the start of 1971, *Vogue* magazine pegged the size of the natural foods industry at about $1 billion, as the "geriatric set" that used to constitute most of the health foods customers now expanded to include "the alienated young who are as skeptical of foods sold in supermarkets as they are of dicta from Washington."[17] *Harper's Bazaar* magazine put the number at $2 billion in late 1972, while sounding some cynical notes and questioning whether health foods might not turn out "to constitute one of the costlier rip-offs of these times."[18] The *Wall Street Journal* even ran a front page story about yogurt, consumption of which they reported had increased to 100,000 tons per year in 1971, up a third since 1969.[19]

Another reason conventional stores appeared to be a possible outlet for the natural foods companies was that the word "natural" was starting to appear with some frequency on mass market products. Many of the Big Food manufacturers had decided to capitalize on America's growing obsession with health by adding that word, in all its gushy vagueness, to many of their conventional products—occasionally parsing their descriptors carefully to provide plausible deniability, should it come to that. Thus, Pillsbury came out with "natural chocolate flavored chocolate chip cookies," which actually contained BHT and artificial vanilla flavoring. Anheuser-Busch had a "natural light beer" that was made with chemical additives. And American Bakeries' "Langendorf natural lemon flavored crème pie" contained sodium propionate, food colors, sodium benzoate, and vegetable gum; the name was justified by company chairman L.A. Cushman, Jr., because "natural" was only modifying "lemon flavored." He told *Consumer Reports* magazine, "The lemon flavor comes from natural lemon flavor as opposed to artificial lemon flavor, assuming there is such a thing as artificial lemon flavor." By 1980 it was estimated that 7 percent of all processed food products were being promoted as "natural."[20] By 1992 conventional store sales of natural products, however they were defined, topped $1 billion.[21]

But as it turned out, there was still a gulf between the natural and conventional foods world big enough for Evel Knievel to consider jumping. Natural foods retailers were so caught up in their mission of differentiation and saving the world that they generally didn't want to carry any products that had anything to do with the conventional stores, even if it would have brought in extra sales. "Clean" mainstream products like Welch's grape juice and Quaker 100% Natural cereal, for example, seldom ever made it onto the shelves of natural foods stores. In turn, this made it hard for natural foods manufacturers to sell to conventional stores.

Stonyfield Farm, for one, experienced great difficulties in crossing sales channels. The company badly needed the volume of its deliveries to the conventional Stop & Shop stores in order to justify sending a truck into Boston for the natural foods stores. "There's only two ways I could bring my price down without screwing the farmer," recalled Gary Hirshberg. "One is to take a loss and sacrifice the business. And the other is to grow [through conventional supermarkets] and get to scale. And a lot of people don't like that." One who didn't was the biggest natural foods chain in New England, Bread & Circus; they didn't want to do anything "conventionally." So until his ultimate Frisbee buddies intervened, Hirshberg was unable to get his yogurt into the Bread & Circus stores. Tom's of Maine had a similar problem when it started selling to CVS.

Most dramatically, there was the story of Thompson Vitamins, which at one time was the clear leader in its category when the vitamins were sold exclusively through health foods and natural foods stores. But then the company made the fateful decision to begin selling to Safeway. Bill Thompson was a superb networker whose professional gatherings, according to Terry Dalton of Unicorn Village, "were probably the first significant social melding of the counterculture and a trade association; and his numerous industry parties would have made the Prince of Monaco blush." Doug Greene described Thompson as "a philosopher-king and the most respected guy in the business at the time." Thompson had foreseen that natural foods were going to move into conventional channels, and wanted his vitamin company to be a leader in that trend. So he cut a deal with his friend Greg Plunkett at Safeway. But it enraged Thompson's core customers, who realized they could get beaten on price if Safeway wanted to do battle. "Every health food store in America dropped them over the next few years," remembered Peter Roy. "It was unbelievable. His business had just been going like a rocket ship, and all of a sudden it just fell off the planet. Bill was right, but it cost him the company."

Fortunately for the natural foods manufacturers, things were about to change—seemingly all at once. Within a 7-year period beginning in 1974, the retail side of the business exploded with several similar-looking, large-scale, often multi-unit operations popping up all around the country. Stores like Mrs. Gooch's, Bread & Circus, Nature's Fresh Northwest, Whole Foods Market, Alfalfa's, and Wellspring Grocery were much larger than the first generation of natural foods stores. Some of them were able to do more sales volume in a week or two than the likes of New Day Natural Foods and Far-Fetched Foods had done in an entire year. Most had sophisticated new merchandising schemes, and clever marketing to back them up. This wasn't just an evolution of the old health foods stores, which by and large continued to exist; it was spontaneous combustion, a fire raging where moments before there had been none. And in the crackling, super-charged air left behind when the smoke of creation had cleared stood something completely new: the natural foods supermarket industry. It turned out that Elizabeth Lansing of *Life* was wrong: Organic foods and the supermarket economy were compatible after all.

On the vanguard of this new industry was a store in uptown New Orleans at the corner of Cohn and Adams Streets, not far from Tulane University. Small in size but ultimately towering in influence, Whole Food Company opened under the new moon, October 15, 1974, in a building that had housed Fontana's Fine Foods, an Italian grocery, since the 1940s, and had been the home to one grocery or another since 1903. It had white exterior columns, a rounded corner, and a four-blade fan on the ceiling—vintage New Orleans. After 70-year-old Leon Fontana became ill in 1974, his wife, Virginia, could not run the store on her own. So when Jon Maxwell and Kathleen O'Connor rode their bikes up to the store one day to inquire whether they might be able to rent the place, Virginia took a shine to them and offered them a 2-year lease. Along with their friends Patricia Roy and Michael Bushnell, they converted the 1,400-square-foot space into a little natural foods store, with nuts, grains, whole wheat bread, yogurt, raw milk, teas, about 150 different herbs, and some housewares like bamboo rice steamers. They opened with $1,800 worth of inventory, and quickly found an eager customer base.

Patricia was pregnant, however, due in January, and so the store needed help. As luck would have it, her 18-year-old brother, Peter Roy, had just become available. A few weeks earlier, Roy had gone off to Prescott College in Arizona to study marine biology, his only previous work experience having been as a scuba instructor. But the school went bankrupt and closed down on November 20 ("three of the best months of my life," he still jokes), so he returned home to New Orleans, the family's home for five generations. Peter had become a vegetarian a year earlier, and had some interest in natural foods. He started working at Whole Food Company for $1.75 an hour—alongside Virginia Fontana, who kept the books and counted the money. A few months later, Patricia agreed to sell her 15 percent stake in the business to her brother for $800. To come up with the money, he took out a loan from the Whitney Bank, the first one of his life. "That made a huge difference to me, having a piece of the business," he said, echoing the sentiments of entrepreneurs through the generations.

The store did well, but faced competition from a co-op, where most of the hippies bought their produce. Roy and his friends had hesitated to sell their own produce, fearing that they wouldn't do enough volume to turn it. But this co-op model made sense, so they adapted it: For $10 a year, you could become a "member" of Whole Food Company, which allowed you to place orders for produce, to be picked up on Saturdays. They signed up 300 or 400 people in the first year, generating $30,000 to $40,000 in free money. With that, they bought produce coolers, expanded the store into the next room, and the business really started to pick up steam.

By chance, Roy attended the Fancy Food Show, which was taking place in New Orleans, and was amazed to discover that there was an entire network of wholesalers from whom he could buy products. Up to that point, 80 percent of everything Whole Food Company got came from the Florida distributor Tree of Life, but at the trade show Roy met some of the cashew, raisin, and almond companies that were the original producers of the goods. He cut deals with them to eliminate the middleman and reduce his costs. He met with Haddon House, and started buying specialty groceries through them. He also found out about a company called Otto Roth that could help him import cheeses from Europe—thus creating a use for Leon Fontana's old meat coolers, which had been sitting around unused in the vegetarian store. Within a year, cheese became 20 percent of Roy's business, and it created a major change in his customer base. "The hippies were still coming in, but all of a sudden we had the Mercedes-Benz crowd coming up, because people were saying, 'Have you heard about this little grocery store in Uptown New Orleans? You can go get this fantastic brie at $5 a pound, and everybody else is selling it for $8.'" Whole Food Company was becoming a full-service store. In 1978 it expanded again, and was doing $40,000 a week in just 1,800 square feet. At this point, Jon and Kathleen wanted to leave the business, so Peter struck a deal with them: He would buy enough of their stock to give him 51 percent of the business, and would pay them each $2,000 a month for the next 3 years. "It was a leveraged buyout before I even knew what that was," said Roy.

Then, just a few weeks later, that first issue of *Natural Foods Merchandiser,* the one with Mrs. Gooch's on the cover, arrived in his mailbox. Soon Peter Roy would go off on his trip to California, meet Doug Greene, visit Mrs. Gooch's ($135,000 a week in sales!) and Frazier Farms ($200,000 a week!), and return with a single-minded purpose: "I have *got to* find a location to open one of these big stores." He searched around, found a site, and pieced together a half-million dollars in loans through the Small Business Administration, Bank of New Orleans, and the city. The second Whole Food Company store opened on Esplanade Avenue in April 1981, and like Mrs. Gooch's it featured meat and seafood, and huge displays of produce.

Roy went out to California to attend Doug Greene's first Natural Products Expo, and stopped by a cocktail party being thrown by his beef supplier, Warren Ehring of Consumer's Cattle. Ehring's gig was simple: He would buy Holstein bull calves—male dairy calves that no one wanted—for $5 a head, put them in a feedlot, and sell them as natural beef. The product wasn't very good, but he was one of the only ranchers in the country selling natural beef at all. At the gathering there was one of those moments that seemed silly at the time, but proved to be seminal: Ehring, dressed in a leather suit, introduced Peter Roy to a couple of guys from Texas named John Mackey and Craig Weller, who were running a company called Whole Foods Market in Austin. "Peter," Warren said enthusiastically, "let me introduce you to the guys that ripped off your name."

Within a year or two, Mackey began partnering with Roy by sending a weekly truck of goods from his distribution company, Texas Health Distributors, out to Whole Food Company in New Orleans (this helped to establish legitimacy for the distribution business, which until then had just been a straw man front for Whole Foods Market, operating out of Mackey's house). Seven years later, they would make things Whole by merging their companies; 12 years later, Roy would become president of Whole Foods Market, frick to CEO John

Mackey's frack, a warm, practical, people-centric presence to counterbalance Mackey's rough-edged competitiveness, piercing intellect, and philosophical leadership. It would become one of the most fascinating and successful pairings in all of American business.

———•———

Sandy Gooch was not there for Peter Roy's visit in 1978. She was busy building a little empire.

Gooch had been born Sandra Buckner in Altadena, California, in 1940, daughter of a research biologist and a homemaker. It was a nurturing home environment, one that encouraged trust, excellence, and independence (her father painted the oven controls in bright orange so that her mother, who was legally blind, would still be able to find the 360-degree mark). She graduated from the University of Texas, and immediately began what should have been a rather predictable pre-*Ms.* magazine path through adulthood: marriage, a career in teaching, and motherhood. She got married in 1961. She proved to be a superb educator: creative, inspiring, and warm, earning master teacher status while moving around to numerous schools in the Los Angeles area. Her daughter, Kristin, was born in 1966. Everything was proceeding right on schedule.

But Gooch's life took a major detour in 1974, when she became gravely ill following a fairly routine eye infection. She was prescribed tetracycline, and immediately after taking the antibiotic suffered from dizziness and chest pains that radiated down her arm. Gooch was driven to the Scripps Research Institute in La Jolla, California, but doctors there did not know what was wrong. At one point during her 8-day stay at Scripps, she was given a can of Fresca—and after one sip, the chest pain and other symptoms returned. Her father, Buck, who knew a great deal about chemistry, talked to doctors all around the country, but on his own eventually determined that the cause had been a severe allergic response to the brominated vegetable oil in the Fresca, interacting with the tetracycline she had taken to treat the infection. "By researching and reading," she said, "my father had come over to another aspect of 'physician heal thyself.'" Over a 9-month period, Gooch began an intense effort to switch her diet to all-natural foods and begin the recovery process. She drove up and down the Southern California coast, seeking out obscure health foods stores in search of whole grains, tofu, and unpasteurized milk. Her energy and vitality returned, and she felt better than she had in 10 years. She knew that she had found a new life mission: "Providing food opportunities to other people who were as thwarted as I had been, and who had as much of a desire as I did for finding good food."

Gooch envisioned opening a four-unit chain of natural foods stores, and found an old A&P location in West Los Angeles for the first one. At 4,700 square feet, it would be one of the largest natural foods stores in the country. It would be a full-service store, offering packaged goods, produce, meat, seafood, and even books. She planned to call it the Greater Los Angeles Natural Food Emporium, but her lifelong friend Doug Stone, who worked in advertising, disabused her of this idea.

"Sandy," he said, "you are going to have more stores than in just Los Angeles. And that name is much too long. I think you should call it 'Mrs. Gooch's.'"

"What?" she asked. "Nobody will come into a store with a name like that!"

But come they did, even while the employees were still stocking the shelves prior to opening. The hippies and Rastafarians from Topanga Canyon came in their trucks, the Hollywood types from Beverly Hills came in their Benzes, and so did many others. Using skills honed in her elementary school classrooms, Sandy Gooch designed a unique "store experience" that featured elaborate displays, whimsical themed characters, lots of signage and product information, well-trained staff members, and fantastic food. She came to call the merchandising concept "eatertainment and edutainment," and it was enhanced by the appearance of some of the food vendors themselves, like Jay the Juice Man squeezing oranges in store, Gypsy Boots talking about climbing trees to pick Medjool dates, or the dignified Colorado rancher, Mel Coleman, Sr., in his Stetson and boots, discussing his 2,000 head of cattle. The wood slat floors and dingy aisles of the health foods store era seemed Paleolithic by comparison.

The first Mrs. Gooch's Natural Foods Market opened in January 1977 and immediately developed an enthusiastic following. In fact, although Gooch contracted for four ads in the *Los Angeles Times* to promote the event, she called to cancel after the first one ran because the crowds were so big. She gave speeches all over the region, telling the story of how natural foods rescued her from the brink of death. And soon the Hollywood glitterati took notice, with people like Greta Garbo, Telly Savalas, and Danny Kaye not only shopping at the store, but coming to dinner at Sandy's house and turning it into a sort of salutary salon. A second store in Hermosa Beach opened later that year, racking up $135,000 in sales each week in just 1,700 square feet—without any high-ticket items like alcohol. To finance the second store, Sandy sold limited partnerships, because no bank in those days was willing to take a chance on a natural foods entrepreneur, especially one without a Y chromosome. Five more stores would follow in fairly short order, as Mrs. Gooch's eventually grew into a $95 million (annualized) company.

What set Mrs. Gooch's apart was not just its variety and decor, but its obsessive product standards. Gooch carefully screened the products that she allowed into her stores, scouring the labels and chasing down the manufacturers when necessary to ensure that everything met her high standards. There could be no artificial ingredients, no refined white sugar, no refined white flour, no chocolate, no caffeine, no hydrogenated oils, no irradiated products. There certainly would be none of what she called "the unmentionables," alcohol and tobacco. This was a very high bar to set—much more restrictive than the typical health foods store—but because Mrs. Gooch's grew quickly and became the dominant retailer in the natural foods industry, she was able to get what she demanded.

As the largest retailer in a still-small industry, Mrs. Gooch's exerted considerable power over the manufacturers who so badly wanted to get onto her shelves, and, in a style that foreshadowed the way Walmart and Whole Foods Market would later act, often demanded that manufacturers reformulate their products to meet her ingredient standards. Gooch would also have a similar influence over the fight for national product standards, and was highly influential in the shaping of 1994's Dietary Supplement Health and Education Act (DSHEA).

Before long other retailers were copying Mrs. Gooch's product standards, and a common question asked of manufacturers in the industry was: "Is it Goochable?" Harry Lederman, who worked at the distributor Nature's Best when Mrs. Gooch's first opened and later married Sandy, said that the product standards became "the Good Housekeeping Seal" for the industry. "If you could be accepted by Mrs. Gooch's, everybody would accept you. Through the years, that helped the manufacturers and suppliers toe the line and maintain a standard."

Over time the standards were updated because, as Gooch once told a reporter, "When you're writing the book for the industry, you go through a lot of drafts."[22] For example, Mrs. Gooch's was probably first in the country to prohibit products made with genetically modified organisms, or GMOs, a technology that was in its infancy.

Her key standard, though, was always this: Will the customers like it? Unlike the gnarly produce and brown-blah products of the old health foods stores, Mrs. Gooch's foods looked *appetizing*. They were carefully screened for flavor and aesthetics. The delis developed intriguing items like fluffy smoked trout pâté and chicken drumettes with slow-cooked onion-tomato marmalade. The bakery made blueberry-cream cheese tarts with no refined sugar. For the first time, natural foods took a turn toward the upscale end of the spectrum. "Mrs. Gooch's really raised the bar beyond what anybody had really seen before," said Peter Roy. "It is hard to overstate how inspirational her original work was."

———————

Across the country in Massachusetts, just a couple of miles from the Erewhon store at 342 Newbury Street, another natural foods chain had appeared on the scene. The original Bread & Circus store in Brookline had been founded by a husband-and-wife team who sold both natural foods and wooden toys; hence the cute name. The store was purchased in 1975 by a 35-year-old retailer named Tony Harnett, who had the foresight to recognize that there was a huge potential market for natural foods among New Englanders, and that the conventional supermarkets were not well equipped to meet it.

Harnett, like Sandy Gooch, was no ex-hippie, but an erstwhile upright soldier of the Establishment. He had grown up in Ireland, working behind the counter of a grocery store. He left home at age 18, went to work in England, and eventually came to the United States. According to those who got to know him well—and there weren't many, since he kept most people at arm's length—those humble roots motivated him throughout his career. "It was like that was nipping at his heels all the time," observed Peter Roy, who as president of Whole Foods Market would later be involved in that company's purchase of Bread & Circus. "He was going to be very successful and very professional, and he felt that was part of the deal." That was perhaps one reason why Harnett was always crisply attired and encouraged neat uniforms in his stores. There was nobility in the simple shopkeeper's life.

The Irish in Harnett came out in many ways. He enjoyed his beer, and

could be fun-loving; at times he was stern and strict. He was remarkably sincere, often telling disbelieving newspaper reporters that he had never eaten a
Big Mac in his life and had no desire whatsoever to do so. Most of all he was
hard-working, intuitive, and hyper-intelligent. Vincent Fantegrossi, whom
Harnett brought in as CFO, recalled that "he could do math in his head like
nobody I have ever seen in my life." Apparently, it all went back to that store in
Ireland, where the clerks would pull the groceries down from the shelves for the
customer and then write the prices on a paper bag and tally it all up. "You've got
a customer waiting," Fantegrossi recalled Harnett telling him. "You've got to do
the math fast and you better be right. Because if you are wrong, Mrs. Flaherty
will be back to see you, and she will have the paper bag with your handwriting
on it and your math mistake."

Building on the customer base that Erewhon had established, and because
of his own fascination with the macrobiotic diet, Tony Harnett (he became
"Anthony" at the advice of a seer in Austin, Texas, arranged by John Mackey)
developed Bread & Circus into a fast-growing company, the eastern equivalent
of Mrs. Gooch's. He opened a second store in Cambridge in 1979, and a third
in Wellesley the year after. Then came Hadley in 1983, Newton in 1988 (along
with a new corporate office and central commissary), Providence, Rhode
Island, in 1990, and a relocation of the original store to Brighton in 1991.

The marketing challenge for stores like Bread & Circus was that they needed
to position themselves as being like supermarkets (in order to differentiate from
the minuscule health foods stores, and thus appeal to a mainstream audience),
yet also as being different from supermarkets (in order to retain the core health
foods consumer and provide the mainstream consumers a reason to shop there,
given that their prices were higher). It was dangerous middle ground, on which
nearly every natural foods retailer has at some point had to stand.

Both Mrs. Gooch's and Bread & Circus decided to forego traditional supermarket advertising in lieu of more thoughtful and provocative marketing.

The California chain often took the "food is the hero" route with newspaper ads. "Read This For Juicy Information!" screamed one headline in an ad
that promoted Ferraro's Carrot Juice. "All of Ferraro's citrus fruits are squeezed
whole and quite ingeniously," the ad read in part, "so that the juice never
touches the bitter outer peel. . . . In fact, it takes 2½ pounds of carrots to make
every delicious pint of their carrot juice, an item so popular with our customers
that we are the only store to warrant—and get—delivery 7 days a week."

Bread & Circus usually opted for more issues-oriented advertising, including one focused on its ban of irradiated foods. The headline read, "The Department of Energy has a solution to the problem of radioactive waste," and the ad featured an illustration of a mushroom cloud rising from a plate of food. "If you've always wanted your food treated with radioactive Cesium 137, your day has come," the copy began. "The federal government has approved food irradiation, a way of using radiation to rid food of microorganisms." For sheer gall and impact, it was right up there with Lyndon Johnson's 1964 "Daisy" ad, which also used a mushroom cloud to scare people into imagining a world with a President Goldwater.

The radioactive waste ad was the inspiration of Chris Kilham, whom Harnett hired to run his marketing and advertising. Kilham was originally brought into the company as a produce assistant by A.C. Gallo, the former Erewhon employee who had begun to build up an impeccable reputation for his sourcing and merchandising of produce. "You're not macrobiotic, are you?" Kilham remembered Gallo asking him. "I don't want someone who hates fruit." Later Kilham lobbied Harnett for a job in marketing, because he knew that he would bring the ideal mix of media savvy, creativity, and deep-seated philosophical belief in the products. His father had sold radio advertising in Boston, and his mother was a well-known reporter for WBZ TV and radio in Boston. She pulled her son into the business at an early age, and he appeared in commercials for Welch's and pancakes on the Big Bob Emory Show by the time he was 7. In 1970 Chris went off to the University of Massachusetts at Amherst, and at the age of 18 became a yogi, meditator, and vegetarian. He started working at the Yellow Sun food co-op in Amherst, unloading trucks of grain, building shelves, and learning the food business from the bottom up. He lectured for Bill Thompson of Thompson Vitamins. Over the next several years Kilham lived in an ashram and taught yoga throughout the Pioneer Valley to everyone from the pinkie-in-the-air tea drinkers at Smith College, to the inmates at the Hampshire County Jail, to— not surprisingly—the students at that beacon of alternative education, Hampshire College, where people like Gary Hirshberg and Jeffrey Hollender were passing through.

Sinewy and 6 feet tall, with wavy black hair and dark, expressive eyes, Kilham cut a dashing figure. He was quick-witted and charismatic, with a little bit of bluster and no filter for political correctness when there were issues on the table he cared about and phrases on his tongue he knew could skewer. Even in his marketing materials.

Thus, as Chris Kilham set about to put Bread & Circus on the map, there would be no weekly circulars (free-standing inserts, or FSIs, in industry parlance), no price-and-item ads.

"I was always thinking, 'What's everybody else *not* doing? Stop & Shop, Star, and all of the markets, what are they doing all the time? Price price price price price price price.' So I was really clear at the beginning: I don't want to talk price. And I had a lot of fights with people in the company about that. 'But if we put up some specials . . .' And I said, 'Do you really think anybody is going to give a shit that a $6 peanut butter is all of a sudden $4.89? Get with it! Skippy is like a buck and a half. This sale is not going to matter. We will just look like fools. Let's tell them why they *don't* want to eat the *other* stuff, why the other peanut butter will kill them.'"

Kilham read thousands of pages of information from the Food Marketing Institute and the National Resources Defense Council, and started putting out position papers so that Bread & Circus would be viewed as a national leader on food issues. When crises erupted—such as the discovery by the Food and Drug Administration of cyanide traces on Chilean grapes in Philadelphia in March 1989—Bread & Circus was ready.

This deep knowledge of issues helped Bread & Circus to define and refine its product standards, and attract a loyal following. The company adopted the tagline, "The food, the whole food, and nothing but the food," with an implicit you-don't-have-to-read-the-labels-because-we-already-have promise of integrity. In truth, the federal government had not yet defined organic, and "natural" remained even more vague, so the retailers were free to define things for themselves. On most issues, Bread & Circus maintained standards that were about as strict as Mrs. Gooch's, although it sometimes took them a while to get there: For example, Kilham had to encourage Harnett to ban all products with hydrogenated oils from Bread & Circus, even though this would mean losing one of the best sellers, a carob-based candy called Carafection. "One of the great things about Anthony," said Kilham, "he was happy to leap headfirst into the chipper shredder if it meant he was going to have better standards. He did not care. Or rather, he cared in all the right ways; he wasn't afraid."

Occasionally those leaps were too precipitous. In 1988, after getting to know Mrs. Gooch's, Harnett became convinced that Bread & Circus should no longer carry coffee, beer, and wine. He called all his directors together to tell them about his decision, and they were wary. "Anthony," intoned Kilham, "I know you don't want to hear this and I know this is going to piss you off, but I am going to tell you now. After you get a shit-rain of complaints, and after you've been told by the howling masses that this is the stupidest thing you can do, you are going to reverse it." Harnett was incensed. But sure enough, bags full of hate mail started to arrive from customers, and he changed course.

For all of its popularity and crossover appeal to the well-educated and environmentally conscious people of New England, Bread & Circus was not terribly profitable. Cash flow was frequently an issue. Once, when the company was on the brink of running out of money, Harnett offered to mortgage his house. Another time he and Fantegrossi inquired with their distributor, Stow Mills, whether it would be possible to get a 3-week abeyance on paying their bills, which would have freed up about $600,000 in short-term cash had they needed it. There were even some negotiations with Leo Kahn about his investing in the company, before he went off on his own to start Fresh Fields, and also with Mitt Romney at Bain Capital.

One problem was the size of the overhead, especially the expensive commissary. Another was that common fallacy, the expansion trap: Once there were multiple units, and Harnett had to go from being a leader (in the stores) to a manager (in the office), the stores didn't perform as well. "It probably took him to get to four stores to make the same profitability he made when he was running one store himself," said Fantegrossi. Thus, the company became engrossed in a classic entrepreneurial problem: not enough scale to cover all of its expenses, but not enough capital to expand.

—•—

Elsewhere in the country, other natural foods supermarkets were taking off.

- In Austin, Texas, John Mackey was putting all the pieces together. He had learned the power of the mission-based approach to retailing in his Safer Way store, and now was intent on growth. The opening of the 10,500-square-foot Whole Foods Market in September 1980 was a triumph, even though there wasn't enough supply of natural foods at first to fill such a large space adequately, so they built massive case stacks of

Corona beer and filled a big rack in the center of the store with 5-gallon bottles of water. But the sheer size of the place was appealing to Austinites, who were accustomed to the limited selection of tiny health foods stores like the Good Food Store, Wheatsville Co-op, Juice Factory, and of course Clarksville Grocery and Safer Way. So within a few short weeks, Whole Foods Market was generating $200,000 a week in sales. Within a couple of years, it expanded to a second location at Route 183 and Burnet Road in Austin. "We never really thought outside of Texas, for years," recalled cofounder Craig Weller. "I think John was the optimist thinking maybe someday we would have six stores in Texas, if we were successful."

But then, feeling ambitious, all at once they opened a store in Houston in 1984, a third store in Austin, and a restaurant called Wildflowers.

"I think we expanded too quickly," said Weller. "We took on too much, and that became a real challenge for the company. We came close to going out of business at that point. And it wasn't because the store wasn't doing great in Houston. But the more money they made, the more money we lost, because we didn't have the right kind of systems in place for three stores. When you have one store you know everybody, you know how much money you take in, you know how much money goes out. It's pretty easy. But . . . with three stores and a restaurant to boot, and a distribution facility, it just took us a while to get those systems in place." The Wildflowers debacle alone reportedly cost the company $880,000.[23]

Whole Foods eventually got things straightened out, however, and in 1986 purchased the Bluebonnet Natural Foods Grocery in Dallas. This was the company's first acquisition, and it was a strategy Mackey and his partners would pursue often in the years to come. As Weller recalled, the Whole Foods partners "saw the benefit in merging with other companies because not only did you have the locations that were existing and doing well, but you also had great team members that could come in and be a benefit to the company, where we could learn from them and they could learn from us, and we could be much better much quicker, if we could somehow get everybody on the same page. Which was always sort of a challenge."

- In Portland, Oregon, after building the annual sales at the first Nature's Fresh Northwest store on SW Corbett Street to $800,000 by 1978, Stan Amy took his show on the road. His second store opened in 1980, and then came five more, including some larger-format ones, several of which were generating $200,000 or more a week.

- In North Miami Beach, Florida, Terry Dalton's Unicorn Village arrived in 1979 and made quite an impression. It grew at an annual clip of 28 percent through the next several years; by 1989 the restaurant and market were generating $8 million a year in sales, with an almost unprecedented gross profit margin nearing 58 percent (48 percent on the supermarket side alone), precipitating a move to the splashy Waterways complex in Aventura the following January. "The big guys had years and years of experience doing this, and had mastered the efficiencies and logistics and labor and all of that," said Dalton. "And here you've got all these punk hippies opening supermarkets. At least I had a captive market, which gave me the opportunity to figure out what the hell we were doing."

- A half-hour up I-95 from Unicorn Village, in Fort Lauderdale, Florida, an old-style 1,300-square-foot health foods store called Bread of Life, which had been losing money, suddenly revived with the new interest in natural foods and a pair of dynamic new owners. Richie and Julie Gerber had arrived in town on July 4, 1980, in a Ford Fiesta towing a tiny U-Haul trailer full of big dreams. By that point the Gerbers, in their early thirties, had already amassed a lifetime full of unusual experiences—he, growing up in Brooklyn, fending off the tough kids of his East New York neighborhood with characteristic humor, going on to become a teacher, inventor, stand-up comic, and jazz saxophonist; she, fleeing the Castro regime in her native Havana in 1961, landing in Brooklyn, studying yoga. They had both been among the muddied masses yearning to breathe free at Woodstock. A year later they met, fell in love, married, and followed the usual path of Jewish-Cuban couples by moving to Maine to become organic farmers and dog breeders.

  Eclectic as they were, for the Gerbers it always came back to food. Richie was an avid vegetarian who could fondly recall watching his father, Sam, help the customers at Gerber's Miracle Grocery in Brooklyn with a pinch of blue humor and a sprinkling of Yiddish. "He always taught me that when people are giving you money, if you can get them to laugh, it is the most powerful thing you can do in customer service." When customers were getting ready to check out, Sam would open up a barrel bag, pull the fat carpenter's pencil from behind his ear, and write the prices of each item on the side of the bag upside-down, facing the customer. Then he would add them upside down so the customer could check his math. "That's what I call customer service!" said Richie. Julie gravitated to natural foods, studied macrobiotics with Michio Kushi, learned how to make her own tofu and sprouted loaves of bread, and became friends with Samuel Kaymen, founder of Stonyfield Farm. Sometimes she sent Richie off to work with a lunch bag of rice balls and yeast-baked tofu. He would gobble them down, telling his astounded colleagues in the teacher's lounge, "I bet you didn't even know that rice had balls."

The Gerbers fled Brooklyn for Maine in 1974 in search of organics, fearing that their diets heavy in conventional produce exposed them to too many chemicals. "We were getting more pesticides, insecticides, fungicides, and herbicides," said Richie, working up a slow-building joke as if he were on stage at Grossinger's, "so we were kind of committing suicide, and decided to not take sides." The Gerbers viewed themselves as modern-day pioneers, who lived close to the land, built a house out of a huge barn that they moved from 3 miles away, and even devised their own version of the Clivus Multrum, a waterless composting toilet. Richie, of course, then started a band called the Compost Blues Boys.

But after 6 years of toughing out the winters and Julys of Maine, Julie longed for the tropical weather of her youth and convinced Richie to move to South Florida. There they found lots of pill shops but no natural foods store that could meet their needs; so they decided to buy Bread of Life and convert it into a true natural foods store, with a juice bar and prepared foods and breads made by Julie. "All of a sudden," recalled Richie, "we became the hottest thing in town. It was like a vertical climb because there was such a need." Bursting at the seams, they relocated the original store to larger digs in 1984, and then partnered with a brilliant lawyer/MBA named Jim Oppenheimer who helped to make Bread of Life into a real business. Together they opened a larger store in Plantation, Florida, and signed a lease for a third store in Coral Springs. (It certainly didn't hurt that they started getting lots of plugs from Richie's close relative, Howard Stern, as his controversial radio program became syndicated in South Florida and much of the rest of the country. "Go to my Cousin Richie's store," Stern would intone his listeners. "When you are there, go say hello to Richie's wife, Julie, the Cuban Bombshell.") Bread of Life became a local phenomenon with national reach.

- In the Gore-Tex Vortex, Mark Retzloff and Hass Hassan's Pearl Street Market proved that its first-year sales of $1 million were only the start of something much bigger. According to Lyle Davis, one of the original investors and the general manager of the store, it was clear from the start that this could grow into a chain of new-age supermarkets. "Hass envisioned his stores being more than just little health food stores," he later told *Natural Foods Merchandiser*. "He early on saw markets . . . and then supermarkets. He saw one-stop stores with access to a broad consumer base."

  Retzloff and Hassan expanded into 12,000 square feet when they moved in 1983 and became Alfalfa's, and Boulder's alpha natural foods store surged in popularity. They built very strong programs in natural meats and food service, and added a juice bar. They won awards for their advertising—vendor-focused and issues-oriented, like Mrs. Gooch's and Bread & Circus—and became very active in Boulder. "Alfalfa's did a tremendous amount to stimulate that community," said Retzloff. "We were involved in all kinds of community activities. For years, Alfalfa's was known as the place to meet your soul mate." *Supermarket News* dubbed it "the supermarket of the future."

  Alfalfa's opened a much bigger store in Denver, and then nine more, so that by the mid-nineties Hassan's vision had been realized: It was an 11-store chain of natural foods supermarkets, doing $120 million a year in sales.

- In Raleigh, North Carolina, Wellspring Grocery opened in March 1981. The supermarket-sized vegetarian foods store was the creation of a 29-year-old named Lex Alexander, who was in some ways an unlikely food pioneer. An outstanding golfer who had played on the 1974 NCAA champion Wake Forest team alongside future PGA superstars Curtis Strange and Jay Haas, Lex and his wife, Ann, had been splitting their time between New York, where he served as a teaching pro at the Wingfoot Golf Club in Mamaroneck, and Palm Springs, California, where he served a similar role. But Alexander came from a family in which food was paramount. His grandfather lived two blocks away when Lex was growing up in Charlotte, North Carolina, and had a root cellar and a place where he kept honey and preserves and chow chow. Later, living in Mamaroneck in the mid-seventies, Lex came into contact with quite a few people who were followers of Michio Kushi and the macrobiotic diet. And at the Wingfoot Golf Club, he befriended the French chef, a man named Roget, and would stop by in the morning to find out what was fresh in the kitchen each day. As a result, he ended up ordering things like striped bass and Crenshaw melons instead of the cheeseburgers that the other pros would get. "After I had been there about three weeks," remembered Lex, "the manager of the club came down to see Mr. Harmon [Claude Harmon, the club pro]. He said, 'This new kid from the South . . . he is eating crab meat and Crenshaw melons, and fish. . . . This guy is killing me. My food costs!'"

Lex and Ann soon caught onto the natural foods trend and toured all of the major natural and specialty markets in the country in preparation for opening their own store back home in North Carolina. The thing that was different about Wellspring was that its proprietor always had a great sense of taste and style; the source of food was important to Lex Alexander, as were natural and organic ingredients, but nothing was more important than taste. Thus, he carried natural and organic packaged goods, carefully sourced produce, gourmet chocolates, homemade recipes like Ann Clark's Pumpkin Pumpkin Pie, as well as a category that Alexander called "supermarket legends" that included Pepperidge Farm cookies, Grey Poupon mustard, Heinz ketchup, and Duke's mayonnaise. And his customers responded. By 1986 Wellspring outgrew its original location and moved two blocks away to a former Food Lion space ("Food Li-ar," in Lex's unsarcastic North Carolina drawl), adding a meat and seafood department along the way. In 1989, flush with success, he self-financed an expansion to a new location in Durham, North Carolina, and began thinking about a Raleigh store, too.

And the natural boom was not just limited to the United States. Similar activities were also taking place around the world, including French stores like Biocoop and La Vie Claire, the Danish consumer co-operative FDP, and 2,000 different natural foods stores in Germany. In Britain, natural foods became prominent in both the conventional supermarkets (Safeway, Asda, Sainsbury) and in a small store on Paddington Street in London, founded in 1960 in association with organic pioneer Lady Eve Balfour's Soil Association, called . . . Wholefood Ltd.[24]

———

Although the combustion that created all of these natural foods supermarkets around the country was spontaneous, and nearly synchronous, by the mid-eighties there was also a catalyst helping to stoke the fire. For that was when Peter Roy, the young industry's premier facilitator and "people-person," came up with the idea of creating a collaborative organization of leaders, which he called the Natural Foods Network.

Of course, it is not uncommon for competitors in an industry to develop some sort of social bonds. Usually these efforts are informal, because in the capitalist system there is an innate belief (and plenty of jurisprudence to enforce the idea) that competition is good and collaboration is not. Thus, for example, Doug Greene, the founder of *Natural Foods Merchandiser* magazine and the industry's trade shows, recalled that in his days of running trade magazines in the sporting goods industry, several of the company leaders used to gather regularly on weekends in Malibu, to socialize and play and share information in the quiet of their beachfront verandas; a more formal organization might have smacked of a cartel or trust.

Yet in entrepreneurial companies and nascent industries, there simply isn't a great deal of intelligence available about how things "should" be done. Everyone is flailing about in their own darkness. This was especially true in the pre-Internet era, when information was much harder to come by. Whole Foods' Craig Weller recalled that at first, they cross-trained all store employees to handle all tasks, and did not organize them into teams (produce department, cashiers, etc.). Nowadays a few seconds spent on Google would pull up a dozen business models replete with organizational charts for anyone trying to puzzle through how to structure their business. But back then, a departmental structure simply never occurred to them. "It was sort of a revelation when we came up with that, although they had been doing that in supermarkets for years."

The only related trade association at the time, the National Nutritional Foods Association, was dominated by the people who ran the pill shops in the vitamin industry. Their interests were very different from the food retailers. "And then came all of us with the tie-dye and the long hair," said Roy. "We didn't care about the pills. We wanted to sell natural foods. And it was a very, very unlikely combo. . . . They were concerned about things we were not concerned about at all. And they were really threatened by us, because we were all of a sudden doing more business in a month than they were doing in a year. And they were really concerned that we were starting to sell their products, and sell them at far cheaper prices. So there was just tons of tension. . . . We needed to start our own thing."

An obvious solution was to create a separate group, bringing together the leaders of the pioneering natural foods retailers so that they could share information and help one another out.

There had been earlier attempts at collaboration within the industry. In 1971 a group called Organic Merchants formed with the goal of establishing uniform product standards among its members, requiring signatories to pledge not to carry "any food products containing white sugar, raw sugar, turbinado sugar, corn syrup, bleached white flour, hydrogenated fats, artificial flavor, artificial color, cottonseed products, monosodium glutamate . . . synthetic preservatives, emulsifiers, or any other synthetic food chemicals."[25] It never really caught on. In May 1975, several of the distributors, manufacturers, and retailers—including representatives of Erewhon, Arrowhead Mills, Tree of Life, and other leading organizations—convened at the Brookline, Massachusetts, home of Michio Kushi to begin organizing the Natural Foods Distributors Association, but the attempt foundered due to lack of funding and clearly defined goals.[26]

But Peter Roy was as optimistic as a sunny Saturday morning—rather amazing given that his free time to work on building the Natural Foods Network came courtesy of a bout with bladder cancer. Fundamental to his concept was the belief, in retrospect charming for its innocence, that because of the way the natural foods retailers had each spontaneously developed in different regions, there would never be any direct competition among them.

Certainly there were some good reasons to believe this. Perishable food was still a highly balkanized industry, with almost no national brands in dairy or produce. Most of the manufacturers of packaged natural foods were small scale, with only enough production and distribution capacity to meet the needs of a few states. Most importantly, the entrepreneurs who had founded the retail companies were the high-minded idealists, who had been through the cultural wars of the sixties and emerged with a hope and determination that the fundamental nature of business—including blood-thirsty competition—had to change.

Secure in their regional cocoons, the members of "The Network," as it came to be known, set to work with a remarkable spirit of collegiality. The first meeting was held at a hotel in New Orleans in October 1983, with Sandy Gooch, Stan Amy, Terry Dalton, John Mackey, Craig Weller, Tony Harnett, Mark Retzloff, Hass Hassan, Lex Alexander, and a few others joining Roy. Other meetings followed every 3 to 6 months for the next 2 years, with the members touring stores, going to dinner, and meeting to trade ideas about merchandising, products, suppliers, product standards, management practices, and more. Most remarkably, the members readily shared sales information with one another, and even profit-and-loss statements.

"I think that there was an element of trust, one with another," said Sandy Gooch. "We had developed a similar platform of food and goodness and honesty in the products that we were selling. That was embraced by all of us. So that when I would call up [Anthony Harnett] I would share with him certain things that I was dealing with, or percentages and so forth, gross profit margins, whatever it might be, he would share with me exactly what it was with Bread & Circus. He knew that I would not even tell my partners. I wouldn't tell anybody. And I knew that he wouldn't share with anyone else. And so that is how the trust developed."

"All of us sort of had an expertise," recalled Unicorn Village's Terry Dalton. "I was obviously food service. There were different segments, so we wanted to put it all together. We had different talents in our organizations, and we wanted to have our CFOs meet and our managers meet and all that stuff. But I never really sensed any competitiveness. . . . We exchanged a lot of written information. We didn't have computers back then, per se, to send stuff. And so a lot of financial statements and employee guides and ideas got exchanged. . . . If you called someone up and wanted their most intimate financial information, you got it faxed or overnighted right away. It was pretty nice."

To Doug Greene, an outsider looking at it from the inside, the reason for this spirit of cooperation was obvious: "They needed each other." He likened it to people who live on the edge of the water, who "are really much better neighbors, because they know stuff happens that affects everybody, and you all have to work together to protect each other and save each other. Along the water it is very collegial. You move three blocks in, they don't even talk at all."

Each member chipped in with $10,000, and in exchange they got access, information, some preliminary efforts to begin product testing, and even a primitive form of e-mail, accessed on IBM XT computers by dialing up the GEICO network on a modem. Most of the members were of similar ages, and were all having kids around that time, so the families started tagging along. They went to Hartford, Connecticut, to marvel at the cheese and wine at Rudra Altman's Cheese & Stuff store; they went to Houston to walk through the new Whole Foods Market and offer assessments to Mackey and his team; and they went to the newly opened Beaver Creek Resort in Colorado, not far from where Mo Siegel used to sell posters, mostly just for fun.

By 1986, 2 years in, The Network had run its course. Everyone was busy, and the Natural Foods Expos had grown to the point at which they were playing much the same role. "But the relationships were cemented," said Roy, "and those lasted forever."

Indeed, in the late eighties and nineties, a successor group of sorts developed, called The Wild Men. It began with a trip by seven friends, including Roy, Greene, Harnett, and Mackey, to hike to Wagon Wheel Falls at Yosemite National Park. The trip nearly ended in disaster, as Harnett broke his ankle and a bear ate their food. The next trip, rafting through the Grand Canyon, proved equally adventurous, as Craig Weller got tossed overboard in the rapids, only to be pulled to safety by Stan Amy and Bill Knudsen, and John Mackey broke *his* ankle; little wonder that Whole Foods has never made much of an effort to build its operations in Arizona.

———

Inevitably, the collegiality gave way to competition.

At the Warren Ehring cocktail party when they were first introduced, Roy recalled, Mackey told him, "Yeah, we knew you were over there, but you know, we are in Austin, you are in New Orleans, what difference does it make?" But their intermittent dealings in subsequent years, and contacts through The Network, made it clear that they could do more together than apart. In 1988 they merged their companies. This made Whole Foods Market a two-state company, although there was still the feeling that it was just a regional player. By the following year, however, when Whole Foods decided to move into Northern California, and Roy and Weller set up an office there, it became obvious that Whole Foods, at least, had graduated from collegiality. Sandy Gooch and Harry Lederman had always considered California to be "their" territory, even though all of their stores were in Southern California; but now the sudden presence of their friend just 350 miles to the north changed the rules of the game. In fact, it changed the game itself. Now it was a land grab. Growth—which once had seemed so improbable for this second-rate, mission-driven, overly idealistic industry—was becoming not just a possibility, but a mandate.

Next, Whole Foods tried to buy Alfalfa's—several times. But when a proposed deal was quashed at the last minute by Alfalfa's shareholders in July 1991, Mackey turned to Lex Alexander in North Carolina, and made a deal to buy his two Wellspring stores in November of that same year. It was a big relief for Alexander. "At that point I was dealing with bankers and lawyers and workers' compensation adjusters and real estate people. And by teaming up with Whole Foods, I got to go back and do 100 percent food." He would go on to become "The Food Guy" at Whole Foods, sourcing and producing all sorts of artisanal private label products, and acting as a gadfly on the executive team. But it was very difficult for him to break the news of the sale to his Wellspring employees. According to Tim Sperry, who was then the purchasing director for Wellspring, the tightly knit team never saw it coming. "We were all in shock. . . . It's like our world was coming to an end. A bunch of us actually had meetings and talked about, you know, can we raise the money and buy it?" Alexander tried to reassure them everything would be okay, but when they went down to Houston for the opening of the Wilcrest Whole Foods store to meet their new colleagues, things only got worse. "There was a song that they sang," recalled Sperry, "and we were all looking at ourselves like, 'What the hell is going on here? Did we join some hippie-dippie cult?'"

Now Whole Foods was on a roll. With a presence in several major markets across four states, Mackey & Co. had built up enough cachet to take the company public in early 1992—certainly one of the landmark moments in industry history. Armed with money from the public markets, confident that the industry had huge growth potential, inspired by the development of "category-killers" in other retail industries (such as Circuit City, Home Depot, and Bed, Bath & Beyond), and eager to move quickly lest the hard-charging upstarts like Wild Oats and Fresh Fields make any inroads, they quickly set out to build a national company.

In August 1992, Mackey came calling on his friend Anthony Harnett with another too-logical-to-refuse offer—you can either sell to me or compete against me—and for the Irishman it appeared to be a good time to exit stage right. The Bread & Circus stores were doing well (making perhaps 8 percent profit) but the high corporate overhead (10 percent) was continuing to put a drain on cash; Whole Foods, in contrast, was also making 8 percent in the stores, but with about 2 percent general and administrative costs. A sale price of $26.2 million was secretly agreed upon. Harnett gathered his team together on Saturday, October 10, to make the announcement and say good-bye. Then he walked out, and never set foot in a Bread & Circus store again. The deal closed on Columbus Day, October 12, 1992. Thus, precisely 500 years after the Niña, Pinta, and Santa Maria arrived in the Americas, a modern pioneer of a very different sort set sail . . . and for Whole Foods Market, it marked the discovery of an entirely new world.

By then, Sandy Gooch and Harry Lederman knew what might be coming. Lederman recalled that at a meeting of The Network in Houston one time, Mackey had actually articulated his vision to everyone: "Why don't we consider becoming a national chain?" So it was no surprise to see that vision taking shape. Mrs. Gooch's remained highly profitable, generating about $85 million in sales in its seven stores in 1992, without any beer or wine or caffeine, while Whole Foods (including Bread & Circus) had done about $120 million in its 22 stores. In order to stay alive in the suddenly competitive world, Gooch knew that her company would have to change. "It was a challenge to go on with the existing management team that was involved in Mrs. Gooch's," she said. "And it seemed as if it would be better to just let the stores continue in a different fashion."

She approached an investment bank in an effort to sell the business. Mackey found out about this, and requested a private meeting with Gooch and Lederman. They flew to San Antonio to meet with him and had a pleasant discussion, but didn't know if anything would come of it. At the same time, Safeway emerged as a potential buyer. "They had truly done their due diligence," remembered Lederman. "Safeway identified twenty-five or thirty of their smaller stores, using our Thousand Oaks store, twenty-five to thirty thousand square feet, as a model. . . . If they had acquired us, they would have closed them down completely, spent six months redesigning them to be identical, called them Mrs. Gooch's and [started] a whole separate division. And they wanted John Moorman [Mrs. Gooch's CEO] to be its CEO, and Sandy to continue to be a part of the advertising." Lederman thought Safeway was the better bet of the two suitors, but Gooch's two other partners opted for Whole Foods. The ultimate $64 million deal[27] was announced in May 1993, and yet another of the industry's great pioneers headed for an early retirement. Tellingly, the headline in the *Los Angeles Times* read: "Mrs. Gooch's Natural Markets, Texas Food Chain to Merge."[28] In LA, Whole Foods was still just some chain store, but Mrs. Gooch's was an *institution*.

"They were like family, the employees were," said Gooch, with a trace of wistfulness after all these years. "I went back into the stores a few times at the beginning, after Mrs. Gooch's was acquired by Whole Foods, and employees would come up to me and start crying. Then I would walk out of the store in tears as well. And so I knew that I had given up the child, the baby, in order for it to thrive and survive."

Two months later, Whole Foods' stock split 2-for-1—a certain sign of success.

All the while, through each move across the national checkerboard by Whole Foods, Unicorn Village's Terry Dalton was watching the game play out from his perch in Florida. Dalton had earned a reputation as a food service visionary, an idealist who had found a way to convert the Golden Rule into gold. John Mackey was impressed by Dalton's success in a part of the country Whole Foods had not yet reached, and by his mastery of the restaurant side of the business, something at which Whole Foods had never had any luck. So in the fall of 1994, it wasn't a great shock that the Whole Foods CEO called up Dalton and trotted out his oft-used argument: "You can either sell to me or compete against me." Dalton was at that very moment in the midst of discussions to open a new location in either Boca Raton or Coral Gables and had also been negotiating with Wild Oats; this just struck him as a better alternative. He could pay off his investors, bank a good amount of money, get a $125,000 salary for 5 years in exchange for agreeing not to compete with Whole Foods . . . and he could get to keep the restaurant. "[John] didn't want the restaurant, and I didn't want him to have it. They could have never run it." Things came together fairly quickly, and the Unicorn Village retail operation was sold for $4.5 million in February of 1995. The two men never even met in person to discuss the deal. The closing was done in Dalton's lawyer's office. Whole Foods faxed a document. The lawyer faxed it back. The money was wired and that was the end of it. Dalton left and never went back.

———•———

Thus, though it took only 7 years (1984–1991) for the natural foods supermarket retailers to explode on the scene, it took only 7 more (1988–1995) for them to consolidate through the extraordinary efforts of John Mackey and Whole Foods Market—leaving, perhaps, some rueful entrepreneurs to sift through the wreckage of their considerable accomplishments. The industry was now poised for another major transformation. No longer hiding in hippie outposts on the edge of the woods, the natural foods industry was now visible to all—its foundational premise of changing the world still in evidence, but its new promise of opportunity obvious to anyone who looked.

CHAPTER 6

LAND OF OPPORTUNISM

I n the spring of 1992, the obscure work of some university researchers, government engineers, and private sector technologists who had been tapping away at computer keyboards in dingy offices for years suddenly burst out into the open. All of a sudden, as a result of their efforts, three letters ingrained themselves in the American consciousness: WWW.

The World Wide Web was still relatively tiny, connecting about 1 million computers on 7,500 different networks.[1] But its potential, both symbolic and practical, was staggering. Because now, for the first time in a century, an entirely new way of communicating emerged, one that many people realized could rival the telephone and fundamentally change human lives. The very next year, 1993, Internet service traffic increased by an astronomical 342,000 percent, and the headlong dash toward the future was underway.[2] The heroes of this new industry included people like Steve Jobs of Apple (whose company shipped its 10 millionth Mac in 1993), Marc Andreessen and Jim Clark (who developed the Netscape Navigator browser and whose company soon went public in one of the largest IPOs of all time), and, of course, Bill Gates of Microsoft (whose operating systems and software applications became so famous that in 1995 he appeared on the cover of *Time* magazine next to the headline, "Master of the Universe").

Thus, the geeky-garage-tinkerer-turned-technology-titan became the newest mythic archetype of the American entrepreneur, taking his place in the pantheon of hero worship alongside the yeoman farmer, the rugged-but-pure-hearted cowboy in the saddle, and the rags-to-riches captain of industry exalted by Horatio Alger, Jr.

The idealized notion of the "self-made man"—lionized by French historian Alexis de Tocqueville after his 1831 tour of the country as "ardent in his desires, enterprising, adventurous, and above all an innovator"—coursed through Americans' blood like no other. Benjamin Franklin, John D. Rockefeller, Andrew Carnegie, Thomas Edison, Sam Walton, and, yes, even C.W. Post . . . their entrepreneurial spirit formed the zeitgeist of American business for more than 2 centuries.

At just about the same time, however, another archetype was taking shape in our collective consciousness: the lucky son-of-a-gun who hits it big. *Really* big. The first Powerball drawing in American history took place on April 22, 1992. A successor to the earlier Lotto*America game, Powerball pooled together the ticket purchases and cross-your-fingers financial planning strategy of people in 14 different states to create one enormous lottery. The initial jackpots were around $2 million, but the long-shot dream of becoming an instant millionaire quickly attracted a lot of players. By July 1993—just as Apple was reporting a quarterly loss of $188 million and dismissing CEO John Sculley—a 30-year-old junior high school English teacher from Fon du Lac, Wisconsin, named Les Robins, who had a salary of $30,000 per year, won the Powerball drawing and claimed the richest prize ever won in a US lottery to that point: $111 million.[3] Suddenly, it seemed, there was another way to make it in America, and it wasn't based on ideals or even hard work. It was simply taking advantage of an opportunity.

—•—

What initially struck most people about Mike Gilliland was not his sense of opportunism or his good fortune. Those would come later. What they noticed about Gilliland at first glance were his youthful dirty blond curls and his round face that was devoid of any crags, crow's-feet, or other obvious signs of age. "I thought he looked like a young kid," said WhiteWave's Steve Demos of his first meeting with Gilliland in the late eighties. "Where'd *he* come from? *That* was a curveball."

Maybe Demos and the rest of the Boulder Mafia couldn't recognize Gilliland because, unlike them, he was not a reformed flower child or some hippie-turned-capitalist. He had never marched on Washington, nor lived in an ashram. Gilliland was on the leading edge of what Tom Wolfe called the

"Me Generation," with an outlook on life that was not about saving the world, or even saving one's own soul, but about saving a few bucks. Less idealism, more opportunism.

Born in Iowa in 1958, his family moved around a lot—a couple of years in Marlboro, Massachusetts, a couple of years in the suburbs of Chicago—so the three Gilliland kids never had much of a chance to settle in anywhere. It was a pattern that clearly took root in young Mike, because he would repeat it often.

Thinking he wanted to be a pilot, Gilliland enrolled at the Air Force Academy and spent a couple of years there learning how to jump out of planes. But "that whole authority thing" never sat well with him, so he left Colorado Springs for France and some vague notion of entering the diplomatic corps. In Grenoble he met Elizabeth "Libby" Cook, whom he would eventually marry, but he also found an idea that he thought held some promise: mobile crêpe carts. Back in the United States, with a few months to kill before returning to Colorado to finish his undergraduate degree at the University of Colorado (where Libby would be attending law school), he bought an old horse trailer, converted it into a food cart, devised a crêpe-making machine using a propane tank, hired one guy from a work-release program and two hitchhikers, and took his little business—Freres Jacques' Crêperie—to New Orleans for Mardi Gras. The whole thing was blatantly illegal, since he had no permits, but he kept it going for a little while, taking it around to flea markets in New Orleans and later Miami.

After finishing his degree in Boulder, he and his brother, Pat, came up with another money-making scheme: a parasailing business. The boys tested it out by tying a rope (and Pat) to a fire hydrant on a windy day in Boulder; then they tried to get the company going in the Caribbean, ultimately setting up shop in St. Croix. But it wasn't generating any real cash, and Mike wanted to get back to Libby, so he returned to Boulder and began scouring the *Daily Camera* for business opportunities.

One day in 1984, he stumbled upon a listing for a convenience store that was for sale. He met with the owner, an Iraqi gentleman who told him that the store was generating about $1,000 a day in sales—he wasn't paying taxes so he didn't keep any sales records. He would sell it to Mike for just $70,000, because someone had cut him a similar deal when he was Mike's age (though of course Mike was older than he looked).

Gilliland didn't have much money or credit, and had he been of another time, another generation, he might have dusted off a suit and marched in to see the loan officer at a bank. But this was a child of the age of opportunism, and he understood how to work the system. He, Libby, and partner Randy Clapp signed up for 17 credit cards, charged a little bit and paid them off, charged a bit more and paid them off, until they finally had sufficient credit limits to put his plan into action. On the appointed day, he maxed them all out, took out $70,000 in cash advances, and bought the store.

On Gilliland's first day as the owner of the newly named Stella's Market, he brought in a whopping $200. It was a dud, and the Iraqi had left town with no forwarding address. There was nothing to do but just hunker down. Through some irreverent promotions (a "Lonely Man's Special" that included *Playboy,* a six-pack of beer, and some rolling paper; a sign in the window that said, "What the fuck, save a buck") he got the place going, and it eventually did okay. Over the next 2 years, Mike and Libby bought two more convenience stores in Boulder, and opened a gourmet food store called the French Market, which, like many of his earlier ventures, proved to be a disaster.

But by this time, the natural foods revolution had overtaken Boulder. Mark Retzloff and Hass Hassan had long since moved their retail store from Pearl Street Market to Broadway and Arapahoe, and had opened up another Alfalfa's in Denver. Back at 1825 Pearl, a store called Crystal Market was selling an odd mix of natural foods, crystals, and Guatemalan clothing, and was thriving. At WhiteWave Foods, Steve Demos was still 8 years away from the heavenly profits that would come with Silk, but he had established a real business. Celestial Seasonings had gotten so big that it had been sold to Kraft. Mike Gilliland looked around town, recognized a good opportunity, and after obtaining a $300,000 loan from the Small Business Administration in 1987, bought Crystal Market, which he and Libby soon renamed the Wild Oats Vegetarian Market. "That was our first exposure to natural foods," recalled Gilliland. "We just really fell in love with the business, and all of the trippy people that are part of it." The following year, they converted the French Market into another Wild Oats, and lo and behold, "what used to be a disaster immediately took off as a natural foods store."

Then business really began to accelerate. Gilliland bought a small store in Fort Collins, Colorado. He bought the two remaining Rainbow Groceries in Denver and Aurora, the last business vestiges of the Guru Maharaj Ji and the Divine Light Mission in Colorado. He attended Natural Products Expo

West and came back with pages of notes and contacts. He visited Mrs. Gooch's and Whole Foods stores, and struck up a correspondence with John Mackey—meeting him for dinner in Berkeley, California, on one occasion, and seeking his opinion about prospective store locations on several others. The collegial days of the Natural Foods Network were already over, but still, according to Gilliland, "Everybody was fully supportive of everybody else. The information was coming in so fast and furious, you just couldn't make changes quick enough."

Gilliland saw opportunity around every corner. After a broker offered him a free weekend trip to Santa Fe, New Mexico, Wild Oats opened a store there within a year and followed that with one in Albuquerque. People called about all kinds of other locations and acquisitions. Soon Wild Oats opened in Arizona, and Missouri, and California—a one-off store here, another there. The stores were usually modest in size, averaging perhaps 15,000 square feet. Some of the sites were considered "B" real estate, located in out-of-the-way shopping plazas that lacked visibility or good parking or a dynamic mix of retail neighbors. It didn't matter. The natural foods industry was hot, the build-outs were inexpensive, and Wild Oats was going places. "I think Mike was a little more opportunistic, more business-like, not as committed to values as some of the earlier founders in the industry," recalled Barney Feinblum, who from his perch on the board at Alfalfa's was then competing with Wild Oats. "But he saw trends and with Libby took advantage of putting together an excellent team that was able to compete on a larger scale and was more aggressive than many of the other retailers, because he took it outside of the local market to try to be a national player."

Gilliland's particular genius was his ability to study and identify other companies' best qualities, and then mimic them, often less expensively. "We were shameless in terms of stealing stuff from people," he said, laughing. "I never understood why everybody didn't do that. It's right there. It's not like brain surgery. The worst retailer in the world does something right or he wouldn't be in business. . . . So that was kind of the mentality we had: There is something to steal from everybody."

Thus, in a Wild Oats store one might find produce hand-stacked in the same pyramidal fashion employed with great effect by Bread & Circus—but because the Wild Oats stores were lower volume and did fewer "turns" of produce, they might "dummy up" the displays with internal blocks so that less fresh product was required to build the pyramid. Wild Oats moved strongly into private label products, but instead of the artisanal fare being created by Whole Foods—dipping sauces and small-batch apple butter, for example—the Wild Oats products were more like generic goods with whimsical labels. So it was with their juice bars, the labor staffing levels, the deli departments, the equipment. . . . Gilliland often opted to do things that were derivative, that were just good enough and no better. "We take the low end," he told the *Denver Business Journal* at the time. "We have lower prices, and are more low-key. . . ."4 Mo Siegel, whom Gilliland persuaded to join the Wild Oats board of directors, said this was a frequent topic of conversation. "I would say in meetings, 'Hey guys, this [food tastes like] ground-up Birkenstocks. Do you see what Whole Foods is doing? It's gourmet chocolate sitting there in the bakery. You gotta sugar-coat this stuff, you gotta make it taste good.'" Taste, after all, had been one of his main tenets at Celestial Seasonings since its founding in the late sixties. But in the unbridled nineties, his advice went unheeded. "I don't think Wild Oats ever really got it," he said.

Still, Wild Oats kept growing. It found pockets of real estate that no other natural foods retailer had claimed. The company generally did an excellent job of connecting to its local communities, in part through 5 percent donation days and wooden-nickel fund-raising programs. Wild Oats tailored its product mix to the customer base in each store, created a brand with a fun vibe, and was consistent in executing it. And Gilliland had a great instinctive feel for how to position the brand as a value-conscious alternative to Whole Foods in the areas where they did compete head-to-head.

For the first few years, Gilliland "never thought for a minute about raising professional money." But while helping out at the first Santa Fe opening, he was approached by a blustery older man who wanted to know who owned the place. "I do," said Mike. The man, an ex-con named Eddie Gilbert, didn't believe him—Gilliland looked so youthful!—but came back later and convinced the young owner to accept an investment of $1 million. "He was a character and a half," recalled Gilliland, "but he kind of changed the thinking as to how big this business could be." Less than a year later, the venture capitalists at Western Presidio put in $2 million (after buying out Eddie Gilbert, whom they deemed too unsavory), and then Chase Capital invested, too. Whether it was his opportunistic brand of entrepreneurship or just being in the right place at the right time, this fresh face, this representative of the new generation of Natural Prophets, had hit the natural foods Powerball.

So while Whole Foods used its IPO in 1992 to go out and buy Bread & Circus and then Mrs. Gooch's, further padding its war chest, Mike Gilliland and Wild Oats took another approach. In effect, they charged a little bit and paid it off, charged a little bit more and paid it off, until they had built a surprisingly big company. In March 1993, Wild Oats bought a store called Clearly Nature's Own in Kansas City. In July 1994, it bought the two Kathy's Ranch Markets in Las Vegas, giving the company 16 stores in five states, doing $50 million in sales. Then it bought the remaining Living Foods store in Northern California, and a pair of stores called New Frontiers in Salt Lake City. There was no particular strategy to it all. There was no clustering of stores, as Fresh Fields had done in Philadelphia, New York, and Chicago to facilitate training, or to ensure consistent operations, or to keep the distribution supply lines short. There was no agonizing over individual locations, as Whole Foods had often done. "I didn't have any kind of strategic ability," said Gilliland in hindsight. "So the fact that they were so far-flung, and that there wasn't a lot of thought to infrastructure, [didn't really matter]. . . . Back then you couldn't do any wrong. If you had the product, you were going to be successful. There was no competition to speak of. Whenever you opened a store, wherever you opened a store, people would be in tears. 'Thank God, we've got a Bread & Circus lookalike in our town!' or whatever. So it was kind of off to the races at that point."

By January 1996, with $150 million in sales, the race course took Wild Oats right to the corner of Broadway and Arapahoe in Boulder. The merger with Alfalfa's was announced, the plans for the IPO were set in motion, and Mike Gilliland had himself one mighty big mobile crêpe cart.

———•———

Like Mike Gilliland, Mark Ordan came into the world at the end of the 1950s, though *his* upbringing was as stable as the Flatbush, Brooklyn, home in which he grew up. "I thought we were rich, because our house was not attached to another house. It was covered in stucco, which I thought was an expensive, precious material. I later found out it was *stucco*." Everyone in the extended Ordan family worked in the public school system, including his father, Harry, who was the principal at PS 208, and his mother, Doris, who was a secretary at Midwood High School.

As a kid, his hobby was consumer electronics, though he never had the money to buy much of anything. One day in 1972, he asked his parents to drop him off at the Audio Exchange, which was the best high-end audio store in Brooklyn. In the store, Ordan saw a help wanted sign for a stock boy. He lied on the application, claiming he was 16, and got the job. "I thought, for years, for *years*, that I had fooled them into thinking that I was older. I found out later that when my parents came to pick me up, the guy from Audio Exchange said, 'Your son said he is 16. We know he is not 16. Are you okay with us hiring him?' My father said, 'If my son wants to work, why would I say no?' So I didn't fool them. I wasn't so clever."

He soon went to work, and when things got busy in the store, they asked Ordan to step into the role of salesperson, which he could easily do. He knew all the equipment, and besides, his diction, demeanor, and deep-set eyes always made him appear very mature. That was how Mark Ordan fell in love with high-end retailing. "I couldn't have sold crappy stereo equipment. I couldn't have worked for Crazy Eddie, I couldn't have worked for Korvette's. . . . I realized, and it is true to this day, that if I believed in something, if I loved it, I'll be good at it."

Ordan graduated from high school at the age of 16, working at Audio Exchange throughout. He then went off to college at Vassar, where in 1979 he earned a degree in philosophy—academic training in the rhetorical arts that only further sharpened a mind that seemed to whir at an unusually high RPM. Audio Exchange soon merged with Harvey Sound, but Ordan would come back on school breaks to resume his job as a stereo salesman at its world-class store at 2 West 45th Street in Manhattan ("212-575-5000," he can still rattle right off). After graduating, he would again return to Harvey, this time as director of operations.

He was young, but Ordan was a very good salesman and manager, and an even better observer of people. And it was his powers of observation that taught him important lessons about opportunism.

First, he noticed that one of the veteran salesmen, a fellow named Anton Schmidt who usually stuck to a remote corner of the sales floor, always seemed to pick up the ringing phone faster than anyone else, and would turn those phone calls into qualified sales leads. Ordan could not figure out how he did it. The odds would seem to dictate that everyone had an equal chance at answering the phone, even though the system for doing so—dialing "9" on the old rotary phones to pick up an incoming call—was a bit unwieldy. Eventually, he learned that Schmidt had changed the rules of the game. "His secret was that he replaced the spring in his phone with a much tighter spring, so his phone sprung back [from dialing 9] instantly and was the only one that would really get through. That was one guy that inspired me, because he used his brain to his advantage."

Ordan also noticed that another salesman seemed particularly adept at picking out the right customers to approach in the crowded store. "To me," Ordan recalled, "everybody looked the same. I didn't understand it. So I asked him one time how he did it, and he told me, which was a mistake on his part because we were all jockeying for position." The rival salesman explained that when customers first walked into the store, he would look down at their shoes to decide which ones to approach. "In New York," Ordan remembered him saying, "everybody wears nice suits and dresses, and everybody looks the same, except for one thing. The people who have money, and will spend money, have really nice shoes. . . . " From that day forward, Ordan's sales soared.

Charming and extremely business-savvy, Ordan took his sales tricks and intellectual tool kit off to the Cathedral of Capitalism, Harvard Business School, in the fall of 1981. There he was surrounded by an extraordinary group of people including Peter and John Weinberg (whose family ran Goldman Sachs), Jamie Dimon (future CEO of JP Morgan Chase), Jeff Immelt (future CEO of General Electric), and Steve Mandel (who would go on to become one of the world's most successful hedge fund managers), as well as a marketing executive named Kathy Sklar, whom Ordan would marry a few months after graduating in 1983. He was recruited for a job in securities by Goldman Sachs, a company he respected greatly. "They were people who totally believed in what they did and were unbelievably good at what they did," said Ordan. "They built something fantastic on really great principles . . . and the partners were very philanthropic. That influenced me a lot."

Though at first he didn't know much about what securities were, he became well liked within the firm. Still, nothing interested him more than high-end retailing, especially stereos. "These stereo retailers were all struggling, and I thought there was a better business model. I thought it would be interesting to buy Harvey—it was a public company, a barely public company—and put together a chain of national high-end stereo stores" that might also include Magnolia in the Pacific Northwest, MyerEmco in Washington, Absolute Sound in Florida, and Tweeter in Boston. The board at Harvey's seemed uninterested, so Ordan called the head of Tweeter, Sandy Bloomberg, who set him up to meet with the company's majority owner—a fellow named Leo Kahn, who had made a fortune in the grocery business in Boston, selling the chain Purity Supreme in 1984 for $80 million, and had used some of those proceeds to help start the office-supply chain Staples. They met at the Harvard Club in New York, the feisty bow-tie-wearing 72-year-old Kahn and the brilliant, opportunistic 29-year-old Ordan. "We just kind of fell for each other," remembered Ordan.

In time Ordan grew bored with the work at Goldman Sachs, which seemed to be all about chasing wealthy clients. "It was very lucrative," he acknowledged, "but I also thought, 'If everybody at Goldman is so excited that a client is doing business with them, I would rather be a client.'" Mostly he wanted to find a career in a field he loved, and perhaps pursue his passion for retailing. As a partner at Goldman would later tell him, "The difference between you and me, Mark, is that if I make money in something, I will love it. And for you, if you love it, you will make money at it." He left Wall Street, set up a little figurehead company in Roslyn, New York, called Granite Ventures—he later joked he should have named it Stucco Ventures, though "I still thought stucco was semi-precious and didn't want to be highfalutin"—and began exploring opportunities to go into business for himself. He and Kahn looked into buying Lechmere, and the HeMan Big & Tall Men's Shops . . . and then one day Kahn called to suggest that he take a trip up to Boston to check out a store called Bread & Circus. Armed with a map of local supermarkets, Ordan popped into a couple of Star Markets and Stop & Shops around 10 in the morning, and was nearly bored to tears. Then he went to the Bread & Circus in Newton Corner and couldn't believe his eyes. The place was jammed. There was energy and excitement in the store. He thought the fish department was amazing, and found the high prices that people were paying even more amazing.

"People were falling over each other. And, you know, every car in the parking lot was a high-end car, everybody there was nicely dressed. It looked to me like any food that was being purchased in Newton, Massachusetts, was in that building."

He called Kahn later that day. "Oh my God," Ordan said. "This is incredible! Let's do it." The idea for Fresh Fields was born.

If she had thought back on it, Kathy Sklar Ordan might have realized that they were getting themselves in over their heads with this new food retailing venture. She would be able to run the marketing and advertising, Jack Murphy would handle operations, Mark would raise the money, and Leo—well, he'd be Leo. But who really knew much about natural foods?

There had been that little tipoff a few years earlier, when she returned home from work one night to find Mark tinkering around in the tiny kitchen of their Manhattan apartment.

"Don't come in!" yelled Mark. "I am making dinner tonight. Just stay away, and I'll have everything ready soon."

It was a romantic gesture, and she'd had a long day of work at J. Walter Thompson advertising, so she shrugged and headed toward the living room.

"Only, one thing," said Mark, beckoning her back, holding a hunk of ginger root in his hand. "How much of this is a clove?"

Fresh Fields was not going to be about the food, at least not at the beginning. Natural foods had left a bad taste in Mark's mouth from an early age, when he had been dragged by his aunt to Brownie's, Manhattan's original natural foods restaurant, on East 16th Street, which served dishes like "chile no carne" and "potato blimp ratatouille." He and Kathy took a healthy-cooking class in Lower Manhattan ("The whole notion of getting beans and soaking them, it was all really foreign to me," she recalled), and though he assiduously researched the natural foods industry (traveling to see Mrs. Gooch's, Whole Foods, Alfalfa's, and Unicorn Village, and even getting Anthony Harnett to agree to let him work in a Bread & Circus store for a few days, sweeping and stocking shelves, in exchange for a promise never to open a Fresh Fields in Boston), it wasn't out of a Gene Kahn–like back-to-the-land passion or a Sandy Gooch–like zealotry for pure food. "It wasn't like there was a personal need or a personal idea," said Kathy. "Our inspiration was the idea to start a business. And this was the business that ended up being supported by the key investor, and, happily, by the market." Fresh Fields became the poster child for the age of opportunism.

The original plan was to open in New York, but the real estate market there was not very favorable. Fresh Fields wanted 15,000- to 25,000-square-foot boxes, and there just weren't many of those in Manhattan, in part, ironically, because Kahn's Staples chain had begun moving into the city and buying up former supermarket sites. So after mapping out the existing natural foods retailers in the country, and overlaying various demographic studies, the Fresh Fields team pinpointed the nation's capital as the best place to start their enterprise. The DC area was booming, as the Reagan-era surge of military spending had swelled the payrolls of local defense contractors like Lockheed Martin and Northrop Grumman. Real estate was hot. The population was well educated. The upscale Tysons Galleria Mall had just opened in 1988, alongside the incredibly success-ful super-regional mall, Tysons Corner Center. And, other than a few lonely health foods outlets like the Bethesda Co-Op or Yes! Market, there was no natural foods retail presence in the market.

Unlike the previous generation of natural foods entrepreneurs who had opened tiny one-off stores, Mark Ordan intended to make Fresh Fields big. "We were interested in chains," said Ordan. "Interested to see how we could do it in multiple places. Because for me there was no thought of opening one store, and for Leo that would be organically impossible."

The first order of business was to raise money. The magnitude of the initial cash raise—$14 million—was not at all unusual for the former Goldman Sachs investment banker, but it was absolutely stunning for the natural foods indus-try. Kahn put up $7 million, and Ordan quickly raised another $7 million by tapping into his old network of Goldman real estate moguls and wealthy entre-preneurs, as well as his Harvard Business School contacts such as Steve Mandel, who was with a hedge fund called Tiger Management.

After the initial raise was done, Ordan received a call out-of-the-blue from Charles Lazarus, founder and chairman of Toys "R" Us, and one of the retail legends he most revered.

"I have heard what you are doing," Ordan recalled Lazarus saying, "and I would like to invest $100,000."

Ordan, then just 33, was a bit awestruck. "Mr. Lazarus, I can't tell you how flattered I am. It's unbelievable. But we are full."

"Then I want a million," said Lazarus.

"Mr. Lazarus," Ordan protested, "I don't think you understand. I can't take $100,000, and I can't take $1 million. We've done our equity raise."

Lazarus, unperturbed, continued. "Mark, I will wire you two-and-a-half million dollars *today*."

Ordan finally succeeded in deflecting the offer, but he was stunned. It may have been little more than the "piling on" effect that sometimes happens when investors hear that other smart money firms are involved, but it all seemed too easy, especially in an industry whose tie-dye undershirt was still peeking through the Brooks Brothers jacket it had recently thrown on top.

"I don't know that there was ever a time that he and I were talking that he even knew what business I was in," Ordan chuckled as he looked back on the incident. "He heard Tiger was piling money into something, and my name was Mark Ordan. I don't think he knew whether I was selling guns to Palestinians, or what. Of course, he probably wouldn't have liked that."

Next, Ordan methodically set out to build a top-flight board of directors, including blue-chip investors and the best retailers he could find. Sam Walton, he figured, would not be interested. Bernie Marcus of Home Depot, whom Ordan believed to be the second best retailer in the world, had just invested in Harry's Farmers Markets in Atlanta and was unavailable. But among others, Ordan did eventually recruit Dave Fuente, CEO of Office Depot; Howard Schultz, CEO of Starbucks; Tom Wilson, who in his time at McKinsey Consulting had been one of the inventors of the barcode; as well as Steve Mandel, and directors at T. Rowe Price and Goldman Sachs. From the start, the company was engineered for growth with Wall Street money, Harvard Business School management acumen, investments in technology, and marketing savvy, the likes of which this little industry, still in many ways struggling for legitimacy, had never seen. Whereas most natural foods stores had been started in local neighborhoods by "health foods nuts" who struggled to find startup capital, catered to aging hippies, and therefore typically went many years before generating enough cash flow to open a second or third location, Fresh Fields had been built to succeed from the very beginning, with millions of dollars, a cadre of Ivy League MBAs, a capitalist philosophy bent on highly competitive prices, and a battery of demographic studies indicating that the *new* health foods nuts were well-educated yuppies and mainstream moms in Jeep Grand Cherokees.

The first Fresh Fields was built in Rockville, Maryland, ironically right next to a Big & Tall men's clothing shop. The merchandising concept borrowed a lot from Kahn's and Murphy's experiences in the conventional supermarket world in order to make it feel comfortable to mainstream consumers; but the Ordans helped steer it in an upscale direction, with a playful teal-and-gold color scheme, tiled walls in the perimeter departments, blond-wood fixtures, spotlights, and PermaGrain hardwood floors. There was organic produce stacked high, a seafood department with glistening fresh fish, and a scratch bakery whose aromas permeated the whole store.

On the night before the first store opened, Kahn gathered everyone together to hand out T-shirts and deliver a pep talk. There was a sense of tremendous anticipation in the air, knowing that 2 years of meticulous planning were about to come to fruition. The store looked beautiful, but nobody knew for certain whether the people of Rockville were ready for a supermarket that was packed to the rafters with products like Uncle Dave's ketchup, Lightlife Tofu Pups, Nasoya Nayonaise, Pizsoy frozen pizzas, and R.W. Frookies fruit-juice-sweetened cookies, and not a single Oreo or can of Coca-Cola. As Kathy recalled, Kahn put things in perspective. "Everybody out there in the world right now is completely content with where they are buying their groceries and how they are shopping. And tomorrow morning at eight we are going to open and hope they come in. We have to give them a reason to come, to change their behavior, and that is not easy."

The sun rose on Fresh Fields on the morning of Memorial Day, May 27, 1991, and the 17,000-square-foot store magically came to life. Mark, Kathy, Jack, and Leo all scurried from department to department. Curious customers came in throughout the day. Even more curious managers from the nearby Giant Food supermarket also came in, blatantly obvious in their starched white shirts and narrow ties as they walked up and down the aisles with befuddled and slightly amused expressions. The expensive cash register system didn't work, forcing the cashiers to use hand calculators and backing up the checkout lines, but it was otherwise a big hit. The first great engineering experiment in the natural foods industry had begun.

In the ensuing months, as the upstart startup drained about $300,000 a week away from the conventional supermarkets, the topic of Fresh Fields came up at a board meeting at Giant. That chain, founded in 1936 by Nehemiah "N.M." Cohen and Samuel Lehrman, was the clear market leader, with 107 stores, $2.3 billion in sales, and a 45.8 percent market share in the Washington–Baltimore area.[5] "Should we crush them?" Izzy Cohen, N.M.'s son and chairman of the board, reportedly asked. It was decided that no, Fresh Fields posed no real threat, and it would be allowed to live.[6]

But whether Cohen or anyone else could have turned back the natural tide is doubtful. A second Fresh Fields store opened in nearby Bethesda, Maryland, just before Thanksgiving to enormous crowds. Then came three more in 1992 (some as large as 30,000 square feet), and *eight* more in 1993—including stores in greater Philadelphia and Chicago. In 1993 Whole Foods Market and Wild Oats were the only natural foods companies that even had as many as eight stores, *total*.

Fresh Fields built a rabid and loyal following through marketing that was both bold and sophisticated. Kathy Sklar Ordan created a pervasive radio campaign that featured the well-known avuncular voice of TV character-actor Tom Poston, saying things like "Question for you: How long should you marinate your flounder fillets in pool chemicals before you grill them? At Fresh Fields, we think not even for a second." Another Poston ad promoted Fresh Fields' natural hormone- and antibiotic-free beef that tasted "like beef was supposed to taste before Man messed with it and started drugging the livestock." Poston then urged listeners to pull their cars over whenever they saw cows in a field, "lean over the fence and tell them to just say no." Meanwhile, the company launched a unique loyalty card program, FreshShopper, which enabled the marketing team to target customers—for example, steering those who were only buying groceries over to the more profitable vitamin department, or identifying and communicating with infrequent customers. It was, for Kathy Sklar Ordan, the business opportunity of a lifetime—a living case study that combined all she had taken in at J. Walter Thompson with all she had learned at Harvard, plus all she was discovering as a new mother. It was, moreover, a chance to prove that in *this* era, money plus mission plus marketing could run rings around the competition.

Taking it all in after one particularly long day of work, Mark and Kathy sat at a red light on Nicholson Lane in Rockville, Maryland, just across from their first store, whose parking lot was still bustling with activity even after dinner. They sat in silence, and then watched as an 18-wheeler with a huge Fresh Fields logo crossed in front of them, on its way to make a delivery to another store. "Can you believe it?" asked Kathy. "We did this!"

Behind the scenes, there were signs that perhaps Fresh Fields was growing too fast. The company had such a great need for talent that it hired away some people from other companies without doing adequate screening: One director proved to have a cocaine problem and had to be sent off to rehab. Some stores were hastily designed and had to be changed on the fly. At the Palatine, Illinois, location, for example, Kahn had insisted they should go with only a self-service meat department, but at the last second Ordan and Murphy persuaded him to put in a counter. "With maybe a week and a half to go before opening," recalled

Dave Printz, who was the director of construction, "we were jack-hammering the concrete."

The company was also burning through a lot of cash. Mark Ordan could remember a finance professor at Harvard Business School who, on the very first day of class, had told the students (many of whom were reluctantly taking the course as a requirement) the one thing they would need to know for all time about finance: "Don't run out of cash." Still, in the midst of hiring lots of people and with Kahn pushing for the expansion into Philadelphia and Chicago, that lesson was lost. "You want to be bulletproof," said Ordan in hindsight. "But you take the accumulated losses of new store openings, including some that shouldn't have been opened—you don't get that money back. It put us under an enormous amount of strain." At one point, Fresh Fields CFO Mark Smiley sent a memo to everyone in the corporate office, telling them that purchases of office supplies had gotten way out of hand, and that until further notice, if anyone needed paper clips or rubber bands, they should get down on all fours and hunt around their desks.

Nevertheless, that was all underneath the hood. To the outside world, the company had screeched out of the starting blocks like a souped-up hot rod on Main Street Saturday night. The media reviews, for example, were exuberant. *Warfield's* magazine noted that Fresh Fields' "upscale chic" decor "looks more like an art gallery than a Giant," and included a picture of a smiling Mark Ordan in oversize round-rim glasses with the caption, "King of the organic mountain." The *New York Times* noted the "sparkling produce, impeccable meat cases . . . [and] tempting prepared foods," and quoted one customer as saying, "Gorgeous. It's wonderful and I'm a real cook. . . . The food tastes better. It's presented better."[7] *Brand Week* magazine declared in 1993, "The chain is storming the industry," and speculated that "Fresh Fields is expanding so rapidly to gear up to go public next spring."[8] *Money* magazine, in naming Fresh Fields its 1993 Store of the Year, called it "snazzy," "expansive," and "well-designed," and noted that the store differed from the big natural foods stores elsewhere in the country because of its pricing—"the good-for-you premium at Fresh Fields is only 5 percent or so"—and its "deliberate lack of missionary zeal" that made it appealing to mainstream customers.[9]

The rest of the industry was also impressed. "I thought [Fresh Fields] was fascinating," remembered Wild Oats' Mike Gilliland. "They were appealing to that crossover customer, as opposed to a hard-core natural foods Whole Foods shopper. Because back then, Whole Foods . . . had the hippie edge to them for sure, and Fresh Fields didn't have that at all. They were taking the world by storm." Terry Dalton of Unicorn Village told *Brand Week*, "They've been good for the industry because they brought prices down, and create competitive excitement. Manufacturers love Fresh Fields; they drive hard bargains, they're selling a ton of product and [are] bringing awareness to the industry." Whole Foods' Peter Roy, quoted in the same article, agreed: "Obviously their concept is very viable; their entry's made the industry more competitive and exciting."

—————

Although the Fresh Fields partners had not come from a long tradition of natural and organic foods, they learned the business quickly. Kahn and Murphy had experimented with a natural foods format in Mesa, Arizona, called Ceres, and Kahn knew Chris Kilham from his own days of snooping around at Bread & Circus. Kilham had left that job in 1990, and was hired by Fresh Fields as a consultant to develop the new company's "Guiding Principles of Good For You Foods," which, not surprisingly, echoed many of the standards of Bread & Circus: "No synthetic preservatives, artificial colors or flavors. No refined sugars or synthetic sweeteners. No hydrogenated oils, tropical oils, or cottonseed oil. No bleached or bromated grain products. No meats obtained from animals raised with hormones or other growth-promoting drugs. No irradiated foods. No products tested on animals. No phosphates or chlorine in the household products."

In earlier days, when the natural foods industry was being driven almost exclusively on principle by the high-minded idealists, there would never have been enough "good for you" products to fill all the square footage of a Fresh Fields store. But thanks to Sandy Gooch and the other retail pioneers who had come before, the retail product standards had long ago started to become industry standards. And now the market conditions of the eighties and nineties (a mass audience, a distribution network, available capital, a surge in larger retail outlets) had opened the door for plenty of opportunistic manufacturers to help fill those shelves.

Their motivations for entering the natural-product manufacturing business were complex and varied, but in some regard they were all united by their sense of opportunism and good luck.

On one end of the spectrum were companies whose roots were clearly planted in the soils of idealism, albeit fertilized with a sprinkling of capitalism. One was the longtime organic entrepreneur Arran Stephens, whose desire to help regenerate the soil through organic agriculture evoked notes of J.I. Rodale and Paul Keene. He launched Nature's Path in 1985, and it quickly became a recognizable name in organic breakfast foods. Another was Seventh Generation, founded in 1988 by Jeffrey Hollender, who was still very much in *Silent Spring* mode, primarily concerned with the dangers posed by chemicals of conventional household cleaning products. There were also strains of the "save the world" rationale in Amy's Kitchen, the frozen foods company founded by Rachel and Andy Berliner in 1987, after their daughter was born.

On the other end of the spectrum were the energy bar companies, which were created primarily out of a functional need and a strong profit motive. PowerBar was the first major entrant in the category, founded by Canadian athlete Brian Maxwell in 1986, and targeted toward endurance athletes such as bicyclists and ultra-marathoners. The fact that the ingredients were generally considered natural was incidental. In business terms, PowerBar ended up being a sprinter rather than an ultra-marathoner, lasting only 14 years before selling to Nestlé for $375 million. Maxwell walked away with 60 percent of this. Balance Bar followed PowerBar into the market in 1992, developed in part by a champion windsurfer, in an opportunistic response to the dietary principles laid out by Dr. Barry Sears in The Zone diet. It, too, almost seemed to have been created with an exit strategy already in mind. Balance became a big seller in natural foods stores, and 5 years later in mainstream supermarkets, as a sort of "acceptable" candy bar. It, too, was sold in 2000, for $268 million, to Kraft. (Clif Bars, the energy bars created by bike racer and bakery owner Gary Erickson, were in many ways the anti–energy bars. Erickson came up with the idea after his 175-mile long "epiphany ride," when he was wolfing down PowerBars but realized that a more food-centric energy bar would have greater appeal. He launched his company in 1990 using high-quality natural—and later organic— ingredients. "Clif Bar was never just about the money," he wrote in his 2004 book, *Raising the Bar*. "We choose how we define shareholder value, and we include product integrity, our people, the community, and the earth in the balance sheets."[10] Guided by mission-driven principles, as most true natural foods companies were, Clif experienced considerable growth, and within 6 years was up to $10 million in sales. To this day, it remains an independent company, one of the very few left in the natural foods industry.

In between those endpoints were many, many companies whose stories epitomized the opportunism of the era.

There were, for example, those who built a more natural mousetrap. Annie's Homegrown, for one, became a household name after Annie Withey used most of the $15 million proceeds from the sale of her popcorn company, Smartfood, to start a new company in 1989. Her first product—a Kraft Mac & Cheese knockoff called Annie's Shells & Cheddar, in a distinctive purple box with a rabbit logo—was an instant hit in both conventional and natural foods stores.

Coleman Natural Beef was another. The Coleman Ranch, located in Colorado's San Luis Valley, in the high desert of the southwestern part of the state, had been in continuous operation since 1875. It barely weathered the Depression years, and ran into trouble again starting in the late seventies, when the cattle market took a major downturn. Mel Coleman, Sr., a fourth-generation rancher who was the president and chief executive, didn't know what to do, because the company was on the verge of going broke. Then one night in 1979, over dinner, his daughter-in-law, Nancy, who was a student at the University of Colorado, made an observation that struck Mel Sr. "You know, a lot of my friends at school in Boulder are shopping at natural foods stores, and they are looking for meats that have never been raised with hormones." Coleman, though an articulate man who had earned a degree in electrical engineering from Colorado, had, according to his son, Mel Jr., a one-syllable response: "Huh." But, as Mel Sr. would explain many times in the future, he had goose bumps on his arms. An opportunity had presented itself.

The Colemans had always been responsible ranchers, taking care of the land and raising their cattle without implanted hormones; but once their calves were sold off each fall, the animals were out of their control—and, like most others, would be sent to feedlots where they were administered rations mixed with antibiotics in order to bring them to slaughter weight faster. But it had never occurred to the Colemans that perhaps they could retain control of some of their calves, maintain the "clean" antibiotic-free diet on which they had been raised from birth, and then market their product as "natural."

In order to figure out where to sell their natural beef, one of the Coleman boys, Greg, suggested that Mel Sr. take a trip out to California to see Mrs. Gooch's.

"I can't afford to," said Mel Sr., stubbornly.

"You can't afford *not* to," said Greg.

So Mel Sr. bought an airplane ticket, rented the cheapest car he could find, tore some sheets out of the Yellow Pages from a phone booth, and drove around to visit natural foods stores—sleeping in the car at night. At one of the Mrs. Gooch's stores, he ran into Sandy and she told him: "This is exactly what I am looking for!" And all of a sudden, the orders rolled in.

"We started jumping into the back end of the business, the beef side," said Mel Jr., "talking to specialty retailers like Sandy Gooch, Mark Retzloff and Hass Hassan, John Mackey, Peter Roy and Stan Amy. And some of the things that those idealists believed in—as ranch kids, we were just raised with that. They put really good language to what we were just raised doing."

———

There was an entirely different class of new manufacturers who took advantage of the natural foods revolution to introduce truly innovative and exotic new products.

One was Terra Chips, which made its debut in February 1990, at a time when the $4 billion potato chip category was dominated by Lays and Ruffles. Low-oil chips were starting to surge in popularity, but the last true innovation that had come to the industry was in 1969, when Procter & Gamble introduced Pringles—a product made from dehydrated and reconstituted potato dough (the Potato Chip Institute actually filed a lawsuit to try to prevent P&G from calling these "potato chips").[11] On the natural foods store shelves there were also lots of fairly familiar potato chips, like Kettle and Michael Seasons.

But chefs Dana Sinkler and Alex Dzieduszycki had a different idea. The two had been scratching out a living working at Restaurant Lafayette in New York, under famed chef Jean-Georges Vongerichten, doing some moonlight catering in their spare time to make ends meet, before they decided to start their own company. On one catering job, for *Family Circle* magazine, they provided batches of what they called their "root chips"—potato-chip-like slices of exotic vegetables such as taro, parsnip, yuca, and batata, which they bought at the Hunts Point Market. "Alex called me from the party and said, 'We've got to make these things!" recalled Sinkler. "The people were freaking out, asking 'Where can we buy these?'" Within 9 months, Sinkler and Dzieduszycki opened a pilot production facility in Manhattan at John Macy's Cheesestick plant.

They launched the product, named Terra Exotic Vegetable Chips, at Saks

Fifth Avenue. After a short blurb then appeared in the "Best Bets" section of *New York* magazine, they were besieged by calls from the buyers at the gourmet stores like Zabar's, Balducci's, and Dean & DeLuca. Before long they had contracts with stores in 40 states, and were shipping cases to them via UPS (this became a problem because the distinctive black-and-silver film bags they were initially using could not withstand the pressures of altitude, and popped open inside the cargo holds of airplanes). Then in the fall of 1991, one of their salesmen suggested a visit to the Natural Products Expo East in Baltimore. "Why the hell would we want to do that?" Sinkler asked him. As he reflected, "I was naïve about natural foods, but very quickly learned. Wow, what a movement!"

The first major natural foods deal for Terra Chips was with Fresh Fields, which typically sold a bag for $5.99, more than three times the cost of Kettle Chips or Michael Seasons. By 1993 Terra was producing 150 cases a day, on their way to becoming an $18 million company that in 1998 would be sold to Hain Celestial. "It's easy to create product, but it's real hard to sell it," Sinkler said in looking back at the experience. "We were fortunate that people bought our product. There was a demand for it, there was a buzz out there. And I think the packaging itself jumped off the shelf."

Another unusual product introduced during this time period was Oregon Chai, created by a fascinating variant of the self-made man: the self-made tomboy.

Born in the year of the Summer of Love, 1968, Heather McMillen grew up in Portland, Oregon, and Marin County, California, playing sports, uninterested in school, and developing a vocabulary that was both salty and sixties. She discovered chai—a spicy, tea-based beverage—while taking some time off from her anthropology program at UC Santa Cruz and trekking in the Himalayas ("I was on the 6½-year plan in college," she noted in her typical self-effacing way). When she went back to Santa Cruz to finish her thesis on sustainable businesses (focusing on Ben & Jerry's, Rainforest Crunch, and the Body Shop), "there was a dude making chai all over campus and all over town, and I was like, 'Ohhhhhh, so excited.'" But after graduating in 1992, she moved home to Portland to begin a graduate program in urban studies and couldn't find chai anywhere.

She called LiveChai, a Boulder-based company that made the product, and asked whether they would just ship some cases to a retailer in Oregon, "and of course they didn't call me back. I wouldn't have called me back. But I was thinking, 'I just want my chai!'" So she went to Powell's Books, found some recipes, and with her mother, Tedde, decided to start making it herself. "I kept saying to my mom, 'We should just start a business doing this,' only because no one else was and I was desperate for quick, easy chai, from Starbucks or wherever. But I was lying, because I hated business people. When I was in college, [I thought] they were evil. . . . I didn't want to start a business. I just wanted a fucking cup of chai."

After Tedde obtained a business license, she and Heather (who would later take the married name of Heather Howitt) and some family friends formally launched Oregon Chai in 1994, and started making bigger and bigger batches of it, experimenting with different recipes that included "tons of milk and sugar and spices," and utilizing a nearby kitchen as their initial production facility because they had pets at home and couldn't use their own. Heather started driving around town offering samples to restaurants and coffee houses. Many people balked, either telling her they didn't know what chai was, or that her formulation didn't taste like real chai. "It was as if I was selling acid," she remembered. "People were like, 'Get out of here! No, I don't want your stuff.' But I wasn't trying to be authentic Indian chai, but to be authentic in our own homegrown sort of way. Chai-ish. I was just trying to make what I liked to drink."

Fortunately, she was in Portland, and Nature's Fresh Northwest was in the midst of expanding to bigger stores. After a while, she persuaded Nature's to serve the chai in their cafés. It began to catch on, and Oregon Chai gradually built up a roster of about eight food service clients. Heather fully extended her credit cards to keep buying supplies, but good things started to happen. Starbucks came calling, which if nothing else validated the crazy notion that this funky-sounding beverage might make it in the West. Then the buyer at Nature's, Tim O'Connor, suggested that the product might sell well in retail packages, too, so Heather and the team packed some in mason jars and Xeroxed copies of hand-drawn labels . . . eventually graduating to plastic bottles, barcodes, NutriFacts labels, and professional packaging. Oregon Chai moved from a co-packer with a 50-gallon tank to Sunshine Dairy, which had 500-gallon tanks, to Pacific Foods, which could produce 60,000 gallons at a time.

Dwight Sinclair, who had been one of the people behind the growth of Gardenburgers, pitched in, bringing in an advertising agency and suggesting that Oregon Chai begin exhibiting at the Natural Products Expo. The fledgling company did about $200,000 in sales in 1995, and $1 million in 1996. Within a year and a half of its founding—very early for an entrepreneurial company— Oregon Chai had turned its first profit. It moved to a real office in northwest Portland, where the tomboy CEO who had just wanted a fucking cup of chai installed a punching bag and a climbing wall; she would leave each afternoon to go trail running in Forest Park, bringing along her cell phone so she could take calls (and even fire people) mid-stride. Sales grew to $2.7 million in 1997, $6.8 million in 1998, and before long to an amazing $32 million, as it captured 80 percent of the chai category in the United States.

—·—

The age of opportunism was marked not just by opportunists, but by *opportuneness:* From coast to coast, there was a pervading sense of propitious timing, which opened the door for some new ideas that in the past would simply never have had a chance. And nowhere was this more in evidence than the produce department, where all of a sudden the previously unbroken sea of iceberg and romaine lettuce heads that had bored shoppers since time immemorial began to yield to something entirely new: bags of pre-washed organic "baby" salad greens or "spring mix," with a label that came to feature an illustrated sun peeking out from a red "organic" banner, and green letters on top spelling out the name of what soon became a well-known brand—Earthbound Farm.

Even by their own estimation, the people behind this new concept were among the least likely of organic agriculture entrepreneurs.

Drew Goodman and Myra Rubin spent their high school years living a block away from each other on the Upper East Side of New York, an area that a century earlier had been rural farmland, but which by the time they were born in the early 1960s had more or less eradicated the color green from the visual spectrum.

Drew's parents broke up in 1968, and after that he lived with his dad, who ran the James Goodman Gallery on East 57th Street, which specialized in contemporary artists such as Alberto Giacometti, Willem de Kooning, and Roy Lichtenstein. Meals were often prepared by a housekeeper, just fish and steak and the usual fare. "I ate well," said Drew, "but I never thought about how the food was getting here, or how it was produced."

Myra was the daughter of Hungarian and Polish immigrants who were very much taken with the convenience culture of the times and of New York. When Myra was growing up in Brooklyn, before moving away after the seventh grade, her mother, Edith, believed that TV dinners were well balanced; home-cooked meals consisted of minute steaks sprinkled with Accent, and maybe some frozen spinach. Myra can still tick off her customary routines: "Pick up a bagel or a donut on the way to school. Get a slice of Ray's pizza, pick up a sand-wich on your way home. Go out for Chinese." When she cooked dinner at home for the first time with a teenage boyfriend, he had to show her how to slice an onion. Indeed, there was so little fresh food in Myra's life that her favorite thing to eat was the frozen yogurt served in the basement at Bloomingdale's because it came with cut fruit.

Drew and Myra both attended New Lincoln, an experimental private school on East 77th Street, although Drew was nearly 4 years older so they never really knew each other there. They started dating after a Grateful Dead concert in California, while Drew was at UC Santa Cruz and Myra was at UC Berkeley. After graduating, they started living together on a 2½-acre farm in Carmel Valley, selling heirloom raspberries at a roadside farm stand before she was going to head off to grad school. But, even though they knew nothing about farming (the only jobs she had ever held were as a mother's helper in the Hamp-tons, and preparing frozen pucks of cookie dough one summer at David's Cookies), there was something about this life that profoundly affected them. "Living on this farm and watching things grow and tasting food—tasting a ripe apricot or a ripe plum—and learning how to cook with stuff that you grew and harvested, it was such a mind-blowing experience for me," Myra recalled. "There was just this real feeling of total awe and respect for the earth and the soil . . . that touched me so deeply and woke me up, like I never was before. It was a real epiphany."

Myra put grad school on hold—permanently, as it turned out. They even-tually named the property Earthbound Farm, and began producing "baby" greens—tender leaf crops like green oak leaf, arugula, and frisée, harvested before they had matured. Content with the life they had found, Drew bought Myra an engagement ring with small inset diamonds so that she could keep it on her finger while she was farming, and they got married in 1986.

In the early years of their business, it was all about simply finding a way to stay on the farm. Myra was just 20, Drew 23. They grew their greens organically, shoveling chicken manure from the ranch next door to use as fertilizer. They harvested and washed the baby greens using equipment jury-rigged by Myra's dad, Mendek, a jeweler by trade who had a great instinct for engineering and a proclivity for tinkering. They packaged up the greens in the living room of their 800-square-foot house, and mostly sold them in bulk to high-end food service operations and restaurants like the Monterey Plaza Hotel. "We knew every back door of almost every nice restaurant in town," said Myra. Later they began to realize how important convenience was becoming to consumers, and that there was a market for their greens in retail stores, so they attached Earthbound Farm labels with double-stick tape. They grossed no more than $19,000 a year. "We didn't have these delusions of grandeur," observed Drew. "We were just trying to make it work."

Sometimes the reality of their idyllic world came into plain view, especially when they traveled back home and tried, just for a day or two, to resume their place in the social strata of the Upper East Side. On one occasion, they went to a New York Knicks game at Madison Square Garden with some art dealer friends of Drew's dad and their stylish wives. The friends were astonished when they learned that Drew and Myra were working on an organic farm in California. When they spotted some of their other silk stocking acquaintances in the crowd, the friends would hasten them over with big "c'mere" arm motions, and then point to Drew and Myra. "Tell them what you do, tell them what you DO!" they squealed, as if they were friends of Lisa Douglas, Eva Gabor's hoity-toity character on the sixties sitcom *Green Acres,* who was forced to move from New York to a farm in Hooterville.

Still, as the Goodmans sat in their living room enjoying the vegetables of their labors, their thoughts would sometimes drift back to the Upper East Side and they would whisper to themselves: "Could you imagine if we could get this in the City?"

Soon they did. Drew's stepmother hooked them up with Eli Zabar, king of the gourmet store circuit, and they started FedExing boxes of organic spring mix to New York for sale at his E.A.T. store. At one point, Zabar called them at their California home, steaming mad. "Billy Crystal is here and there's a caterpillar in his salad!" They apologized over the phone. Shortly thereafter, Earthbound Farm started printing a message on their labels: "Pre-washed; please inspect before serving."

Organic produce was starting to come of age. In a lengthy 1989 article in the *New York Times,* Marian Burros declared that organic agriculture was "on the verge of changing from a movement to an industry." She noted that the eight-store Whole Foods Market chain now sold 50 percent organic produce in season, up from 2 to 5 percent in 1980, and that big conventional chains like Ralph's (129 stores), HEB (150 stores), and Kroger (850 stores) were all experimenting with organic produce. A 1988 survey conducted by Louis Harris & Associates for Bob Rodale and *Organic Gardening* revealed that 84 percent of respondents would purchase organic produce if given the choice.[12] And production was steadily ramping up. Indeed, 250 miles southeast of the Goodmans' farm, another organic fairy tale was taking form, courtesy of the real-life Brothers Grimm—Rod and Robert—whose Grimmway Farms had created an organic division, Cal-Organic, which was developing a large-scale carrot farming operation that would eventually expand to include many other vegetables.

But Earthbound Farm became the best-known brand in a business whose commoditization and slim margins had seldom ever led to the creation of brands, save perhaps for Chiquita bananas and Dole pineapples. "We *were* the [organic salad] industry," said Drew, although "the ubiquity of Earthbound on the shelf had more to do with the production engine than some conscious execution of a brand strategy." Step by methodical step, the Goodmans were able to seize each opportunity that presented itself. They made smart decisions, were aggressive but pleasant, and stayed true to their brand.

Early on, for example, they expanded their farm operations to the Salinas Valley northeast of Carmel, one of the most productive growing regions in the country, which was nominally closer to San Francisco but culturally even farther away from the world they knew. (Myra still marvels at the memory of it. "New Yorkers in the Salinas Valley! It was like a different species.") By 1992 they were doing about $3 million a year in sales. But even with the additional acreage, they began to have trouble fulfilling the bulk demand for food service, so they turned to a large conventional grower, Mission Ranches, for help. It turned out that baby greens could be produced easily using organic farming methods, so Mission Ranches began to ramp up its organic production, and 3 years later would become an equity partner in Earthbound Farm, enabling Drew and Myra to significantly expand their capacity.

This arrangement had the ancillary benefit of freeing up cash. Rather than having to suffer the cyclical cash-flow problems endemic to farming (invest in equipment and labor months in advance of the crop being harvested), Earthbound was able to take advantage of the equipment and expertise at the big farms like Mission Ranches and later Tanimura & Antle. "We were frugal," said Myra. "We pretty much grew the business when there was money in the left pocket." Their divide-and-conquer strategy was: You guys grow and harvest it, we will wash it, pack it, and sell it.

Then in July 1992, they finally began moving production out of their home, where they had shared one bathroom with all the employees for years, and into a production facility in Watsonville, California. In that same month they attended the annual Produce Marketing Association food service show in Monterey, California. Somehow they found out that Costco was going to be there. The warehouse store was one of the hottest retailers in the country, having grown from one location in 1983 to become a $6.5 billion retailer in 1992. Myra, realizing that her skin was too thin to deal with the inevitable rejection, wishfully told Drew, "Honey, go meet the Costco people and see if they will buy our product." He dutifully obliged, and simply walked right into a cocktail reception attended by the Costco buyers. He never expected anything to come of it. But by January 1993—just after Costco celebrated its 100th store opening and just after the Goodmans celebrated the birth of their son, Jeffrey—a meeting was set up at the new Earthbound Farm office in Aromas, California. The Costco buyers arrived in their buttoned-down clothes; Myra was in her maternity outfit, nursing and burping the baby. Rabbits scurried in and out of the packing shed nearby. The meeting ended and they shook hands, and when the Costco guys had left, Drew and Myra erupted in laughter. "Yeah *right*, we are going to get *that* account!" Myra said sarcastically. But a few weeks later, the buyers called back and began placing their orders: 1,400 pounds for this region, 2,800 pounds for that one. (Interestingly, Costco at first did not want the packages to say "organic" because they thought that word still connoted expense and poor quality, but the Goodmans ultimately prevailed.) It was an event that came to be known in company folklore as "The Costco Catapult," because Earthbound Farm salads became one of the top sellers in the Costco produce departments and have remained there for 20 years. In turn, the Costco deal attracted the attention of other retailers, and led to additional relationships with other farms.

By 1996, 12 years into the venture, Earthbound Farm owned 80 percent of the packaged salad category in the United States and was on its way to becoming a $500 million, 53,000-acre all-organic operation—the largest

organic produce grower—and one of the two or three most important brands
in the natural foods business.

As the natural foods industry gained momentum throughout this era, growing
at a compound annual rate of about 17 percent in the first half of the nineties,
reaching $9.17 billion in sales and more than 6,600 retail outlets by 1996,[13] it
started to attract some very different kinds of people into its ranks.

Some were highly educated entrepreneurs, MBAs like Mark Ordan who
had begun to realize that this unique industry was becoming a white-hot caul-
dron for experiments in the "triple-bottom-line" approach, emphasizing social,
environmental, and economic outputs, or "people, planet, and profit." In effect,
the natural foods industry, perhaps more than any other industry of the times,
was proving that you could not only do well and do good, but that you could do
well *by* doing good.

There was no better exemplar of this than a brilliant and congenial
32-year-old former nonprofit leader named Seth Goldman, who in the waning
days of the age of opportunism created a lightly sweetened beverage as an alternative to Snapple, which he called Honest Tea.

Goldman had grown up in Wellesley, Massachusetts, the son of two prominent professors who were experts on Soviet and Chinese affairs and were frequently involved in local conservation issues. "We had a lot of dinner
conversations not just about world and global issues, but the idea of what can
you do to affect those issues?" he said. He cited a phrase from Jewish liturgy,
tzedek tzedek, meaning that you should do not just righteous work, but do it in
a righteous way.

As a boy, he could hardly contain his abundant intellectual and physical
energy. He ran lemonade stands, had a paper route, played soccer, took karate
and piano lessons, went to Hebrew school, and wandered through the woods on
the Wellesley golf course collecting errant golf balls, which he and a friend
would re-sell at the nineth tee. He studied Chinese and Soviet economic reform
at Harvard, and then spent time teaching in both China and Russia, working on
Michael Dukakis's presidential campaign, serving as an aide to Texas Senator
Lloyd Bentsen, and in 1993 working on a demonstration program called
Summer of Service, a precursor to AmeriCorps. "I saw tremendous idealism,

tremendous passion, and a terrifying lack of real skills," he recalled. "There were people who were really passionate about the idea of service, and had a vision, but no real sense of what it would take to get there."

Goldman thought perhaps he would head into politics or law, but decided instead on the Yale School of Management (SOM) and a career in business, a fateful decision he still thinks about today. "What I have come to appreciate is that social change can happen from different sectors. This has both been the surprise and the delight of my professional life thus far, that where I expected business was going to have to be about compromise and accepting certain assumptions in order to do it, I have been so gratified to see how much we can have convictions in this business and not have to compromise in order to accomplish what we want."

Goldman thrived in the SOM program, especially after taking a course titled Political and Economic Marketing from Barry Nalebuff, a gifted and somewhat eccentric Rhodes Scholar just 7 years his senior. Nalebuff had gained fame among the SOM students for his complex explanations of game theory and his Socratic teaching method, which generated excitement, nervous laughter, and sometimes even tears of frustration. (A few years earlier, the midterm exam in his Individual Decision Making game theory class was so befuddling that it generated a median grade of just 37 out of 100.) "Barry's reputation at Yale had always been that of a cold-hearted, cold-calling, extremely intelligent but not necessarily personable person," observed Goldman. "I was never intimidated by that because my parents were both professors and I was used to lively discussions." Seth and Barry hit it off when Goldman submitted an outstanding proposal to the Yale Business Plan Competition (for, of all things, a urinary tract infection diagnostic), and also when they discussed a case study related to the beverage industry. Thus, it was almost predictable that, after spending the first two and a half years out of business school marketing socially responsible mutual funds at the Calvert Group, Goldman teamed up with Nalebuff to launch Honest Tea, a company they envisioned as being the "anti-Snapple."

By this time, of course, the natural foods industry was well established, so there were a few models to turn to for inspiration. Goldman was particularly taken with Stonyfield Farm, because the company had developed a health-oriented product and brought that to a mainstream audience, all while keeping its mission of supporting the organic farmers intact. Goldman got to know

Gary Hirshberg through the Social Venture Network, and Hirshberg, in turn, was impressed with both Goldman and his idea. "I saw kind of a younger version of me, a smarter version of me," said Hirshberg. "And I thought, 'Gosh, this guy ought to be able to make it.'"

Hirshberg helped, at first with advice and later by investing in Honest Tea. "There was one poignant moment, at the Expo East in Washington," Hirshberg recalled, "where I could see in his eyes—he was raising money now, he was sort of on that treadmill—and I could see a little bit of that 'I'm not sure I know what I am doing' kind of look." Hirshberg ended up making personal and company investments in Honest Tea of more than $6 million. "The idea there was to sort of take him under our wing and see if we could help replicate some of the success we had had. . . . Part of the problem when you are charismatic and have an appealing product is that money gets, I won't say thrown at you, but the avenues for raising capital get presented. And sometimes you are better off being lean and not taking the money. The learnings that you get by gritting it out are much more valuable than getting someone's money, spending it, and getting a little learning. And I was concerned that he was heading down into a vortex where he would ultimately have no ownership. So that was sort of a driving interest to me."

Goldman was also intrigued by Snapple, which had been a regional beverage company when it went public in December 1992, jumping 45 percent on the first day of trading to a market cap of $1.2 billion.[14] "That was sort of the dotcom or the Facebook of the time," remembered Goldman. "Not that it was a product I wanted to emulate, but this was a brand that had emerged as a healthy alternative to sodas. And ironically, Snapple isn't that much healthier. It's the same ingredients without the fizz." Nantucket Nectars was another interesting model, since it had just been sold to Ocean Spray, and Nantucket cofounder Tom Frist, according to Goldman, "had a way to make it sound deceptively not simple, but doable."

Honest Tea launched in 1998, with an order of 15,000 cases from Fresh Fields. "That was the chain that had been successful at taking natural foods and making them accessible and marketable," said Goldman. He had a "Northeast mindset," because even though Honest Tea had aspirations of becoming a national brand, he and Nalebuff had never given any thought to how to build a distribution network. In the Northeast, with everything fairly close together, it wasn't all that difficult; getting Honest Tea into central Nebraska would be a lot harder.

With all of that intellectual firepower, however, it was only a matter of time. Honest Tea ended the first year with sales of about $250,000. The following year it expanded into more Whole Foods and Wild Oats stores, as well as some conventional supermarkets, and hit $1.1 million in sales. Goldman was famously thrifty around the office—using the backs of invoices as fax cover sheets, or stretching payables to the bottle supplier each January to cover potential cash shortfalls—and applied much of his innate restlessness and enterprising mindset to drive the company forward. Soon Honest Tea samples were being handed out at dozens of supermarkets and community events. Honest Tea shifted to all-organic ingredients, became a strong supporter of Fair Trade agreements with growers, and began publishing an annual "mission report" to give an honest appraisal of how well the company was fulfilling its commitments. Honest Tea reached break-even after 6 years, in 2004, and had about $23 million in sales in 2007 before an agreement was reached to sell 40 percent of the company to Coca-Cola for a reported $43 million in 2008, along with a "path to control"—which Coca-Cola exercised in 2011. Goldman told *Inc.* magazine: "Our mission is to democratize organics. The best way to protect what we have done is to make it big."[15]

Another group of newcomers to the industry in the 1990s were the mid-level managers who came from conventional foods companies, bringing with them considerable experience in packaging, marketing, and brand management. In the past, those with conventional foods backgrounds had often been castigated as conventional thinkers by the soapbox idealists of the natural foods community. But as the barriers between conventional and natural began to fall, the new workforce ushered in a fresh set of skills and a level of professionalization that the fledgling industry needed badly. In turn, their desire for analytical tools such as those they had utilized in their Big Food jobs created a huge new opportunity on the natural foods side of the fence. An opportunist was needed to fill the void.

That would come in the person of Paddy Spence, a humble and visionary marketing executive whose corporate brainchild, SPINS—an acronym for Spence Information Services—was as uniquely linked to the opportunities of the era as was the World Wide Web.

Spence had grown up in Cambridge, Massachusetts, where he unwittingly lived something of a natural foods childhood, because his mother shopped at Bread & Circus. "I thought it was normal to come home from school and dinner was steamed tofu," he recollected with a laugh. He graduated from Harvard and eventually earned an MBA from Harvard Business School as well. Hoping to find work for a bicycle manufacturer or a sporting goods company, he would send out 75 or 80 inquiry letters at a time to companies like Trek, Cannondale, and KHS Bicycles. Instead, he landed a job as the VP of sales and marketing for Kashi, a company in La Jolla, California, run by "professional Californians" Phil and Gayle Tauber that made multigrain pilafs and breakfast cereals. Phil and Gayle had bounced from a houseplant business called Plant Pushers to a bodybuilding business called Vince's Gym to the real estate game before becoming vegetarians and starting Kashi. It certainly wasn't the quick payday or path to fame and power that many of Spence's Harvard classmates were pursuing. "I was from the MBA side, but joined the natural products industry before there was money in it, so it wasn't even necessarily opportunistic, it was just luck to find a great job with a growing brand."

The job offer came in late February of 1992, 3 months before graduation from business school, and this left Spence ample time to consider it. He traveled to Natural Products Expo West in March and stopped by the Kashi booth, where they were offering samples of their Seven Grain Pilaf, Seven Grain Sesame, and new Puffed Kashi Cereal. One of Phil and Gayle's kids, 12-year-old Jerra, was dressed up in a giant Kashi box with holes cut out for her head, arms, and legs. Spence thought the whole thing was quirky, but promising, and so he accepted the job and moved to California after graduation.

Over the next couple of years, as Kashi took off, it sold a lot of product into both conventional and natural foods channels. Spence was able to utilize ACNielsen reports to gauge Kashi's success in conventional supermarkets, but there was no such service available for the natural foods stores.

Three years later, in the fall of 1995, he would remedy that problem by starting his own service. The idea behind SPINS was to collect product movement data from distributors and retailers, create reports about market share and category management, and sell these to the manufacturers. Until then, brand managers in the natural foods industry had generally been relying on observation, instinct, and vague warehouse pull reports to figure out how well their products were selling . . . if they even cared.

There were, in fact, many in the young industry—both brand managers and retailers—who rejected the idea of utilizing reports and data as being out of character for their homegrown, dirt-under-the-fingernails little businesses. But as in so many other ways, the rise of SPINS in the second half of the decade demonstrated that change was in the air, and that henceforth things would be different.

Spence moved to San Francisco, hired a couple of key people from ACNielsen, and then marched into a CompUSA store on Market Street with his American Express card to buy $45,000 worth of servers. Over the next few years, SPINS would grow to become one of the most clever and important support companies for the industry, providing metrics about market share, helping retailers to identify leading products around the industry that were missing from their shelf sets, and injecting a data-driven sense of legitimacy that had always been lacking.

Paddy Spence, the quintessential entrepreneur in the industry's age of opportunism, sold SPINS in 2004, and would go on to several other prominent roles in the natural foods industry, including CEO of Zevia, the stevia-sweetened soda that—in large part due to his masterful data analysis and brand building—has become the only top-20 low/zero calorie soda not owned by Coke, Pepsi, or Dr Pepper Snapple. But the data reporting idea was not the most important thing he ultimately took away from his days at Kashi. Many years later, he would marry Jerra Tauber, the little girl in the Kashi box costume at Expo West in 1992. As Thomas Edison once said, "We often miss opportunity because it's dressed in overalls and looks like work."

————•————

The smart money, it is said, stays on the side, but that time had now come and gone. Having witnessed the enormous boost in organic sales that came from the Alar scare in 1989 and the passage of the Organic Foods Production Act in 1990, and now further reassured by the presence of a dominant, publicly traded retailer, the bulls came rushing over from Wall Street.

Because of their anti-establishment roots, natural foods entrepreneurs had long shunned the idea of institutional investments, even while they struggled mightily with cash flow issues; Matt Patsky, who closely followed the industry while working as an analyst at Lehman Brothers, Robertson Stephens, and

Adams, Harkness & Hill, recalled getting a cold shoulder from Ben Cohen of
Ben & Jerry's when he had approached the ice cream maker for help on a report
about the social impact of sustainable businesses: "Oh," Cohen had said, "you
are one of those 'necessary evils.'"

But that was then. Now venture capitalists, investment banks, and private
equity investors began gorging themselves on natural foods, and were welcomed. Hambrecht & Quist, Piper Jaffray, Montgomery Securities, Dain
Rauscher, Merrill Lynch, Bear Stearns, Bain Capital, Goldman Sachs, and
North Castle Partners all began to put their money where the American mouth
was. Patsky sponsored his first Healthy Living Conference in 1996 in an effort
to get the institutional investors comfortable with people like Michael Funk of
the newly merged and publicly traded distributor United Natural Foods, Inc.;
Funk, characteristically casual, came to Wall Street with his ponytail and pur-
ple high-top sneakers. Doug Greene and New Hope put on two financial conferences at the Plaza Hotel in New York that were also extremely well received.
"People left there thinking, 'Wow, this is not the business everybody complains
about,'" said Greene.

The availability of capital helped a lot of manufacturers to expand their production and operations rapidly. It also led to a consolidation movement that in
some ways paralleled what had happened on the retail side of the business, with
Hain emerging as the Whole Foods of the vendor world. Following its purchase
by Kineret Acquisition Group in 1994 for $22 million, and aided by debt financ-
ing as well as equity investments from H.J. Heinz and George Soros, Hain went on
an unprecedented buying spree, purchasing Westbrae, Breadshop, Garden of
Eatin', Arrowhead Mills, Terra Chips, Nile Spice, Health Valley, and Earth's Best,
among others, by 1999. CEO Irwin Simon then spent $390 million to acquire Celes-
tial Seasonings in March 2000, and the newly dubbed Hain Celestial Group continued on with the purchases of Walnut Acres, Mountain Sun, Millina's Finest,
Imagine/Rice Dream, Yves Veggie Cuisine, and companies across the entire spectrum of natural foods products—including, appropriately, Spectrum Organics in
August 2005. Some of these brands Hain invested in heavily, upgrading their
packaging, marketing, and distribution; others it simply took out of circulation,
the better to consolidate an advantage in certain categories. The money was there
to do as they pleased. "Every time I went out and did another deal," Simon told
Inc. magazine in 2002, "I risked the company, because I was borrowing $30 mil-
lion to $40 million. . . . And I always just felt bigger is better."[16]

But as it so often does, the money also had a seamier side—perhaps more so here because many of the founding entrepreneurs were so idealistic and so unschooled in finance. When Terry Tierney brought in outside money for his first natural foods company, Rocky Mountain Natural Foods, he soon found himself getting out-voted on key issues, such as whether to focus on retail or food service. "In raising that capital, we had diluted ourselves out of owner-ship," he said. Similarly, by the time Earth's Best organic baby food was sold to Heinz, founders Ron and Arnie Koss had been squeezed out by investors and were mostly just observers: Arnie was informed on February 14, 1996, by the lawyer representing Heinz that his ownership consisted of only 42 shares of common stock and a warrant to buy 60 more. "It was all plenty of nothing, cleverly disguised as something," he later wrote.[17]

Certainly one of the most dramatic examples was that of Oregon Chai, which Heather Howitt had bootstrapped up from nothing in 1994, mostly on friends-and-family investments, maxed-out credit cards, and a loan from the Small Business Administration. In August 1995, after she set up a small display at the Fancy Food Show in New York, an article appeared about Oregon Chai in *Newsweek*. "Drinking it is a bit like sipping spice cookies," it said.[18] Immedi-ately, the money started flowing in more readily—first $450,000 from the likes of investors at Cantor Fitzgerald, then, in 1999, $4 million from a new invest-ment fund called Sherbrooke Capital, which installed a couple of its officers on the five-person board of Oregon Chai.

The money helped Oregon Chai gain liquidity and expand its business. But there was plenty about the deal that Howitt did not understand. This came to light in 2002, when Mo Siegel of Celestial Seasonings made a "soft offer" of $30 million to buy Oregon Chai. Howitt recalls that one of the Sherbrooke board members said, "Well . . . it's not really $30 million, it's 25. Because you pay us back our 4, plus 10 percent a year. And then our shares convert to common and we get paid again." Howitt had no idea what they were talking about. "I was like, 'Huh? What did they just say?'"

It turned out that Oregon Chai's lawyer had mistakenly included in the orig-inal investment agreement something called "series A convertible participating preferred shares," which give the investors a yearly dividend that goes unpaid until the company is sold, at which point they take priority. The discovery of this clause in the investment contract created some confusion and set in motion a series of events that resulted in Howitt being ousted as CEO and placed on the board instead. "Once you bring in money, things change," said Howitt. "They are going to do what they need to do to protect their shareholder base."

Howitt made out fine in the end, when Oregon Chai was sold to the Kerry Group in 2004 for $75 million—yet another truly amazing example of great wealth being created out of nothing in this industry that until recently had struggled for legitimacy, idling on the fringes of society. But as with so many natural foods entrepreneurs, it was always less about the money than the mission for Heather Howitt. Her wistfulness over it lingers to this day, especially when she stops by the Oregon Chai booth at Expo West, and the employees don't know who she is and can't figure out why this well-informed tomboy businesswoman seems so interested in the mission of the company.

But not everyone is even that lucky. These sorts of Faustian bargains are all too common in the world of venture capital, and have earned it the nickname of "vulture capital." Like Howitt, most CEOs of companies that take on venture capital eventually end up getting replaced; unlike Howitt, some of them pocket nothing in the process. A recent study by professors at Indiana University and Harvard found that the common investors in about half of all venture-backed deals ended up with nothing when the company was sold, even if the sale was for tens of millions of dollars.[19]

Nobody, it turns out, is more opportunistic than Wall Street.

CHAPTER 7

CULT OF COMPETITION

O n Thursday, June 14, 1996, with 6 minutes and 42 seconds left in game four of the NBA Finals in Seattle, Michael Jordan of the Chicago Bulls was called for a double-dribble violation. Jordan was incensed, and got right up in the face of referee Billy Oakes to protest, gesticulating and cursing and furrowing his brow in almost cartoon-like fashion. The outburst was volcanic but brief, as Jordan had already received a technical foul and a flagrant foul earlier in the game, and didn't want to be ejected.

And why, exactly, the Mount Saint Helens reaction? His team, which had won the NBA championship for 3 straight years from 1991 to 1993 before he had taken a nearly 2-year hiatus to try his hand at baseball, was already up three games to none in this series, and was one inevitable win away from another title. They had already set an NBA record for wins by going 72-10 in the regular season. And at the moment of the double-dribble, they were trailing by an insurmountable 23 points. The answer was simple: The competitive nuclear fuel in his inner core had reached the point of meltdown. He just couldn't help himself.

One of Jordan's teammates, Randy Brown, told reporters after the game: "I saw that look in Michael's eyes today. It's one of those looks where you know he is going to come out and try to end it tomorrow. I'd be scared."[1] Jordan didn't end it the next day, but he did lead his team to victory in game six.

Almost from the day he first stepped on a basketball court, Jordan had That Look in his eyes. He was a competitive firebrand the likes of which the game—any game, for that matter—has seldom seen. He led the league in scoring 10 different times, elicited maximum effort and talent from his team-mates, and when games got heated or were on the line, he always seemed to have an extra gear, some miraculous way to rise above the other garden-variety superstars. After Jordan scored a record 63 points in the first game of a playoff series against the Boston Celtics in 1986, Larry Bird—thought by almost every-one at the time to be the NBA's most competitive player, and never one for much hyperbole—said about Jordan: "He is the most exciting, awesome player in the game today. I think it's just God disguised as Michael Jordan."[2]

For Jordan, competition was the very battleground of manhood, whether played out with daily desperation under the white-hot spotlight of a nationally televised basketball game or on the bucolic quiet of a golf course. He was noto-rious for trash-talking opponents during games (he once even did so to Presi-dent Bill Clinton on the golf course, goading him not to play from the closer-in "little girls' tees"), and famously once punched teammate Steve Kerr in the nose during a scrimmage after Kerr had talked back to him.[3]

Jordan was thus in many respects the perfect symbol of an era in which competition in nearly all aspects of American business, especially retailing, was elevated to unprecedented levels of ferocity. Throughout the 1990s, while Jordan was leading the Bulls to six championships, many different retail sec-tors broke out into a bare-knuckled duopolistic brawl, fueled by changes to the Federal Trade Commission's guidelines on comparative advertising in 1979 that had given a green light to naming and even disparaging competitors in advertising. Throughout the decade, Home Depot duked it out with Lowe's, Bed Bath & Beyond with Linens 'n Things, Circuit City with Best Buy, Staples with Office Depot, Barnes & Noble with Borders, PetSmart with Petco, CompUSA with Computer City, CVS with Walgreens, Blockbuster with Hollywood Video, and Walmart with Target. Meanwhile, with all of these "category kill-ers" opening bigger stores and pouring more money into advertising, many old-time retailers still on the scene in 1990, including Abraham & Straus, Caldor, Montgomery Ward, Bradlees, F.W. Woolworth, McCrory Stores, and Hills Department Stores, all quietly disintegrated into the retail dustbin before the end of the decade.

As business became blood sport, many of the leaders of the top companies emerged from the obscurity of the boardroom to become pugnacious capitalist celebrities who penned books on management and entrepreneurship and were regularly feted on the spate of business-centric cable TV shows that seemingly popped up out of nowhere, such as CNBC's *Squawk Box*, MSNBC's *The Site*, and CNN's *Lou Dobbs Tonight*. Jeff Bezos of Amazon, Michael Dell of Dell Computers, Bill Gates of Microsoft, Steve Jobs of Apple, Martha Stewart of Omni-Media, and Jack Welch of General Electric all became as Jordanesque heroes for the Wall Street crowd; among the best-selling business books of the decade were works by CEOs such as Howard Schultz of Starbucks, Dave Thomas of Wendy's, Andrew Grove of Intel, and Michael Eisner of Disney.[4]

There were other CNBC celebs, including management consultants Warren Bennis, Stephen Covey, Tom Peters, Jim Collins, and Peter Drucker, all of whom rode the surging wave of business interest through the nineties. Their business philosophies, often captured in best-selling books and quoted by adoring members of the press corps, both reflected and redirected the changing views on leadership and management of the era. Bennis, a professor at USC whom *Forbes* magazine called "the dean of leadership gurus" in 1996, published three separate books in 1993 and four in 1997, arguing in part that collaboration and authenticity were too often missing from leadership, and, signaling the triple-bottom-line approach, that the next generation of leaders would need to balance economics, ethics, and ecology.[5] Covey's 1989 best seller, *The Seven Habits of Highly Effective People*, focused on aligning one's internal values with a set of "universal and timeless" external principles.[6] Drucker had been lecturing, consulting, and writing about leadership for decades, but in the nineties his beliefs in the importance of a nonprofit-like sense of community, the need for decentralization and outsourcing, and the superiority of corporate culture over strategy all gained new currency.[7]

Meanwhile, all of the capitalist kingpins, and most of the battles in the retail wars, were carefully chronicled by the business magazines, whose popularity also peaked in the nineties. By the middle of 1995, the circulation of *Business Week* was more than 877,000, with *Fortune* (777,000) and *Forbes* (752,000) not far behind.[8] But ironically, the publications themselves fell prey to the very surge in business competition that they were covering, as Americans' fascination with business leaders and excitement over the dot-com boom spawned a whole new set of entrants into the field, including *Wired* (1993), *Red Herring* (1993), *Fast Company* (1995), *The Industry Standard* (1998), and *Business 2.0* (1998).

The country sometimes seemed to be obsessed with business competition in this era, and this was perhaps best captured by that ultimate parabolic microphone of parody, the Fox TV show *The Simpsons,* which debuted on December 17, 1989, and began regularly skewering the competitive consumer culture. In the coming years, it would mercilessly lampoon many of the consumer brands and leaders who came into prominence and battled so relentlessly throughout the 1990s, with spoofs such as Lackluster Video, CostMo, Bloodbath & Beyond Gun Shop, Pest Bye, IPO Friday's, Sprawl-Mart, and Trader Earth's Organic Market. In 1999 *The Simpsons* did a send-up of the decade's ultimate competitive warrior, Michael Jordan—sans furrowed brow. And in 2009 the show featured an organic supermarket called Wellness Foods, where a cashier with tattoos and piercings unapologetically told Marge Simpson that their products spoil quickly.

Facing a transformed mano-a-mano business climate and a cable-come-lately roster of hyper-competitive role models at every turn, the natural foods industry—petri dish of 1960s communitarian principles, 1970s idealism, and 1980s collegiality—contemplated some existential questions. Could mission and values compete with money? Was consolidation unavoidable? As natural and organic foods became more popular, did that inevitably mean that the industry would just become a variant of what it had been fighting against—in effect, Big Clean Food?

So it was that as the battle for retail supremacy and the soul of the industry headed toward confrontation in that tipping point year of 1996, the brilliant, innovative, often combative CEOs of its leading companies, John Mackey of Whole Foods, Mark Ordan of Fresh Fields, and Mike Gilliland of Wild Oats, emerged with That Look in their eyes.

—————

Virtually everyone who has gotten to know John Mackey over the years has come away with a strong reaction of one sort or another—awed by his facile mind, impressed by his literary references, wowed by his philosophical and strategic vision, belittled by his bluntness, surprised by his intensity, confused by what might be called his "serene argumentativeness," put off by his on-the-sleeve libertarianism . . . but most of all, blown away by his rip-roaring competitiveness.

"My initial impression was, '*Man,* that guy is competitive!'" said Michael Funk of Mountain People's Warehouse (later UNFI), when he first attended one of Mackey's annual "sports weekends" at his 720-acre ranch in the Hill Country west of Austin, Texas. "Whether he was playing backgammon or volleyball, you know, he was out to win."

"He is so competitive," said Mo Siegel of Celestial Seasonings fame, who has served on the Whole Foods Market board with Mackey for years. "John just moves forward in all conditions."

"He is as competitive as he could possibly be, and when he decides he is going to make a competitive move, he doesn't hold back," observed Hass Hassan, who rebuffed Mackey's numerous attempts to buy Alfalfa's over the years, but eventually sold his London-based Fresh & Wild business to Whole Foods and has served with him and Siegel on the board since then. "He does absolutely the best that he and the organization can do, and they are great at it."

"Pathologically competitive," laughed Mackey's former colleague, Peter Roy.

Of all of the natural foods pioneers, concluded Chris Kilham, the industry consultant who used to head up marketing for Bread & Circus, "the only one who really wanted to dominate the universe was John."

Craig Weller, one of the cofounders of Whole Foods, said that the hard edge is tempered by a softer side. "John is a very competitive person, but he is also a very loving person. It is hard unless somebody knows him to see that part of him sometimes."

Mackey's will to win certainly springs in part from his upbringing. His late father, Bill, the Rice professor-turned-hospital-management-mogul, "liked to have a nice argument at dinner every night—it was sport," according to Roy, who got to know the senior Mackey well during the many years he served on the Whole Foods board. When he was a senior in high school, John used those debating skills to his advantage, persuading his parents to move to a neighboring town so he could play basketball there after he had been cut from the varsity team at his school. (Basketball has long been Mackey's favorite showcase of competition. At Whole Foods he organized—and often won—fantasy basketball leagues, and he exalted when his hometown Houston Rockets won back-to-back NBA championships in 1994 and 1995—an opening made possible, in all probability, only because Michael Jordan was in the midst of his dalliance with baseball.)

But for John Mackey, the competitiveness is more a case of nurture than nature. For it is apparent to many of those who have watched him over the years that as Whole Foods grew bigger, he became more outspoken and contentious, ultimately transforming into a larger-than-life industry anti-hero who more than occasionally over-revved his fundamentally gentle soul.

Even fun and games could sometimes take an ugly turn. As the company expanded through the 1980s, the leadership network from the stores and central office would get together in Austin each month for meetings, after which they would frequently blow off steam by playing volleyball. But with the CEO on the court, whipping the competition up to a froth, the games got very, very competitive. Mackey simply couldn't stand to lose. When his teammates screwed up, remembered Roy, Mackey would sometimes scream at them. It was just John being John, but the games eventually had to be stopped.

John Mackey has certainly evolved into one of the more polarizing, fascinating, and, in some ways, enigmatic business figures of the modern era. He defies easy categorization, although his detractors—and there are many, including the unions, some competitors (who, according to the *Austin American-Statesman,* "find his cutthroat style at odds with the live-and-let-live image of the industry"[9]), and not a few Whole Foods shoppers who recoil at his increasingly strident political pronouncements—are quick to want to slap labels on him.

Mackey's sometimes cathartic transformation from an intensely private idealist into a conscious and conspicuous capitalist has been well chronicled by hundreds of major media outlets, including *Fortune* magazine, the *Wall Street Journal, 60 Minutes, Fast Company* magazine, numerous books, and, in 2010, in a remarkable article in the *New Yorker* magazine that even in 9,125 words struggled to capture the essence of his curious contradictions. The article's author, Nick Paumgarten, referred to Mackey as "a right-wing hippie," a "crazy uncle" to the Whole Foods team members, "an unrepentant foot-in-mouther, as often a fount of exasperation as inspiration," a "blend of guile and guilelessness [that] is peculiar," and a self-described "philosopher-king" whose stores are like "Mackey's mind turned inside out . . . an incarnation of his dreams and quirks, his contradictions and trespasses, and whatever he happened to be reading and eating, or not eating."[10]

Paumgarten had multiple meetings with Mackey to conduct his interview, and ample time to reflect on him. But in most settings, including the business meetings and negotiations where Mackey has made his mark, people only have one chance and usually have to labor mightily just to keep up with him in conversation. His mind moves too fast, and is wrapped in layers of intellect and

connectivity that linear thinkers cannot easily unravel. He has engaged in public debates with the likes of the late economist Milton Friedman and the jour-
nalist Michael Pollan, and in private debates with—well, nearly everyone he has
met. Stan Amy, who as CEO of Nature's Fresh Northwest got to know Mackey
through the Natural Foods Network—and who is no intellectual slouch in his
own right—said that he always had "challenging conversations" with him. "It
was hard to get on an equal footing." Vincent Fantegrossi, who was the CFO of
Bread & Circus when Whole Foods purchased it in 1992, was surprised at
Mackey's command of financial details. "I remember once he came to the office
[and] sat down with me for an hour, just going over the numbers. . . . He was not
the financial guy, he was the CEO, but he really knew the numbers. I was pretty
impressed with him."

And that is not all that is enigmatic about John Mackey. Although reportedly an atheist, Mackey is a deeply spiritual person who has embraced various
practices and beliefs that mainstream thinkers might brand as wacky. These
have included, at various times, open marriage, Grofian psychological therapy
grounded in deep breathing, a Jesus-channeling philosophy called A Course in
Miracles, a profound belief that a "spiritual cohort" has come together to form
the natural foods industry, and a deep-seated fascination with a "trance channel" named Catherine who had a nice house in the Austin suburbs, two hus-
bands, and declared herself to be doing very important work for the universe.
In a husky voice, Catherine claimed to be "Father Andre," who had personally
taken over the mantle of power from Herakhan Baba, one of the most famous
and legendary of Himalayan yogis. Mackey and his then-girlfriend (now-wife),
Deborah, apparently received several readings from Father Andre and often
brought friends and guests to see her/him. One was Tony Harnett, the CEO of
Bread & Circus, who was told in his reading to "assume your full power and use
your full name," and would henceforth and forever more be known as
"Anthony." According to Chris Kilham, "He went absolutely apeshit when people slipped and called him 'Tony,' which we had been doing for like 15 years, so
it was really hard to adjust."[11]

Kilham himself was invited for a reading by Father Andre in 1990, after he
had left Bread & Circus and was being recruited by Mackey to run marketing
for Whole Foods. "My mumbo jumbo meter was redlining at that point," he
recalled. Kilham had actually known the Herakhan Baba, had met hundreds of
swamis, psychics, seers, and sages during his own travels in Asia, and didn't

believe a word of what he was hearing in Austin. "It was just massive dump-truck loads of total cosmic nonsense," he said, and he let Mackey know his feelings. Not surprisingly, after an otherwise good interview at Whole Foods and an enjoyable weekend of staying with Mackey, eating Mexican food and windsurfing with him on Lake Travis, Kilham awoke the next day, went down to the breakfast table in Mackey's home, and found a note saying that Whole Foods would not be needing his services.

Still, though Mackey's personal and professional beliefs are often inter-twined like a Gordian knot, he brought a remarkable clarity of thought to his business. He alone, or at least well before anyone else, developed the vision of how important the natural foods movement could be and how big the industry could become. In pursuit of this vision, he studied other companies both inside and out of the natural foods industry. According to Doug Greene of New Hope Communications, who often brought industry leaders together for roundtable discussions at the Expos, "John Mackey was always on point. He was always asking questions. He was among the most curious [people] in the room." Though he never earned a college degree, Mackey is exceedingly well read—sometimes digesting a dozen or more books at a time—and has a singular talent for integrating his learning and putting it into action. "Where I could look at a problem and [find] one way to solve it, John's method was to look at it and see six different ways to approach it," remembered his Whole Foods cofounder Craig Weller. "Sometimes that meant we butted heads a lot, and sometimes it forced me to think out of the box more."

Perhaps because of Mackey's often contradictory characteristics (ruthless competitive fire yet profound love and respect for friends; intellectual curiosity yet egalitarian suspicions about traditional corporate structure; innate under-standing of consumer trends yet leftover hippie idealism), Whole Foods was a different kind of company from the very start. Early in Whole Foods' history, Mackey articulated a management philosophy that was centered on the pri-macy of corporate culture and the alignment of incentives (financial and oth-erwise) among all stakeholders in a business. This appealed to the graying counterculture types, as well as to the newer mission-driven entrepreneurial generation, so Whole Foods was able to attract very high-caliber employees.

In Mackey's company, decentralization became not just a form of organi-zational structure but an almost metaphysical moral code. You either believed in it and were in, or you resisted it and were way, way out. All the key hiring and decision-making power was enthusiastically pushed away from the central office and out to the extreme edges of the organization. The bakery team at the Shepherd store in Houston, for example, could make meaningful decisions about the factors that affected them most, including the right to hire people, to give themselves raises, and to vote people out as employees (what Whole Foods calls "team members").

Most Whole Foods team members largely bought into the culture of "empowerment," an evolved variant of the collectivism of the 1960s counterculture and co-op food movement whence it had sprung and one of Mackey's larger contributions to the more enlightened workplace in which much of 21st century business now operates. Empowered workers, the theory went, make a deeper commitment, take more pride in their work, and make better decisions.

With that culture came some unusual practices, such as the right for anyone in the company to access a binder listing everyone else's compensation—which in the Trusting World of Whole Foods is viewed as motivational instead of threatening.

Free speech and free choice were also fundamental aspects of the culture of empowerment. By and large, the teams, stores, and regions made their own decisions and the central office stayed out of it— a clear victory of states' rights. As Lex Alexander, the founder of Wellspring Grocery who had sold his company to Whole Foods and become "The Food Guy," once described it, "At Whole Foods, job satisfaction is defined as being able to do your own thing"— much to his frustration, since he would sometimes encounter stores refusing to sell some of the artisanal private-label products that he had worked so hard to source. At one point in the nineties, Mackey rejected the idea of creating a centralized database of photos even though he knew that each regional marketing director was wasting money by paying to have essentially the same pictures taken of the same products; what the company lost in efficiency, he theorized, it would make back in process, because the marketing directors would all feel like they were calling their own shots, and hence would feel empowered, work harder, be more creative, and stay with the company longer. It was a fascinating philosophy that few traditional businesses or CEOs would ever condone; but at Whole Foods, it worked. On the few occasions when a policy *was* imposed by the central office, it ran the risk of being decried by team members as a "cramdown," and might even be sabotaged by people in the field. For example, when Whole Foods launched a glossy magazine called *Flavors*, which sold tens of thousands of copies, some stores reluctantly accepted their shipments and then put them on display behind the automatic doors, where customers would never see them—simply because they didn't want any centralized program to succeed. And in a very real sense, that was okay with Mackey.

Personnel in the stores would occasionally be very direct and vocal in their criticism of the CEO. On one such occasion, team members in the Austin store that was located directly beneath the Whole Foods central office protested one of his policies by pasting photocopied pictures of Mackey's face all over the shelves of the store. Message received—but the knowledge that there would be such protests had always been part of John Mackey's larger plan.

In the Whole Foods system, the regional presidents were accorded most of the power in the company, since they had control over the budgets. When they locked rhetorical horns with Mackey, as they often did, they usually lost . . . until they invoked the fail-safe argument that Whole Foods is supposed to be all about empowerment.

Rich Cundiff, the strong-willed president of the Southern California region in the mid-nineties, once wrote to Mackey to argue that he should be allowed to proceed with a controversial advertising campaign to help get the former Mrs. Gooch's stores back on track. The stores had operated with the dual name of "Mrs. Gooch's Whole Foods Market" from the time of their acquisition in 1992 up until December 1996. At that point, it was decided, there had been enough time for customers to get accustomed to the new name and the loosening of the original product standards, and the "Mrs. Gooch's" name was removed from all the stores overnight—resulting in an instantaneous drop in sales of 45 percent and a sustained loss of 10 to 20 percent of the business.[12] The customers, according to Cundiff, felt that "this interloper who had conquered Mrs. Gooch was clearly lacking in values, lacking in any sort of ethical background," and for all they knew had slit Sandy's throat and left her to bleed in the back alley. The $1 million radio ad campaign Cundiff was fighting for would shift attention away from that mess, and establish a name for Whole Foods in its own right by making customers lose their appetites for the conventional alternatives. "Baseball, hot dogs, apple pie, and nitrates," read one headline. Mackey wouldn't approve it, because, he said, "Fear campaigns never work." Cundiff was about to lose the battle, until he resorted to the fail-safe plan.

"As a regional president I am responsible for all aspects of the success and failure of this region," he wrote to Mackey on March 17, 1997, "so please allow me to do the thing that I have total conviction about the region needing right now. Many times in the past I have seen you allow your key players to do things with which you disagreed because you respected them, their intentions, and their savvy. . . . Will you please consider allowing us to pursue this campaign with your noted skepticism?"[13]

Mackey acquiesced, but not before making Cundiff bet his raise and bonus that the campaign would generate at least 5 percent comp growth. "He would let you prove him wrong," Cundiff recalled about Mackey, "but you better be right."[14]

The ads ran, the stores eventually recovered their lost volume, Cundiff got his bonus and raise, but the battle would go on, as it does to this day. In March 1999, when another regional president argued for the freedom to run a radio campaign of his choosing, Mackey warned him in an e-mail.

> "[As] a Regional President you have a discretionary marketing budget that you can spend as you see fit. If you wish to spend that on radio ads I won't make a command decision to stop you. . . . [A]t the end of the day you are free to run your own experiments and make your own mistakes (within established parameters). You will be held accountable for the overall performance of your Region. As a General Rule I tend to interfere much more in Regional affairs when we miss a quarter—especially when the main reason we missed the quarter is mismanagement of direct store expenses. I have been thoroughly reprimanded for the first quarter by the Board and I have been beat up very badly by numerous investors. I am not a very happy C.E.O. right now! I will likely be in many people's faces for the next few quarters until we are solidly back on the growth track."[15]

In *The Omnivore's Dilemma*, Michael Pollan described Whole Foods' marketing positioning as the "supermarket pastoral narrative," something he said was both "seductive" and "beguiling." Pollan wrote: "One of the company's marketing consultants explained to me that the Whole Foods shopper feels that by buying organic he is 'engaging in authentic experiences' and imaginatively enacting a 'return to a utopian past with the positive aspects of modernity in tact [sic].'"[16] That surely overstates things. With Mackey opposed to traditional marketing, and the business almost never needing it, Whole Foods has rarely worked on its "positioning," has seldom ever hired marketing consultants or spent any real money on advertising other than to undertake simple activities like sponsoring local road races and making small donations to the communities it serves. The "supermarket pastoral narrative" sounds interesting, but it is a categorization created after the fact by outsiders, not a willful construct of Whole Foods itself.

Indeed, Mackey would probably bristle at the notion of his company expending any effort to create such a campaign, since the very topic of marketing usually brings out the gladiator in him. In the same month that he chided his regional president about radio advertising, he also issued a strategic plan to the entire company, which continued to lambaste the idea of advertising.

> "Ongoing media advertising doesn't work and is a waste of money . . . ," he wrote. "Look at our industry. The companies that spent a lot of money on media advertising all ran into huge G&A problems; the only survivors have been those who have relied on the 'radical' idea of community-based marketing. There are simply no examples of large media advertising spending ever being able to increase sales of any non-startup or non-repositioned store on a sustained basis! Our company has wasted millions of dollars in ambitious advertising programs, which simply haven't worked over the long term and never will."[17]

Of course, as the company grew in size, it only made sense to centralize some programs. Mackey generally resisted this direction, and frequently clashed over it with Peter Roy,[18] but he was always willing to experiment in an effort to find the right balance. He believed that such exercises strengthened the company culture. Indeed, in a striking example of his self-described "dialectical" style, Mackey often deployed a concept he called "thesis/antithesis/synthesis." The idea was that if you allowed two opposing points of view (a thesis and an antithesis) to oppose each other, they might blend together to arrive at a heightened solution (a synthesis). Hence, there were times when Mackey would instruct someone in the central office—say, human resources—to proceed with a plan, and he would also encourage the people in the regions to proceed with a different plan. If they were both passionate supporters of their respective plans, Mackey believed they would produce the best (and sometimes an unexpected) solution.

Thus, despite his better judgment, starting in the mid-nineties Mackey allowed factions within Whole Foods to develop several centralized programs, including produce purchasing, grocery purchasing for "national deals," vendor co-op funding, health care, e-commerce, and some marketing. But there was no grander experiment than 365, the value-oriented private label line launched in 1998. It was the creation of two outside consultants, Denis Ring and Bob Johnson, who approached Mackey and then–Northern California regional president Walter Robb with the idea of creating a company-within-the-company, in order to be sure to send a message to the recalcitrant team members in the field that this was a program they couldn't undermine in their never-ending zeal to "do their own thing." Ring recalled Mackey stiffening up when the proposal to create a separate company was made.

"Why wouldn't you want to work [directly] with us?" Mackey asked.

Ring replied: "We don't want to be employees because I have heard too many horror stories about how decisions are getting made within Whole Foods and how fragmented it is."

Mackey understood, and at a follow-up meeting in November 1997, in the high-ceilinged Whole Foods conference room in the former Hamm's Brewery building in San Francisco, Mackey threw a contract proposal down on the table that would create the entity 365, 52 percent owned by Whole Foods and 48 percent owned by Ring and Johnson.

"Here it is, take or it leave it," Johnson recalls Mackey saying, matter-of-factly.

Johnson and Ring looked at each other. "Well, can we read it first?" Johnson asked, hesitatingly.

"Yeah," said Mackey, "but take it or leave it. If you guys want it, take it; if you don't, well, thanks for coming to see us."

But if Mackey was sounding cavalier, it was just a negotiating tactic. He had thought about the concept extensively, and would soon formulate a strategy for rolling out 365 brand products that would include a mandated plan placing them on aisle end caps in every store. According to Ring, "[this] drove the regional buyers crazy. For the first time in the company's history, their authority over a product that was in the store that they had to carry had been usurped by Whole Foods central for the benefit of the shareholders and for the benefit of the customers." Russell Parker, the national purchasing director, was given the task of going out to the regions to turn around what he deemed their "extreme opposition" to the program. "The regional presidents didn't like it. They thought it would kill margins and dictate prices, shelf placement, and ordering." But Mackey also had a stroke of genius: To gain buy-in and ensure compliance, he aligned part of the store teams' bonus plans with their sales of the Whole Foods private label lines. In effect, thesis/antithesis/synthesis: He wanted to make 365 a program the stores would fight for, not against, and perhaps even work to improve.

The 365 program went on to become a game-changer for Whole Foods, softening its "Whole Paycheck" image and giving it a weapon to use in its growing competition with Trader Joe's. It also made a lot of money for everyone involved, including the manufacturers of the products. Years later, in 2002, when internal jealousies forced Mackey to engineer a buyout of Ring and Johnson by Whole Foods, the CEO invited them to his house and thanked them for all they had done. "I don't want to buy you out," Ring recalled Mackey saying. "You guys have added huge amounts of market capitalization to the stock of Whole Foods, and you have made millions of dollars for me personally. I would love to leave you guys exactly as it is, but I can't." They soon parted ways.

Whether it was programs like 365, the smooth integration of acquisitions, or just his ability to attract great people and then delegate meaningful work to them, Mackey emerged as one of the most important CEOs and business philosophers of his time.

"I give John Mackey an awful lot of credit for building a culture and an organization that empowered people but demanded excellence," said Barney Feinblum, who has interacted with Mackey many times over his long career with Celestial Seasonings, Horizon Organic, Alfalfa's, and others. "He wanted to treat people well, but create financial incentives. John grew up in a very financially sophisticated family. He understood business very well. He probably rejected it, like many of us, when we went off to school and tried to find an alternative, but I think he always understood that discipline and skills were required to be successful because it's a competitive world out there and you've got to be good to win."

———

While John Mackey was in the midst of his alchemic organizational experiments, building Whole Foods Market from a single health foods store into a public company, a national brand, and an icon ultimately worthy of Simpsonian satire, Mark Ordan had turned up the flame to "high" under Fresh Fields. From its first store opening in Maryland in 1991, the company had grown out and grown up, and by the end of 1995 operated 20 stores that were generating $213.6 million in sales—a little bit less than half the size of the 15-year-old Whole Foods Market, and rapidly closing the gap.

Some of this could be attributed to the execution of Leo Kahn's original concept. Fresh Fields COO Jack Murphy, who had worked with Kahn since 1979, called him "a real retailer's retailer," a "fanatically driven individual [and] brilliant visionary . . . for whom no detail was too small." Mark Kiriakos, who worked as a meat buyer under Kahn, remembered one occasion on which Kahn had discovered a missing shopping cart miles down the road from his store and towed it back with his left arm sticking out of his slow-moving Mercedes-Benz. "He held up traffic to retrieve this $200 shopping cart," said Kiriakos, "and I went and looked later and saw that it had really scratched up the door of his Mercedes. That was Leo. He didn't care."

Though he had two Ivy League degrees, including a master's in journalism from Columbia, Kahn had devoted his life to retailing and put his entire career's learning to use in creating Fresh Fields. Murphy said that Kahn had first articulated his vision after carefully studying the health foods stores and then Bread & Circus; he then figured out where that path would lead. The answer was Fresh Fields: the natural evolution of the earlier concepts, done on a larger scale, in which he opened up the look of the stores, added some conventional twists, but still hewed to a mission and a rigid food philosophy.

However, by the time Kahn had brought Murphy and Ordan together to begin working on the Fresh Fields concept, in 1990, he was already in his seventies and had grown curmudgeonly and difficult to deal with; and once the stores were open, his role was never clear. He walked up and down the aisles of each store taking notes on a pad, constantly fussing with merchandising details. He clashed with Kathy Sklar Ordan on what tone the advertising should take. And it was his ill-advised push to open hastily in Chicago (he was afraid of replaying the scenario from Staples, when a lack of growth had inspired a disaffected board member to split off and create Office Depot) that spread the company too thin.

Mark Ordan smiled at the memory of how on one occasion, Kahn was meddling in everyone's business and they couldn't wait to get away from him. As luck would have it, Kahn had to return to Boston for a week to attend a wedding, and as Ordan walked him out to his waiting cab, Kahn turned to him with his piercing blue eyes, stopped in his tracks, and said, "Maybe I shouldn't go."

Ordan recalled: "If I had gone back inside and told people Leo was staying— we had just had enough!—they would have lynched me. I said, 'What do you mean? You're going to a wedding! You're going to have such a nice week! You'll eat clams! It's fabulous. You'll go.'" And then, to convince him that it was okay, Ordan told him, "'Leo, if anything big happens, I am not going to make any decision without calling you.' And he looked right at me with those eyes of his and he said, 'Mark: I am not worried about the big things. The big things we all get together, we talk about it, and we make decisions. And if we make a mistake, we'll fix it. I worry about all the *little* things that people don't stop to think about. You make those decisions and you wake up one day and say: How the hell did we get here?'"

Ordan was amazed. But then Kahn got in the cab and Ordan breathed a big sigh of relief. "It's really one of the greatest management things I have ever heard," he later acknowledged.

Not long after that, Kahn, growing disenchanted and wanting to cash out, sold his shares of Fresh Fields to The Carlyle Group.

Left to their own devices, Ordan and Murphy hit the accelerator hard. Maybe too hard. They opened stores faster than any other retailer in the natural foods industry had ever done, sometimes with spectacular results—a relocated Rockville, Maryland, store averaged $497,448 a week for its first month in 1994— and occasionally with some clunkers. They began experimenting with all kinds of ideas, often changing course without slowing down—a maneuver that became known within the corporate office as "doing U-turns at 55 miles an hour," and which in many ways was the manifestation of the young CEO's mercurial nature, lack of industry experience, and turbo-charged gear-shifting mind.

For example, Fresh Fields opened a store in Richmond, Virginia, on Valentine's Day of 1993, and closed it on November 1 of the same year after a strong response by the local conventional supermarket chain, Ukrops, and after persistent media reports about how a Coleman Beef sample from the Fresh Fields store showed traces of the antibiotic dihydrostreptomycin. (No other Coleman samples taken from Fresh Fields stores tested positive, and Ordan later learned through FDA Commissioner David Kessler that the sample had likely been tampered with in the laboratory; he speculated that it may have been by supporters of the conventional beef industry who were upset at Fresh Fields' "just say no" radio ad.)

The company veered from one advertising strategy to another, switching from radio to newspaper to direct mail and back, burning through four marketing directors in 5 years. Ordan added a group of "crossover products" to the shelves—items like Cheerios, Hellman's Mayonnaise, and Snackwell's. This program was reminiscent of Lex Alexander's "supermarket legends" at his Wellspring stores in North Carolina, but the Fresh Fields items were marked with signs that were the equivalent of a skull-and-crossbones, warning customers that these products didn't meet Fresh Fields' standards but had been added for their convenience. In 1995 Ordan then pushed through a major campaign to lower prices in the Chicago market (followed quickly by other markets), with ad copy that read, "Ever since we came to Chicago, you've said everything about us was out-of-this-world. Little did we know, that included our prices." Mary Kay Hagen, Whole Foods' Midwest regional president and the ex-wife of John Mackey, told *Supermarket News,* "They're moving into more of a conventional niche."[19] But she missed the point: Fresh Fields had always been in more of a conventional niche.

All of these moves were attempts to try to tweak the model, to find the right formula and the systems that would reverse the more than $30 million in losses the company had absorbed in its early years. Because although it had been born out of opportunism, Fresh Fields always had attracted employees and customers who believed deeply in the mission of bringing "good-for-you foods" to the world, and wanted desperately to see it succeed. The good news was that the top line continued to grow, as Fresh Fields expanded into new markets and opened stores at a furious pace. It also got better and better at food procurement, with more organic items, excellent all-natural bakery and seafood departments, and a new prepared foods program developed by Washington restaurateur Nora Pouillon—who in 1979 had opened the country's first organic restaurant, Restaurant Nora, supplied in part by prime cuts of meat from Walnut Acres.[20]

But the company seemed to lack the clarity or vision or discipline to translate these moves into profitability, as Whole Foods had done on its own and then with its acquisitions. "It was never a question about the concept or the team or what we were doing," said Jack Murphy. "Because you could see from the volume, sooner or later we were going to get the profitability right." He recalled Howard Schultz, the Starbucks CEO, telling the rest of the Fresh Fields board: "Look, we have a big idea here. And we have a great company, a great management team. This is the beginning struggle. We are ultimately going to get the management of all these things right."

Perhaps no single event better illustrated the lack of clarity for the organization than a focus group held on a foggy night in May 1995 in Potomac, Maryland, to gauge customers' reactions to the forthcoming addition of crossover products. While Ordan, Murphy, and members of the marketing team watched from behind a two-way mirror, a facilitator led a group of eight customers through the concept—and one by one, they all soundly rejected it as a betrayal of the principles for which they felt Fresh Fields stood. As Murphy recalled, "Mark was getting hotter and hotter and hotter," feeling that the facilitator was not doing a good job of communicating the rationale for the program. Suddenly, he couldn't take it anymore. "Mark burst into the focus group room and just started convincing people that no, what you are saying is not really what you should think. He blew the entire focus group to smithereens," and persuaded each of the focus group participants that crossover products were okay. Such was his passion and undeniable personal charm. But when he returned back to the observing room, one of the marketing people said, "*Great.* Now can you do that with each of our other 2 million customers?" According to Murphy, "I think that is the anecdote that demonstrates Mark's management style. If there was a poster child performance, that was it."

Ordan worked around the clock, and for better or worse surrounded himself with other type A personalities who responded to his expansive and quicksilver personality. Typical of early-stage, fast-growth companies, Fresh Fields thus developed an imbalanced culture, slanted dangerously toward all work and no family life. Executives and store managers almost always worked on the weekends; new employees earned no vacation days until their second year on the job.

With his trenchant wit and a mind that awaited openings in conversations like a spring-loaded trap, Ordan also developed an unusual didactic leadership style that was by turns tricky, instructive, and humorous.

On one occasion, he summoned produce buyer Craig Bishop to his office and held out two tomatoes, saying that he couldn't understand why the one he had picked up at Trader Joe's seemed better than the one he had bought at Fresh Fields. Bishop weighed the two, sniffed them, cut into them and tasted them, and did his equivocating best to come up with an explanation. "Actually, I bought them both at Fresh Fields," admitted Ordan. "I just wanted to see how confident you were in the tomatoes you were selling." It was, perhaps, an unwitting page out of the playbook of his hero, President Franklin Delano Roosevelt, who according to Ordan "had a lot of very brilliant people around him, but they weren't sure where he was going with things."

On another occasion, he confronted the cheese buyer, who had been caught rifling through papers in Ordan's office.

"You have two choices," said Ordan sternly. "You can tell me why you were going through those papers, or you can be fired."

The flustered buyer told him he had wanted to get some information about who the board members were.

"Great," said Ordan, "thank you for coming clean. You're fired."

"What do you *mean*?" the buyer protested. "I thought you said I could tell you or I could get fired!"

"I didn't say those were the *only* two choices," said Ordan.

At times Ordan was manic, frantically checking his watch in the middle of a meeting only to realize that he was supposed to have picked up his daughter, Jackie, from preschool 10 minutes ago; the meeting would then go mobile, with an executive or two packed into his Audi as he sped off. At other times he was incredibly patient, displaying his deeply caring and supportive nature by helping coworkers with personal or medical problems, and, after the tragic suicide of the head of the Fresh Fields bakery in December 1994, continuing to pay a salary to his widow for more than a year.

———

Whole Foods and Fresh Fields and their two iconoclastic leaders had eyed each other warily from the start. As the consummate company of the high-minded idealist era, Whole Foods realized that Fresh Fields presented a more vexing problem than other competitors. For although they derided Fresh Fields as a "command-and-control" company, Mackey and his team knew that the threat it posed as a shrewdly engineered, Wall Street–backed, marketing-driven, opportunistic, capitalistic company was not just competitive; it was existential.

"The Fresh Fields thing was different," said Peter Roy, who served as president of Whole Foods from 1993 until 1998. "Mark Ordan was not somebody that came up through the same root system that we came through. He was a Goldman Sachs investment banker that teamed up with Leo Kahn, whom we certainly had known. When Fresh Fields came on the scene, we knew that this was a very different animal that we were going to be dealing with. . . . Clearly there was a level of professionalism and a level of capital that had been brought to bear that the industry had never seen before. The whole thing got John's competitive juices just going insane."

The real competition between Whole Foods and Fresh Fields had begun in Chicago.

Whole Foods got there first, with a beautiful, bustling store on North Avenue on the edge of the city's Lincoln Park neighborhood, with wide aisles, a huge produce department off to the side, and a mezzanine-level restaurant named the Quixotic Cafe. The lease had been secured a week after the purchase of Bread & Circus, in the fall of 1992. Whole Foods VP of real estate Jean-Claude Lurie had urgently summoned Mackey and Roy to go from Boston to Chicago so they could sign the lease the next day. They flew into O'Hare International Airport, rented an Avis car, and in order to avoid construction on the Kennedy Expressway, took North Avenue in from near the airport, through about 15 miles of combat zones and housing projects.

Roy, usually gentle and mild-mannered, was beside himself.

"I cannot believe you got us on a fucking plane to come and see this place!" he yelled at Lurie before the Avis doors had slammed shut.

"What are you talking about, what you are talking about?" asked Lurie.

"Jean-Claude, we just drove in for 15 miles and I haven't seen anybody who would shop at a Whole Foods even if the food were *free!*"

It quickly became clear that Roy and Mackey had taken the "scenic route" and had not gotten a true feel for Lincoln Park. The landlord drove them around the rest of the neighborhood, densely filled with gentrified brownstones and yuppie-occupied lofts, and they shook hands on a lease by 1 p.m. A few months later, on March 29, 1993, the Whole Foods Lincoln Park store opened and immediately became a winner, averaging $248,000 a week in sales in its first 3 months, and topping its year-two $13 million projection before the end of year one. More importantly, North Avenue proved that a store like Whole Foods could thrive in an urban environment. "That store changed the trajectory of the company," said Roy.

Fresh Fields wasn't far behind, with stores in suburban Palatine, Illinois, and Naperville, Illinois, that both opened on July 9, 1993. Kahn had led the charge for expansion into Chicago, and in one respect, at least, it made good sense, since the Bluhm family—minority owners of the Chicago Bulls—were among Fresh Fields' investors.

But the rapid move into Chicago made Ordan and COO Jack Murphy uneasy. They knew that expansion would greatly stretch the company's cash. Fresh Fields' centralized management structure would test their logistical ability to train employees, oversee operations, and deliver goods to these remote stores. Stow Mills, their primary distributor, was based in New Hampshire and did not have established routes to the Midwest. Moreover, Palatine and Naperville were ho-hum locations in questionable suburban outposts that lacked the density of the highly educated consumers who had driven the company's success in places like Rockville and Bethesda, Maryland. (Whole Foods, watching keenly from a distance, scoffed at the Illinois site selections, and realized that for all the things that Fresh Fields was doing consistently well, real estate was not among them.) Still, the stores opened reasonably strongly, with first week sales of $360,000 and $315,000, respectively.

Just as those stores were opening, however, a unique site with much greater potential became available on Ridge Avenue in the town of Evanston, Illinois: an original General Motors dealership, most recently operated by Toyota. Ordan loved it, sent his real estate team over to check it out, and decided he wanted to move ahead with it. The only problem was that Whole Foods also had its sights set on the location.

The landlord set up meetings with both companies on the same day, Fresh Fields first, Whole Foods second, probably thinking he could play them off of each other. Ordan found out about this schedule and hatched a scheme. On the appointed morning, he phoned the landlord to apologize that his plane had been delayed; he would come by in the afternoon. In truth, he was already in town. He then drove to the site and sat in a rental car across the street, read a book, and watched while Mackey arrived for his meeting. Shortly after Mackey left, Ordan went in for his meeting, topped the Whole Foods offer, and got the site.

It was game on for two fierce competitors and the paradigms they represented, and it only escalated over the next couple of years, as the media, always eager for war reportage, jumped in with snarky truculence. "Tofu Fight!" the *Chicago Reader* declared in a 6,200-word article that detailed each company and chronicled the devastating impact they were having on local health foods stores. "You can sum up their in-store personalities by the on-hold music," observed *Brand Week* magazine. "Call Whole Foods headquarters and they're playing Lyle Lovett; call Fresh Fields and it's Kenny G."[21]

The Fresh Fields store in Evanston opened in May 1994 with $372,000 in

weekly sales. Another new store, on Elston Avenue just a mile from Whole
Foods' North Avenue location, opened a month later. Ordan—a World War II
buff—had his team prepare an aggressive marketing plan that was laced with
martial language and images. Whole Foods, in due course, soon announced its
own location for Evanston, and several more in the Chicago area.

Now it was 1995, and a wild card emerged out in Boulder: Hass Hassan of
Alfalfa's was ready to sell his business. His former partner, Mark Retzloff, had
long ago left to create Horizon Organic Dairy, and Alfalfa's was getting to the
point at which it needed new blood in order to keep growing. "I don't think at
the time I was one of those people that had the desire to say, 'Okay, I want to go
out and raise public money and build an organization that competes on that
level,'" Hassan recalled. "I wasn't that enthralled about it, wasn't motivated to
do that. I like the business a little smaller, I guess. I like the creative phase and
not the organization phase, not the 'let's do 100 locations' phase. Not my skill
set. Not my passion."

Since Alfalfa's and Wild Oats were located in the same town, and since the
always-enterprising Mike Gilliland had proven to have an appetite for acquisitions, it only made sense that Hassan might sell to him. Of course, a hard-
charging Wild Oats to the west and a fast-growing Fresh Fields to the east
threatened to open a two-front war that Whole Foods probably couldn't win, so
John Mackey continued to pursue a merger with Alfalfa's, even well into 1995
when it was widely rumored that an Alfalfa's–Wild Oats deal was near.

But Mackey also had a plan B.

Mark Ordan, it turned out, was not the only military buff. Mackey had
seemingly internalized the strategies of *The Art of War* and figured out how to
apply them to modern-day retailing. And so, in a brilliant strategic move,
Whole Foods identified two sites right in Fresh Fields' backyard, in the Georgetown neighborhood of Washington, DC, and in Arlington, Virginia. If
approved, the stores would open up under the Bread & Circus Whole Foods
Market name in early 1996, and could deliver a bruising hit to Fresh Fields'
comp store sales in Rockville and Bethesda, Maryland, which might have the
effect of delaying or canceling the much-rumored IPO and perhaps bringing
Fresh Fields to its knees—maybe even to the bargaining table.

The Georgetown store, in particular, was a great site, but the build-out would be exceedingly expensive because of a café, an underground parking garage, high labor costs, and other factors. It looked like it might take $7 million to $8 million, two or three times what Whole Foods usually spent on a new store. Mackey had to sell it to his board members, who were shocked at the price tag.

"It doesn't matter how much we spend," Peter Roy remembered Mackey protesting. "It doesn't matter if this store itself is profitable, if we end up getting Fresh Fields."

By this time, Goldman Sachs owned about 40 percent of Fresh Fields, and there were certainly people there who saw things the other way: Whole Foods might be ripe for the picking. Their stock had dipped as low as $10.50 a share and was languishing. Another possibility was the Fresh Fields IPO. But the team at Goldman Sachs also knew that Fresh Fields had some bad sites in its portfolio, and that the company was burning through a lot of cash; a sale to Whole Foods might be the quicker path to liquidity. There had even been some back-channel communications between Whole Foods and Goldman, as the former tried to establish an investment banking relationship; news of this, of course, got back to Ordan.

So, unsure of which course to pursue, Ordan contacted Mackey and requested a meeting in mid-1995. The purpose was simply to talk and explore various possibilities. Ordan flew to Austin on a Saturday and met up with Mackey at the Whole Foods office on Sixth and Lamar. It was dark, and there was no one around.

At first the meeting was cordial but cautious, two prizefighters dancing slowly about the ring in the first round, sizing up the opponent. Then Ordan excused himself to go to the men's room. Mackey followed.

"You know," said Mackey, as they walked toward the urinals, "if you ever buy this company, there will be nothing left of it when you get here."

Ordan paused for a millisecond, startled, staring at Mackey, perhaps thinking back to the scorched earth policies of Joseph Stalin and Albert Speer that he had read about in his books on FDR. He realized that Mackey had gotten it all wrong, and was fearing that Fresh Fields and its powerhouse board might somehow attempt a hostile takeover. Always quick on his feet, Ordan smiled demurely and joked, "Why didn't you tell me that before I came down here? I could have saved a day of flying."

Ordan reported back to Goldman Sachs that Mackey wasn't interested. But this set in motion a series of tit-for-tat moves behind the scenes. Mackey sold his board on the idea of over-spending on the two new stores in Fresh Fields' backyard in order to force his rival to the negotiating table on his terms; Ordan retaliated by dispatching Maurice Kreindler, his head of real estate, to Austin and Dallas to set up a relationship with the most prominent commercial real estate brokers in town, ostensibly to begin looking for store sites there, but really just as a warning. And sure enough, it took no time at all for that news to reach the Whole Foods central office. Ordan also hurriedly signed a lease to create a new store in a second-rate location in the Tenleytown section of Washington, DC. His hope was that Tenleytown might steal a little bit of the thunder from the opening of the Whole Foods store in nearby Georgetown, though Ordan also joked that perhaps the only way to derail the Whole Foods grand opening would be to drive a car to the entrance of its parking garage and yank out the distributor cap.

At the same time, Fresh Fields' cash situation grew tighter. It had opened up a line of credit with a bank but was "on the edge," according to Ordan. Neither Goldman Sachs nor The Carlyle Group, the two largest shareholders, wanted to put in any more money. Ordan could have gone out and raised additional capital through new investors, but that would have been dilutive to the original shares, and nobody wanted that. Ordan and his board continued to discuss the one possible plan for salvation, an IPO, and held some preliminary discussions with William Blair & Company, Goldman Sachs, and Montgomery Securities. But with the uneven collection of stores, there was no real confidence that Fresh Fields had gotten the model right, and therefore no real guarantee that Wall Street would react favorably to the IPO.

Fresh Fields rushed through the construction of the Tenleytown store, which opened on January 5, 1996, amid a blizzard that more or less shut down the city for several days. The store recovered and averaged $374,000 a week in sales for the first month, a very solid number. But by the end of that month, the much bigger and better located Whole Foods store in Georgetown opened to much acclaim and nearly identical sales numbers to Tenleytown; and then the beautiful Whole Foods store in Arlington, Virginia, opened on February 29 with another $370,000 in average weekly sales.

And in the midst of it all came the long-awaited announcement from Boulder: Alfalfa's and Wild Oats would join forces by July. This would create a company of 39 stores and $260 million, leapfrogging past Fresh Fields and closing the gap with Whole Foods considerably. Moreover, it was widely reported that the combined company, under the Wild Oats name, would be filing with the Securities and Exchange Commission to announce a public offering later that year.

The Fresh Fields board took notice of all these developments and realized that their company was not easily going to be able to compete. So a few weeks later, when John Mackey—the idealist turned capitalist—called Mark Ordan—the capitalist turned natural foods impresario—and said he would like to meet to discuss buying Fresh Fields, they were all ears.

Ordan was not surprised—in fact, he was a bit relieved. He knew that this might be a way to satisfy the needs of the increasingly impatient capital on his board, and also preserve most of the jobs in the company. They met halfway, at a United Airlines conference room at O'Hare International Airport (not far from Chicago Stadium, the home of the Chicago Bulls, where the John Mackey of the NBA played), and serious negotiations got underway.

Ordan brought with him the sales volumes and square footages of each store, and said to Mackey, "Tell me what you can pay."

Mackey looked his rival squarely in the eyes and asked, "But am I wasting my time? Because I know you don't want to sell. You're like me."

"I'm not like you," Ordan replied, aware that his personal feelings about the deal mattered little. "I have shareholders [direct investors on the board]. It's up to them."

Mackey seemed surprised. He had thought that his rival shared his never-accept-defeat ferocity. He also knew that Fresh Fields was a young company that had simply been too impatient to work out its kinks. When they were talking about the deal, Ordan later reported, Mackey told him, "I can't believe your company is actually selling because you have so many stores that are so immature."

Ordan remained steadfast in his belief in Fresh Fields, but was also painfully aware of his mistakes. "We just grew too fast," he said in retrospect. "[I]f we had grown in Washington and New York [instead of expanding to Chicago], I think Whole Foods would have sold to Fresh Fields. But we were spread very thin. I always thought that we would out-compete them. . . . We were in many ways better than Whole Foods. Our good stores were better. Our Greenwich store was better than anything they had. Our Bethesda store was better. . . . Our produce department was better than theirs. Our seafood did a better job. But the history of Fresh Fields was that we pushed it very, very hard, and we grew very fast. . . . If you take the accumulation of the good things that we did, and the bad things that we did, in the short time we did it, it made it very tough."

The game was nearing an end. Before long, Whole Foods came back with an offer that was too good to turn down: $24 to $28 per share (depending on the fluctuation of Whole Foods' stock price prior to the closing of the sale), amounting to more than $134 million, to purchase a company that had never earned a dime of profit. The deal was struck, in secret, and concluded within weeks. And on Tuesday, June 18, 1996—one week after rumors of the sale had first surfaced at the Fresh Fields Naturals softball game at Broome Park, and just 2 days after Michael Jordan had earned his fourth championship in 6 years—it was announced to the world.

Although Whole Foods had gradually evolved into the hippie hero of Wall Street, and Fresh Fields into the respected East Coast beacon of the natural foods movement, the deal was viewed by many within the industry as a singular victory for mission over money. As *Conscious Choice* magazine publisher Jim Slama wrote, "[I]n this first real competition between traditional natural products retailers and mainstream industry, the natural products industry won out."[22] John Mackey's daring real estate strategy won the day, and to close observers it was apparent that the entire Whole Foods culture of decentralization, mission, and empowerment had been vindicated. It could, in fact, compete with the best that Wall Street and Harvard Business School had to offer!

And yet, this was that most cliché of mergers in which there really were no losers. Almost all of the approximately 3,000 Fresh Fields employees kept their jobs, and went on to work for a company that would soon regularly be named one of *Fortune*'s "100 best companies to work for," while also crashing the Fortune 500. Ordan and Murphy both walked away with a big payday, but more importantly, as Murphy reflected, "I think I hit the lottery in an accomplishment sense. To start with nothing, no stores, no people, two guys in a room at 654 Madison Avenue, and to have built that over a five-year period to twenty-five stores doing $300-plus million? And although it is under a different name . . . the real guts and principles endure to this day? I absolutely think that I won." Meanwhile, Whole Foods would work hard to absorb and learn from Fresh Fields' expertise in technology, merchandising, marketing, and flat-out gumption. And, stripped of some of the inflated overhead and wasteful changes of direction, which had resulted in a net operating loss of $6.5 million in 1995, the Fresh Fields stores would quickly become profitable and build Whole Foods' new Mid-Atlantic region into a dynamo.

There would be some work ahead to blend the companies and cultures together (a fact that was never more evident than on the day when Whole Foods CIO Carl Morris showed up at the Fresh Fields office in Rockville, Maryland, in his customary ponytail and flip-flops to meet his counterpart, the deadpan, square-jawed, consummately professional Bruce Fleegal; the two eyeballed each other from head to toe at the reception desk, and then broke out into laughter). But the merger went smoothly, and with it, John Mackey's gradual metamorphosis from idealist to capitalist was now complete. This was precisely the event that was needed to move the industry out of the age of opportunism and into a new as-yet undefined era in which the lessons that had been internalized over decades of struggle would now be externalized—transforming other industries and, in small but important ways, even American society itself.

———

With Fresh Fields out of the way, the combined Wild Oats–Alfalfa's company was left as Whole Foods' chief nemesis within the natural foods industry.

It was not at first clear what kind of a competitor the new Wild Oats would be. The merger had paired the light-hearted, hyper-casual, throw-caution-to-the-wind Gilliland— whose office, according to *Natural Foods Merchandiser*, was "a study in chaos" including "a carelessly folded nylon sleeping bag tossed in one corner"[23]—with the cerebral, meticulous, quality-focused Hassan. Many insiders wondered whether perhaps they weren't the Oscar Madison and Felix Unger of the natural foods industry. Hassan himself later acknowledged that it took him "maybe a day" to determine that he wasn't interested in a subordinate management role, and that he didn't really enjoy the push to make money for money's sake. But he stayed on for a while, out of loyalty to the people who had helped to build Alfalfa's.

The rivalry heated up in the fall of 1996, when Wild Oats went public, but in the inner circles of Whole Foods, the Boulder company was seen more as an annoyance than a credible threat. Wild Oats' real estate was second rate, its operations were lacking, and Mackey simply could not brook a company that built its business model around imitation instead of innovation.

Still, in need of a new competitive foil, John Mackey found one in Mike Gilliland, the baby-faced 38-year-old CEO of Wild Oats who had ridden opportunity hard for a number of years. Though the two men seldom met, they squared off in a playful and slightly edgy behind-the-scenes tussle. Gilliland acknowledged that his staff often "trash-talked" Whole Foods internally, and he himself kept a statue of St. Michael stabbing Lucifer in his office, with a picture of Mackey pasted over the devil's face. Mackey, for his part, told the *Austin American-Statesman*: "They don't like or trust us. And the feeling is mutual."[24] He often told friends that he would "short" Wild Oats stock, believing that since it was inevitably going to go down, he might as well bet against it.

Gilliland always did a superb job of working the media, keeping Wild Oats in the national conversation. After Mackey repeated his brilliant Fresh Fields strategy—telling his leadership team and Wall Street analysts that "[w]e are going to blow up the factory where they make the weapons," and then overspending on a big, beautiful store in Boulder, right in Wild Oats' backyard, in 1998—Gilliland earned a lot of ink for Wild Oats by telling reporters that Mackey was like "Chainsaw Al" Dunlap, the ruthless CEO of Scott Paper and Sunbeam. Mackey then sent Gilliland a package with the war-strategy board game "Risk" in it, and a note that said, "Forewarned is forearmed." It was signed, "Chainsaw John Mackey." (Gilliland didn't know what was in the package and actually had his secretary bring it out into the Wild Oats parking lot to open it, just in case.) Gilliland got his revenge in a sly way, which presumably Mackey never knew about: When he sent packages containing dope from his Colorado home to his Arizona home, Gilliland said he always listed the return address as John Mackey, Whole Foods Market, Austin, Texas.

Mackey and Gilliland sometimes found themselves in bidding wars for people, store locations, and even companies. In 1997, for example, Richie Gerber of Bread of Life reached out to Mackey to see if he might be interested in selling the Unicorn Village store, which Whole Foods had acquired a couple of years earlier from Terry Dalton and which was not doing well. Mackey flew to Florida and met with the Bread of Life team in a Barnes & Noble on University Drive in Coral Springs. After several hours of discussions, Mackey came back at Gerber with a novel suggestion. "Instead of you buying the Unicorn and Whole Foods leaving Florida, how about we buy the Bread of Life?" Gerber remembered him saying. "We get you, Julie [Gerber], and Jim [Oppenheimer] to run it. We'll start a new region, the Florida region, and you guys run the Unicorn and then build stores for us." Two weeks later, Mackey submitted an offer to Gerber—and during the ensuing negotiations, somehow, Gilliland found out about it and desperately tried to put in a bid of his own, offering Gerber more and more money. But it was to no avail: Gerber liked Mackey, and ultimately made a deal to sell Bread of Life to Whole Foods for $2.15 million.

In the ensuing years, Whole Foods made some preliminary efforts to try to acquire Wild Oats itself, but Chris Hitt, who took over as president of Whole Foods after Peter Roy resigned in 1998, always argued against it. "Why do you want to buy these guys?" he asked Mackey. "Based on everything you are trying to do, John, the size of stores and the basic feeling we want to create in these stores, why would we buy them at this point? What are they offering us of any value?" Wild Oats served more of a purpose in just keeping Whole Foods on its toes.

Whole Foods hit 100 stores and $1.6 billion in sales in 1999. Despite an overly aggressive and distracting move that year into e-commerce—WholePeople.com opened a huge operation near Boulder, and Mackey actually moved there, the moth drawn to the natural flame—Whole Foods fairly quickly reached a scale and level of operational efficiency that elevated it beyond the ranks of mortal companies and into an iconic realm.

Wild Oats, meanwhile, continued to open more retail outlets and buy new ones, and actually surpassed Whole Foods in number of stores, with 110 in 22 states and Canada by the end of 1999 (although, at $721.1 million, its sales were less than half those of Whole Foods).[25] But in many ways it was an empire built on a house of cards. For one thing, the stock languished for many years and cash remained tight; late in 2000 Wild Oats closed stores in New York, Salt Lake City, and elsewhere, and took a $14 million to $15 million write-down. For another, Wild Oats was constantly tinkering with new concepts. It tried small stores and large ones. For a while, Gilliland tried to "out-do Sandy Gooch" and become the purist's natural foods store. In 1999 Wild Oats acquired the Henry's stores in California and became enamored with that chain's farmers' market format. "We had a lot of fits and starts, and tried different things," said Gilliland. "It was the flavor of the moment. . . . We were always trying to anticipate, [but] the customer doesn't always go with you. So we made a number of mistakes."

One of those was buying Stan Amy's seven Nature's Fresh Northwest stores (from interim owner GNC) in 1999, which Gilliland called "the worst deal I ever did." He acknowledged that he made some major miscalculations. "I just didn't understand Portland. I didn't understand the culture [of Nature's]. I remember having our employee meeting. 'Okay, here's the deal, guys. We paid this much money, we got to have a reasonable return on investment. We are not trying to kill anybody here, but we need to change some things up.' And [the response] was like, 'Fuck you! We don't care if you ever make money!' And half of them ended up quitting and the stores were a disaster." Only years later, when Gilliland's daughter, Stella, went to college in Portland, did he finally realize how much he had misjudged the market. "I love that town. It is so provincial and they are so proud of it. . . . But I want nothing to do with Portland from a business perspective!"

Gilliland was clearly an entrepreneurial success, but close observers always had the sense that for him it wasn't a game of win-or-die. It was Mike and his brother, Pat, and all of Wild Oats with a parasail on their backs and a tenuous tether tied to a Boulder fire hydrant. "We were definitely more seat of the pants, and we used to take pride in our ready/fire/aim kind of approach," Mike Gilliland reflected. "And I think it ultimately cost us, the infrastructure in the organization and that kind of thing. Things did start getting competitive, and you needed systems, you needed a certain critical mass—we suffered for it. So that was probably lack of strategic vision on my part." And as for his rival? "Whole Foods just has that strength of culture, that strength of conviction that we didn't have, frankly," he acknowledged. "As they got more flexible, you realized, 'Man, you can't go anywhere without being exposed to them.' I didn't think we were going to win that race. I knew there was plenty of running room for us for forever, that we would have a market niche. But I didn't really think about besting them in the game." Gilliland left his post at Wild Oats in 2001.

Nevertheless, the competitive fire continued to burn inside Mackey. Later that same year, the *Wall Street Journal* reported, he first met Gilliland's successor, Perry Odak, at a retailing conference in New York and supposedly told him, "I'm going to destroy you."[26] By this time, Mackey had also discovered and apparently gravitated toward the vitriolic world of online message boards. And so, over the course of 8 years, he posted about 1,300 messages anonymously on the Yahoo! Finance Board that often praised Whole Foods and occasionally its CEO ("I think his hair is cute!"), and at least 240 times mentioned (and often denigrated) Wild Oats. On June 21, 2006, for example, Mackey posted (using his pseudonym, Rahodeb), "The Company [Wild Oats] still stinks and remains grossly overvalued based on very weak fundamentals. The stock is up now, but if it doesn't get sold in the next year or so it is going to plummet back down. Wait and see."[27]

Readers didn't have to wait long. Whole Foods finally consummated the inevitable deal, agreeing to purchase Wild Oats in February 2007 for $565 million. The deal was held up by the Federal Trade Commission for months, while the Securities and Exchange Commission (and also the Whole Foods board) looked into Mackey's Yahoo! waggishness. But, in the end, it was confirmed that he had done nothing more than exercise bad judgment, much as Michael Jordan had done in taunting Bill Clinton on the golf course with the media lurking nearby. Mackey himself, in his 2013 book, *Conscious Capitalism,* continued to express surprise at the reaction the whole incident had generated. "No one participating took this activity seriously," he wrote. "It was just a form of play and entertainment. . . . The whole thing was so bizarre to me because I was just having fun when I did those postings. I didn't see how anyone was being harmed. . . ."[28]

But perhaps the real reason he did it, as with so many of the other things that this truly remarkable entrepreneur has done over the years in his competitive quest to change the worlds of food, retailing, and business itself, was much simpler than that. He just couldn't help himself.

CHAPTER 8

DUELING BUSINESS MODELS

I n September 1982, a curious-looking set of newspaper coin boxes began appearing on the streets of major cities from coast to coast. The boxes sat on top of pedestal columns and had a bright white base coat, rounded corners, and a sleek black modern façade through which the colorful newspapers inside peered out. The whole thing was suggestive of a television set—and that was precisely the intent.

Gannett's *USA Today* was a new kind of newspaper: national in scope, jingoistic in tone, highly graphic in design, compartmentalized in structure, and lightweight in content. Its motto—"An economy of words. A wealth of information."—was squarely targeted toward the TV generation, which pollster Lou Harris had told the Gannett board of directors "is not going to fight its way through dull, grey newspapers, however good they are."[1]

It was not just a new newspaper *brand,* but an entirely novel newspaper *model,* one that was radically different from even the other 79 newspapers then owned by Gannett. It wouldn't rely on either classified ad revenue or a subscription base of home delivery, but on newsstand sales, display advertising, and revenue from third-party "blue-chip circulation" distributors such as hotels and airlines. It wouldn't build its reputation on journalistic heavy hitters and far-flung foreign bureaus, but on a stripped-down newsroom staff churning out pithy blurbs, opinion polls, and infographics. It wouldn't seek to become a pillar of any one city or local community, but a mouthpiece for the entire nation and a source of bite-size state-by-state information for those who were traveling or who longed for news of home. It wouldn't be limited to traditional black-and-white newspaper halftone images or the hand-drawn "hedcut" style of the *Wall Street Journal,* but would have plenty of splashy color photographs. Other than the cover feature, it wouldn't run any front page stories that needed to jump to another page. It would always have an entire section devoted to celebrities and lifestyles. And it would use satellite technology to print in as many as 33 locations throughout the country. "The *New York Times* is edited for the nation's intellectual elite, its thinkers and policy makers," wrote the *American Journalism Review* in 1997. "The *Wall Street Journal . . .* is edited for business leaders. *USA Today* is edited for what has been called Middle America—young, well-educated Americans who are on the move and care about what is going on."[2]

It was, in more theoretical terms, what management science has come to refer to as a "disruptive innovation." In their influential 1995 *Harvard Business Review* article entitled "Disruptive Technologies: Catching the Wave," Joseph L. Bower and Clayton M. Christensen illustrated how the business models of established companies sometimes keep those companies too close to their customers, resulting in an endless cycle of continuity: They just create more of the same products/services that got them to this point. Therefore, "[w]hen a technology that has the potential for revolutionizing an industry emerges, established companies typically see it as unattractive: it's not something their mainstream customers want, and its projected profit margins aren't sufficient to cover big company cost structures." The established companies stay on the sidelines while new companies "invade" the market with a new business model that makes it structurally difficult for the established companies to respond; by the time the old companies realize what has happened, it is too late to do much more than disparage the upstart. Disruptive innovation is all about trade-offs: offering diminished performance along one dimension (e.g., journalistic depth) in exchange for new benefits related to simplicity, convenience, and low price.

When Gannett first announced that it was going to launch *USA Today,* the company had enjoyed 86 consecutive quarters of earnings growth. It *was* the Establishment. But Gannett had a forceful and visionary chairman/CEO in Al Neuharth, who recognized that American society was becoming more rootless, impatient, and information-hungry. *USA Today* was the perfect "disruptive" antidote. He predicted that it would take 5 years for his new paper to reach profitability, and the Gannett stock immediately took a dive. "Wall Street thought we were nuts," he recalled in an interview in 2007. But he knew better. "Your decisions cannot be based on quarter-to-quarter report cards to Wall Street. If they are, you won't do anything that has long-term possibilities."[3]

Although the newspaper sold out all 155,000 copies of its first edition, the Establishment skeptics soon came out in force. Some called it "McPaper." David Hall, executive editor of the *St. Paul Pioneer Press,* said that reading it was like "reading the radio." Ben Bradlee, publisher of the *Washington Post,* said that if anyone considered *USA Today* one of the nation's better newspapers, "then I'm in the wrong business." John Morton of the *American Journalism Review* said, "A national daily newspaper seems like a way to lose a lot of money in a hurry."[4] But one month later, the circulation had more than doubled, to 362,879, and by April 1983 it topped 1 million. By the end of its third year, it trailed only the *Wall Street Journal* in circulation, and it would surpass that scion in 1999.

Like many disruptive business models, this one was not born fully formed and had to be tweaked. Within 2 years of launch, *USA Today* added a home-delivery subscription service, and within 7 years that accounted for about half of the newspaper's distribution.[5] It improved the journalistic gravitas; redesigned the editorial pages to accommodate guest columnists; switched to all-digital production, which helped push the deadlines back to include late-night sports scores; and in 1991 added front-page advertising. By then Gannett's once-healthy balance sheet had taken a big hit, with the investments in *USA Today* amounting to an $800 million loss. But in 1993 the paper turned its first yearlong profit, $5 million, and that doubled in 1994. From there, it went on to become one of the most profitable newspapers in the country and, ironically, also one of the most influential. As Neuharth said in 1997, "It has had a tremendous impact on newspapers for better or for worse."[6]

The growth of *USA Today* came at precisely the same time as the explosion of the natural foods industry—and in many regards, the two were equally disruptive to the conventional industries they sought to displace. (Moreover, as the new self-anointed chronicler of all contemporary trends, "America's newspaper" ran many, many stories about the natural foods movement. "Our growing appetite for 'natural snacks,'" read one headline on August 21, 1987. "Organic supermarkets sprouting up like weeds," read another on July 24, 1991. Then there was "Buyers prefer organic produce" [March 20, 1989], "Is organic food worth the price?" [March 19, 1990], "The food fight over pesticides" [June 24,

1993], "New 'organic' labels will ease consumer confusion" [April 22, 1991], "Bringing home the bacon, healthfully" [September 12, 1994], "Whole Foods to gobble up rival Fresh Fields" [June 19, 1996], "Organics cropping up everywhere, Natural superstores cater to families hungry for chemical-free food" [October 7, 1997], and plenty of others.) And among those contributing to the disruption were a few natural foods companies which created products that, just like *USA Today,* might have looked familiar to mainstream America, but whose pure ingredients, highly entrepreneurial founders, and unusual business plans marked a radical departure from the norm.

————

Fruit juice had long been a staple of the American pantry. What could be more pure and simple? One of the earliest and most successful juice brands was Mott's, which began bottling apple juice in 1842 using the runoff from apples crushed by a horse-drawn press. Welch's (1893), Martinelli's (1898), Ocean Spray (1930), and Sunsweet (1932) were other early national "shelf-stable" juice brands, most of which, in their original formulations, would have met today's standards as "all-natural." Orange juice, because it is a perishable product, was frequently produced by local dairies and distributed door-to-door by the milkman. Florida's Natural (1938) and Minute Maid (1946) were among the first national orange juice brands.

In the era of mass markets and mass production, as juice producers began shipping products over great distances and therefore required a longer shelf life, it became commonplace to develop juice "blends" using highly acidic ingredients like cranberry or lemon juice to act as preservatives. Tropicana adopted the flash pasteurization (rapid heating) process in 1954 to help kill microorganisms and achieve longer shelf life, though the process was known to have a deleterious effect on nutrients and flavor.

After World War II, as with so many other foods, the chemical revolution overtook the fruit juice industry. Hawaiian Punch, developed in the 1930s but not distributed nationally until 1955, was typical of the wave of postwar processed juice products in its use of artificial preservatives, such as potassium sorbate, and minimal use of actual juice: The ingredients included small amounts of apple, apricot, orange, pineapple, papaya, guava, and passion fruit juice, but about 90 percent water and sugar, as well as artificial flavors, colors, sweeteners, and preservatives. (Amazingly, though Hawaiian Punch remains a best seller to this day, with a market share in excess of 12 percent, it has been kicked around a lot over the years; its owners have included R.J. Reynolds, Del Monte, Procter & Gamble, Cadbury Schweppes, and Dr Pepper Snapple.)

That was the backdrop against which, in 1980, three musicians decided to launch a fresh-squeezed juice company they called Odwalla. Greg Steltenpohl, Gerry Percy, and Bonnie Bassett were living in Santa Cruz, California, playing occasional avant-garde improvisational jazz gigs with their band, known as The Stand. In need of money, they picked up an idea in a book called *100 Businesses You Can Start for Under $100,* and began creating fresh-squeezed orange juice in the 26-year-old Steltenpohl's backyard using a secondhand $225 juicer. They delivered the juice to local restaurants in the requisite 1968 VW Microbus. Apple juice and carrot juice would follow.

Santa Cruz was a good place to start such a business. Long a bastion of liberal thinking and social activism, by the 1980s it already harbored a strong market for natural foods. It was the home of Harmony Natural Foods, Staff of Life Natural Food Market, and an old pear packing plant. The upscale restaurants of San Francisco were only 80 minutes away, and it was also close to the source of the fruit: Santa Cruz County contained more than 2,000 acres of apple orchards and was not far from the citrus centers in the San Joaquin Valley and Inland Empire. There were even some local juice companies to serve as inspiration: Mr. Natural Apple Juice, which had been started by John Battendieri in 1972 when he began to revitalize some of the abandoned orchards in the Santa Cruz Mountains, and a fresh line called Mrs. Wiggles Rocket Juice, which originated a drink made with spirulina. Ferraro's, Hansen's, Langers, Escondido Juice, Heinke's, and Knudsen were all located within a couple hundred miles, as well.

The Odwalla partners began to find some success in natural foods stores like Living Foods and The Good Earth, and formally incorporated the business in 1985. The company grew right along with the natural foods industry (which in 1985 stood at $2.75 billion and by 1991 had more than doubled to $4.64 billion[7]): By 1991, spurred by deals with Safeway and Costco, Odwalla was up to about $6 million in sales.[7]

The business model was as unusual as the name (which was borrowed from an Art Ensemble of Chicago song-poem called "Illistrum").

First and foremost, all of the juice products would be fresh and non-pasteurized. Steltenpohl, who had a degree in environmental science from Stanford, understood that the heat from the pasteurization process used by most companies to achieve shelf-stability resulted in a loss of flavor, nutrients, and enzymes. But this decision had a whole series of implications. Without pasteurization, the juice would be highly perishable, which meant it would have to be maintained in an unbroken "cold chain" from production all the way to consumption, much like dairy products: no more than 40°F, and preferably 36°F to 38°F. This, in turn, would mean that Odwalla would have to be delivered in refrigerated trucks, preferably via direct store delivery (DSD) rather than through an intermediary, in order to maximize the freshness and minimize the cost. And *that,* in turn, would mean that its distribution radius would be limited—probably just to the Bay Area at first, maybe up and down the West Coast once the volume so dictated.

Additionally, the Odwalla name lent itself to the creation of a colorful, fun, and whimsical brand. The bottle labels and delivery trucks were designed with flighty hand drawings of odd-looking birds that wouldn't have seemed out of place on an Egyptian sarcophagus. Odwalla launched product names like Strawberry C Monster, Femme Vitale, and Mango Tango and used the tagline "Juice for humans." Mott's and Welch's began to sound like relics from Ward and June Cleaver's pantry.

Another key plank in the Odwalla business model was that because of the integrity of the cold chain, the structure of the company needed to be oriented around the DSD system. Once a relationship was established with a retailer, Odwalla would not only deliver the product there, but would also set it up, rotate it, reorder it, and compensate the store for any returns (with a shelf life of only 3 days, there were times when juice was made on a Monday night, delivered on Tuesday morning, and then picked up from the same store if it hadn't sold by Tuesday night). It was a turnkey approach that saved the retailer considerable expense, in exchange for which Odwalla would keep more of the profit margin. For example, if a typical bottled juice might command a 33 percent profit margin at the store, Odwalla might limit it to 25 percent and pocket the extra 8 percent.

Steltenpohl, CEO Stephen Williamson (who came on board in 1991), and VP of market development and expansion Paul Orbuch (who joined in 1993 after having built an ingenious delivery system as CEO and cofounder of the tofu/distribution company Wildwood Natural Foods, which had helped to boost sales of Mrs. Wiggles Rocket Juice) eventually developed an extensive DSD system. It put the truck drivers—route sales people, or "RSPs" in Odwalla-speak—front and center, and made them into the rock stars that Steltenpohl and his original founders had never themselves become. Energetic and outgoing, the RSPs received honks and shouts of love from passing drivers throughout the Bay Area, who recognized them as like-minded souls. "It wasn't just that they were 'hail fellow well met,'" Orbuch said of the RSPs. "They were the customer. They were people who believed in health and in the new age, the human potential. They exemplified the lifestyle that Odwalla fit into."

The RSPs were issued state-of-the-art handheld Fujitsu computers to track their accounts and key metrics such as "dollars per route day." According to Steltenpohl, "That became the economic engine for the company. . . . All of a sudden you had the information flow. I could know exactly what the driver was doing, hire motivated people, give them a feedback system, pay them better, and give them a piece of the action." They were converted from clock-punching hourly employees into base-plus-incentive entrepreneurs, partners in the growth of their routes who were encouraged by their area business managers to get to know the store personnel and to distribute their "O-Zone" in-store Odwalla-branded refrigerated cases wherever they could.

The unusual business model began paying big dividends. By 1993 Odwalla was doing about $13 million in annual sales from about 20 different types of juice, each selling for $1.50 to $2.00 a pint. It had grown to 200 employees. After watching a handful of other natural foods companies go public earlier in 1993, including Wholesome & Hearty Foods, Celestial Seasonings, and the Hain Food Group, Odwalla did the same with a small early-stage offering in December 1993, which brought in about $7 million. A subsequent offering raised $18 million to $20 million more. The stock then took off, and, in the overheated financial markets of the next couple of years, at times hit a price-to-earnings ratio in the triple digits. Odwalla built a big new 65,000-square-foot production facility in Dinuba, California, in 1994, and a corporate office in Half Moon Bay, just south of San Francisco, in 1995. The company received lots of media attention, including reports that both Steve Jobs and Bill Clinton were big fans. Revenue tripled from 1994 to 1995, surpassing $50 million. "Managing Odwalla's rapid growth was challenging but exhilarating," Williamson later told *Fast Company* magazine. "We were sourcing, squeezing, mixing, blending, bottling, shipping, and delivering our products to more retailers and more consumers every day."[8] And although it had barely made a dent in either the shelf-stable juice market or the single-serve beverage business, its fast growth was creating disruptive dreams. "Odwalla was big on trying to inculcate the vision of what we were about," said Orbuch. In some of the meetings, the leadership would even talk about the brand's "share of stomach" versus Coca-Cola, trotting out a picture cofounder Gerry Percy had snapped of an Odwalla truck passing a Coke truck on the road. "We really thought of ourselves as competing with everybody who was making beverages. We didn't see ourselves as being in a different business as these unhealthy drink purveyors. If anything, we were going to take them over!" Steltenpohl estimated that Odwalla would hit the $100 million mark around 1999.[9]

But the business model still had a big built-in constraint, because the DSD system was limited to the range of the trucks picking up juice in Dinuba; even with advancements in controlled atmosphere and sanitation, shelf life was still no more than 18 days. That meant that if the company ever wanted to get its products into more distant markets—and Fresh Fields, for one, was itching to bring Odwalla to the East Coast—it would have to find another way.

One means for expansion would be to build another production facility on the East Coast and essentially replicate the entire Odwalla model there. Flush with cash from the public market, the management team looked into the possibility of building a plant in Palm Beach County, Florida.

But a much easier alternative was growth through acquisition.

On January 31, 1995, Odwalla announced the purchase of Just Squeezed Juices in Denver, Colorado, for $2.5 million. "We looked at their volumes and we knew they were underperforming," recalled Orbuch. "*They* didn't know that. We knew that. We needed to sort of take over their position. We always knew Odwalla was a better brand because of everything we could do with the creativity on the trucks and the coolers. We weren't going to re-create that with [Just Squeezed]. The main thing was to displace them. . . . We basically wanted their relationships. We wanted their market position."

The subsequent purchase of the Dharma Juice Company extended Odwalla's reach into Seattle. Then in October 1996, Orbuch flew to Austin, Texas, and negotiated with Whole Foods and the University of Texas to start bringing fresh juice there, too. The East Coast, however, was still a missing piece in the Odwalla jigsaw puzzle, so they began to take a look at a small company in Saco, Maine, called Fresh Samantha.

———◆———

Despite the fact that he grew up in Belgium, Doug Levin was not really into food. The aioli, fries, and chocolate didn't excite him. He was a picky eater who liked the fresh pear juice that he could get in the malls in Brussels, but not much else.

He returned to his native United States to attend college at Wesleyan, in Connecticut, where he met the woman he would marry, Abby Carter. He graduated in 1984 and then went on to a couple of jobs as an art director at the big New York advertising agencies Doyle Dane Bernbach and Saatchi & Saatchi— periodically flying up to Maine on the chaotic discount airline, People Express, to see Abby's family. Those visits were intriguing for Levin, in part because Abby's mother, Julie, who had been a part of the food co-op movement in the sixties, was a fabulous cook who made broccoli dip and hummus and guacamole, and grew alfalfa sprouts under heat lamps in her basement. But Levin was also feeling downcast about his future in advertising.

"I felt really lost," he said. "I had always perceived myself as more of an artist than a businessperson, and, you know, a lot of people sort of end up in the advertising world when they think of themselves as artists but can't make any money." He tried his hand at photojournalism for a while, but on another visit to Maine in 1991, it suddenly hit him: "I just want to work with these people. I don't want to do what I'm doing anymore."

The Levins moved to Maine, and Doug started delivering Julie Carter's alfalfa sprouts and hummus around town in a truck. "I thought this could be a really cool product, so I started going down to Boston, the suburbs of northern Boston, and delivering the hummus DSD, telling them I'd buy it back if it went bad. And of course, I'd often buy back puffed-up containers of hummus. That was the system: We bring it, and we guarantee the sale."

On one delivery to a Shop 'n Save in Portland, he spotted a bottle of a local product called 24 Carrot Juice on the shelf. "I went in there and saw the bottle of juice and I almost had a religious experience! I saw a little halo around it. I thought, 'This is for me! I just know it's for me!' I tried it, and I loved the taste. And that was it."

He sought out the owner of 24 Carrot Juice to see if he could start delivering his bottles of carrot and orange juice during the alfalfa sprouts runs, and, although he was initially rebuffed, he got a call back a few weeks later asking if instead he would like to buy the business. "He called us up and said he didn't want to make carrot juice anymore, he wanted to travel around the world. So we unburdened him of his business for a small amount of money." Bob and Julie Carter cashed in a life insurance policy so they could buy the 24 Carrot juicer and refrigerator. They allocated a section of their basement sprout plant so that Levin could run the juice business, which began in 1992 with the production of fresh-squeezed unpasteurized juices, packed into bottles that had whimsical hand-drawn labels. He named the company Fresh Samantha, in honor of his newborn daughter. At this point, Doug Levin had never even heard of Odwalla.

By his own admission, Levin had no idea how to build a business. He relied on his family for the technical aspects—Abby created the label artwork, and her brother, Michael (a former physics major and oil rig worker), designed and built some of the production facilities. But when it came to a business strategy, Levin didn't quite know what to do. Employing the same DSD model he had used for the hummus, he tried to interest convenience stores and gas stations in Fresh Samantha juices. "Off I went with my little cooler to the gas stations and I said, 'Here, put these in. Don't worry, we'll buy it back.' And they put it on the shelves, and of course I bought it all back. Nobody in a convenience store and a gas station wanted to buy fresh carrot juice for $4 or $3.50 or whatever we were charging at the time. And these juices were exploding on their shelves. So not only did I have to buy it back, I had to clean up their shelves." There was no funding to expand the business. There was no marketing plan. There was no business model at all. "Without any business plan," he said, "I realized that I was missing something. It wasn't working. It wasn't happening. It wasn't clicking."

By chance, Levin got lost in Medford, Massachusetts, one day while finishing up a delivery of sprouts, and found himself in front of Tufts University. He went to see the head of the university's food service, who told him that Tufts had just signed a contract with Naked Juice, then owned by Chiquita, which produced a similar line of fresh juice products. Levin pleaded, saying that it would be better to go with a New England company, and left behind about 20 samples of Fresh Samantha. Before he even got back to Maine that night, all of the bottles had sold out and Tufts was asking for more. "Until I got lost and found Tufts," said Levin, "there was no future. But the future happened at that moment."

Soon Fresh Samantha was in all of the major colleges in New England and in Bread & Circus, too. In 1994 it grossed $300,000. Levin became more savvy with each passing day. He set up contracts with fruit growers and companies to provide frozen fruit purées. He consulted with Gary Hirshberg of Stonyfield Farm, by then the dean of New England natural foods entrepreneurs. He studied another New England juice business, Nantucket Nectars, and realized that was basically just a marketing company that was outsourcing all of the production and distribution. He took inspiration from Odwalla, copied its in-store refrigerated case system, and, knowing that the California juice company might someday come into New England, "scoured every street, every little store" in an effort to achieve full market penetration for Fresh Samantha. He brought the retail price down below $3, and expanded the product list beyond carrot and orange to include flavors like Big Bang Body Zoom Juice, Raspberry Dream, and Desperately Seeking C; still later, there would be soy drinks and seasonal flavors, such as Watermelon Whirler and Fuchsia Lemonade. Under Michael Carter's direction, Levin built a 24,000-square-foot production facility in Saco capable of producing 600,000 bottles a week. He approached Seth Goldman of Honest Tea just as that business was getting going, offering to buy it mostly so that he could make better use of his trucks and warehouse capacity. He even launched TV ads, featuring a sassy talking moose inspired by the Sid and Marty Kroft TV puppet show *HR Pufnstuf*—a bit of a strange campaign, especially for an ad agency veteran, that unfortunately drifted away from what Levin called the "warmth, coziness, and New Englandness" of the brand and moved it toward what he later realized was "an edgy urban kind of farce." But it didn't matter. In 1998 Fresh Samantha hit $15 million in sales, and in 1999 it reached Levin's goal of $38 million before his 38th birthday; as a reward, he took his 400 employees on a cruise to Nova Scotia.

Through it all, the DSD system remained central to the Fresh Samantha model. "We put so much money, so much effort, into that direct store delivery system. The drivers were salespeople. They were marketing people. The avant-garde, the forward point of our research. When they came back to the warehouse, we found out so much about what was going on with our business! And for a while it was a huge advantage for us. . . . We knew exactly what was going on. It was moving at Tufts, you know, but it wasn't moving in the small little convenience store right next to Tufts. So we could find out these things very, very quickly and make adjustments."

The main problem was the Maine problem. With a production facility tucked away in an inaccessible corner of the country, far from both the orchards and the retail stores, expenses were always going to be high. At first Levin thought New York would be "the outer limit of our possibilities." But he also had grand visions, and before long was building a complex and expensive network of refrigerated warehouses up and down I-95—in New York; Washington, DC; Raleigh-Durham, North Carolina; Atlanta; and eventually Miami. In order to fund this expansion, he could no longer just rely on cashed-out insurance policies and bank loans. For the first time, Fresh Samantha turned to outside money, and brought in Bain Capital as investors. "It was the only way to get the money in and to expand, but at the same time it was sort of doomed," recalled Levin. "[Moving] South was our undoing."

Coming back from Austin on that night in October 1996, Paul Orbuch was feeling good. But then, as he relaxed back into his seat on the plane, he received a message on his pager from Michael Young, the VP of operations at Odwalla: "Don't go home. Come to Half Moon Bay. Important event."

Because it didn't pasteurize its juice, Odwalla had always cleaned the raw fruit with a phosphoric acid wash and whirling brushes. But apparently, the company had gotten a shipment of apples that had been picked from the ground instead of the tree, and this sanitation process had failed. And now the word came from health officials in the state of Washington: The fruit, and the juice made with it, had become infected with the E. coli 0157:H7 bacteria, killing a 16-month-old girl and sickening what would ultimately be 66 other people. Apparently, food safety experts had convinced the production coordinators that E. coli could not live in the acidic environment of apple juice, so Odwalla hadn't tested for it.

The management team gathered at Half Moon Bay that night to put an emergency plan in place. "We are Odwalla, these are our core values," Steltenpohl told his team. "Having one extra moment of risk for a consumer is not acceptable. We own a DSD system, so let's pull off a complete recall and see how fast we can do it." The company would plan to have the RSPs pick up every bottle of Odwalla containing apple juice within 48 hours—a $6.5 million product recall, covering 4,600 stores.

Steltenpohl and Williamson faced the press the next day, saying, "This is not who we are" and vowing to take care of any medical problems that arose. Nevertheless, a firestorm of bad publicity immediately rained down on Odwalla and, to a certain extent, on the entire natural foods industry. It may have seemed a bit ridiculous to some that the entire fresh juice industry was being condemned while products laden with artificial chemicals were being sold in massive quantities every day. But the death of a 16-month-old will do that. Odwalla's stock price plummeted 34 percent overnight. Sales dropped by 90 percent. Customers filed more than 20 personal injury lawsuits, and 2 years later Odwalla ended up paying a $1.5 million fine, at that point the biggest criminal fine in a food injury case in the history of the FDA. Even Fresh Samantha's sales were affected, clear across the country, as supermarkets immediately began calling to say, "Get your product out of here!" According to Doug Levin, "Everything changed at that point. The joy went out a little bit. And the taint on the category didn't go away for a while."

As a result of the incident, both companies (and Naked Juice as well) changed one of the basic tenets of their business models and began flash pasteurizing their juices, sacrificing taste and nutrition for food safety. "Probably in the end you just needed to have pasteurization if you were going to do things on this scale, or on even a scale one-tenth the size of this, if you wanted to guarantee that you were going to be safe," Paul Orbuch said.

Still, Odwalla soldiered on, powered in large part by the strength of its brand and the DSD model. The company suffered a net loss in 1997, but shortly thereafter entered the food bar market and began making soy-based Future Shakes. Additionally, there was a silver lining to flash pasteurization: It extended the shelf life of juice. Hence, Odwalla was able to expand into the former Fresh Fields stores in Washington, DC, and Philadelphia in 1998 without having to build an East Coast production facility or buy an East Coast company. By the end of 1998, gross revenue exceeded the pre-incident levels.

In this changed world, where fresh pasteurized juice products could now go through distributors, DSD became less important than cash and brand strength. Fresh Samantha was stuck with a network full of expensive distribution centers, talking moose ads, and needy outside investors. Moreover, tastes were shifting a bit, as a host of new fad diets (Low-Carb, Atkins) called attention to the fact that fresh juices like Fresh Samantha, Odwalla, Naked, and those made to order at Jamba Juice were loaded with calories. "You could feel it in the atmosphere," recalled Levin. "The frenzy was gone."

In February 2000, Doug Levin sold his company for $29 million—a fraction rather than a multiple of sales—to Odwalla. Steltenpohl was impressed by Levin ("Doug was a sales maniac. His metabolism was one of the highest of anyone I have ever met!"), and brought him out to Half Moon Bay to serve as president of the combined company for a while. But Odwalla itself was sold to Coca-Cola in 2001; Levin and his family moved back to the East Coast, where they have lived a quiet life ever since; and the Fresh Samantha sub-brand was retired forever in 2003.

Nevertheless, the disruption to the traditional beverage business caused permanent changes. Fresh, refrigerated juices (especially single-serve) became a mainstay of the natural foods supermarkets and are today once again one of the most active areas of entrepreneurial development in the food business. Among others, Bolthouse Farms, Evolution Fresh, Purity Organic, Columbia Gorge Organic, BluePrint, and Greg Steltenpohl's newest venture, Califia Farms, are all active producers. And in recent years, fresh-squeezed juice bars have begun catching on again, with companies like Organic Avenue, Sweetgreen, and Juice Press leading the way.

Through all of Mark Retzloff's many experiences in the years since he cofounded Eden Foods at the University of Michigan—running the Erewhon store in Seattle, living in the Divine Light Mission ashram in Denver, planning the Millennium '73 celebration for the Guru Maharaj Ji, building Alfalfa's into a powerhouse retailer in Boulder—he had always remained entranced by the simple power of organic farming. Given the right conditions, he knew that organic foods could be regenerative for the food industry and perhaps for all of American business, just as organic farming was regenerative for the soil. But that was a big "given."

Part of the problem was what author Michael Pollan, in *The Omnivore's Dilemma,* called "the perverse economics of agriculture," which, he said, "would seem to defy the classical laws of supply and demand."[10] The first Farm Bill, passed in 1933 at a time when the price for farm-raised food had fallen by more than 50 percent while farm production costs had fallen by only 32 percent, established a precedent by paying farmers not to grow, in an artificial attempt to balance supply and demand. This then became an entitlement. In the early 1970s, Secretary of Agriculture Earl Butz famously urged farmers to "adapt or die" and to "get big or get out." He switched away from the Soil Bank concept, which paid farmers to let land lie fallow, to a method of direct payments to farmers that would make up for the shortfall in crop prices. Thereafter, a larger and larger share—in fact, nearly half—of farm income came to depend on those subsidies. With each subsequent passage of that omnibus Farm Bill, there would be more money for subsidies and virtually no incentives for organic research. Indeed, the laws were set up so that as soon as a farmer stopped using chemicals and began the switchover to organics—typically a 3-year process—he would lose most or all of the federal crop subsidies.

Moreover, by 1990, after nearly half a century of "chemical farming," the agrichemical and Big Food industries had become so accustomed to their way of doing things, and the enormous profits that came with it, that they were unwilling to cede even the paltry 1 to 2 percent market share that organic foods had won back. So they mounted a ferocious counteroffensive—lobbying lawmakers, subsidizing research at universities—that left all efforts to create legislative support for organics in disarray.

Individual states did begin to pass legislation to define and standardize organic farming, including Colorado in 1989, but they weren't consistent, and this only served to create confusion among consumers about what each manufacturer meant when it labeled a product "organic." It was akin, in some respects, to the days before 1883 when the United States finally adopted standardized time: Prior to that, "current time" was defined differently and was usually pegged to a local landmark like the clock on a church steeple, creating havoc for people trying to catch a train or attend a meeting in a nearby town.

"It became clear to me as a retailer that we needed to get that sorted out," said Retzloff. "I couldn't be having doubts about whether something that I was selling was organic. I wanted to be sure." He left Alfalfa's in 1990 to devote himself to this problem, and cofounded the Organic Food Alliance as sort of an offshoot to Peter Roy's old Natural Foods Network. He spent a great deal of time in Washington, DC, and along with the efforts of many others in the industry, such as the Organic Foods Production Association of North America and its successor, the Organic Trade Association, helped to secure the passage of the Organic Foods Production Act as part of the 1990 Farm Bill. The Act itself was really just a starting point in what would become a 12-year process, stipulating the creation of the National Organic Program (NOP) to require and oversee mandatory certification of organic production, and the National Organic Standards Board to advise the secretary of agriculture in setting the standards for the NOP.

In the process of all his lobbying, Retzloff scrutinized the way Alfalfa's and other retailers were marketing organics in each department throughout the store, and made one of those stunningly obvious observations that are apparent only after one gets some distance from the subject: There weren't many organic products in the dairy department. He stood there and watched how many customers picked up conventional milk to go along with the organic produce or organic packaged goods in their baskets. Having spent a great deal of time with the rancher Mel Coleman, Sr., he knew all about how hormones were being implanted behind the ears of cows, and he had closely followed the conference organized in 1990 by the National Institutes of Health about the safety of rBST—a cloned version of a hormone that Monsanto and others were pushing for approval to use. Retzloff was also concerned about whether pesticides were working their way from the crops into the feed and on into the milk.

Along with his friend Paul Repetto, who had been one of the key people at the natural foods companies Westbrae and Little Bear, he commissioned a study to look into the feasibility of producing milk organically in a big dairy, capable of generating enough to supply retailers like Alfalfa's and Bread & Circus and the other large natural products stores. The answers were encouraging. So even though it had never been done before, even though there was no national brand of milk except Lactaid (which had launched in 1984, and had a 6-week shelf life due to its high-heat ultra-pasteurization), even though they had no idea how to create a business model that would support shipping organic dairy products to stores across the country affordably, Retzloff and Repetto each invested $100,000 to launch Natural Horizons in 1991. The company name would soon be changed to Horizon Organic Dairy, and it would go on to become the leading organic brand of any food in the country.

Retzloff and Repetto did not own any cows, and Boulder was not exactly dairy country, anyway. So they made a deal to get their milk from the newly formed Coulee Region Organic Produce Pool (CROPP), a co-operative of 12 organic farmers (including five dairy farmers) in southwestern Wisconsin, and cut a separate deal with a milk processing facility in Madison, Wisconsin. Their first product line, yogurt, debuted in April of 1992, and in order to make up for their higher production costs, they made a key decision: to offer it in 6-ounce cups for about the same price that Dannon and other yogurts were selling 8-ounce cups. Consumers, Retzloff knew after all his years working in retail, would be willing to pay a slight premium for organic, and this was a fairly understated and painless way to extract it. By the end of 1992, their organic yogurt had generated $460,000 in sales spread out over 2,000 stores from coast to coast.[11]

Fluid milk, however, was still very much on Mark Retzloff's mind, because he knew it had enormous symbolic value. "The notion of milk as a gateway product for consumers to get into organics was pretty much imbedded," he said. He understood that organic milk, unlike most of the other organic products then available, had the potential to become a best seller in conventional stores, not just natural foods stores. But he also knew this would require a novel business model.

From roughly the time the first cows had been brought to Plymouth Colony in 1624 up through the end of the 19th century, milk had been produced locally and distributed in buckets by milkmen. The Thatcher's Common Sense Milk Jar, sealed with a wax paper disk, had become the industry standard by 1889. In the early 20th century, milk tanker trucks were developed to transport milk over longer distances, and the 1922 Capper-Volstead Act gave dairies the legal right to band together for processing and marketing—so milk was now treated as a commodity, with several regional dairies combining their output into a single tank. Square cartons with printable side panels came into vogue in the 1950s and 1960s, opening up the first serious possibility of marketing milk under a brand name.[12]

But what Retzloff envisioned was a national model, where Horizon Organic would source milk in different parts of the country, contract with a series of processing and pasteurizing plants, and ship from there under a single brand name. When it became clear that CROPP could not grow fast enough to keep up with Horizon's demand, he extended the notion of vertical integration to include opening and operating his own big dairies. In 1993 he and Repetto did a stock swap with their silent partner, Marc Peperzak of Aurora Dairy, so that they could acquire a conventional 4,000-acre dairy farm in Idaho, which they began converting to organic by developing the pastures without pesticides and by sourcing organic grain. With $1.5 million in additional venture capital helping to offset their $5 million transition cost, they purchased 1,000 head of Holstein cows and made the farm operational in July 1994.

Horizon Organic began selling its milk at Ralph's in Los Angeles, at about a 40-cent premium over conventional milk, and quickly ran short on supply. Soon Horizon expanded to other conventional chains in Los Angeles, Denver, and New York, as well as to natural foods stores. All of Retzloff's theories, honed over 20 years in every aspect of the natural foods business, proved to be correct. Mothers who were otherwise loading up their carts with Fruit Loops (red 40, yellow 6, BHT) and Hidden Valley Ranch Dressing (MSG, artificial flavors, calcium disodium EDTA) were nevertheless opting for organic milk. And it certainly didn't hurt that when Monsanto was given FDA approval for use of its rBST hormone, Posilac, in 1994, there was a huge consumer backlash. By the end of 1994, Horizon had added sour cream to the product mix and established itself as the first national organic dairy brand, with total sales reaching nearly $4 million.[13] By 1995 sales hit $7 million.[14]

Horizon took off from there, but not without further adjustments to its business model. In its second incarnation, that model called for milk that was produced in Idaho to be shipped to Des Moines, Iowa, for processing, and then shipped from there to markets—including back to Idaho and points west. But Retzloff—the man who had worked through the logistics to help feed tens of thousands of Premies at the Houston Astrodome during Millennium '73—saw how inefficient that was. "We realized very quickly that we weren't going to ship milk from one processing plant in the middle of the United States when most of our business was on the coasts." The transportation costs alone would make Horizon milk cost-prohibitive. Fortunately, the surge in demand for Horizon products and some additional venture financing soon provided the capital to establish milk sheds (production regions) around the country, to build processing facilities on the farm in Idaho, and to contract with processors in Reno, Denver, and elsewhere, including Petaluma, California—35 different facilities in all—which in turn helped Horizon to expand the product line to butter, cheese, cream cheese, and other dairy products. (In 1997 the company would also add an organic dairy farm on Maryland's Eastern Shore to its holdings, with 556 head of cow.)

Retzloff tapped his fellow member of the Boulder Mafia, Barney Feinblum, to become president and CEO, and his financial acumen helped to steer the company—which in 1996 did $16 million in sales but still lost $5 million—toward profitability. Feinblum had engineered the successful second Celestial Seasonings IPO in 1993, and would do the same with Horizon. He took the company public in June 1998, and arranged a private placement with the Brazilian conglomerate Suiza Foods that raised additional cash. By the end of 1998, Horizon turned a small profit of $486,000 on its sales of $49.4 million. From there, a variety of different licensing agreements, international and domestic acquisitions, expansions of supply, and marketing efforts brought Horizon into rarified air within the natural foods industry, with sales exceeding $100 million ($127.2 million) in 2000. The company was acquired in 2004 by Dean Foods—the largest conventional dairy producer in the country.

———

Competition, like Mother Nature, abhors a vacuum. So not surprisingly, other dairies began to fill the void. Stonyfield Farm, the leader in organic yogurt since its founding in 1983, thrived. Buoyed by the surge of awareness Horizon brought to the dairy department, and by the controversy generated by the rBST issue, Stonyfield's sales, which had been averaging about $5 million a year, exceeded $42 million in 1998. "The speed of change in the industry has been staggering," Gary Hirshberg told the *New York Times* in 1999. The Straus Family Creamery, which had been founded in the 1940s and was faltering in the early nineties, switched to organic in 1994 and quickly turned around.

And then there was that little co-op of 12 organic farmers in the Coulee Region of southwestern Wisconsin. The theory behind an agricultural co-operative is straightforward. Farming is hard work, and expensive work, requiring lots of inputs (seeds, fuel, machinery, labor, capital or credit) and lots of outputs (storage, packaging, transportation, marketing). Instead of each farmer buying materials in small quantities—a single tractor can cost $125,000 or more—or setting up a distribution network for his goods, why not pool resources?

Though farming is a largely solitary endeavor, the barn-raising spirit has always permeated farming communities, so there has often been a philosophical alignment for co-operatives even while the farmers themselves have maintained their fierce independence on other issues. Among the earlier and more important agricultural co-operatives in the United States were the Tillamook County Creamery Association (founded in 1909, but whose roots date back to 1854, when farmers banded together to build a schooner to transport butter from the Tillamook Valley to Portland, Oregon); Sunkist (formalized in 1893 as the Southern California Fruit Exchange, which launched one of the first branded co-op ad campaigns ever, in 1907, to try to deal with a surplus of oranges); Blue Diamond (formed in 1910 as the California Almond Grower's Exchange, now comprised of 3,500 growers); Land O'Lakes (founded in 1921 by 320 creameries in Minnesota for the purpose of marketing butter, now with 3,200 members); and Ocean Spray (created in 1930 by three Massachusetts cranberry growers, now with 600 members).

George Siemon knew a little bit about that history when in 1988 he convened a meeting of 140 farmers at the Vernon County Courthouse, 20 miles east of where the Mississippi River divides Wisconsin and Minnesota. Then 37 years old, he had spent the previous 10 years as a dairy farmer, doing everything by hand, but had become disillusioned when the price of milk dropped precipitously in 1987, and sold his cows. "Wasn't just me that felt disgusted," he recalled in his soft, almost scratchy voice, peering intently into the past through his round wire-frame glasses. "The money was poor and we felt insulted." Many of the Midwest farmers of that era had been born into farming families that had discouraged their kids from staying on the farm because they envisioned a better life for them. "There was that much droning involved, hard work and not being rewarded, never missing a milking," said Siemon. "It wasn't a happy place. So out of that, those people that started the co-op with me, they were hungry to try something different. They were frustrated. We really didn't care if we succeeded or not."

But it was not at all clear on that cold January day in 1988 that the answer was going to be an organic dairy co-op, because co-ops, according to Siemon, had a bad name. "We started a co-op not liking co-ops. But there was no other model to turn to. We always used to use the Constitution—you know, you started the United States government not liking governments, so you put chains on it. We always had that perspective. Co-ops can be good or bad. Depends on how well you build the foundation for it."

Siemon himself was a rather improbable leader for the group. Though he was a child of the sixties who "went to rock festivals and all that stuff" and once joined an antiwar protest that took over the highway in Miami, he did not consider himself a "disinheritor." He was a gentle soul who was respectful of others and especially of the environment. "Born and raised a naturalist. Nature-lover, Boy Scouts, bird-watching. My mother was a huge Rachel Carson fan, so you know, I am 10 years old and my mother is pushing *The Sea Around Us*." As a kid, he got to spend a couple of weeks here and there on farms owned by relatives in Alabama and Iowa, but his world was in Palm Beach, Florida, where his father ran a chain of seven office supply stores called Halsey & Griffith, and served as president of the Downtown Merchants' Association. "Every store was in a downtown," he recalled. "I can remember my grandfather in the early sixties driving by the first mall and saying, 'See that? That's the death of community.'" Soon Office Depot set up its headquarters in their district, and Halsey & Griffith went bankrupt. But in a Darwinian sense, that was just the way of the world. George swore he would never become a businessperson.

In college, at Colorado State University, Siemon studied forestry and animal science. Sometimes he took jobs as a hired man on nearby farms, most of which were heavily into using chemicals, but he had only respect for the farmers. "They were saying they needed chemicals. They were saying they needed fertilizers. So it was hard for me to be that arrogant to say, 'Yeah, but you are all wrong.'" It wasn't until he moved to Iowa in 1974 and met some old-time organic farmers that he "got the bug"—a rather ironic turn of phrase for a man who would soon build a hugely successful brand using natural methods of pest management.

Siemon and the other organizers met a couple more times in the winter of 1988 before formalizing the CROPP co-operative in March. They began studying the model established by Mondragon, a federation of worker co-operatives in Spain's Basque country that was in the midst of aggressive expansion. They thought perhaps they would create a produce co-op, a goal that Siemon said in retrospect was "dreamy-eyed" because they would have had to start from scratch and pioneer the whole thing. Instead they turned to dairy, which was familiar to them, and specifically to organic dairy—which, with the growth in the natural foods industry around the country, held the promise of higher prices, a decent life for the farmers, and a big boost for sustainable farming.

"Some were saying, 'This is a big undertaking. We shouldn't try to do anything this year, we should pull back,'" Siemon remembered. But they pushed ahead, bringing together support from "conventional ag" (including co-packers), the National Farmers Organization (a sometimes-radical group that had practiced collective bargaining to get a fair price for farmers), and the even more radical organic dairy farmers. Their first product was cheese, sold to another co-op in Madison, this one called North Farm.

A bit later came the call from Mark Retzloff, seeking a source of organic milk for the yogurt he was about to begin manufacturing. CROPP entered into a contract with Horizon, and was its sole supplier for a few years. "But," said Siemon, "they had made it clear all along that they had this urge to do a big dairy. . . . We debated [internally], of course that, 'Gee, these people could succeed. We could be starting a competitor here.' But the truth is we needed them. . . . They brought professionalism, they brought funding, they brought management skills. They brought a lot of things we didn't have. . . . They taught us a lot."

Perhaps the key thing Horizon taught CROPP was that it was possible to build a national organic brand. But for George Siemon—who continued to farm but gradually devoted more time to running the co-op as its "C-EIEI-O"—it wouldn't be built with a big, centralized dairy operation. It would be done by growing the co-op business model to scale, from coast to coast, ensuring that the first priority was to create a stable living wage for farmers, regardless of the price vagaries of the market, in order to keep them on the land. Thus, the man who started a co-op not liking co-ops became one of that business model's most ardent supporters. "In a co-operative it's easier to have a mission-based business," Siemon would later tell the Social Venture Network. "You're more about your mission and who you want to be versus any of the struggles of ownership value. . . . [I]t's not a stock company that has valuation or only looks at return on investment."[15]

In 1990, with more farmers now on board, CROPP was able to mount enough marketing effort to create a brand, which was called Organic Valley. Whereas Horizon was putting its bet on a business model that relied on a couple of large corporate-owned organic dairies, and all of the attendant logistics of processing and transportation, Organic Valley used a decentralized model: The milk would be produced at hundreds of locations around the country (typically farms with only 70 to 80 cows), and then processed and distributed regionally, all under one unifying brand.

For a few years, it was unclear if the model could be sustained. CROPP insisted on paying farmers higher-than-market rates for their milk through good times and bad, and therefore could not always hit its very modest profit goal of 2 percent. It began selling to Walmart in 2001, and soon was supplying that company with 1.3 million gallons a year, as America's biggest retailer was on its way to becoming America's biggest organic milk retailer; but supply became a big issue, especially after a (non-CROPP) case of mad cow disease in 2004 created a huge surge in demand for organic milk. Organic Valley began allocating to its other customers in order to keep up with Walmart. Finally, Siemon and his vice president of sales made the difficult decision, on a day in November 2004 they dubbed "Dry Thursday," to drop Walmart and several other customers who would not tolerate allocations, and walk away from a potential goldmine. The natural foods stores, which represented 50 percent of Organic Valley's business and had supported and helped to build the Organic Valley brand from its infancy, were placed first in line for the milk. Besides, Horizon was knocking on Walmart's door and seemed willing to undercut Organic Valley's price. "No sense fighting a fight you can't win," Siemon told *Inc.* magazine.[16]

But in the end, it hardly mattered. CROPP sales grew by 15 percent in 2005, and by 37 percent in 2006. The brand, and the business model, had proven its worth.[17]

By 2013 CROPP had become the largest farming co-operative in North America, with 1,814 members in 35 states (and three Canadian provinces)—representing about 9 percent of the certified organic farmers in the United States.[18] Its 2012 sales were $860 million.[19] Perhaps more significantly, the strength of its decentralized, farmer-owned model was illustrated by the company's resilience after a fire destroyed half of the corporate office in May 2013. "This co-op has been through a lot in the last 25 years, and this is just another chapter," said Siemon in a YouTube video released the day after the fire, standing in front of the burned-out building wearing a tartan work shirt, a baseball hat over his stringy shoulder-length hair, and a ready-for-anything expression on his face. "I know we can count on the tenacity of our employees to pull this off."[20] Farmers like Siemon and all of his co-op advisors, it would seem, are accustomed to dealing with adversity. Sure enough, Organic Valley didn't miss a single pick-up or shipment as a result of the fire, and was back up and running at full strength within days.

In their own ways and with their own vastly different business models, Horizon and Organic Valley collectively succeeded in kicking the pail out from underneath the stodgy old dairy business. Today, less than 25 years after those companies began the first commercial production of branded organic milk, organic represents 53.9 percent of all milk sales in natural foods stores and 42.8 percent in conventional supermarkets.[21]

—•—

While the fresh-squeezed juices and organic milks were battling it out, utilizing their unusual business models to thrive in the natural foods stores, some new developments in the cookie category began to disrupt the well-established order of the conventional supermarkets, too.

For a century, the formula for commercial cookie success had been clear: Create a tasty recipe, come up with a clever brand name, and advertise the heck out of it. This was the basic pattern followed by Nabisco with all of its famous cookies, including the Fig Newton (introduced in 1891), the Oreo (1912), the Mallomar (1913), Chips Ahoy! (1963), and Nilla Wafers (1967), as well as by other major manufacturers like Keebler and Pepperidge Farm. Ingredients never mattered much (Oreos, for example, included lard in the crème filling from their earliest days until 1993); a "healthy cookie," after all, was a contradiction in terms. But advertising mattered a lot—from Nabisco's early 20th century "Oh! Oh! Oreo" print ads, to its 1950s Saturday morning TV commercials with a cowboy singing, "Yer darn tootin', I like Fig Newtons," to the 3-decade-long Pepperidge Farm advertising campaign that featured old-time radio star Parker Fennelly in a straw hat, bow tie, and suspenders, waxing nostalgic in a crusty New England accent about how "Pepperidge Fahm remembuhs."[22] As long as a company could concoct a personality for its cookie brand, it seemed, it could make a lot of money.

And then, suddenly, everything changed when Nabisco introduced Snack-Well's in 1992, upending the category it already dominated. SnackWell's were not all-natural, but this line of cookies and crackers *was* made without tropical oils and included several low-fat or fat-free versions—a fact that apparently helped assuage the average American's guilt over binge snacking. The brand caught fire: 6 months after its introduction, *USA Today* ran a story entitled, "No-fat chocolate cookies spark insatiable demand."[23] Sales hit $490 million in 1995. With supplies short, some fanatical consumers actually chased delivery trucks down the street.[24] SnackWell's Reduced Fat Crème Sandwich Cookies actually overtook Oreos as the best-selling cookie in the country.[25]

In retrospect, the SnackWell's phenomenon proved to be more fatuous than virtuous, part of the fat-free fad of the nineties that also brought us the reduced-fat McDonald's McLean DeLuxe (born 1991, died 1996) and Sara Lee's short-lived Free and Light frozen desserts (which the *New York Times* eulogized as "the food-business equivalent of Kevin Costner's fiasco with the film 'Waterworld'").[26] Supermarket sales of SnackWell's plummeted by 35 percent from 1995 to 1997, and by the following year the formulation was changed to add more fat and flavor.[27] But what exactly was it that had paved the way for such a disruptive new product? Not surprisingly, it was the incursion into the conventional supermarkets of two products from the natural foods world whose "personalities" were real rather than invented on Madison Avenue—and whose business models were as different from each other as a Nilla Wafer was from a Keebler Opera Crème Cookie.

Richard Worth blew into the cookie business with all the subtlety of a Nor'easter.

Blame it, perhaps, on his family. His grandfather was a serial entrepreneur who had lost a $2 million fortune in the stock market crash of 1929, but refused to let the world get the best of him. He bounced back to found the first ready-to-wear women's clothing store in Boston, Worth of Boston. By the time Richard was 11 or 12, his father, Stanley, was running the store, and he would occasionally bring his son along to New York to help select the fashion lines for the next season. The ones Richard picked always sold the best. As did the Hawaiian jewelry he chose. "I would say to people, 'Do you want to see something special? REALLY special?' And I would take out a slab of these things. 'How gorgeous are THESE?' I could sell shit to anybody!"

Worth went on to earn a degree in psychology at Hobart, with a minor in East Asian studies, and spent much of his twenties hopping from one entrepreneurial opportunity to another in what he now insists, unconvincingly, was all part of a larger plan: selling bread in upstate New York, marketing underground sprinklers in Boston, unloading tuna boats in Canada. Once he even burst into a small real estate office in Calais, Maine, and told them they needed to make him a partner—which they did. ("This is how Worth works," he said of himself. "He sees no walls; he respects no titles.") Saying no to Richard Worth has never been easy to do.

In 1975, inspired by what he later told *People* magazine was "a cosmic desire to live with nature,"[28] he bought a farm in rural New Brunswick, Canada, for $9,500. The notion of Worth—a Jewish kid from Brookline, Massachusetts, who had grown up in the world of women's fashion, and had grown into a chunky man with a walrus mustache and a smoker's cough—becoming an organic farmer in Canada might have seemed far-fetched to some. But he was nothing if not resolute, and for 7 years he raised organic blueberries, turnips, potatoes, and livestock. Yet the farm was generating very little income—only $3,500 a year—and he had just become a father after a scary home birth that frightened and humbled him, so in 1978 he decided to start a business that had a little more earning potential: manufacturing organic jams, which he named after his farm, Sorrell Ridge.

It wasn't an especially well-conceived plan. The farm was at the end of a dirt road, across a covered wooden bridge, miles from the nearest neighbor; tractor-trailers had a devil of a time reaching him. The expensive production techniques meant that the product would have to retail for $2.49, much higher than the category leaders like Smucker's. And there was no real marketing plan, other than the label he slapped on the jars with the tagline, "The fruit and nothing but the fruit." But through the sheer force of his typhoon-like personality, Richard Worth built Sorrell Ridge into a million-dollar business within 2 years, and into a $10 million business within 5 years.

On one occasion he called up the head of marketing at Häagen-Dazs in an effort to set up a deal to get Sorrell Ridge jam included as a topping. "We don't get involved with anybody else," Worth was told. "Good," he said. "What time on Wednesday would you like to talk to me about not getting involved? Ten or eleven?" The meeting happened, and so did the deal. On another occasion, in order to challenge Smucker's, he mimicked its formula by filling a jar with 45 percent candy raspberries and 55 percent sugar and brought that around to supermarket buyers. Representatives from Smucker's heard about it, and Chairman Tim Smucker and his head of sales visited Worth at his plant.

"You are demeaning our product," Worth recalled them telling him.

"No, I am not," Worth shot back. "*You* are demeaning your product. These are your ingredients!"

Smucker's later tried to sue Sorrell Ridge, but Worth fought back hard, even though he secretly liked them and respected the family's farming background. "All I do in business is either create for myself or destroy the competitor," he said.

The lesson that Worth had learned was that times were changing and the chumps in the world of Big Food hadn't realized it. "I changed the way large companies saw natural foods," he immodestly observed. "They said, 'This guy is selling jam at $2.49 and he is gaining 10 percent market share. . . . We don't believe this! Why are they buying it?' Dumbbells. It's called health, stupid. Americans wanted health in the mainstream manufacturing."

Itching to take his brazenness and braggadocio to a larger stage, Worth sold Sorrell Ridge in 1983 and set his sights higher: the $4 billion cookie category. "If they love jams without the sugar, they are going to love cookies without the crap!" He experimented with numerous recipes, going through 2,000 pounds of dough, and then in 1987 came out with a fruit-juice-sweetened cookie that he unsurprisingly named after himself: R.W. Frookies. It made $400,000 in profits in just the third month.

Worth's new company was brilliantly conceived in many regards. The packages were what one writer described as "a weird and compelling ultraviolet contraption."[29] The wacky product names were spoofs on well-known mainstream brands: Frookwich, Animal Frackers, Froyster Crackers. To finance it, he invested $500,000 of his own money but also sold one-third of the equity in the company to some of his suppliers and distributors to get them to back the products. He targeted conventional supermarkets right from the start—Kroger was his first account—and sidestepped the slotting fees that the big boys were paying by sending most of his product in cardboard "shippers" that lived outside of the aisles.

And then, of course, there was that force of nature called Richard Worth.

"He would just pick up the phone and [cold] call the supermarket buyers," said Bruce Nierenberg, who was a natural foods broker. "'I am sending a truck,' he would say. 'I know you don't want it. I am sending it anyway. It'll be there next week.' Click. He was passionate, aggressive, brilliant, but manic."

Distributors often took in his products even if they didn't want them, because they knew his track record was good, and besides, he would probably just argue with them until he got what he wanted. Worth said that he had more than a dozen people approach him at the Natural Foods Expos and say they didn't want to talk to him because he was crazy. Instead, they'd say: "Just place an order and ship it, on all your products."

He posed in a chef's toque for television ads. In interviews and behind the scenes, he disparaged his competitors (calling Health Valley "Death Valley" and SnackWell's "SmokeWell's," because Nabisco was owned by the tobacco company R.J. Reynolds). It also became well known in the industry that when Worth was hiring salesmen, he would ask if they had "skids" on their underwear; if in his candor or embarrassment someone answered no, Worth concluded that he "is either a fucking liar or he is not a salesman. Because all good salesmen are bored after their second wipe! They have to get out of there and sell something!"

Frookies sold 70,000 cases and did $2 million of business in the first 3 months. By the ninth month, Worth's cookies were in more than 50 percent of all supermarkets nationwide, becoming perhaps the most readily adopted natural foods brand in conventional store history. The company did a remarkable $17.5 million in sales in its first year, and was soon featured in the *New York Times*, *Inc.* magazine, *People* magazine, and on ABC's *20/20*, among many others. Worth was interviewed on several TV news programs, including a segment about "self-made millionaires" on *CBS This Morning*. With his round features, high forehead, prominent mustache, and forceful personality, he greatly resembled the actor Dennis Franz, who was then starring as Detective Andy Sipowicz on *NYPD Blue*. Worth himself starred in two prominent national TV commercials for Avis, with its Worthy tagline, "We're trying harder than ever."

Armed with the energy of the high-minded idealism that had given birth to the industry, but empowered by cutthroat capitalism and a 24-gauge double barrel shotgun of a personality, Richard Worth and R.W. Frookies were the consummate brand of a changed industry. Worth's original goal of building a $100 million company in 5 years soon gave way to something even larger and more disruptive—perhaps even hubristic: He intended to buy Keebler, and gradually remove the trans fats and sugar from its products. "They would become a non-negative company," said Worth, "and a positive force when they saw their margins jump and . . . moved into health. The country would be more healthy. The country would have more organic farmers like me. The country would change Europe!"

And with Frookies riding the crest of the biggest, most sustained sales wave the food industry had perhaps ever seen, it wasn't that implausible. In April 1994, Frookies pulled off a leveraged buyout of the Delicious Cookie Company, which was three times its size, creating a $65 million business that was larger than all but four other cookie companies in the United States. Worth then began discussions with friends on Wall Street about a potential $500 million buyout of Keebler.

But it was all too good to be true. The marriage with Delicious Cookie quickly went south because of bad purchasing, deal making, and accounting. Frookies sales declined for 4 straight years. In August 1997, Worth accepted a buyout package that included stock, 5 years of consulting fees, and a licensing agreement for one of the other product lines he had started, Cool Fruits. Carl Icahn purchased a 16 percent stake in Delicious Frookies in April 1999 to prop it up temporarily, but the following year, the assets were sold to a subsidiary of Parmalat SpA, the Italian company, which shortly thereafter got involved in financial fraud and money laundering. Frookies disappeared from the shelves forever, almost as quickly as they had appeared.

In the end, the Frookies story turned out to be more myth than fairy tale, and Richard Worth more Icarus than Alger's *Ragged Dick*. Frookies changed the natural foods industry, along with other popular crossover brands like Earthbound Farm, Odwalla, Horizon, and Organic Valley. For a while, it was a disruptive brand; ultimately, however, all that Frookies disrupted was the meteoric rise of its indefatigable founder.

Worth would go on to other ventures, and in his life has now notched 11 different businesses on his entrepreneurial bedpost. Today, in his sixties and living in semi-retirement in Asheville, North Carolina, the fire still burns within. He insists that he could still create a new business in 4 days. And, even though he almost never goes into a natural foods store, he says he has a "third eye" so he knows that the cookie category is mediocre. "If I came back?" he said with a glint. "If I got funded? I'd wreck it. *I'd wreck it!* I'd be number one within six months!"

———•———

A somewhat subtler entrance into the cookie category was made by someone who knew the color of money even better than did Richard Worth.

Paul Newman had used some of the earnings from his long acting career to start an all-natural food brand called Newman's Own in 1982, beginning with salad dressings and later including pasta sauce, salsa, and other items. But there was a twist to his business model: Though the company was organized as a for-profit enterprise, Newman would donate 100 percent of the profits he received to charity. Utilizing a licensing program, every time a Newman's Own product was sold, a royalty would be generated, which was then given away to charity by the actor (and still is, by the Newman's Own Foundation). Newman always had an expansive world view and supported humanitarian and social causes (though usually as a "white knight" who rode in and out quietly, rather than as a sustaining donor); Newman's Own would be the perfect way to capitalize on his legendary name and support his passion for philanthropy at the same time.

Around 1992, Newman was beginning to think about what else he could do with product development, and called his daughter, Nell, who was living in Santa Cruz, California, working for the Predatory Bird Research Group. She suggested that he think about organic foods, since that aligned well with his interest in land preservation. He mulled it over, and after she surprised him with an all-organic Thanksgiving dinner, came back to her with the idea for a new business: Newman's Own Organics, The Second Generation. She called her friend Peter Meehan, who lived nearby in Santa Cruz and had known the Newman family back in Connecticut, when he owned a swimming pool business. "Wow, you should jump all over that," Meehan told Nell Newman. "He has baked the cake and iced it for you."

The Newmans pulled Meehan into the business as CEO because of his tenacity and entrepreneurship, "knowing full well that I wasn't from Kraft or Unilever. . . . I was the guy who used to be at the bottom of his pool painting or scraping." Paul gave Nell and Peter $125,000 in seed money, lowering his glasses and peering out over them with his legendary blue eyes: "It's a *loan*. This needs to get repaid because it is charity money I would have given away." There would be no failure to communicate here.

Newman's Own Organics launched its first product, pretzels, in 1993. The company followed up with chocolate bars in 1995. The packages featured a picture of Paul and Nell on the front, in the pose of Grant Wood's "American Gothic." The unusual business model meant that the cost of goods sold for every Newman's Own Organic product would always include ingredients, production, overhead, packaging, brokers' fees, distributors' fees . . . and a charitable royalty, something no competitive product would face. The resulting higher costs forced the team to be very selective. Moreover, they needed to make sure that the price points weren't so high that consumers would feel like they were underwriting the Newman's Own Foundation. "It has to taste good and it has to be reasonably priced," Meehan said. "Then the mission works and people feel like it is a dividend. People don't eat mission. It doesn't taste good."

The company managed to do reasonably well in its first few years, and then came the introduction in 1997 of Fig Newmans (which Paul thought was "the greatest name I have ever heard"). When they first talked about it, Meehan remembered, "some of our brokers said, 'Don't go into cookies. It's a dead category.' But we couldn't find [an organic] cookie that tasted good. They were terrible. They weren't even, like, okay. Fig Newmans changed everything." The key was the combination of brand recognition, trust (Newman's Own had been in the market for 15 years already, and Paul Newman was a revered figure), great taste (the company bought every organic fig on the market, and soon began using organic palm oil to add a little fat), and packaging that used trays with an overwrap instead of boxes (which not only cut down on costs but enabled the cookies to be merchandised "off-aisle" in cardboard shippers). In 1999 Newman's Own Organics introduced chocolate chip cookies, and in 2001 its Oreo knockoff, dubbed Newman-Os. "Everything had to be something that my father, who was born in 1925, would look at, recognize, and eat," Nell told the *New York Times*.[30] She might well have stolen his line as Brick Pollitt from *Cat on a Hot Tin Roof*: "People like to do what they used to do after they've stopped being able to do it."

Of course, Newman's Own Organics cookies also had to compete directly with Frookies, and it was challenging. Peter Meehan likened the situation to the Cold War, "where one side didn't have any missiles in the silo so the other side way overspent." He saw this happen with Muir Glen versus Millina's Finest pasta sauce, and with Kashi versus Nature's Path cereal, and then it happened to him. "Frookies . . . was a serious discounter. We were organic, so they had more margin, and Frookies was dominating with promotional activity. At least it appeared that way." So Meehan had to decide whether there was really anything in those silos, and how much he should spend to fight back. Yet, because of the combination of celebrity appeal, organic ingredients, and the charitable tie-in, he was able to carve out space in stores throughout the country, right alongside Frookies.

The Newman's Own Organic cookies "were really game-changers for us," Meehan said in looking back, because they helped the brand cross over into conventional stores. "They went into every natural foods set in every supermarket chain. They were cornerstones for Stow Mills, Cornucopia, and everybody else who was trying to get space for natural." According to Meehan, the grocery buyers for those distributors saw this as such a monumental breakthrough that they even referred to it as "parting the sea." It would also lead to another remarkable breakthrough in 2008, when the owner-operators of the 640 McDonald's restaurants in New England decided to start selling Newman's Own Organic Fair Trade Coffee through a partnership with Green Mountain Coffee Roasters. They have continued to do so ever since, even after the McDonald's parent corporation came out with its own premium coffee products.

Newman's Own Organics separated from Newman's Own in late 2000, and a few years after that the parent company actually introduced a few organic items. When he heard about that, Meehan said, "It was one of the most exciting days I ever had." Paul Newman died in 2008, proud that his efforts had raised hundreds of millions of dollars for charity, but perhaps unaware of the role his unique business model had played in the natural foods revolution. "He did know it was a big thing," Nell said, "but I don't think that he realized he changed snacking in America. . . . He probably would have laughed at that."[31]

CHAPTER 9

FROM CO-OP TO
CO-OPTATION TO CLOUT

S pring reliably comes to Austin, Texas, by the end of January each year. The temperature warms up into the mid-60s—sometimes higher— and the roadsides of Texas State Highway Loop 1 ("Mopac," to locals) come alive with a carpet of bluebonnets pretty enough to slow down traffic from its usual 70 mph to a true Texas crawl, maybe 68.

On January 24, 2000, just a few short weeks after Lyle Lovett had helped the "capital of live music" ring in the new millennium with a huge street party—and after the tech-centric core of Austin businesses had breathed a collective sigh of relief with the uneventful passing of "Y2K"—CNBC, cable TV's oracle of the Internet age, decided to take advantage of the good weather and broadcast its *Power Lunch* show live from a park on the south side of Austin called Auditorium Shores. A sizeable crowd of onlookers gathered, many of them eager just to get an autograph from Bill Griffeth, the show's host, who had obsequiously donned cowboy boots for the day.

Power Lunch's popularity was simply one more piece of evidence that the dot-com revolution was at hand, with lots of media-fueled talk about the "new paradigm" in American business. Anything and everything online was "in," the information economy was king, and suddenly cash flow and profits mattered less than Web metrics like "page views," "monetizing eyeballs," and "stickiness." How the world had changed! Companies that nobody had ever heard of, that created software services and tech equipment that few understood, suddenly soared to market capitalizations that dwarfed the pottering old bricks-and-mortar organizations that had driven the American economy for its first 224 years. Eight such companies had gone public in 1999 in Austin alone, including DrKoop.com, Garden.com, Crossroads Systems, and Vignette Corporation, and several of their CEOs were on hand at Auditorium Shores to bask in the klieg lights of CNBC.

One of Griffeth's first interviews was with Brian Smith of Crossroads Systems, a "provider of storage routers for storage network systems," whose company had begun trading on the NASDAQ market on October 20, 1999, at $18 a share, and closed that first day at nearly $79 a share, after reaching as high as $85.81. Its 337 percent first-day gain was then the fourth largest ever, trailing only three other dot-coms: TheGlobe.com, MarketWatch.com, and AskJeeves.com. As Smith now appeared on CNBC from Austin, his marketing team watched from behind the cameras, making cell phone calls to monitor the company's stock price minute by minute; their E*Trade accounts waited at the ready.

Also on the program was Greg Peters, CEO of Vignette, a provider of "content management software" for aggregating and delivering Web materials. At the time of Peters's appearance on another CNBC program, *The Edge,* in February 1999, there was considerable chatter on the investor message boards: "Interview went as they normally do," said one person who posted on SiliconInvestor.com. "CEO was very confident and covered what they do well. While they talked, they had boards up that listed top customers, etc. (Like BAY, CNET). . . . Typical stuff, nothing earthshattering."[1] On that day, the VIGN stock closed at $39.81 a share. On this day at Auditorium Shores, less than one year later, it was trading at more than $220 a share.

It was a financial feeding frenzy, fueled by little more than air and airtime, and if one slowed down just a little bit more, it might have appeared that the flowers on the side of Mopac were not bluebonnets at all, but Dutch tulips.

The bubble didn't last long. The Crossroads stock dropped from $79 on the day of *Power Lunch* to $4.69 by year's end. Vignette closed 2000 trading at $18 a share, and was sold a few years later. Garden.com was gone by November 2000. DrKoop.com ceased operations in December 2001.

On this January day in Austin, however, things still looked rosy. And maybe that was why, just for balance, CNBC also invited one of Austin's stodgy old-world businesses to be on the show, a 20-year-old company that had 100 honest-to-goodness bricks-and-mortar operations (imagine!), $1.6 billion in actual revenues, $536 million in real gross profit, and $42 million in bona fide net income from operations: Whole Foods Market.

The natural foods retailer was the odd man out on *Power Lunch,* but the odds-on-favorite to actually make some money. And that is precisely what happened. From the start of 1999 until January 24, 2000, the Whole Foods stock had traded rather narrowly in the $30 to $40 range. But as the rest of NASDAQ seemingly got trapped in the sticky mess of the burst dot-com bubble, Whole Foods' stock soared, closing the year 2000 at $61.13. Within 5 years it would join the ranks of the Fortune 500, en route to becoming a true financial juggernaut and one of the most talked-about companies in America.

How the world had changed, indeed.

Having evolved during the age of opportunism from a group of dreamy-eyed do-gooders into capitalist converts to the church of the triple-bottom-line, the companies of the natural foods industry entered what might be called the age of influence. It would be a time of consolidation, co-optation, pragmatism, and hybridization—but mostly an era in which the lessons of those who had already succeeded would illuminate the path for a huge influx of aspirants and entrepreneurial newcomers, and in which the industry itself would recast the meaning of success for other industries. With natural foods' unremitting growth—from an estimated $2 billion in gross revenues in the early seventies, to $9 billion in 1995, to $32 billion in 2000, to $65 billion in 2010, now approaching $100 billion, solid 5 to 10 percent annual gains while the food industry as a whole remains mired at about 1 percent annual growth[2]—it has emerged as a major force, a case study nonpareil in the apparent value of mission, transparency, authenticity, and trust in a changed business world.

Along the way, the industry's most visible leader, Whole Foods Market, transformed itself from a good company into a great one. It shed its hippie heritage to become the apotheosis of 21st-century trendiness, the high-class haunt of the healthy, and the quintessential symbol of the aspirations of upper middle classdom. It seamlessly integrated the strengths of its many acquisitions—a process that Chris Hitt, the company's go-to guy for cultural and business integration, ascribed to "understanding who you've got to work with and what they can do, and marrying the good from us and the good from the new company." There was never a set formula for how to handle an acquisition. The former Wellspring Grocery stores were allowed to keep selling their gourmet items with some unnatural ingredients for years, but Fresh Fields' crossover items were instantly eliminated; Unicorn Village's *The Nature of Things* mailer was cut, but John Mackey—citing the fact that Whole Foods was a "big tent" company that could accommodate lots of different people, thoughts, and ideas—allowed Bread of Life to keep working with Howard Stern, despite the shock jock's salacious antics and comments that some viewed as derogatory toward gays and lesbians, key constituents of the Whole Foods customer base.

Perfectly suited to the changing times, and perhaps a catalyst of them, Whole Foods thrived—surpassing $2 billion in sales in 2001, $5 billion in 2006, and, after the controversial Wild Oats acquisition was completed in 2009, $10 billion in 2011. Whole Foods opened in Canada in 2002, and landed in Europe in 2004 with the acquisition of Hass Hassan's Fresh & Wild. In order to complement and implement John Mackey's constantly evolving vision, it built a smart and well-rounded management team on the capable shoulders of the brilliant retailer-turned-preeminent-leader Walter Robb, and management inherited and integrated from its many acquisitions including A.C. Gallo and David Lannon (Bread & Circus), Ken Meyer (Fresh Fields), and, for a while at least, Russell Parker (Mrs. Gooch's) and Lex Alexander (Wellspring). "One of John's great strengths," said Chris Hitt, "is that he never feared finding talent." Whole Foods figured out how to execute at an extraordinarily high level, using the company's unique culture and decentralized structure to ensure both consistency and creativity a long way from Austin. It came to New York City in 2003, opening a 59,000-square-foot store in the new Time Warner Center in Columbus Circle in 2004 that for its sheer size, visibility, and *buzz* was perhaps the single most important food store to open in America's food capital since Balducci's or Zabar's, decades earlier.

Whole Foods also adapted: for a while, building bigger and bigger stores—sometimes 80,000 or 90,000 square feet, with creative options like hot Indian meals, outdoor farmers' markets, chocolate enrobing fountains, herb gardens, barbecue stations, and beer on tap—and then downsizing again to more human proportions when it realized it had started to become a victim of its own excesses. The company implemented groundbreaking programs to support sustainable fisheries, animal welfare, wind energy, and fair trade; voluntarily eliminated plastic bags long before local ordinances compelled it to do so; and created unusual self-funded health-care programs to encourage team members to lose weight and quit smoking so they could live the healthful lifestyle they were selling. Much of this redounds upon its brilliant cofounder and his vision. "If you really look into why Whole Foods is successful," said Hitt, "John Mackey deserves the recognition that people like Steve Jobs and Bill Gates have gotten. The company has contributed as much or more than those companies."

With such a solid core, Whole Foods weathered the Great Recession in reasonably good shape. Walter Robb told a class of MBA students at UC Davis in 2009 that at first the company couldn't understand why its year-over-year ("comp store") sales, which had always been around 8 percent, were faltering, and tried to adjust with more sales and promotions. "Then," he said, "we realized this was a complete reset, and we just had to hunker down." As Robb later told *Business Week* magazine, it was "a drop that I have never seen in 32 years of retail. Customers left us in droves."[3] Whole Foods made a conscious decision to slow its growth overnight, and late in 2008, to stabilize its cash situation, sold 17 percent of the company to Leonard Green and Partners; a few months later, Ron Burkle of Yucaipa Companies purchased another 7 percent on the open market. But the company's turnaround after that was stunning. The stock soared ninefold, not only recovering its losses but hitting an all-time high by February 2012. One analyst called it "one of the biggest success stories of the post-crash era, an almost inexplicable outcome."[4]

Still, Whole Foods has plenty of critics, even within the industry, who charge it with everything from haughtiness to hypocrisy to betrayal. Some have become critical of its size: As of 2013, Whole Foods reports that it is the eighth-largest food and drug store company in America, and the professional services firm Deloitte notes that Whole Foods is one of the 100 largest retail chains in the world.[5] The whole notion of this kind of "industrial organic" company has rankled many purists, who have taken umbrage at the scale (and, to a certain extent, methodologies) of Whole Foods and some of its big organic brethren, like Earthbound Farm, Horizon, and Aurora Dairy (a successor to Horizon created by Mark Retzloff in order to help fill the need for private-label organic milk).

Gene Kahn, one of the original high-minded idealists, said that he finally decided to leave Cascadian Farm because of Whole Foods. But it wasn't so much because of their size as their attitude. "When you hate your largest customer, and you cannot enjoy being in their presence, you know it is time to go away. I could no longer stand Whole Foods Market. I just literally couldn't abide them, either socially or business-wise. I felt they were so self-righteous and so self-congratulatory that I wanted nothing to do with them. Now, that's not about reality, that's about how I felt. So I knew I had to get out of Dodge."

(Kahn, of course, has long been an outspoken critic—one of the most passionate and vocal supporters of letting the natural foods industry, especially its organic component, expand in a pragmatic way so that it can reach scale. As a member of the National Organic Standards Board, which has battled over the sum and substance of the industry for many years, he fought for the inclusion of certain synthetics such as xanthan gum and ascorbic acid on "the national list of allowed and prohibited substances" in organic foods. In a storied and slightly ornery exchange, Columbia University nutrition professor Joan Dye Gussow asked in an article if such loosening of organic standards meant that perhaps there should be an organic Twinkie; Kahn replied, "If the consumers want organic Twinkies, then there should be organic Twinkies. . . . Organic is not your mother."[6] Similarly, when Kahn sold Cascadian Farm for the third time, to General Mills in 2003, he was criticized by some for accepting a job there as VP of sustainable development. But after 32 years at the helm of Cascadian, he knew a good thing when he saw one. "General Mills is so obsessive about product integrity that they probably improved my product integrity by a factor of 10. An example: [At Cascadian] I would make a sincere effort to wash out and clean out every last bit of conventional grain that might be in a harvesting machine or a combine. General Mills would *tear the damn machine apart*.")

Just as Whole Foods' supposed haughtiness incensed Gene Kahn, it has frustrated many others. Certainly it is true that hundreds of manufacturers owe their livelihoods to Whole Foods, and Mackey maintained in *Conscious Capitalism* that a core respect and "partnering mind-set" for vendors is still a basic tenet of the business.[7] Nevertheless, it is commonplace throughout the natural foods industry to hear vendors bemoan how difficult it is to do business with Whole Foods. They reserve particular venom for the Whole Foods decentralized buying system and the attitude that often accompanies it. In most cases, in order to sell a product to Whole Foods, a vendor must make separate pitches to the buyers in all 12 regions, and possibly even set up different ordering and distribution systems for them. When Whole Foods' few central buyers *do* conduct "category reviews" to determine which products to bring in, they make the vendors fly to Austin at their own expense, limit them to two people in the room, and give them exactly 10 minutes to state their case. Some of the buyers have actually been known to put an iPad on the desk and start the countdown clock running backwards from 10. This is clearly a self-preservation technique by a company that has in some ways become more successful than its infrastructure can support. It is hard to imagine that this paragon of progressivism has failed to see how contemptuous it sometimes appears to its vendors; but it is also hard to imagine that the company's leaders will permit the problem to linger.

——•——

The natural foods industry's amazing growth from 1996 on could not have happened on the strengths of one retailer alone. Sure enough, as the industry started to accelerate and prove itself to be a reliable source of both innovation and profits, the mainstream retailers began to horn in on the action, and soon a fascinating back-and-forth battle of co-optation broke out between natural and conventional retailers, with the manufacturers in the middle.

At first there was virtually no product overlap between natural and conventional food stores. Until the 1970s, of course, the vast majority of products sold in natural foods stores were bulk items, herbs and produce that typically bore no labels. Erewhon, Lundberg, Hain, and Arrowhead Mills were among the only recognizable packaged goods. The few national brands whose ingredients might otherwise have qualified them to be sold as natural or organic were often rejected by the co-ops and health foods stores on philosophical grounds, since these items were part of the Big Food complex that the "food faddists," hippies, and back-to-the-landers were fighting against.

Conversely, there was little incentive for the conventional stores to stock natural products, since they were more expensive, tasted awful, and would take up valuable shelf space with little prospect of attracting incremental sales from the fringe health foods consumers; as Warren Belasco noted in his book *Appetite for Change,* all of the food co-ops in Washington, DC, together grossed $2 million in 1974, one-eightieth of what Safeway alone sold in that city.[8] One of the only mainstream supermarkets that paid any attention to natural foods in the early years was Raley's, in Northern California, and that was primarily because one of their executives, Greg Plunkett, had become friends with some of the natural foods pioneers like Peter Roy, Anthony Harnett, and Doug Greene through the "Wild Man" trips that had grown out of the Natural Foods Network.

But starting in the 1970s, some innovative high-quality natural products with professional packaging began to appear, and the conventional retailers were not going to let that opportunity pass them by. Celestial Seasonings (at Safeway), Tom's of Maine (at CVS), and Stonyfield Farm yogurt (at Stop & Shop) were among the first major natural brands to cross the divide; Odwalla, Earth's Best baby food, Frookies, Coleman Beef, Earthbound Farm, Organic Valley, and Horizon were part of the next and much more visible wave. Consumer demographics were shifting, with the maturation of the well-educated and well-heeled Baby Boomers. Sensibilities toward food and health were also changing, due in part to a string of food safety crises (from cyclamate to saccharin to Alar to mad cow disease) and the visibility created by the large–format natural foods retailers like Mrs. Gooch's, Bread & Circus, and Whole Foods Market. As a result, many other natural foods manufacturers would also start to pursue a multichannel distribution strategy and try to get into the mainstream grocery stores.

With those upstart natural brands showing up on conventional supermarket shelves, conventional food manufacturers took note and began to fight back. At first many of them developed their own set of "health foods"—some of which were just lower-fat versions of their best sellers. Quaker 100% Natural Granola (1972), General Mills' Nature Valley Granola Bars (1973), Lite Beer from Miller (1973), Kellogg's Nutri-Grain Cereal (1981), Nestlé's Stouffer's Lean Cuisine (1981), and Campbell's Home Cookin' 100% Natural Soups (1983) were among the first ones introduced.[9] As early as 1980, nearly a third of all consumers reported that they were buying natural products.[10]

There had to have been some concern among food manufacturers that the creation of healthier products might cast an unwanted spotlight on their less-healthy lineup of foods already in the pantry. Nabisco, for example, introduced an all-natural whole wheat cracker called Sesame Wheats, which threatened to cannibalize some of the sales of its popular Wheat Thins and Cheese Nips, which contained artificial colors.[11] But the potential for profits outweighed all other concerns, paving the way for a whole new class of brand extensions that would eventually include Heinz Organic Ketchup (2002), Kellogg's Organic Rice Krispies (2006), and—onward, Richard Worth!—Keebler Toasteds Organic Harvest Wheat Crackers (2006).

Many conventional manufacturers also tried to short-circuit the development process by buying their way into the natural foods business. The first major acquisitions were made in 1984, when Kraft purchased Celestial Seasonings for $40 million and Smucker's bought R.W. Knudsen & Sons, a California juice company. Terry Tierney, who was then a brand manager at Kraft, said that the consumer packaged-goods giant didn't really know what it was buying. Kraft's usual approach to business planning was to break out a big leather-bound book that on page one told the 80-year history of the company, and on page two essentially said, "Don't screw it up." According to Tierney, "They were all about dominating the category, 80 percent market share, improving your margins, pricing up, spending it back against the business. That was the playbook." That stood in stark contrast to the natural foods industry's "risk-be-damned" philosophy. As a result, said Tierney, when Kraft purchased Celestial, "We saw a brand, but we didn't have the foggiest idea what to do with it."

Nevertheless, these deals gave the Big Food companies an entrée into a new line of business, and led to a trickle of merger activity over the next few years. In 1990, after getting over-extended because of investments made in the wake of the Alar scare, Gene Kahn sold a majority stake in Cascadian Farm to Welch's. Smucker's broke out its checkbook again in 1992 to buy Santa Cruz Naturals from John Battendieri.

But then, with the surge of Wall Street interest in the natural foods industry after the retail mergers of 1996, Big Food went on an unprecedented buying spree. Risk *could* be damned. Heinz bought Earth's Best in 1996 for about $30 million. M&M Mars bought Seeds of Change in 1997. Dairy giant Dean Foods bought equity positions in both WhiteWave and Horizon in 1998, later taking control of both companies; Dean also bought Alta Dena in 1999. General Mills bought Small Planet Foods (a combination of the post-Welch's Cascadian Farm and Muir Glen) in 1999, and Larabar in 2008. Kellogg bought Worthington Foods in 1999 for $307 million, Kashi in 2000 for $33 million, and Wholesome & Hearty Foods (Gardenburger) and Bear Naked in 2007 for a combined $122 million. Kraft became more active in the natural foods market, purchasing Boca Foods in January 2000, Balance Bar 3 days later, and Back to Nature in 2003. Nestlé acquired PowerBar in 2000 for $375 million. ConAgra bought Lightlife in 2000 and Alexia Foods in 2007. Group Danone took a 40 percent stake in Stonyfield Farm in 2001, and another 45 percent in 2003. Coca-Cola bought Odwalla in 2001 for $181 million, and a 40 percent interest in Honest

Tea for $43 million in 2007 (and the remainder in 2011). PepsiCo bought Izze beverages in 2002 and Naked Juice in 2006. Hershey Foods bought the organic chocolate brand Dagoba in 2006. The incredible crush of deal making was like a power lunch for the hungry Big Food interests, and the only thing missing was Bill Griffeth.

Paul Keene, the poetic pioneer of Walnut Acres, watched the start of this trend unfold with great interest and began commenting on it as early as 1985.

> "[T]he large multinational food companies," he wrote in one of the Walnut Acres catalogs, "having first unmercifully ridiculed the truth-seekers' eccentricity, began ever so cautiously to reverse themselves. They came to see that they could not, no matter how valiantly they tried in their advertising, transmute the dross of artificiality and devitalization into the gold of life-giving completeness demanded by the people, who were just beginning to rejoice in their new-found independence. And so the large companies carefully and gradually changed their approach, testing the waters with each reversal of policy. Unable to hold back the wave of the future, they decided to ride it in. . . . Bit by bit they began to 'discover' natural foods. They could make it appear that they themselves were the very first to think of this marvelous new approach to foods. The word *natural* was squeezed and twisted to make it fit new, self-serving definitions."

The pattern, he said, was characteristic of the phases of growth of *any* new idea: "First, people reject it; second, they ridicule it; third, the claim it as their own."[12] It was, in other words, an ineluctable journey from co-op to co-optation.

Keene ultimately came to feel that the co-optation of natural foods was acceptable: "Walnut Acres could not feed the whole planet, and half a loaf is better than none." But others railed against it every chance they got. There certainly were some egregious examples of co-optation, such as in 1984 when Kraft switched its description of Velveeta—a creation of scientists and chemists, often ridiculed as the archetypical "plastic" food—to "a blend of natural cheeses and other wholesome ingredients."[13] There were also more insidious examples, which the outspoken public health lawyer Michele Simon dubbed "nutriwashing." She cited companies that "jumped on the zero trans fat bandwagon, whether or not their product ever contained trans fats," and pointed out others that reformulated their products with whole grains (e.g., General Mills' Whole Grain Lucky Charms) but still had low fiber, high sugar, and plenty of artificial ingredients.[14] In the end, however, the power and influence of the natural foods industry's triple-bottom-line model would prevail, attracting more copycats than cheaters from the world of conventional foods, and thereby leading to what all but the most hard-line holdouts of the high-minded idealists would admit is tremendous progress.

Today, a walk down the aisles of just about any supermarket reveals an enormous variety of mainstream brands that have developed natural products or reformulated artificial ones: Ovaltine with no artificial flavors, Chef Boyardee Spaghetti and Meatballs with no artificial preservatives, Natural Jif, 100% Natural Lipton Citrus Green Tea, All Natural Roasted Garlic and Black Bean Tostitos Tortilla Chips, and more. Jack Murphy, the former COO of Fresh Fields, who in 2008 became CEO of Earth Fare, a rapidly growing chain of natural foods stores based in Asheville, North Carolina, has welcomed several of these types of products to his shelves, and espouses a philosophy that could never have held sway in an earlier era. "My position is that if this industry is ultimately going to succeed long term, we have to celebrate the national manufacturers that are coming over to what we believe are the best ingredients to have. We need to celebrate those people, not denigrate them. . . . Our simple rule at Earth Fare is, if it fits the food philosophy, and if we think we can sell it, we will carry it." Though old-school natural foods retailers seldom deigned to allow mass-market brand names into their stores, in the 21st century that is clearly changing. "It's not about the company or the CEO or how many planes they have or what their carbon footprint is," said Murphy. "It is all about the ingredients."

Late to the game, the conventional supermarket industry tried to figure out how best to capitalize on the natural foods boom. "They were operating in a world that they didn't recognize anymore," said Terry Dalton of Unicorn Village. "They had to go back and not only add natural SKUs [stock-keeping units, a synonym for "individual products"], but sort of think about ways of being more transparent and sustainable, because that's what the natural foods pioneers stimulated in the consumer base."

They weren't very good at it. Stocking a few of the natural and organic top-sellers was a defensive strategy, aimed at keeping some of their more progressive customers from making a "second stop" at the natural foods supermarket and, presumably, learning how much deeper their selection was, how much better their pricing, and, in some cases, how much more enjoyable their shopping experience. Many of the larger chains simply carved out small sections to create a "store-within-a-store," in some instances laying down faux wooden flooring and hanging an overhead sign that said something simplistic and imitative such as "Nature's Pantry." Safeway, for example, was reported to have 770 stores with natural foods sections in 1987.[15] By the early 1990s, most conventional supermarkets had also added at least some organic produce. In her "Eating Well" column in the *New York Times* on August 28, 1996, Marian Burros said that "experts predict that within 10 years it will be difficult to tell a Whole Foods from a Safeway."[16]

A few conventional chains went further, and built their own natural foods stores. In 1994 HEB opened its first Central Market store in Austin—a free-flowing 61,000-square-foot "amusement park for food lovers" that quickly surpassed Whole Foods as the most buzz-worthy food store in town. A handful of additional Central Market stores would follow throughout Texas. While not explicitly called a natural foods store, it posed a challenge that Whole Foods could not (and still has not) figured out how to counter: the everything store. It featured a huge assortment of local, gourmet, and conventional foods in addition to thousands of natural and organic items. Wegmans would pursue a similar format when it moved outside of its upstate New York home in the late nineties. For several years, these stores clearly influenced Whole Foods to shift to larger store formats and to incorporate more gourmet offerings.

The first conventional company to open a real natural foods store—appropriate, since it was also among the very first to have opened a regular supermarket, back in 1930—was King Kullen. In November 1995, it converted a 25-year-old King Kullen in East Setauket, New York, into a beautiful 18,000-square-foot store called Wild by Nature, with a circular café, colorful up-lighting, and a scratch bakery. For inspiration, it turned to Fresh Fields and Whole Foods. "They have already perfected the concept, but we have looked at their concept, and we see that there is truthfully a need for this type of market on Long Island," Tom Cullen, vice president of government, industry, and public relations for King Kullen, told *Supermarket News*.[17]

In Boston, where so many of the natural foods innovations had started 3 decades earlier, conventional grocer Star Market launched its natural foods business, Wild Harvest, with a store in Medford in 1996. This was a new sort of hybrid store that, in a sense, formalized the "crossover product" concept that dated back at least to Pearl Street Market and which had been tested by Wellspring Grocery and Fresh Fields, among others. "Given all the resources that we can put behind it as a big company," Star's chairman Henry Nasella told public radio's *Living on Earth* program in December 1996, "we can be very successful and also at the same time do the right thing in expanding, if you will, this whole natural food industry to more and more people that otherwise wouldn't have been exposed to it. . . . I like the quality, I like the ambiance of some of those stores, but I really have to shop more than one place and it's not convenient. You know, I like a Diet Coke or I want a Ben and Jerry's Ice Cream or I want whatever. But if in fact they were going to go to a second store anyway and going to buy those products, why not save them time? I mean, time is the currency of the year 2000."[18]

Wild Harvest never really gained traction. Ironically, though, in the same month it opened, Leo Kahn, then 80, launched his last-gasp entrepreneurial effort: a new natural foods store called Nature's Heartland in Bedford, Massachusetts. Kahn built Nature's Heartland into a four-store chain, and then sold it to Whole Foods in 1999 for about $25 million, perhaps earning the last laugh with John Mackey, after all. Kahn passed away in 2011, his estate and legacy secure.

This trend continued even well into the new century, with the opening in 2007 of the first of three GreenWise Markets, a natural offshoot of the Florida mega-supermarket chain Publix. By then, however, many of the conventional supermarkets had settled upon another tactic to steal business from the natural foods stores: private-label natural and organic brands. (Indeed, GreenWise started off as a private-label brand.) This was perhaps an inevitable development, since on average private-label products generate a 35 percent gross profit margin, compared to 25.9 percent for national brands;[19] however, until 2005 or so there simply was not enough manufacturing capacity among co-packers to produce large volumes of private-label natural or certified organic foods. In 2003, for example, when manufacturing capacity was still limited, only 35 new organic private-label products were introduced; by 2007 that number skyrocketed to 540.[20]

One of the most successful of the conventional retailer "clean" private-label efforts was the O Organics brand, launched by Safeway in 2005. Its success came as little surprise to people in the natural foods industry, however, because they knew that it was the creation of Denis Ring, who had built the 365 program for Whole Foods (remarkably, neither Ring nor his former business partner, Bob Johnson, were ever required to sign a noncompete agreement when they left Whole Foods). Along with the Open Nature and Eating Right lines, which came later, Safeway developed hundreds of healthier private-label products. In 2012 those products generated more than $750 million in sales.[21]

There were many others. In 2001, Hannaford Supermarkets in Maine created a store brand called Nature's Place. In 2008 Supervalu, which owns numerous supermarket banners, including Shaw's, the successor to Star Market, resurrected Henry Nasella's Wild Harvest name for its line of private-label natural and organic foods. The nation's biggest supermarket chain, Kroger, originally got into the game in 2000 with its Naturally Preferred line, and extended it in 2006 with Private Selection Organic; in 2012 these were united under the name Simple Truth, which within one year of launch became a billion-dollar brand.

To most consumers, the brand names mattered little and anyway were probably conflated in their minds into a giant morass of consolidated, co-opted, feel-good, farmers' market foods—the grocery equivalent, perhaps, of faux wood paneling on the side of a Subaru Outback L.L. Bean Edition.

But by this time, it wasn't about brands anymore. It was about ubiquity. The taste, quality, variety, packaging, and value of natural foods had improved to the point of near parity with conventional foods, so they gained much wider acceptance. Additionally, the new generation of Millennials was coming of age with a holistic interest in natural foods but an indifference to where they were purchased. Whereas in 1991 only 7 percent of all organic products were sold through conventional retailers, by 2006 mass-market retailers had surpassed natural foods retailers as the number one channel for organic food sales (46 percent to 44 percent).[22] The larger natural products category is also now about evenly split (41 percent through natural retailers, 40 percent through conventional retailers as of 2012).[23] As Doug Greene said, "When I see natural food in a gas station, or anywhere, I am excited. . . . The big thing is getting somebody on the path of thinking better, eating better, feeling better. There's a lot of doors to that path, and you can't be too judgmental about them."

Because of all these developments—natural foods selling in conventional stores; some conventional foods selling in natural foods hybrid stores; conventional manufacturers launching their own natural and organic versions; conventional stores opening natural stores-within-a-store or natural retail subsidiaries; and just about everybody creating a natural and organic private-label brand—the balance of the industry had shifted dramatically. The barriers between the retail channels, which so many of the early natural foods retailers had worked so hard to erect, came tumbling down. And as the differences between natural and conventional retailers diminished, new opportunities opened up for those who were motivated less by principle than by pragmatism or profit.

Accordingly, a next logical step would have been for a major conventional supermarket retailer to buy its way into this profitable new business by acquiring a natural foods chain. But it never happened.

At first the conventional supermarkets had a hard time figuring out whether the natural foods stores posed a real threat, like the new warehouse format and membership clubs did. Most conventional companies reacted in about the same manner as Izzy Cohen of Giant Food had toward Fresh Fields: "Should we crush them?" followed by a period of wait-and-see.

But from the point at which Sandy Gooch spurned Safeway and chose to sell her business to Whole Foods in 1993, there were no serious attempts at market miscegenation. Internally, Whole Foods Market executives often speculated about whether they might be a tempting takeover target for a conventional grocer, but concluded that because their motivation was to balance the needs of all stakeholders (including customers, team members, vendors, and the environment, and not just investors) they were bulletproof. A conventional chain wouldn't be able to figure out what to do with them. Stan Amy did sell Nature's Fresh Northwest to the vitamin retailer GNC in 1996; but according to him, that was a strategic acquisition, not a territory acquisition. "They knew they had filled all the 'A' sites for a GNC store," recalled Amy. "And they knew the stock market was going to beat them up if they didn't continue to have topline growth. So they were looking for a new way to grow and that's why they acquired us." Similarly, the warehouse chain Smart & Final bought the quasi-natural foods company Henry's Farmers Markets in 2007 as a strategic complement. But in general, the conventional supermarkets kept to themselves.

Instead, the move toward hybridization came from the natural side of the once insuperable barrier.

First, when GNC's stock fell from about $40 to $10 a share in the middle of 1999 following rumors that it was going to switch to a discount format, cash grew tight and the vitamin retailer turned around and sold Nature's Fresh Northwest to Wild Oats. Mike Gilliland and his team talked about using a "best practices approach" in marrying the two companies, but mostly they tried to run Nature's from Boulder using the Wild Oats system, which included some symbolically stupid moves like searching employees' bags when they left the store. "It turned into a bad territory acquisition," said Stan Amy, "one that was destroying the value that was there, and not just the economic value but the human value." Lots of employees quit.

Brian Rohter, who was running Nature's at the time, told Amy how fed up he was trying to operate under the Wild Oats system, and that got them thinking that perhaps there was a better alternative. In response, Amy called his friend Chuck Eggert at Pacific Foods, with the idea of piecing together an investment team that could start a new retail operation and hire the disaffected former Nature's employees. "We know how good these people are," Amy told Eggert. "We know what they can do. This is a pretty good bet. You are betting on a management team, and you are looking at a competitor in Wild Oats that doesn't know what the fuck they are doing." So Rohter, Amy, and Eggert sat down at Widmer Gasthaus Pub in Portland, Oregon, and drew up plans for a new company that they would call New Seasons.

There was more than a little irony in the name. The idea was not just to move beyond their disenchantment with Wild Oats, but to create a new hybrid model store that would cross over from natural to conventional as smoothly as autumn crossed into winter. "[Y]ou can find everything from pasture eggs and organic baby food to Frosted Flakes and Coca-Cola in our aisles," reads the mission on their current Web site. "We're here to please the whole family."[24]

According to Amy, the hybrid model was an "essential definition" of the concept, a way of getting to the core of what they wanted to do. "We don't own customers. If you don't offer the convenience of selection, you then can't locate your stores close enough to each other to provide the convenience of location. And you are restricted to higher demographic profiles. So you can't offer access to good food to people who would otherwise buy it." A hybrid store would solve the problem.

He cited as an example the New Seasons store in the Arbor Lodge neighborhood in North Portland, which opened in 2005. At the time, demographic
studies showed that the neighborhood contained only 18 percent college graduates; yet the store, in a mere 22,000 square feet, is now doing about $500,000 a
week in sales. "Kicking butt," he said with pride. "Whole Foods would *never*
consider going into a neighborhood like that. But we have the opportunity to
provide access to good food, the opportunity to support far more sustainable
acres out there in production, and the obligation to balance broadening the
product with going deeper in the niche." And all because the store sells Coke
alongside the natural sodas like Zevia.

A similar, though decidedly less intellectual, approach was taken by the
Boney Family when they started what became known as Henry's Farmers Markets in 1997, and then created Sprouts Farmers Markets in 2002 (the companies
were united in a merger in 2011).

Henry Boney had gotten his start in the business with a fruit stand in San
Diego in 1943, and went on to create many other ventures, including the very
successful chain of convenience stores called SpeeDee Mart, which eventually
became 7-Eleven; his son and grandson developed the farmers' market format
stores, having been reared in the tradition of convenience stores with cheap
prices and without any product standards. At Henry's and Sprouts, there would
be no wrangling over whether to sell items with white sugar or hydrogenated
oils, as all of the true natural foods stores had done. There would be little
emphasis on organic produce, which the Sprouts team always believed customers don't care much about and which therefore for years was shunted off to a
dark and remote corner of the store, just as conventional supermarkets had
done in the beginning. Even "natural" was never truly in the Sprouts retail
vocabulary, any more than an apostrophe was in its punctuation of the word
"farmers"; both were implied, and apparently optional. So in the Sprouts stores,
right alongside Nature's Path Organic Hemp Plus Granola and bulk bins full of
lentils and quinoa would be artificially colored gummy worms, deli meats pre-
served with nitrates, and freshly baked muffins made with so many ingredients
that they do not even fit on the product signs. In the new order of things, it did
not matter. The convenience of a hybrid selection and low prices on less-than-
perfect produce has proven to be a winning formula. By 2013 Sprouts grew into
the second largest chain in the history of the natural foods industry, with more

than 150 stores and $2 billion in sales, without product standards or high-minded inspirational leadership at all. Its big growth push simply came along at the right time, just as the country was heading into the Great Recession and as the natural foods industry was heading into its era of hybridization. Indeed, at the time it went public in 2013, Sprouts' majority owner was Apollo Global Management, which earlier in the same year had purchased from the bankrupt Hostess Brands the ultimate symbol of artificial food that the natural foods community had been fighting against for all those years: Twinkies.

And then, of course, there was Mike Gilliland. The man who would have been natural foods king had built a fortune at Wild Oats in part by being so good at observing and mimicking his competitors. Gilliland had become enamored of the Boneys' model, and in 1999 bought the Henry's stores. "Some of their stores were 20 and 30 years old, and were still comping in the double digits," he said. "It was crazy to me. They seemed invulnerable. I loved their saying in the old days, 'a steppingstone to better health.' I loved that concept, of someone who is making a transition and really can't afford it. . . . There is a whole universe of people who are not comfortable shopping at Whole Foods. And so I was pretty impressed with that concept."

When he left Wild Oats in 2001, he was still thinking about that model, and his entrepreneurial motor was still running. He talked to the Boneys about investing in what would become Sprouts, but when they couldn't come to terms, figured he would just do it himself. Thus, in 2002, right after Sprouts opened its first store in Arizona, Gilliland launched a concept that he called Sunflower Farmers Market. "We saw Sprouts doing it in Phoenix, and [at first] we still kept trying to reinvent the wheel. So we tried to do bigger stores, and huge food service, and large liquor stores. I lost my ass the first couple of years. More than I needed to." But then the industry's great imitator went back to basics. "We just dumbed it down enough that it ended up being a replica of Sprouts." Indeed, the store layout, the hybrid product mix, even the ads were so similar that many customers didn't know the difference. "I am sure the average person walking in couldn't even tell if it was a Sprouts or a Sunflower," said Gilliland.

Gilliland ultimately built Sunflower into a 35-store chain. He was forced to resign as CEO in 2011 because of legal and personal difficulties, but the kingpin of the natural foods industry's age of opportunism still made one last opportunistic move: He sold Sunflower to Sprouts in 2012, and has eased into an early retirement in a beautiful home in Paradise Valley, Arizona—just a couple of miles down the road from Sprouts' corporate headquarters.

The fight for legitimacy—waged so valiantly by the high-minded idealists and the Rodale family—had been won. The contest of wills between the early natural foods pioneers and the Big Food Establishment—Mo Siegel trying to defend his goofy tea company to C.W. Cook of General Foods—had been decided. The issue-oriented ads of the Mrs. Gooches and Bread & Circuses—the Department of Energy's solution to the problem of radioactive waste—had worked, so that a sizeable swath of the population now understood the dangers of chemical farming and the value of eating well. Natural foods had transmogrified into a big business, and the only battle remaining would be one of market share: *How* big?

As of 2013, even after nearly 50 years of effort to restore some "natural balance" to the world of food, it is estimated that natural foods represent only about 5 percent of total food sales—and organic farmland only about 5 percent of all farm acreage—so there is great opportunity, and perhaps a long struggle, still ahead.

To measure the industry's impact in mere percentages, however, misses the mark. Unnatural food—be it chemically farmed, highly processed, or laden with artificial ingredients—is and probably long will be the dominant paradigm of our diets; and the soulless, standardless, linoleum-lined supermarkets will continue to obscure their more progressive brethren with the glare of their garish lights. Instead, like a faint star, one must use averted vision and look off to the side to appreciate the true accomplishments, and significance, of the natural foods revolution.

First, there is the professionalization of the industry itself. The days of Michael and Kay Greer cutting a hole in their apartment floor so that customers at the Nature's Food and Tool store down below could summon them with a bell, or of Gary Hirshberg promoting Stonyfield Farm yogurt by presenting a radio DJ with a cup full of camel manure, are not all that far removed. It was 1995—well into the Internet age!—when Heather Howitt was Xeroxing copies of hand-drawn labels to convert Oregon Chai from a food service product into a retail package. Today, not that far past the tipping-point year of 1996, Whole Foods and The Fresh Market are widely admired for their sophisticated merchandising and customer service; the yogurt manufacturer Chobani runs TV commercials during the Academy Awards; and there are sophisticated packaging innovations happening all across the natural products world, such as the all-cardboard liquid laundry detergent bottles launched by Seventh Generation in 2011. The natural foods industry's combination of sustained growth and warm-and-fuzzy save-the-world sensibility has also begun to attract top-level talent, including many recent MBA graduates who in the past would never have contemplated a career in this industry, and who wouldn't have been welcomed in it, either.

Another sign of this professionalization is that the natural foods industry remains a hotbed of entrepreneurial activity, long after its period of white-hot growth. Venture capitalists poured $350 million into food projects in 2012, mostly natural, organic, and/or vegan, and overall investment deals were up 37 percent for the year. (The language used to describe this trend by the *New York Times* sounds remarkably familiar: For investors, they say, the "ultimate goal is nothing short of . . . transforming the food industry.")[25]

There has also been a strong movement toward natural, organic, and vegan fast-casual restaurants. Terry Dalton's Chestnut and Unicorn Village restaurants in Florida were early leaders, and Gary Hirshberg modeled a newer concept with a small chain called O'Naturals in 2001. But in recent years there have been some major successes scored by True Foods Kitchen, Organic Avenue, Native Foods Café, and something called Lyfe Kitchen. On CNBC's *Squawk Box* in November 2012—in a segment called "The Disruptors"—Lyfe's CEO, Stephen Sidwell, said that his goal is to produce supermarket products and open 250 restaurants within 5 years. He told the panel that Lyfe had raised $30 million from "friends, family, associates, suppliers"—though he neglected to mention that the concept was cofounded by Mike Roberts, former global president and COO of McDonald's, who had tried to bring healthier items to the Golden Arches, including mango strips, yogurt, and a vegan McNugget.[26]

Meanwhile, Expo West, the largest of the trade shows that Doug Greene had created in the early eighties to try to facilitate some spontaneous combustion, now draws nearly 70,000 people to the Anaheim Convention Center each March, making it the largest show at that enormous venue. Of the 2,248 vendors who exhibited there in 2013, approximately 650 were new to the show—a remarkable sign of entrepreneurial vitality. Many of these were classic mom-and-pop operations, crammed into the Convention Center's underground Hall E, which event organizers used to refer to as the "Hash Den" for all of its funky, avant-garde exhibitors, and where the industry's huckster heritage is still partially on display: *An earnest but overly enthusiastic man in a baseball cap stands in front of his booth for something called Bonk Breaker Bars and solicits passersby with his elevator speech. "Have you heard of us? Give us a try! All-natural protein bars, gluten-free, dairy-free, soy-free!" There are CEOs handing out T-shirts, "booth babes" in nothing but flesh-toned Spandex holding trays of samples, and more than a few "spin to win" wheels making their clackety-clack noises. A sign at the Saffron Road booth promises "certified humane 100 percent vegetarian feed pasture-raised" products. Nearby are booths for Trophy Farms "snacking tubes"—basically, sleeves of nuts—Nature Vites gummy multivitamins, the Sweetwood Cattle Company, Quirky Jerky, NadaMoo coconut milk, and Incredible Cravings ("nutritious foods for moms and moms-to-be").*

In 2013 even French's Mustard made an appearance in the Hash Den, with a sign that said "100 percent natural" and a booth backdrop ever-so-carefully designed to look like it was handwritten. And while French's may be an old-time brand that debuted at the 1904 St. Louis World's Fair, long before most of the miracles of the food laboratories, many of the companies exhibiting at Expo these days are new brands that can easily be carbon-dated to the modern natural foods revolution, when just about any nature-evoking words can be mashed together to form a new company name: Orchard Valley Harvest, Forces of Nature, Freshly Wild, Purefit Nutrition, Organika Health Products, Nature's Earthly Choice—they're all there, too.

But in this modern era, there is also a level of sophistication that is evident right from the startup. Many of the entrepreneurs drawn to the natural foods industry because of its "values and value" orientation are well educated, well advised, well funded, and they are arriving with well-thought-out business models that are driven first and foremost by a clear, compelling mission.

Runa, for example, is a company that makes a caffeinated tea from the Amazonian guayusa tree leaf. But the product is simply a means to the end, which is its mission of supporting the values and economic needs of the farming communities in the Ecuadorian Amazon. This isn't just another example of corporate social responsibility, the laudable movement that had led many companies to attach themselves to a charity and donate 2 percent of the proceeds, but which usually remained peripheral to the main mission of profit making. It is a cause built into a company.

Runa was founded by two Brown University graduates named Tyler Gage and Dan MacCombie, who had conceived of the idea while traveling in South America during time off from college, and then formalized their business plan in an entrepreneurship class in the fall of 2008. After graduating in December of that year, Gage passed up a Fulbright scholarship and MacCombie declined a consulting job so that they could move to Ecuador and begin work on their mission. They assembled a board of advisors, including their entrepreneurship professor at Brown, Danny Warshay, who urged them to think big and to establish clear, bold differences from everything else in the marketplace (*the only tea with as much caffeine as coffee; twice the antioxidants of green tea; the only Amazonian tea on the market,* etc.). They studied aspects of other natural foods companies, such as the market-driven restoration model created by Guayaki to assist with reforestation in South America, and the triple-bottom-line approach of Sambazon, which had been launched in 2000 with a goal of helping family farmers in the Amazon. They looked at nonprofits such as Sustainable Harvest International and the One Acre Fund. They leveraged their liberal arts training and network to help problem-solve on a stunningly diverse range of issues, including FDA regulations for new products, import rules, product design, manufacturing, co-packing, factory construction in Ecuador, accounting, and government relations. And, at least vaguely aware of Gary Hirshberg's incisive recap of the history of natural foods startups—"hopeless infinite naïveté about cash flow"—they gradually raised *a lot* of money: $2.4 million in rolling convertible debt, mostly in small $5,000, $10,000, and $20,000 chunks from a group of 80 investors, in lieu of going the textbook route of a few strategic investors who carried a lot of weight. "We were very busy," said Gage of all that learning and fundraising, "but that's one of the benefits of having a pretty highly caffeinated product."

Mission is the primary driver for Runa, and this has increasingly become the norm in the natural foods industry. As John Mackey wrote in his book, "Money-making enterprises need to discover or create their higher purpose beyond profit maximization in order to realize their full potential."[27] Organic Valley sells dairy products at a reduced profit margin so that it can continue to pay high prices for raw organic ingredients and keep the small family farms alive. Revolution Foods sees its mission as "leading the conversation on childhood health," and does so primarily through partnerships with schools, where it serves more than 200,000 healthy meals a day and also offers vending machines that sell all-natural products. When Annie's Homegrown filed its S-1 with federal securities regulators in 2011 prior to going public, the company stated its primary mission as "to cultivate a healthier, happier world by spreading goodness through nourishing foods, honest words and conduct that is considerate and forever kind to the planet."[28] This is not to say that profit isn't one of the main missions—for as Paddy Spence, the Harvard MBA/Kashi VP/founder of SPINS and now CEO of Zevia noted, "Natural products has been the most consistent industry I can think of over the past 20 years in terms of generating wealth for entrepreneurs." It's just that the bottom line now factors in people and planet as well as profit.

Unquestionably, this unique orientation of the natural foods industry has exerted a strong influence on other industries. In article after article about mission-driven businesses, and study after study, leading natural foods companies are featured as prime examples. A Google search in May 2013 for "mission driven business" and "Whole Foods" yielded more than 260,000 results. The Cone Communications "2011 Cause Marketing and CR Trends" study of the top mission-driven programs cited Stonyfield Farm, Annie's Homegrown, and Honest Tea—alongside non-food companies like Patagonia, Nissan, Lush, and Levi's. Cone's research also showed how deeply consumers now embrace mission-driven companies, with 94 percent of Americans saying they were likely to switch brands if there were a comparable one that had the mission of supporting a social cause.[29] "We are changing all sorts of other things besides just the food in this country," said Mark Retzloff, who cofounded Eden Foods, Alfalfa's, Horizon Organic, and many other industry companies. "I am proud to have been a part of that from the beginning. It's about how we build communities, how we take care of each other, how we build a better world."

Meanwhile, Stonyfield has also attracted a wide variety of non-food companies to its Climate Counts global warming initiative, including L'Oréal, Time Warner, Kimberly Clark, Nokia, Liz Claiborne, and News Corp. A commonality among all these companies is a fundamental belief in the power of business to do good, which if nothing else has been bolstered by the industry-wide success of natural foods. As Gary Hirshberg wrote in his book, *Stirring It Up*, "It's going to take a lot more than moral rectitude and virtuous principles to set us on a truly sustainable path. . . . Business is the most powerful force on the planet; it got us into this mess and is the only force strong enough to get us out."[30]

Perhaps most significantly, the enormous success of some natural foods companies has created a road map for other companies—the very thing that the early natural foods pioneers lacked. Numerous high-profile companies have materialized since the explosion of the natural foods industry in 1996 that are equally mission-centric, including Toms Shoes (which donates a pair of shoes to a child in need for every pair sold), Zipcar (which seeks to improve mobility and reduce fossil-fuel consumption through car-sharing), World of Good (an importer of handcrafted products, acquired in 2010 by eBay, which seeks to promote fair trade policies), and IceStone (which transforms waste glass into countertops). Dow Jones launched its Sustainability Indexes in 1999, to measure the economic, environmental, and social performance of 2,500 companies. In 2007 the concept of a B Corp (benefit corporation) was introduced— something that has been described by Jay Coen Gilbert of B Lab as "like the Fair Trade label but for a whole company, not just a bag of coffee."[31] As of mid-2013, there were more than 780 B Corporations registered around the world. Blake Mycoskie, the founder of Toms, said that the economic philosophy of Milton Friedman, which held that the only social responsibility of business was to increase profits, "is out of date and out of gas. Social and economic priorities are merging. Companies realize that a profits-only focus risks alienating customers and partners. They also know that if they want to attract the best talent, they have to pay attention to having a positive social impact."[32]

Such efforts represent the new ethic of "social entrepreneurship" in the purest sense—a variant of the notion of "right livelihood" that had driven WhiteWave's Steve Demos and some of the early industry pioneers, infused with a little pragmatic 21st-century capitalistic drive. "We are not doing it out of some massively idealistic or revolutionary framework," said Tyler Gage about Runa and some of the other mission-driven startups. "I think we are ambitious and very values-driven, and have a very clear focus and specific missions that we know we can make a dent in."

———

Along with mission, the issue of transparency has long been at the core of the natural foods industry, in part because the chemical-food revolution had led to so much obfuscation. In his influential 1972 book, *Eat Your Heart Out,* Jim Hightower noted that the Mounds and Almond Joy candy bars, then manufactured by Peter Paul, were coated with an ingredient that, at that time, was termed "an undisclosed brown substance," and even the president of the company said "I'm not exactly sure what it is." Hightower also cited a company called International Multifoods—a name seemingly right out of Fritz Lang's 1927 masterpiece *Metropolis,* but which was very real and later sold to Smucker's—and its ingredient product called Merlinex. International Multifoods advertised Merlinex as "Instant Anything," which could be used as a substitute for real ingredients in a wide variety of products. "It is the silly putty of the food world," wrote Hightower, "that you eat as an extender in colby cheese, as phony fig paste in fig bars, as imitation strawberry filling in pastries, and as a texturizer in brownies, to mention only a few of its uses."[33]

Nowadays, with more than 5,000 food additives available, food labels are less transparent than ever, with pleasant euphemisms like "dough conditioners" taking the place of their actual names, such as sodium stearoyl lactylate or diacetyl tartaric ester of monoglyceride, otherwise known as DATEM. As Melanie Warner pointed out in her fascinating 2013 book, *Pandora's Lunchbox,* there are also some 3,750 "food-contact substances" such as lubricating oils and cleaning chemicals that are used on the machines that process food, which could show up in trace amounts in the products but which you will never see on a food label itself.[34]

Natural foods, on the other hand, were intended to be all about transparency. As Paul Keene of Walnut Acres once wrote, "We have always insisted on telling what we know about the way in which our products are raised, about exactly what is contained in each one."[35] Chuck Eggert, the founder and CEO of Pacific Natural Foods, imposed a rule in his company that if anyone wants to use more than seven ingredients in a formula, they must plead their case to him about why the eighth ingredient is needed. This came about because he read lots of old food-science books and understood the Rube Goldberg–like process that had resulted in such complex foods. "After World War II, they started using preservatives," said Eggert. "And if they used a preservative, the flavor went away. So then they had to put in flavor. Then those two didn't like each other and they had to put in an emulsifier. And now you get into this whole chicken noodle soup that has 40 ingredients. Why? When your mom made it at home she just had chicken broth and noodles."

It is also transparency, more than anything else, that is the beating heart of the heated battles over "the national list" of acceptable organic ingredients (octadecylamine? xanthan gum?) and the labeling of genetically modified organisms (GMOs). "It's not necessarily what information they are providing, it's what transparency they are giving," said Eggert.

Nevertheless, from Annie Withey printing her address and home phone number on the packages of Annie's Mac & Cheese, to Bob's Red Mill's cellophane packaging that enables customers to see his stone-ground grain, to Whole Foods' binder of employee salaries, to Odwalla's no-excuses handling of its product recall, the industry's leaders and leading companies have usually believed that their products and business practices should have nothing to hide—and indeed, that they will become better companies if they hold themselves accountable for their mission in a very public way. Stonyfield Farm and Honest Tea, for example, both publish annual report cards on their activities that contain impressive lists of accomplishments, but also some case studies in self-circumspection. In Honest Tea's *Keeping It Honest 2010 Mission Report,* for example, it stated that the purpose of the report was "not [to] be a cheerleading document, but rather one that discloses progress, shortcomings, and opportunities for improvement." The report included a scorecard showing the percentage of women (36 percent) and minorities (13 percent) among the employee base, and detailed the amount of carbon emissions resulting from the company's production processes, including the average of 640 miles that each case of tea travels before it reaches a store. The report noted that "We exist in a contradiction" because despite Honest Tea's corporate commitment to sustainability, "the bulk of our products are sold as single serve packages, the majority of which are not recycled." It also openly discussed the company's controversial move toward a new plastic bottle that was 22 percent lighter, but which some customers viewed as "cheap tricks" or "trying to sell them more air."[36]

Many of the companies now entering the natural foods industry, and working their way up from the Hash Den to the main exhibit hall in the Anaheim Convention Center at Expo West, are highly transparent. They have been born that way.

For example, there is Back to the Roots, a company created by UC Berkeley students Nikhil Arora and Alex Velez after they discovered that used coffee grounds could be a good growing medium for mushrooms. The pair developed kits for growing mushrooms in this manner, and their success led to millions of dollars in sales and an invitation to meet with President Barack Obama during a roundtable of 15 small-business owners at the White House in November 2012.

In building the company, Alex and Nikhil never really sat down and declared that transparency was one of their core values; it just was. "Graduating in '09, in the heart of the financial mess," said Nikhil, "people of our age were like, 'There has got to be a better way to do this. Let's not do that again.' You heard about Lehman Brothers and all this chaos, and that's not who we wanted to be. There were other examples of transparency in the natural foods space we knew we could follow." They sought assistance from many of the natural foods companies in the Bay Area, including Clif Bar, Annie's Homegrown, Numi Tea, Plum Organics, and Whole Foods. They were also influenced by Patagonia, which on its website is very open about the company's shortcomings, including working conditions and its carbon footprint. Alex and Nikhil aggressively began marketing their business through demos and social media, always responding to customers and managing to come through as real people who were feeling their way through the travails of a startup instead of as slick entrepreneurs. "The world has gone from clever marketing to transparent marketing, and that's what people respect; we totally believe in that," Nikhil said.

Of course, there is an argument to be made that in the Internet age, and especially in its social media phase, greater transparency is unavoidable. Companies no longer control their brand voice or information flow; all they can really do is join in the dialogue. This, according to Steve Demos, "has brought companies to show what they are authentically made of and what they stand for. It was all sensory, but now sensory is at parity. Price is at parity. Marketing cuteness is at parity. So where is the differentiation in brand? It comes from the ability of the company to represent in the world of social change something that is greater. They will learn this over some long period of time."

Some of the conventional food companies are already starting to learn about the power and necessity of transparency. When Gary Hirshberg sold a controlling stake in his company to Group Danone, and then helped Seth Goldman to do the same in selling Honest Tea to Coca-Cola, he created a new sort of entrepreneurial model in which the founder of the acquired company stays on and begins to inculcate some of the mission and transparency into the new parent company. Goldman, for example, is frequently pulled into Coca-Cola corporate meetings in Atlanta, and has had a lively dialogue with the Coke executives on issues such as fair trade, high-fructose corn syrup, and even the controversy over GMO labeling in 2012's California Proposition 37. "As a company we are less than a half-percent of Coca-Cola's sales, so the idea that we are going to be dictating to Coca-Cola what their policies are is just not realistic," Goldman said. "But there are internal conversations." It was thus unsurprising to see Coca-Cola announce the inclusion of calories on the front of the label worldwide in 2013, and to begin test marketing "Coca-Cola Life," a natural, stevia-sweetened, lower-calorie product with a green logo, sold in fully recyclable plant-based bottles in Argentina. In the past, Coke's response to soda's link to obesity had been to form something called the Beverage Institute for Health and Wellness, which, according to *PR Week* magazine, made "outlandish industry-science yarns . . . to diffuse concerns that sugary foods are a culprit in America's obesity epidemic."[37]

PepsiCo, too, is making strides toward healthfulness and transparency, years after it bought the natural foods brands Izze and Naked Juice. In 2011 CEO Indra Nooyi charged her Frito-Lay division with eliminating all artificial ingredients; and in 2013, at the behest of a 5-year-old who garnered 200,000 signatures on a petition, the company decided to eliminate the controversial brominated vegetable oil from Gatorade.[38] (Remarkably, this was the very same ingredient that nearly killed Sandy Gooch in 1974—although Gatorade decided to replace it with the emulsifier sucrose acetate isobutyrate, which is merely "generally regarded as safe.")

This "inoculation" model is now well established. As Eric Ryan, cofounder of the environmental cleaning products company Method, told the *New York Times*, he had always felt that an acquisition by one of the large conventional soap companies would "give us the chance to work from a bigger, global stage, and . . . try to change those companies from the inside out."[39]

"This idea of becoming part of the DNA of these larger companies is maybe infuriating or misunderstood by a lot of folks, but it's the only solution," said Hirshberg. "For organic to get into the double digits, we need the kind of efficiencies and reach of these large companies. It's not like we are going to knock them off the shelf. With the speed that we need to correct the imbalances and broken aspects of our food system, we are better off making one plus one equal three by getting our DNA into their host organism. [By] sensitizing them more to the needs of the natural and organic consumer, [we are] also helping to stabilize and build our supply chains."

And the example set by many of the natural foods companies is certainly proving to be influential well beyond the food industry. Our newly transparent business world, a columnist in *Forbes* magazine commented in March 2013, proves that listening is now more important for a business than talking; companies like Patagonia and Zappos have shown that "it is no longer possible to leave a gap between what a brand says and what the brand does."[40] In a May 2013 front-page story, the *New York Times* reported that consumers are now beginning to demand transparency from the clothing industry so that they can understand more about outsourcing, environmental issues, and working conditions. And companies such as Nordstrom, Nike, Walmart, Lush, and one auspiciously named Honest By are responding. "The revolution that has swept the food industry is expanding to retail," the article stated. "[O]rigins matter."[41]

———

In the earliest days of the natural foods revolution, there was a sort of open-ended rhetorical joke that often went around the co-ops: What happens if the mission actually *succeeds*?

Here in the second decade of the third millennium, there can be little doubt that the mission has succeeded—perhaps not to the extent that the high-minded idealists might have hoped, but then again far beyond what any realistic person might have predicted. The natural foods movement has turned out not to be a fad, as the early critics charged, or a bubble akin to the dot-com mania of the late 20th century, but an unprecedented and revolutionary movement whose growth has been sustained for decades. The revolution has held off the inexorable advances of Big Food and agribusiness; rolled back more than 2.5 million acres of cropland to organic; rewritten the agenda for health, diet, and sustainability; and established a nearly $100 billion business that has already proven to be more influential on attitudes, consumer and business behavior, and the health of the planet, than any other industry in our lifetimes. And even as innovative new companies and products enter the natural foods marketplace in pursuit of their missions and their triple-bottom-line green gold, the pioneers who led that revolution, the Natural Prophets, are emerging in the historical dialogue as among the most fascinating and influential entrepreneurs in American history.

AFTERWORD

aul Keene once said: "By being close to the center of the natural food and farming movement for many years, first helping hold it together, and later sharing its strong forward thrust, we've seen the future sweep into the present with a tremendous rush. Let's hope that the renewed awareness represented by this movement will be one of the saving elements so desperately needed now, to lead us moderns away from ourselves and our unbearable cocksureness into a quiet, thankful understanding and acceptance of life's limits and controls." He wrote those words in 1986, and they are just as true today. Keene largely stepped away from Walnut Acres the following year, but lived long enough to see the company sold to a dot-com baron in 1999; to watch the Penns Creek facility shuttered after the dot-com crash in 2000; and to witness the brand getting sold again to Hain Celestial in 2003, for about $10 million. Paul Keene died in 2005 at the age of 94. Today Walnut Acres lives on a few labels that help to maintain the trademark, but is otherwise relegated to the dusty Museum of Brands That Were—though its influences are still in the soil that nourishes the roots of the industry.

Mo Siegel still lives in Boulder, Colorado, still climbs mountains, and still serves on the board of Whole Foods, though he is largely retired. When he visits the huge Celestial Seasonings factory and headquarters on Sleepytime Drive, there is an excitement in the air, and one can hear him coming from well down the hall, as even employees who never knew him in the old days come out from behind their desks and greet him by his first name.

Gene Kahn left General Mills in 2010 and, through his connections with the Bill & Melinda Gates Foundation, is now the head of global market development for Harvest Plus, which is working on the "biofortification" of crops like sweet potatoes to improve their nutrient levels, especially in sub-Saharan Africa. It is important work, and he doesn't care too much whether the crops are chemically grown or organic . . . whatever it takes to secure quick adoption and therefore make the greatest impact.

In Portland, Oregon, Stan Amy continues to serve on the board of New Seasons, though most of his considerable analysis and deconstruction of business these days is concentrated in real estate. Sometimes, however, those worlds collide. He is, in fact, still the landlord of the store at 15th and Fremont that was once a Nature's Fresh Northwest, later a Wild Oats, and is now a Whole Foods.

Michael Funk still serves as chairman of United Natural Foods, Inc. He lives on a solar-powered estate in the Sierra Nevadas spanning several hundred acres, including some organic orchards—no gloves required to pick the fruit. His hair is grayed, but he still has a ponytail and a beard.

Gary Hirshberg stepped down as CE-Yo of Stonyfield Farm in January 2012, but he has been unable to step away from the industry. He is heavily involved in advocacy efforts related to climate change, organic marketing, and GMO labeling, and is frequently in Washington, DC, meeting with people in Congress or the White House. Many friends and admirers have urged him to run for office, but in his mind he is still just a yogurt entrepreneur—and sure enough, he shows up at the Stonyfield office most days in his New Balance sneakers with a backpack slung over one shoulder, seemingly ready to go out and run some demos.

Mark Retzloff and Barney Feinblum have lost some of their hair, but none of their drive. They are still fixtures in Boulder, providing leadership, advice, and funding to many of the area's food entrepreneurs through their investment company, Greenmont Capital Partners, which also includes their good friend and fellow Boulder Mafia member, Hass Hassan. On Earth Day 2011, Retzloff and Feinblum opened the new incarnation of Alfalfa's at Broadway and Arapahoe, and they are getting ready to open a second location soon.

The store at 1825 Pearl Street in Boulder that once housed Retzloff's and Hassan's Pearl Street Market, and then Crystal Market, and then Wild Oats, is today a charming boutique food store called Cured, selling handmade salamis, fresh-baked loaves of bread, and organic Grenada Chocolate bars for $5. Its wide, worn, wood plank floors seem to have history etched into them.

Restless as always, Steve Demos keeps an organic homestead north of Boulder, a residence in Costa Rica, and is frequently traveling around to places like India and Africa to pursue his passion for wildlife photography. "Life has to be greater than commerce," he says. Since he always said he was unemployable, he has made sure to let the professionals run GoodBelly, his follow-up business to WhiteWave, which produces probiotic juice drinks. He is proud of what his team accomplished with Silk, but is distressed about the fact that its subsequent owner, Dean Foods, moved away from organic ingredients and the concept of right livelihood. "Silk stood for something, and they tore it down." Dean spun off WhiteWave as a separate, publicly traded business in May 2013.

When he left Whole Foods in 1998, Peter Roy had spent 24 years in the industry, but was still only 42 years old. He was immediately in hot demand by several companies that wanted him to serve as a board member, and he joined several, including WhiteWave, North Castle Partners, Stonyfield Farm, and the National Outdoor Leadership School. But, ever the networker, he also set about to build his dream home, on the Intracoastal Waterway in South Carolina, which he could use as a base for hosting many get-togethers with family and industry friends.

Roy's good buddy, Doug Greene, sold New Hope Natural Media to Penton Media in 1999. "We were like a state, and things were getting so complicated," Greene says. "The day of independent stand-alone media companies like New Hope was nearing its end, and we needed to merge to bigger companies." The money and freedom that came from the sale have allowed him to explore his passion for music, and to become a citizen of the world, with homes in Boulder, Malibu, Amsterdam, Barcelona, and Australia. Greene looks like the aging rock star he is. He likes to stay out of the limelight, but when he comes back to Expo West, as he usually does each March, he is surrounded by grateful friends and well-wishers. He looks around the Anaheim Convention Center with awe at what this industry has become, and allows himself to enjoy a few quiet moments of self-congratulation.

Sandy Gooch is now in her seventies, but there is an aura about her, a mantle of matriarchal wisdom that has settled into her graceful countenance, and her lifetime of healthy eating has left her looking far too young to be the industry's grand dame. She and her husband, Harry Lederman, are frequent guest speakers, serve on some boards, and split their time between homes in Southern California and Arizona—entertaining, hosting their grandchildren, cooking a lot, and trying to figure out which of their 600 cookbooks is in which house.

After selling Bread & Circus in 1992, in what certainly seemed to be a reluctant move, Anthony Harnett briefly ran an integrative pharmacy in Boston, and then got involved in some investment initiatives in the natural foods industry.

But that is all in the rearview mirror now, and he is glad to forget it. "I simply have no interest in the business world," he says, "and even less in the past."

Mike Gilliland watches Whole Foods and Sprouts with admiration, even as he lives very comfortably because of them. He seems serene, but his sense of opportunism is only barely contained. "I still think there is another iteration out there, and I hope to do the next chapter."

Mark Ordan, who rode Fresh Fields so hard but only so far, got back into food retailing after his noncompete agreement with Whole Foods expired, buying Sutton Place Gourmet in 2002 and rebranding it as Balducci's. But that lasted for only 3 years. Since then he has become a turnaround specialist, taking over as CEO of companies such as the specialty mall developer The Mills Corporation and Sunrise Senior Living, righting their ships, and then selling them. In so doing, he has become quite wealthy—fulfilling the destiny that had started at Harvard Business School and Goldman Sachs, before it was so rudely interrupted by his passionate pursuit of retailing.

John Mackey turned 60 in 2013, and is now well into his third decade at the helm of Whole Foods Market—though these days, he spends more of his time giving interviews and writing books, including a forthcoming history of Whole Foods. But neither his success nor his unquestioned status as the industry's greatest iconoclast has dimmed the competitive flame that burns within: He declined to participate in *Natural Prophets* first and foremost, he said, because "I see [it] as a partial competitor to my own book."

And each September, on an evening when the sun's waning warmth yields to the approaching autumnal air, with a pleasant chorus of crickets and katydids in the background, a few dozen people converge on an old fieldstone barn in Kutztown, Pennsylvania. They come from around the country, agronomists and activists, farmers and food manufacturers, retailers and restaurateurs, composters and civil servants. Some fly into the Lehigh Valley Airport, very close to the Rodale homestead in Allentown, Pennsylvania, where J.I. first took up organic farming. They drive along US 22 and exit into the rolling hills of the Lehigh Valley, which are dotted with small plots of farmland, old homes with white columns, grain silos, tall oaks, guy wires twisted with vines reaching up to telephone poles—in one of the few places in the country where good old-fashioned telephone lines are probably still needed—and corn fields gone fallow for the season. There, sprawled out along 333 acres on either side of Siegfriedale Road, is the Rodale Institute—founded by J.I. in 1947 to study organic practices and healthy soil management, and relocated here by his son, Bob, in 1980—with its pick-your-own herb gardens, patch of 10-foot-high sunflowers, honeybee colonies, water purification eco-center, goats and hogs and barnyard chickens. As the sun sets and the sweaters come out, the guests at the Organic Pioneers Awards are taken by tractor-pulled carts out to the soybean and corn fields of the Farming Systems Trial (FST), site of a systematic side-by-side comparison of organic and chemical agricultural techniques that has been running continuously since 1981 (and which has recently added genetically modified crops to the test, as well). The FST has proven beyond a shadow of a doubt the superiority of organic agriculture for soil health, energy inputs, greenhouse gas emissions, crop yield (especially in times of drought), and overall profitability. To these guests, this is not just farmland. It is holy land. For this is where it all began—the revolution, the Natural Prophets—and where it continues to this day.

ENDNOTES

PROLOGUE: THE TIPPING POINT

1. Marian Burros, "Eating Well; Health-Food Supermarkets? Why, Yes. It's Only Natural," *New York Times*, January 8, 1992, http://www.nytimes.com/1992/01/08/garden/eating-well-health-food-supermarkets-why-yes-it-s-only-natural.html.
2. Mark Hamilton Lytle, *The Gentle Subversive: Rachel Carson, Silent Spring, and the Rise of the Environmental Movement* (New York: Oxford University Press, 2007), 175.
3. Ronald D. Michman and Edward M. Mazze, *The Food Industry Wars* (Westport, CT: Quorum Books, 1998), 11.
4. Whole Foods Market, *10-K Annual Report,* September 29, 1996, http://www.getfilings.com/o0001010549-96-000323.html; also, Lani Luciano and Elif Sinanoglu, "*Money*'s 1993 Store of the Year: Riding the crest of eco-consciousness, Fresh Fields serves up 'good for you' foods and products in snazzy supermarkets—for only 5 percent more than you would pay for the ordinary stuff," *Money,* December 1, 1992, http://money.cnn.com/magazines/moneymag/moneymag_archive/1992/12/01/87661/index.htm.
5. "Wild Oats Markets, Inc. History," fundinguniverse.com, accessed February 4, 2013, http://www.fundinguniverse.com/company-histories/wild-oats-markets-inc-history.

CHAPTER 1: THE MILKMAN OR THE COW

1. Google Images, accessed May 5, 2013, http://www.google.com/search?hl=en&site=imghp&tbm=isch&source=hp&biw=1920&bih=971&q=Postum+ads+1903&oq=Postum+ads+1903&gs_l=img.12 . . . 1940.7943.0.9810.15.8.0.7.7.0.134.990.0j8.8.0 . . . 0.0 . . . 1ac.1.12.img.aN3No5msesk#imgrc=03IIT5DYIHVqkM%3A%3BIbwgD8XKPqn70M%3Bhttp%253A%252F%252Fecx.images-amazon.com%252Fimages%252FI%252F51ZUAosLksL._SL500_SS500_.jpg%3Bhttp%253A%252F%252Ft.co%252Fjj2MXpjH%3B500%3B500.
2. Maria Rodale, *Organic Manifesto* (Emmaus, PA: Rodale, 2010), 19.
3. Ibid., 47.
4. Samuel Fromartz, *Organic Inc.: Natural Foods and How They Grew* (Boston: Mariner Books, 2007), 48–49.
5. Charles Duhigg, "Debating How Much Weed Killer Is Safe in Your Water Glass," *New York Times,* August 22, 2009, http://www.nytimes.com/2009/08/23/

us/23water.html. Seventy-six million pounds of Atrazine are used in the United States each year, although it is banned in the European Union and in Switzerland—home of Syngenta, the company that manufactures it. Also see Rodale, *Organic Manifesto* for further context.

6. Siel Ju, "232 Toxic Chemicals Found in 10 Newborns," mnn.com, posted December 2, 2009, http://www.mnn.com/health/fitness-well-being/blogs/232-toxic-chemicals-found-in-10-newborns.

7. As quoted in Michio Kushi and Stephen Blauer, *The Macrobiotic Way: The Definitive Guide to Macrobiotic Living* (New York: Penguin, 2004), 10, citing research from Samuel S. Epstein, MD, *The Politics of Cancer* (Garden City, NY: Anchor Press. Doubleday, 1979).

8. Rodale, *Organic Manifesto*, x.

9. Vaclav Smil, "Eating Meat: Evolution, Pattern, and Consequences," *Population and Development Review* 28 (4), December 2002, 609–610. Also see "A Nation of Meat Eaters: See How It All Adds Up," npr.org, accessed October 2, 2013, www.npr.org/blogs/thesalt/2012/06/27/155527365/visualizing-a-nation-of-meat-eaters.

10. Advameg, Inc., "United States of America—Agriculture," *Encyclopedia of the Nations,* accessed March 18, 2013, http://www.nationsencyclopedia.com/economies/Americas/United-States-of-America-AGRICULTURE.html.

11. Michael Pollan, *The Omnivore's Dilemma* (New York: Penguin, 2006), 104. Also Katherine Harmon, "Global High Fructose Corn Syrup Use May Be Fueling Diabetes Increase," blogspot.scientificamerican.com, posted November 27, 2012, http://blogs.scientificamerican.com/observations/2012/11/27/global-high-fructose-corn-syrup-use-may-be-fueling-diabetes-increase. According to reports from the Centers for Disease Control and Prevention, US obesity rates were stable at about 15 percent from 1960 through 1980; by 2010 the number had reached 36 percent, and it is forecast to rise to 50 percent by 2030. See Nanci Hellmich, "State Obesity Rates Could Soar by 2030," *USA Today,* September 19, 2012.

12. In one of the more remarkable stories of 19th-century industriousness, guano deposited over the centuries by cormorants, pelicans, and terns was harvested from the Chincha Islands off the coast of Peru and shipped to the United States, starting in the late 1820s. The supply had largely been exhausted by 1860. Will Allen, *The War on Bugs* (White River Junction, VT: Chelsea Green Publishing, 2008), 25–32.

13. Wilfred W. Robbins, Adlen S. Crafts, and Richard N. Raynor, *Weed Control: A Textbook and Manual* (New York: McGraw-Hill, 1952), 80.

14. Ibid., 121.

15. Adelynne Hiller Whitaker, *A History of Pesticide Regulation in the U.S. to 1947* (Emory University doctoral dissertation, 1974) as referenced in Allen, *War on Bugs,* 114.

16. Allen, *War on Bugs,* 63.

17. Ibid., 42.

18. Mary Bellis, "Frozen Foods—Clarence Birdseye," about.com, accessed February 15, 2013, http://inventors.about.com/library/inventors/blfrfood.htm.

19. James Trager, *The Food Chronology* (New York: Henry Holt, 1995), 457.

20. Ibid., 461.

21. "Radio in the 1930's," radiostratosphere.com, accessed February 15, 2013, http://www.radiostratosphere.com/zsite/behind-the-dial/radio-in-1930.html.

22. Allen, *War on Bugs,* 35.

23. Ibid., 35, 37.

24. From an editorial titled "New Insecticides," in a 1943 issue of *California Cultivator,* as quoted in ibid., 149.

25. From *Time* magazine, June 30, 1947, as referenced in ibid., 226.

26. John H. Martin and Warren H. Leonard, *Principles of Field Crop Production* (New York: Macmillan, 1949), 265, 384, 517, 680.

27. Allen, *War on Bugs,* 158.

28. As quoted in Rodale, *Organic Manifesto,* 11.

29. Lytle, *The Gentle Subversive,* 134.

30. "A Triumph and an Obligation," *Life,* January 3, 1955.

31. Ibid.; also Pollan, *The Omnivore's Dilemma,* 71.

32. Fromartz, *Organic Inc.,* 53.

33. "A Triumph and an Obligation," 3.

34. Melanie Warner, *Pandora's Lunchbox: How Processed Food Took Over the American Meal* (New York: Scribner, 2013), 41–49.

35. "A Triumph and an Obligation," 2.

36. From informational signs at Smithsonian Museum of American History, January 2013.

37. Peter Jennings and Todd Brewster, *The Century* (New York: Doubleday, 1998), 334.

38. John Seabrook, "The Spinach King," *New Yorker,* February 20, 1995, http://www.booknoise.net/johnseabrook/stories/self/spinach/index.html.

39. Ibid; also "Biggest Vegetable Factory on Earth," *Life,* January 3, 1955.

40. From informational signs at Smithsonian Museum of American History, January 2013.

41. Edward C. Hampe, Jr., and Merle Wittenberg, *The Lifeline of America— Development of the Food Industry* (New York: McGraw-Hill, 1964), 346.

42. Jennings and Brewster, *The Century,* 322–324.

43. "Mr. Khrushchev Goes to Washington," onthemedia.org, posted July 10, 2009, http://www.onthemedia.org/2009/jul/10/mr-khrushchev-goes-to-washington/transcript.

44. Jerome Lawrence and Robert E. Lee, *Inherit The Wind* (New York: Bantam, 1976), 83.

45. J.I. Rodale, "Introduction to Organic Farming," *Organic Farming and Gardening,* May 1942.

46. Daniel Gross, *Our Roots Grow Deep: The Story of Rodale* (Emmaus, PA: Rodale, 2008), 69.

47. Ibid, 69.

48. J.I. Rodale, "15 Years," *Organic Farming and Gardening,* June 1957.

49. Rodale, *Organic Manifesto,* 146.

50. Gross, *Our Roots Grow Deep,* 99.

51. George DeVault, "Walnut Acres Founder Paul Keene Dies at Age 94," rodaleinstitute.org, posted May 12, 2005, http://newfarm.rodaleinstitute.org/depts/readermail/200505/0512_1.shtml.

52. Paul Keene and Dorothy Z. Seymour (editor), *Fear Not to Sow Because of the Birds* (Chester, CT: Globe Pequot Press, 1988), 4.

53. Ibid., 59–60.

54. George DeVault, "What Became of Walnut Acres?" *The Natural Farmer,* Spring 2006, www.nofa.org/tnf/ . . . /The%20Walnut%20Acres%20Story.pdf.

55. Keene and Seymour, *Fear Not to Sow,* 92.

56. DeVault, "Walnut Acres Founder Paul Keene Dies at Age 94."

57. Keene and Seymour, *Fear Not to Sow,* 113–115.

58. Ibid., 128.

59. Ibid., 28.

60. Rachel Carson, *Silent Spring* (Boston: Houghton Mifflin, 1962), 158–160.

61. Lytle, *The Gentle Subversive,* 124.

62. Carson, *Silent Spring,* 165–168.

63. Ibid., 30, 25, 3.

64. Lytle, *The Gentle Subversive,* 166.

65. Keene and Seymour, *Fear Not to Sow,* 24.

66. As quoted in *Lytle, The Gentle Subversive,* 165.

67. As quoted in ibid., 175.

CHAPTER 2: A FEW GNARLY PIECES OF FRUIT

1. Jane Stern and Michael Stern, *Sixties People* (New York: Alfred A. Knopf, 1990), 172.

2. Allen, *War on Bugs,* 171.

3. Carson, *Silent Spring,* 17; also Rodale, *Organic Manifesto,* 19.

4. Allen, *War on Bugs,* 166.

5. Hampe, Jr., and Wittenberg, *Lifeline of America,* 341–343.

6. "Fact-filled Flood of Figures," *Life,* November 23, 1962, 143.

7. The best available numbers are 65 percent for newspaper in 1972, and 50 percent for TV in 1973. Warren J. Belasco, *Appetite for Change: How the Counterculture Took on the Food Industry* (Ithaca, NY, and London: Cornell University Press, 2007), 155.

8. Martin Lindstrom, *Buy*Ology: Truth and Lies About Why We Buy* (New York: Doubleday, 2008), 37.

9. Belasco, *Appetite for Change,* 135.

10. Ibid., 144.

11. Stern and Stern, *Sixties People,* 23–24.

12. "Source of the River of Abundance," *Life,* November 23, 1962.

13. See http://www.youtube.com/watch?v=wQCKqDJksuE.

14. Belasco, *Appetite for Change,* 4.

15. Belasco, *Appetite for Change,* 161. Also, "Source of the River of Abundance," *Life* magazine, noted that there were 27,000 supermarkets at the start of 1962.

16. Belasco, *Appetite for Change,* 91.

17. Akasha Richmond, *Hollywood Dish* (New York: Penguin, 2006), 78.

18. James Trager, "Health Food: Why and Why Not," *Vogue,* January 1, 1971.

19. "What's So Great about Health Foods," *Life,* September 29, 1972, 45.

20. Nancy Gittelson, "The $2 Billion Health Food . . . Fraud?" *Harper's Bazaar,* November, 1972.

21. Michio Kushi, Aveline Kushi, and Alex Jack (editor), *Macrobiotic Diet* (Tokyo: Japan Publications, Inc., 1993), 5.

22. George Alexander, "Brown Rice as a Way of Life," *New York Times,* March 12, 1972.

23. Ibid.

24. Eunice Farmilant, *Macrobiotic Cooking* (New York: New American Library, 1972) 191–203.

25. Kushi, Kushi, and Jack, *Macrobiotic Diet,* 6.

26. Ibid., 63.

27. William Shurtleff and Akiko Aoyagi, *History of Erewhon: Natural Foods Pioneer in the United States* (Lafayette, California: Soyinfo Center), 272.

28. Kushi, Kushi, and Jack, *Macrobiotic Diet,* 16–20.

29. Ibid., 15, 20–21.

30. Shurtleff and Aoyagi, *History of Erewhon,* 24.

31. Ibid., 157.

32. Ibid., 56.

33. Ibid., 20.

34. Ibid., 46.

35. Ibid., 45; also Gross, *Our Roots Grow Deep,* 69. Swanson had become a vegetarian around 1928 and was well known for bringing her own food to public outings. She became quite friendly with Aveline Kushi and at one point bought her a Toyota Celica, the very car she drove after she gave up her Rolls Royce. Kushi was once stopped on the Hollywood Freeway for driving this car too slowly. Swanson lived to be 84. See Shurtleff and Aoyagi, *History of Erewhon,* 46; also Christopher P. Anderson, "At 76, Gloria Swanson Has a New Crusade—And a New Mate to Go with It," *People,* February 16, 1976, www.people.com/people/archive/article/0,,20066161,00.html.

36. Shurtleff and Aoyagi, *History of Erewhon,* 66.

37. Ibid., 10–11.

38. Ibid., 159.

39. Pat Domowitz, "Health food firm sues 5 retailers," *Hartford Courant,* March 23, 1977.

40. Shurtleff and Aoyagi, *History of Erewhon,* 7.

41. Melvin Maddocks, "The Seeds of Idealism," *Christian Science Monitor,* August 31, 1972.

42. Shurtleff and Aoyagi, *History of Erewhon,* 67.

43. David Whitford, "Smith & Hawken Founder Paul Hawken Believes That Business Is Destroying the World. Maybe That's Why the Author and Environmentalist Wants You to Turn Your Small Business Upside Down," *Fortune Small Business,* May 1, 2002, http://money.cnn.com/magazines/fsb/fsb_archive/2002/05/01/322803/index.htm.

44. Robert Rodale, "The Organic Way of Life," *Organic Farming and Gardening,* April 1962, 22.

45. J.I. Rodale, "20 Years of Organic Gardening," *Organic Farming and Gardening,* June 1962, 17.

46. Rodale, "The Organic Way of Life," 23.

47. Keene and Seymour, *Fear Not to Sow*, 89–90.

48. As quoted in Wade Greene, "Guru of the Organic Food Cult," *New York Times*, June 6, 1971.

49. Enid Nemy, "Adelle Davis: 67 and Going Strong," *New York Times*, June 14, 1971.

50. United Press International, "Adelle Davis, Nutritionist, Best-Selling Author, Dies," *New York Times*, June 1, 1974; also Wolfgang Saxon, "An Outspoken Believer," *New York Times*, June 1, 1974.

51. Ibid.; also Dan Hurley, *Natural Causes: Death, Lies and Politics in America's Vitamin and Herbal Supplement Industry* (New York: Broadway, 2007).

52. United Press International, "Adelle Davis, Nutritionist, Best-Selling Author, Dies."

53. Lytle, *The Gentle Subversive*, 208–209.

54. Though seemingly, the globe just started spinning faster after that: 9 days later, US troops entered Cambodia; 3 days after that came the shootings of four students by the National Guard at Kent State.

CHAPTER 3: THE RISE OF THE HIGH-MINDED IDEALISTS

1. Mark Pendergrast, *Uncommon Grounds: The History of Coffee and How It Transformed Our World* (New York: Basic Books, 2010), 285.

2. When a student was killed, some critics asked Reagan if that didn't mean he had blood on his hands. Reaching back to the sponsor of his old *Death Valley Days* TV program, he said, "Fine, I'll wash it off with Boraxo." Stern and Stern, *Sixties People*, 215.

3. "PCC History," pccnaturalmarkets.com, accessed March 19, 2013, http://www.pccnaturalmarkets.com/about/history_text.html.

4. As quoted in Belasco, *Appetite for Change*, 161.

5. Ibid., 29.

6. Stern and Stern, *Sixties People*, 150.

7. Ibid., 147.

8. Gary Hirshberg, *Stirring It Up* (New York: Hyperion, 2008), 2.

9. Barry Newman, "No Grape, No Nuts, No Market Share: A Venerable Cereal Faces Crunchtime," *Wall Street Journal*, June 1, 2009.

10. John Kallas, "Euell Gibbons The Father of Modern Wild Foods," *Wild Food Adventurer Newsletter*, November 25, 1998, www.wildfoodadventures.com/cuellgibbons.html.

11. In a eulogy in the *New York Times*, writer John McPhee said that Gibbons had become "a household figure of a cartoon sort." John McPhee, "Wild Man," *New York Times*, January 10, 1976, http://www.nytimes.com/2010/09/26/opinion/etc-mcphee.html.

12. "Celestial Seasonings, Inc. History," fundinguniverse.com, accessed August 26, 2013, http://www.fundinguniverse.com/company-histories/celestial-seasonings-inc-history.

13. Allen, *War on Bugs*, 62.

14. Sharon Begley, Gerald C. Lubenow, and Mark Miller, "Silent Spring revisited," *Newsweek*, July 14, 1986.

15. Allen, *War on Bugs*, 176–179; also Timothy Egan, "Apple Growers Bruised and Bitter After Alar Scare," *New York Times*, July 9, 1991; and M. Beck et al., "Warning! Your food, nutritious and delicious, may be hazardous to your health," *Newsweek*, March 27, 1989. Ironically, the same *Newsweek* issue contained a "Better things for better living" ad for DuPont.

16. Belasco, *Appetite for Change*, 76, 161.

17. John O'Mahony, "'A hodgepodge of hash, yoga, and LSD,'" *Guardian*, June 2, 2008, www.theguardian.com/music/2008/jun/04/worldmusic.india; also, Walter Isaacson, *Steve Jobs: A Biography*. (New York, Simon & Schuster, 2011), 527; also, Jill Mangino, "2006 Marks 60th Anniversary of Autobiography of a Yogi," awarenessmag.com, accessed August 28, 2013, www.awarenessmag.com/novdec06/nd06_2006_marks.htm.

18. "Cultures with a conscience," *Prepared Foods*, October 1991.

19. Wendy Zellner, "John Mackey's Empire: Peace, Love and the Bottom Line," *Business Week*, December 12, 1998, http://www.businessweek.com/stories/1998-12-06/john-mackeys-empire-peace-love-and-the-bottom-line.

20. San Gwynne, "Born Green," *Saveur*, May 26, 2009, http://www.saveur.com/article/Kitchen/Born-Green.

CHAPTER 4: THE BOULDER MAFIA

1. John Schwartz, "Highway Expansion Encourages More Than Just Driving," *New York Times*, June 20, 2013, http://www.nytimes.com/2013/06/21/us/a-highway-projects- focus-discouraging-driving.html?_r=0. As of 2013, it is also in the midst of a massive reconstruction project that will add a bike lane and reintroduce a toll, for single-occupancy cars only—an effort to cut down on the 80,000 to 124,000 cars that drive on it each day.

2. Florence Williams, "Twenty-Five Miles Surrounded by Reality," *New York Times*, March 30, 2008, http://www.nytimes.com/2008/03/30/style/tmagazine/30boulder.html?pagewanted=all&_r=1&.

3. Shelley D. Schlender and Reed Glenn, *The Insiders' Guide to Boulder & Rocky Mountain National Park* (Boulder, CO: Boulder Publishing Company, 1995), 2.

4. Matt Woolsey, "America's Top 25 Towns To Live Well," forbes.com, May 4, 2009, www.forbes.com/2009/05/04/towns-cities-real-estate-lifestyle-real-estate-top-towns.html; also Jason Stevenson, "The Best Cities To Raise An Outdoor Kid: The Winning 25," *Backpacker*, August 2009, www.backpacker,com/august_09_the_best_cities_to_raise_an_outdoor_kid/articles/13125; also G. Scott Thomas, "Brain Bounty or Brain Busted," upstartbusinessjournal.com, December 1, 2010, www.upstart.bizjournals.com/news/wire/2010/12/01/boulder-colorado-tops-portfolio-2010-ranking-of-city-brainpower.html?page=all; also Carla Fried, "The 10 Happiest (and Saddest) Cities in the U.S." moneywatch.com, March 17, 2011, www.cbsnews.com/8301-505123_162-41142308/the-happiest-and-saddest-cities-in-the-us/

?tag=mwuser; also "AARP The Magazine Names the Top 10 Healthiest Places to Live in America," aarp.org, July 23, 2008, www.aarp.org/about-aarp/press-center/info 07-2008/aarp_the_magazine_names_the_top_10__healthiest_pla.html; also Andrew Knowlton, "America's Foodiest Town 2010: Boulder, Colorado," bonappetit.com, September 9, 2010, www.bonappetit.com/drinks/wine/article/americas-foodiest-town-2010-boulder-colorado; also Sean Fennessey, "The 40 Worst-Dressed Cities in America," gq.com, accessed August 28, 2013, www.gq.com/style/fashion/201107/worst-dressed-cities-america#slide=1.

5. Schlender and Glenn, The Insider's Guide to Boulder, 1.

6. Ibid., 19.

7. "You're a Perfect Master," Newsweek, November 19, 1973, http://www.prem-rawat-bio.org/magazines/1973/newsweek_191173.html; also Lord of the Universe, produced by TVTV (Hudson Marquez, Allen Rucker, Michael Shamberg, Tom Weinberg, and Megan Williams), 1974.

8. "A Call to Millenium [sic]," prem-rawat-bio.org, accessed December 20, 2012, http://www.prem-rawat-bio.org/dlm_pubs/aiid/millenium/acalltomilleniump13.html.

9. TVTV, Lord of the Universe.

10. Stern and Stern, Sixties People, 153.

11. TVTV, Lord of the Universe.

12. "You're a Perfect Master."

13. Ibid.

14. Interestingly, it was from the pool of conscientious objectors that the government drew many of its volunteers for the testing of genetically modified foods, though Retzloff was not among them.

15. "A Call to Millenium."

16. TVTV, Lord of the Universe.

17. Mick Brown, The Spiritual Tourist: A Personal Odyssey Through the Outer Reaches of Belief (London: Bloomsbury Publishing, 1998), 197.

18. Richard Levine, "When the Lord of All the Universe Played Houston, Many Are Called But Few Show Up," Rolling Stone, March 14, 1974.

19. "Site Insight Lifts New Store To $1,650 A Day," Natural Foods Merchandiser, December 1979, 28.

20. Wallace Stegner, Recapitulation (New York: Penguin, 1997), 185.

21. "Steve Demos. The Soy Wonder: Building a 'Right Livelihood,'" The New Wellness Revolution, accessed December 8, 2012, http://webcache.googleusercontent.com/search?q=cache:vd9FUxaqoDYJ:thewellnessrevolution.paulzanepilzer.com/stevedemos.php+steve+demos&cd=1&hl=en&ct=clnk&gl=us.

22. "The Natural Wonder of Boulder: We're Going to Revolutionize the Way People Eat," thefreelibrary.com, accessed March 14, 2013, http://www.thefreelibrary.com/The+natural+wonder+of+boulder%3A+'we're+going+to+revolutionize+the+way ... -a0130217616.

23. Julia Sommerfield, "Our Social Dis-ease," Pacific Northwest, Seattle Times, February 13, 2005, http://seattletimes.com/pacificnw/2005/0213/cover.html.

24. Julie Guthman, Agrarian Dreams: The Paradox of Organic Farming in California (Berkeley and Los Angeles: University of California Press, 2004), 15.

25. William Shurtleff and Akiko Aoyagi, *Mildred Lager—History of Her Work With Soyfoods and Natural Foods in Los Angeles (1900–1960): Extensively Annotated Bibliography and Sourcebook* (Soyinfo Center, 2009), 17.

26. Ibid., 18.

27. Mary Ann Galante, "Judge OKs Sale of Irvine Ranch Farmers Market," *Los Angeles Times,* August 1, 1989, http://articles.latimes.com/1989-08-01/business/fi-713_1_irvine-ranch.

28. "Trader Joe's Company History," fundinguniverse.com, accessed March 27, 2013, http://www.fundinguniverse.com/company-histories/trader-joe-s-company-history.

CHAPTER 5: SPONTANEOUS COMBUSTION

1. Brian J. Ford, "The Big Burn Theory: Why Human Beings Spontaneously Combust," *New Scientist,* August 12, 2012; also William H. Brock, *Justus von Liebig: The Chemical Gatekeeper* (Cambridge: Cambridge University Press, 1997), 286.

2. As quoted in Joe Nickell, "Not-So-Spontaneous Human Combustion," *Skeptical Inquirer,* volume 20.6, November/December 1996, http://www.csicop.org/si/show/not-so-spontaneous_human_combustion.

3. Begley, Lubenow, and Miller, "Silent Spring revisited."

4. Donald L. Bartlett and James B. Steele, "Monsanto's Harvest of Fear," *Vanity Fair,* May, 2008, www.vanityfair.com/politics/features/2008/05/monsanto200805; also Michael Winerip, "You Call That a Tomato," *New York Times,* June 24, 2013; also "Monsanto's Dirty Dozen," gmo-awareness.com, posted May 12, 2011, www.gmo-awareness.com/2011/05/12/monsanto-dirty-dozen/.

5. *Whole Earth Catalog* (March 1969), 15.

6. Tom Alexander, "The Hysteria over Food Additives," *Fortune,* March 1972.

7. "Food expenditures by families and individuals as a share of disposable personal income," USDA Economic Research Service, accessed October 23, 2012, http://www.ers.usda.gov/datafiles/Food_Expenditures/Food_Expenditures/table7.xls.

8. "The Move to Eat Natural," *Life,* December 11, 1970.

9. Guthman, *Agrarian Dreams,* 25, 130.

10. Total pasture/rangeland plus cropland was 935,450 acres in 1992, 1,346,558 in 1997, and 4,289,957 in 2007. "U.S. Certified Organic Farmland Acreage, Livestock Numbers, and Farm Operations, 1992–2008," USDA Economic Research Service, September 24, 2010, http://www.ers.usda.gov/datafiles/Organic_Production/Nutritional_Tables/Farmlandlivestockandfarm.xls.

11. According to Katherine DiMatteo, who in June 1990 became executive director of the Organic Foods Production Association of North America, which would later change its name to the Organic Trade Association (OTA), the strongest influence was being exerted by the Organic Food Alliance (the industry group cofounded by Mark Retzloff) and by a series of non-governmental organizations, including the Natural Resources Defense Council, The Humane Society, Food & Water Watch, The Environmental Working Group, and a program inside the Center for Science in the Public Interest. OTA was advocating to set the industry standards itself, but the

other groups, as well as most farmers and food producers, feared that self-regulation wouldn't build enough consumer confidence in organics.

12. In 1995 the NOSB came out with its initial opinions on what to incorporate within the "organic" definition, which included highly controversial recommendations allowing the use of sewage sludge fertilizer, genetic modification, and irradiation for organic foods. Two more years would pass before the USDA fully reviewed those recommendations, and even then their proposal for organic standards was roundly criticized, drawing more than 275,000 comments requesting stricter standards. It was not until 2001 that the National Organic Program was settled upon, and not until October 21, 2002, that it went into effect.

13. Trager, *The Food Chronology*, 578.

14. "It's natural! It's organic! Or is it?" *Consumer Reports*, July 1980, 411.

15. At various times, the FDA, concerned about specious health advice, seized copies of books by both Fredericks and Hauser.

16. "The Move to Eat Natural," *Life*.

17. Trager, "Health Food: Why and Why Not."

18. "The $2 Billion Health Food . . . Fraud?"

19. John E. Cooney, "Oh, No, Not Yogurt! Many People Hate It, Yet Many Now Eat It," *Wall Street Journal*, February 28, 1972.

20. "It's natural! It's organic! Or is it?" 410–411.

21. Betsy Spethmann, "Nature's Bounty," *Brand Week*, September 6, 1993. *Brand Week* cited natural foods sales in conventional stores as $1.02 billion, and in natural foods stores as $1.1 billion.

22. Shara Rutberg, "Sandy and the Seven Stores that Changed an Industry," *Natural Foods Merchandiser*, March 2, 2009, http://newhope360.com/business-directory/sandy-and-seven-stores-changed-industry.

23. "Whole Foods Market," answers.com, accessed November 26, 2012, http://www.answers.com/topic/wholefood.

24. Geoffrey Jones, "Entrepreneurship in the Food and Beauty Categories Before 2000: Global Visions and Local Expressions," working paper (Harvard Business School, August 28, 2012), http://hbswk.hbs.edu/item/7088.html.

25. Shurtleff and Aoyagi, *History of Erewhon*, 60.

26. Ibid., 101.

27. The original price was set at $56 million, but it was a pooled partnership all-stock deal, and a surge in the stock price raised the final tally.

28. Jill Bettner, "Mrs. Gooch's Natural Markets, Texas Food Chain to Merge," *Los Angeles Times*, May 13, 1993, http://articles.latimes.com/1993-05-13/business/fi-34908_1_texas-food-chain.

CHAPTER 6: LAND OF OPPORTUNISM

1. "Computer History Museum," computerhistory.org, accessed April 2, 2013, http://www.computerhistory.org/internet_history/internet_history_90s.html.

2. "Hobbes' Internet Timeline 10.2," zakon.org, accessed April 2, 2013, http://www.zakon.org/robert/internet/timeline.

3. "Timeline of Steve Jobs' Work at Apple," foxnews.com, August 24, 2011, http://www.foxnews.com/tech/2011/08/24/timeline-steve-jobs-work-at-apple; also "English Teacher, 30, Is Buyer of the Ticket Worth $111 Million," *New York Times*, July 10, 1983, http://www.nytimes.com/1993/07/10/us/english-teacher-30-is-buyer-of-the-ticket-worth-111-million.html. Today Powerball is run in 45 states and occasionally reaches jackpots with annuity and cash values exceeding a half-billion dollars, with more than 280 million tickets sold for a single drawing.

4. "Wild Oats Markets, Inc. History," fundinguniverse.com.

5. Susan J. Stocker, "Shoppers Food Gains Ground at Expense of Giant, Safeway," *Washington Business Journal*, June 24, 1991, http://www.accessmylibrary.com/article-1G1-11005439/shoppers-food-gains-ground.html.

6. The story was told to Mark Ordan by Izzy Cohen.

7. Burros, "Eating Well; Health-Food Supermarkets? Why, Yes. It's Only Natural."

8. Spethmann, "Nature's Bounty." The article also quoted the company's biggest natural foods convert, extolling the virtues of its food offerings: "It's foods you want in a healthy version," said Fresh Fields director of marketing Kathy Sklar Ordan. "We're not just talking about bean sprouts; were talking about chips, [pudding]—regular fare, but healthier versions."

9. *Money*'s 1993 Store of the Year."

10. Gary Erickson and Lois Lorentzen, *Raising the Bar: Integrity and Passion in Life and Business: The Story of Clif Bar, Inc.* (San Francisco, CA: Jossey-Bass, 2004), 21, 26.

11. Trager, *The Food Chronology*, 598.

12. Marian Burros, "A Growing Harvest of Organic Produce," *New York Times*, March 29, 1989, http://www.nytimes.com/1989/03/29/garden/a-growing-harvest-of-organic-produce.html.

13. Whole Foods Market, *10-K Annual Report*.

14. "Does Snapple Have the Juice to Go National?" *Business Week*, January 17, 1993, http://www.businessweek.com/stories/1993-01-17/does-snapple-have-the-juice-to-go-national.

15. Andrew Park, "Did Seth Go to the Dark Side?" *Inc.*, May 1, 2008, http://www.inc.com/magazine/20080501/did-seth-go-to-the-dark-side.html.

16. Hesh Kestin, "The Apprenticeship of Irwin Simon," *Inc.*, March 1, 2002, http://www.inc.com/magazine/20020301/23926.html.

17. Ron Koss and Arnie Koss, *The Earth's Best Story: A Bittersweet Tale of Twin Brothers Who Sparked an Organic Revolution* (White River Junction, VT: Chelsea Green Publishing, 2010), 343.

18. Laura Shapiro, "Hot Cha Cha, Hot Cha Chai," *Newsweek*, August 14, 1995.

19. Steven M. Davidoff, "In Venture Capital Deals, Not Every Founder Will Be a Zuckerberg," *New York Times*, May 1, 2013.

CHAPTER 7: CULT OF COMPETITION

1. As quoted in Mike Wise, "NBA Finals; Sonics Get Lesson in Jordan Rules," *New York Times*, June 14, 1996, http://www.nytimes.com/1996/06/14/sports/nba-finals-sonics-get-lesson-in-jordan-rules.html.

2. As quoted in "NBA's Great Moments: 'God Disguised as Michael Jordan,'" nba.com, accessed April 19, 2013, http://www.nba.com/history/jordan63_moments.html.

3. Tony Manfred, "17 Examples of Michael Jordan's Insane Competitiveness," businessinsider.com, posted February 15, 2013, http://www.businessinsider.com/craziest-michael-jordan-stories-2013-2?op=1.

4. "List of books written by CEOs," wikipedia.org, accessed April 19, 2013, http://en.wikipedia.org/wiki/List_of_books_written_by_CEOs.

5. "Warren Bennis," businessweek.com, accessed August 28, 2013 at www.businessweek.com/authors/2536-warren-bennis.

6. "Voices on Leadership: Stephen R. Covey," Q&A on washingtonpost.com, posted July 17, 2008, www.washingtonpost.com/wp-dyn/content/discussion/2008/07/16/DI2008071602427.html.

7. Leigh Buchanan, "The Wisdom of Peter Drucker from A to Z," *Inc.*, November 19, 2009, accessed August 28, 2013, www.inc.com/articles/2009/11/drucker.html; also Rick Wartzman, "Insourcing and Outsourcing: the Right Mix," businessweek.com, February 5, 2010, www.businessweek.com/managing/content/feb2010/ca2010024_507452.htm; also Sean Culley, "Leadership and Culture: Part I—The Case for Culture," europeanbusinessreview.com, accessed August 28, 2013, www.europeanbusinessreview.com/?p=6529.

8. Associated Press, "Fortune Magazine Accuses Forbes Editors of Pandering to Advertisers," *Daily Gazette,* January 16, 1996, http://news.google.com/newspapers?nid=1957&dat=19960116&id=CZJGAAAAIBAJ&sjid=gOkMAAAAIBAJ&pg=5740,3275254).

9. R. Michelle Breyer, "All-Natural Capitalist," *Austin American-Statesman,* May 10, 1998, 1.

10. Nick Paumgarten, "Food Fighter. Does Whole Foods' C.E.O. know what's best for you?" *New Yorker,* January 4, 2010, http://www.newyorker.com/reporting/2010/01/04/100104fa_fact_paumgarten.

11. Information about Mackey's beliefs comes from the *New Yorker* article cited above, interviews with Chris Hitt and Chris Kilham, and the author's own experiences and interactions with Mackey.

12. Per interview with Rich Cundiff. Regarding the loosening of the old ingredient standards, Harry Lederman said: "Bless John's heart, he had a different vision: to be the bridge to natural foods. 'I am going to be the Pied Piper leading them to a Sandy Gooch.' What he didn't do was keep the Sandy Gooch store after he led them there, so he could have had the best of both worlds. . . . Everything else transferred. The real estate. The employees. But not the trust."

13. E-mail from John Mackey to Rich Cundiff, March 17, 1997.

14. Cundiff was one of many at Whole Foods who came to appreciate Mackey's passion and forgive his hard-core tactics. Today Cundiff regards his former boss as "like a father or brother for me," and fondly recalls an encounter at a dinner after Cundiff had gone to work for Earth Fare, a Whole Foods competitor. "He is with the enemy," Mackey told people that night with a twinkle in his eye, "but we still like him."

15. E-mail from John Mackey to Michael Besancon, March 24, 1999.

16. Pollan, *The Omnivore's Dilemma,* 137.

17. John Mackey, "Strategic Plan for Whole Foods Market," updated March 1999.

18. Russell Parker, who had been the director of purchasing at Mrs. Gooch's, remembers when Peter Roy approached him at the NNFA trade show in Las Vegas

in the summer of 1993 and asked him to take on a similar role within all of Whole Foods. "The odds are against you, it won't work, and John is opposed to it. Are you interested?" Parker was, and held that role until the summer of 2000.

19. Pamela Blamey, "Fresh Fields Mows Down Prices in Chicago Stores," *Supermarket News,* December 4, 1995.

20. Officially, the USDA did not allow beef to be certified as organic until 2002, but the restaurateurs trusted the farmers to know how it had been raised.

21. Dennis Rodkin, "Tofu Fight! The Nation's Top Two Natural-Food Chains Have Chosen the Chicago Market for Their First Head-on Battle. Some Local Operators Are Going to Get Hurt," *The Chicago Reader,* October 21, 1993, http://www.chicagoreader.com/chicago/tofu-fight/Content?oid=883045; also Spethmann, "Nature's Bounty."

22. Jim Slama, "Reflections on Whole Foods," *Natural Foods Merchandiser,* November, 1996.

23. Emily Esterson, "Sowing the Seeds of a New Company," *Natural Foods Merchandiser,* September 1996.

24. Breyer, "All-Natural Capitalist," 9.

25. Wild Oats Markets, Inc. *10-K for the Fiscal Year Ended January 1, 2000,* accessed April 19, 2013, http://www.getfilings.com/o0000899733-00-000020.html.

26. David Kesmodel and Jonathan Eig, "Whole Foods CEO John Mackey in Hot Water. Unraveling Rahodeb. A Grocer's Brash Style Takes Unhealthy Turn: Were Posts by Mackey, CEO of Whole Foods, A Case of Ethics, or Ego?" *Wall Street Journal,* July 20, 2007, http://www.mindfully.org/Industry/2007/Whole-Foods-Rahodeb20jul07.htm. Walter Robb of Whole Foods says that Mackey wasn't quite so confrontational.

27. As quoted in ibid.

28. John Mackey and Raj Sisodia, *Conscious Capitalism* (Boston: Harvard Business Review Press, 2013), 207.

CHAPTER 8: DUELING BUSINESS MODELS

1. Nat Ives, "USA Today's Al Neuharth Chases New Generation," *Ad Age,* June 11, 2007, http://adage.com/article/media-people/usa-today-s-al-neuharth-chases-generation/117239.

2. James McCartney, "USA Today Grows Up," ajr.org, accessed April 20, 2013, http://ajr.org/Article.asp?id=878.

3. Ives, "USA Today's Al Neuharth Chases New Generation."

4. McCartney, "USA Today Grows Up."

5. William M. Pride and O.C. Ferrell, *Marketing: Concepts and Strategies* (Stamford, CT: Cengage Learning, 2006).

6. McCartney, "USA Today Grows Up."

7. "History of Natural Product Sales" *Natural Foods Merchandiser,* June 1993, 1.

8. Anni Layne, "How to Make Your Company More Resilient," *Fast Company,* February 28, 2001, http://www.fastcompany.com/63866/how-make-your-company-more-resilient.

9. "Odwalla, Inc. History," fundinguniverse.com, accessed April 19, 2013, http://www.fundinguniverse.com/company-histories/odwalla-inc-history.

10. Pollan, *The Omnivore's Dilemma*, 48.

11. "Horizon Organic Holding Corporation History," fundinguniverse.com, accessed April 24, 2013, http://www.fundinguniverse.com/company-histories/horizon-organic-holding-corporation-history.

12. "Historical Timeline: A Brief History of Cow's Milk, From the Ancient World to the Present," milk.procon.org, posted August 25, 2011, http://milk.procon.org/view.resource.php?resourceID=000832.

13. "Horizon Organic Holding Corporation History," fundinguniverse.com.

14. Marian Burros, "Eating Well; A New Goal Beyond Organic: 'Clean Food'," *New York Times*, February 7, 1996, http://www.nytimes.com/1996/02/07/garden/eating-well-a-new-goal-beyond-organic-clean-food.html.

15. As quoted in Camille Jensen, "George Siemon Surprised to Use Business for Environmental Change," svn.org, accessed March 9, 2013, http://svn.org/george-siemon-surprised-to-use-business-for-environmental-change.

16. Kermit Pattison, "Case Study: Could Organic Valley Thrive Without Wal-Mart?" *Inc.*, July 1, 2007, http://www.inc.com/magazine/20070701/casestudy.html; also Jensen, "George Siemon Surprised to Use Business for Environmental Change."

17. Pattison, "Case Study: Could Organic Valley Thrive Without Wal-Mart?"

18. "Organic Valley to Celebrate 25th Anniversary," organicvalley.com, accessed January 14, 2013, http://www.organicvalley.coop/newsroom/press-releases/details/article/organic-valley-to-celebrate-25th-anniversary.

19. "Organic Valley Ends Challenging Year with Resiliency: Farmer-Owned Cooperative Furthers Mission, Experiences Growth Despite Severe Drought and Farming Hardships," organicvalley.com, accessed January 14, 2013, http://www.organicvalley.coop/newsroom/press-releases/details/article/organic-valley-ends-challenging-year-with-resiliency.

20. "George Siemon on OV Headquarters Fire," posted May 16, 2013, http://www.youtube.com/watch?v=Ud2HP0bQpQE.

21. Statistics from 2011, reported in "Organic Milk Gains Share," *Supermarket News*, October 2012, http://supermarketnews.com/datasheet/oct-1-2012-organic-milk-gains-share.

22. Fennelly died in 1988, but the campaign lives on to this day through parodies on shows like *Family Guy* and *Futurama*, and has now become an online meme. See http://knowyourmeme.com/memes/pepperidge-farm-remembers and http://www.hark.com/clips/sczrrsqkpr-futurama-pepperidge-farm-remembers, accessed June 9, 2013.

23. Nanci Hellmich, "No-fat Cookies Spark Insatiable Demand," *USA Today*, February 18, 1993.

24. Constance L. Hays, "Fickle Finger of Fat; Nabisco Gives in as Consumers Shun Snackwell's, Demanding Taste," *New York Times*, May 1, 1998, http://www.nytimes.com/1998/05/01/business/fickle-finger-fat-nabisco-gives-consumers-shun-snack-well-s-demanding-taste.html.

25. Trager, *The Food Chronology*, 709.

26. Glenn Collins, "Low-Fat Food: Feeding Frenzy For Marketers," *New York Times*, September 27, 1995, http://www.nytimes.com/1995/09/27/business/low-fat-food-feeding-frenzy-for-marketers.html.

27. Hays, "Fickle Finger of Fat."

28. Dan Chu, "Fortune Frookies," *People,* September 30, 1991, http://www.people.com/people/archive/article/0,,20110948,00.html.

29. Joe Mullich, "Worth it!" joemullich.com, accessed December 7, 2012, http://www.joemullich.com/article6.htm.

30. Kim Severson, "And Then There Was the Food," *New York Times,* September 30, 2008, http://www.nytimes.com/2008/10/01/dining/01paul.html.

31. Ibid.

CHAPTER 9: FROM CO-OP TO CO-OPTATION TO CLOUT

1. "Technology Stocks: Vignette Corporation," siliconinvestor.com, February 22, 1999, http://www.siliconinvestor.com/readmsgs.aspx?subjectid=25395&msgnum=25&batchsize=10&batchtype=Previous.

2. Whole Foods Market, *10-K reports for 1996, 2001, 2006, 2011;* also "NFM Market Overview 2012: Natural Stays on Perennial Path to Growth," newhope360.com, posted May 27, 2012, http://newhope360.com/nfm-market-overview/nfm-market-overview-2012-natural-stays-perennial-path-growth.

3. Leslie Patton and Bryan Gruley, "Walter Robb on Whole Foods' Recession Lessons," *Business Week,* August 9, 2012, http://www.businessweek.com/articles/2012-08-09/walter-robb-on-whole-foods-recession-lessons.

4. Joshua M. Brown, "What Whole Foods Learned from the Recession," stocktwits.com, accessed April 27, 2013, http://www.thereformedbroker.com/2012/08/12/what-whole-foods-learned-from-the-recession.

5. "Fast Facts," wholefoodsmarket.com, accessed May 7, 2013, http://media.wholefoods market.com/fast-facts/; also "Global Powers of Retailing 2013," deloitte.com, G22, accessed August 6, 2013, http://www.deloitte.com/assets/Dcom-Australia/Local%20Assets/Documents/Industries/Consumer%20business/Deloitte_Global_Powers_of_Retail_2013.pdf.

6. As quoted in Pollan, *The Omnivore's Dilemma,* 156.

7. Mackey and Sisodia, *Conscious Capitalism,* 115.

8. Belasco, *Appetite for Change,* 93.

9. The natural foods community sometimes reacted with cynical amusement to these moves. The headline of a 1979 Hain Pure Food Company ad read, "The 'naturalness' of the food giants is getting hard to swallow." The copy began: "Having labored solely in the natural foods business for more than half a century, we really question the sincerity of all the 'born again' corporate giants who've recently jumped onto the natural foods bandwagon." It featured a cartoon drawing of the "General Meals" factory with a carrot-shaped façade thrown on the front. See *Natural Foods Merchandiser,* December 1979, 26.

10. "It's natural! It's organic! Or is it?" *Consumer Reports,* 411.

11. Belasco, *Appetite for Change,* 186.

12. Keene and Seymour, *Fear Not to Sow,* 61.

13. Ann Vileisis, *Kitchen Literacy: How We Lost Knowledge of Where Food Comes from and Why We Need to Get it Back* (Washington, DC: Island Press, 2008), 219.

14. Michele Simon, *Appetite for Profit: How the Food Industry Undermines Our Health and How to Fight Back* (New York, NY: Nation Books, 2006), 96, 108.

15. Jeffrey A. Trachtenberg and Edward Giltenan, "Mainstream Metaphysics," *Forbes*, June 1, 1987, http://www.forbes.com/forbes/1987/0601/156_print.html.

16. Marian Burros, "Eating Well," *New York Times*, August 28, 1996, http://www.nytimes.com/1996/08/28/garden/eating-well.html.

17. Lisa A. Tibbitts, "King Kullen to Open Organic Foods Store," *Supermarket News*, April 24, 1995, http://supermarketnews.com/archive/king-kullen-open-organic-foods-store.

18. "Natural Foods Gain Ground," transcript of "Living on Earth" radio program, week of December 6, 1996, loe.org, http://www.loe.org/shows/segments.html?programID=96-P13-00049&segmentID=6.

19. Annie Gasparro, "Supermarkets Aim to Win Back Health-food Shoppers," marketwatch.com, posted September 24, 2012, http://www.marketwatch.com/story/supermarkets-aim-to-win-back-health-food-shoppers-2012-09-24.

20. Carolyn Dimitri and Lydia Oberholtzer, *Marketing U.S. Organic Foods* (United States Department of Agriculture Economic Research Service, Economic Information Bulletin Number 58, September 2009), 6.

21. Eric Schroeder, "Safeway Sets Sights on Health and Wellness," foodbusinessnews.com, posted March 12, 2013, http://www.foodbusinessnews.net/articles/news_home/Food-Service-Retail/2013/03/Safeway_sets_sights_on_health.aspx?ID=%7B11776CA6-19E3-4BF5-936A-E2033A05FE46%7D&cck=1.

22. Dimitri and Oberholtzer, *Marketing U.S. Organic Foods*.

23. "NFM Market Overview 2012: Natural stays on perennial path to growth," newhope360.com, accessed May 1, 2013, http://newhope360.com/nfm-market-overview/nfm-market-overview 2012-natural-stays-perennial-path-growth.

24. New Seasons Market—Grocery; newseasonsmarket.com, accessed May 1, 2013, http://www.newseasonsmarket.com/our-departments/grocery.

25. Jenna Wortham and Claire Cain Miller, "In Silicon Valley's Kitchen: Venture Capitalists Are Making Bigger Bets on Food Start-Ups," *New York Times*, April 29, 2013.

26. "Disrupting the Food Chain," CNBC's *Squawk Box*, November 27, 2012, http://video.cnbc.com/gallery/?video=3000131602&play=1; also Leslie Brokaw, "Can the Ex-COO of McDonald's Bring Healthy Food to the Masses," *MIT Sloan Management Review* blog, posted August 9, 2012, http://sloanreview.mit.edu/article/can-the-ex-coo-of-mcdonalds-bring-healthy-food-to-the-masses.

27. Mackey and Sisodia, *Conscious Capitalism*, 65.

28. Annie M. Hamilton, "Still Farming, Annie's Founder Stays Close to Roots as Company Wows Wall Street," *Hartford Courant*, July 25, 2012, http://articles.courant.com/2012-07-25/business/hc-annies-homegrown-20120711_1_annie-withey-wall-street-enterprise.

29. "Nearly All Consumers Likely to Switch Brands to Support a Cause This Holiday Season," prnewswire.com, December 1, 2011, http://www.prnewswire.com/news-releases/nearly-all-consumers-likely-to-switch-brands-to-support-a-cause-this-holiday-season-134834278.html; also "Cone Communications 2011 Cause Marketing and CR Trends," conecomm.com, accessed May 2, 2013, http://www.conecomm.com/stuff/contentmgr/files/0/b312c873541362dbddf3c52b52f744f0/files/2011_cone_cause_marketing and_cr_trends.pdf.

30. Hirshberg, *Stirring It Up*, xvii.

31. As quoted in Hilary Howard, "Socially Conscious Companies Have a New Yard-stick," *New York Times,* November 8, 2012, http://www.nytimes.com/2012/11/ 09/ giving/a-new-yardstick-for-socially-conscious-companies.html.

32. Blake Mycoskie, *Start Something That Matters* (New York: Spiegel & Grau, 2011), 164.

33. Jim Hightower, *Eat Your Heart Out* (New York: Vintage Books USA, 1976), 105–106.

34. Warner, *Pandora's Lunchbox,* 109.

35. Keene and Seymour, *Fear Not to Sow,* 90.

36. Honest Tea, *Keeping It Honest 2010 Mission Report,* (Bethesda, MD, 2010), 2, 4, 6, 7, 10, 11, 15.

37. Stephanie Strom, "In Ads, Coke Confronts Soda's Link to Obesity," *New York Times,* January 15, 2013; also Associated Press, "Coke Goes Global with Anti-Obesity Campaign," *Arizona Republic,* May 9, 2013; also Simon, *Appetite for Profit,* 188.

38. Stephanie Strom, "PepsiCo Will Halt Additive Use in Gatorade," *New York Times,* January 26, 2013.

39. Rod Kurtz, "A Soap Maker Sought Compatibility in a Merger Partner," *New York Times,* January 17, 2013. Instead, Method was sold to the Belgian natural products company Ecover.

40. Avi Dan, "The Most Important Job Facing CMOs: Creating a More Transparent Business Model," forbes.com, March 18, 2013, http://www.forbes.com/sites/ avidan/2013/03/18/the-most-important-job-facing-cmos-in-a-newly-complicated-world-is-the-creation-of-a-more-transparent-business-model.

41. Stephanie Clifford, "Some Retailers Reveal Where and How That T-Shirt Is Made," *New York Times,* May 9, 2013.

ACKNOWLEDGMENTS

The idea for this book popped into my head one day, and would have remained there but for a few conversations that quickly followed.

The first was with Peter Roy, with whom I have consulted about many oddball ideas in the decade-and-a-half since the one brief year during which I had the great privilege to work by his side at Whole Foods. He reached me by phone while I was standing in a Barnes & Noble store, and that seemed like validation enough. But he immediately course-corrected my initial concept, and later was predictably generous with his time and encouragement.

The second was with Walter Robb, co-CEO of Whole Foods and one of the most thoughtful, incisive human beings I have ever met. In the space of perhaps 10 short minutes, he grasped the concept and framed it for me perfectly. He makes only a couple of brief cameos in the text, much less of a role than is deserved, but his guiding hand is there throughout.

The third was with Chris Hitt, who like Roy before him and Robb after him served as president of Whole Foods. Chris was the one who articulated the theory that the natural foods pioneers deserve their place in the pantheon of great modern-day entrepreneurs—a theory that became the driving force for the entire project. He later welcomed me back into his North Carolina home to provide hours and hours of stories, reflections, and inspiration that proved enormously helpful.

And the fourth was a dialogue with Maria Rodale that began via e-mail and continued one magical evening at the Rodale Institute. She deftly handed me off to her publishing division but made it clear that she believed in me and in the merits of the project—and in so doing, enabled me to sidestep the traditional process of pitching a book concept that can be so daunting to a first-time author.

What followed were 5 months of research, 13 intensive weeks of writing, and then 4 months of back-and-forth editing.

During the research phase, many, many people provided time and assistance. These included Lex and Ann Alexander, Stan Amy, Bob Anderson, Nikhil Arora and Alex Velez, John Battendieri, Shannon Bennett, Linda Boardman,

Bob Burke, Samantha Cabaluna, Matt Chappell, Mel Coleman, Jr., Rich Cundiff, Terry Dalton, Steve Demos, Katherine DiMatteo, the incredibly inspirational Chuck Eggert of Pacific Foods, Vince Fantegrossi, Barney Feinblum, Bruce Fleegal, Michael Funk, Tyler Gage, Julie and Richie Gerber, Mike Gilliland, Seth Goldman and his great team at Honest Tea, Sandy Gooch and Harry Lederman, Drew and Myra Goodman, Doug Greene, Hass Hassan, Gary Hirshberg, Janet Hoffman, Jeffrey Hollender, Phil Howard, Heather Howitt, Gene Kahn, Chris Kilham and Zoe Helene, Bob Johnson, Maurice Kreindler, Doug Levin, Theresa Marquez, Peter Meehan, Melanie Melia, Bob Moore, Jim Morano, Lou Morsberger, Jack Murphy, David Neuman, Bruce Nierenberg, Paul Orbuch, Mark Ordan, Scott Owen and Bill Crawford of New Hope, Russell Parker, Matt Patsky, Steve Petusevsky, Rick Prill, David Printz, Diane Radley, Mark Retzloff, Denis Ring (who always makes time for me), Heidi Rodale, Jimmy Searcy, Bill Shurtleff, Mo Siegel, George Siemon, Dana Sinkler, Kathy Sklar (on whom falls much of the blame for bringing me into this industry in the first place), Mark Smiley, the much-admired Paddy Spence, Greg Steltenpohl, Tim Sperry, Terry Tierney, Kevin Tisdale, Blake Waltrip, Craig Weller, and Richard Worth. Some of their stories, alas, ended up on the cutting room floor—this time. Thanks also to Beth Shepard for all of her timely advice.

While I was writing I am sure I was not a lot of fun to live with. But Julie Zagars, the great love of my life, has put up with stretches like that before, and as usual kept me motivated and smiling throughout.

And then, as we entered the editing phase, my family of writers proved invaluable, including my very literary parents, Alan and Vicki, and my sister, Julie, in whose footsteps I have been following my entire life. Special thanks to my brother, Marty, with whom I just seem to share editing biorhythms. Growing up, we were rivals who selfishly dreamed of future careers we didn't want the other one to pursue; thank God writing wasn't one of "Those Things," and that we became such great friends.

Most importantly, I want to acknowledge the guidance and patience of Alex Postman, my editor at Rodale Books, and the outstanding team behind her. An accomplished magazine editor, acknowledged foodie, and mother of three, Alex had the perfect training for this project—though I am not sure which part of her background was most crucial. Authors and books, like great meals and kids, require some encouragement, prodding, and creative inspiration, and from that first night at the Rodale Institute through the entire process, she provided them all.

INDEX